Midwestern Methodists
Four Thrall Generations

Midwestern Methodists

FOUR THRALL GENERATIONS FROM BONE GAP, ILLINOIS, 1809–2018

Including allied families Britton, Campbell, Flint, Gould, Jones, Leighton, Morgan, Pifer, and Schofield

by Harold A. Henderson, CG

Harold A. Henderson
2020

Midwestern Methodists: Four Thrall Generations from Bone Gap, Illinois, 1809–2018

Creative Commons Attribution-NonCommercial-ShareAlike (CC-BY-NC-SA)
https://creativecommons.org/share-your-work/licensing-types-examples/#by-nc-sa

2020 by Harold A. Henderson, CG, La Porte, Indiana
librarytraveler@gmail.com

Subjects: Genealogy, Family History, Bone Gap, McKendree College, Thrall, Morgan, Gould, Campbell, Flint, Jones, Schofield, Britton, Leighton, Pifer

First Printing: September 2020
ISBN: 978-1-7343752-1-3

Printed in the United States

Dedication

in memory of Rosalie (Thrall) Carmichael (1907–1999), genealogist and librarian,

who trod this path first and marked it well,

when it was much steeper

Table of Contents

FAMILY FINDER BY DESCENT AND CHAPTER 0

PEOPLE FINDER BY DESCENT AND CHAPTER 0

Introduction 1

Family Overview 3

    Map 1: Thrall and Gould migrations 6

    Map 2: 1891 Bone Gap and railroads 10

SEVENTH GENERATION
(1809–1875, presidents Jefferson to Grant)

Chapter 1. WORTHY^7 THRALL &
    HANNAH JAMES 13

EIGHTH GENERATION
(1827–1925, presidents Jackson to Coolidge)

Chapter 2. MARY ELIZABETH^8 THRALL &
    AMOS MORGAN 27

Chapter 3. LAURA LUCINA^8 THRALL &
    SOLON GOULD 33

    Tree 1: Allied Gould–Thrall Families 45

    Story 1: A walk in the orchard 46

Chapter 4. H. CAROLINE^8 THRALL &
    CHARLES CAMPBELL 47

Chapter 5. LEONIDAS^8 THRALL, EDITH MARIE
    FLINT, EMILY JONES 59

    Tree 2: Allied Jones–Thrall Families 74

    Story 2: Housework in Kansas, 1878 75

NINTH GENERATION
(1852–1979, presidents Fillmore to Carter)

Chapter 6. MILTON[9] MORGAN, CLEMENTINE CLARK, AMANDA TEACHOUT 77

Genealogical puzzle 1: Beyond this chapter, how much of Milton's life in Nebraska can be told? 86

Chapter 7. ALLYN T.[9] MORGAN, ROSINA SMITH, LOUISA JONES (THRALL) GASH, MARY CATHERINE SCHOFIELD 87

Tree 3: Allied Flint–Morgan Families. 103

Tree 4: Allied Schofield, Thrall, Morgan Families 104

Genealogical puzzle 2: Who were the parents of Lulu Irene Geoffroy? 105

Chapter 8. WILBUR A.[9] MORGAN & ELIZA JANE SMITH 109

Chapter 9. LUCRETIA[9] MORGAN & JOSEPH W. BRITTON 117

Tree 5: Allied Thrall, Morgan, Gould, Britton Families 125

Chapter 10. ALTA ARETA GOULD[9] & EDW. G. BRITTON 127

Chapter 11. LEIGHTON–PIFER–GOULD CONNECTIONS 133

Chapter 12. VIRGIL N.[9] GOULD & DORA S. LEIGHTON 139

Chapter 13. Edith E.⁹ Gould,
Flora A.⁹ Gould..............................145

Chapter 14. Etta J.⁹ Campbell &
Harvey Marshall 149

*Table 1: Etta's and parents' stated
birthplaces*......................................151

Chapter 15. Leo F.⁹ Campbell &
Fleeta M. Cantwell 153

*Table 2: Leo's parents' stated
birthplaces*......................................155

Chapter 16. Edith Laura⁹ Thrall 159

Chapter 17. Victor W.⁹ Thrall &
Carrie Jones 163

Chapter 18. William F.⁹ Thrall &
Enola L. Keisling 171

*Story 3: Locating the high-school
track meet*.......................................180

Chapter 19. Gertrude Gerking 181

Chapter 20. Harold⁹ Thrall &
Elizabeth Schriber 185

*Story 4: Horse and Buggy from Noble
to Weedman, 1911*......................193

Chapter 21. Mary Virginia⁹ Thrall &
David Cover 195

TENTH GENERATION
(1874–2018, presidents Grant to Trump)

Chapter 22. EDGAR A.*¹⁰* MORGAN &
   ADDIE GOULD 199

Chapter 23. MYRTLE*¹⁰* MORGAN &
   CHRISTOPHER COLLINS 213

Chapter 24. RAYMOND*¹⁰* MORGAN &
   ADA P. VENSEL 217

Chapter 25. EZRA LEONIDAS*¹⁰* MORGAN &
   MARY FLINT 221

Chapter 26. EARL A.*¹⁰* MORGAN &
   EFFIE BANKSTON 225

Chapter 27. EVART*¹⁰* MORGAN, ELSIE DRURY,
   EVA BRINES 229

Chapter 28. HALE E.*¹⁰* MORGAN &
   EDNA WHEELER 233

Chapter 29. GLEN*¹⁰* MORGAN, MINA SIMS,
   AVA B. [–?–] 237

   Genealogical puzzle 3: Who was Glen's 2ⁿᵈ wife? 241

Chapter 30. WILLARD*¹⁰* MORGAN &
   WILMA SNIDER 243

Chapter 31. WILLIAM*¹⁰* BRITTON,
   SARAH CASTILE, HELEN ROSS 247

Chapter 32. FLOYD*¹⁰* BRITTON, GLADYS GAUNT,
   HAZEL (RECK) (CROCKER) THORSNESS 251

Chapter 33. Lucile[10] Britton & Timothy McKnight 257

Chapter 34. Vivian[10] Britton & Harry I. Hannah 259

Chapter 35. Waldo Vincent[10] Britton 263

Chapter 36. Elsie M.[10] Britton & Verla Crawley 265

Chapter 37. Ethel[10] Britton & Milton Hartman 269

Chapter 38. Ernest[10] Britton & Martha Hughes 273

Chapter 39. Kathleen V.[10] Pifer & Hugh McNelly 277

Chapter 40. Edwin M.[10] Gould & Rhodean Perdue 283

Chapter 41. Victor[10] Gould, Ella Lippert, Geraldine Hacke 287

Chapter 42. Paul Glenwood[10] Gould, Ada Shaffer, Rosa (Burdette) Germanini 291

Chapter 43. Areta H.[10] Gould & Emery H. Martin 295

Chapter 44. Margaret Louise/Lucille[10] Pifer & George Y. King 299

Chapter 45. Cecil Melvin[10] Pifer, Rosalie Galeener, Kathryn Williams 303

Chapter 46. Carrie Eleanor[10] Marshall & Howard Lee Daughenbaugh 309

Chapter 47. Beulah[10] Marshall 313

Chapter 48. Leona M.[10] Campbell & Chester E. "Jackie" Pearson 317

Chapter 49. Mary A.[10] Campbell & Edward Kohler 321

Chapter 50. Edith F.[10] Thrall & George A. Mooers 323

Chapter 51. Evelyn G.[10] Thrall & Jess Jennings Bird 327

Chapter 52. Victor W.[10] Thrall Jr. & Donna Brown 331

Chapter 53. Rosalie[10] Thrall & Colin Carmichael 335

Chapter 54. Robert M.[10] Thrall & Natalie Hunter......................... 341

Chapter 55. Elizabeth Rose[10] Thrall & Ronald Athol Henderson 345

Chapter 56. Miriam R.[10] Thrall & George N. Foster 351

Chapter 57. H. James[10] Thrall & Joan E. Walker.......................... 355

Chapter 58. William H.[10] Cover & Ruth Alice Palmer 361

Chapter 59. David Leonidas[10] Cover, Billie J. Taake, Ava M. (Simmons) Goddard 365

Index... 369

Family Finder by Descent and Chapters

CHAPTER 1 **Worthy**[7] **Thrall**, pp. 13–26

Morgan Descendants
CHAPTER 2 **Elizabeth**[8] **(Thrall) Morgan**, pp. 27–32
CHAPTERS 6–9, pp. 77–125
CHAPTERS 22–36, pp. 199–267

Gould Descendants
CHAPTER 3 **Laura**[8] **(Thrall) Gould**, pp. 33–46
CHAPTERS 10–13, pp. 127–148
CHAPTERS 37–45, pp. 267–307

Campbell Descendants (adoptive)
CHAPTER 4 **Carrie**[8] **(Thrall) Campbell**, pp. 47–57
CHAPTERS 14–15, pp.149–157
CHAPTERS 46–49, pp. 309–322

Thrall Descendants
CHAPTER 5 **Leonidas**[8] **Thrall**, pp. 59–75
CHAPTERS 16–21, pp. 159–198
CHAPTERS 50–59, pp. 323–368

People Finder by Descent and Chapter

Name & Spouse	Life & Places	Descendant Chapters
Gen. 7 1809-1875		Presidents Jefferson-Grant
1. Worthy Thrall m. Hannah James	1809 VT-1852 IL 1809 OH-1875 IL	2-5
Gen. 8 1833-1924		Presidents Jackson-Coolidge
2. Mary Eliz. Thrall m. Amos Morgan	1833 OH-1903 IL 1827 VA-1865 IL	6-9
3. Laura L. Thrall m. Solon H. Gould	1835 IL-1898 IL 1837 IL-1914 IL	10-13
4. H. Caroline Thrall m. Charles Campbell	1845 IL-1924 LA 1851 IN-1922 LA	14-15
5. Leonidas W. Thrall m1. Edith Marie Flint m2. Emily Jones	1850 IL-1918 IL 1845 IL-1898 IL 1865 IL-1957 IL	16-21
Gen. 9 1852-1976		Presidents Fillmore-Ford
6. Milton Morgan m1. Clementine Clark m2. Amanda Teachout	1852 IL-1899 IL 1849 IN-187? NE 1863 MI-1946 CA	22-24
7. Allyn T. Morgan m1. Rosina Smith m2. Louisa T. Gash m3. M. C. Schofield	1856 IL -1931 IL 1856 NY-1880 IL 1861 IL-1888? 1862 IL-1932 IL	25-27
8. Wilbur A. Morgan m. Eliza Jane Smith	1858 IL-1945 1862 IL-1945 CA	28-30
9. Lucretia Morgan m. Joseph W. Britton	1863 IL-1906 IL 1855 OH-1925 IL	31-36
10. Alta Areta Gould m. Edw. Geo. Britton	1865 IL-1957 IL 1862 OH-1953 IL	37-39
11. Leighton-Pifer-Gould Connections		39, 44, 45
12. Virgil N. Gould m. Dora S. Leighton	1868 IL-1959 IL 1871 VA-1957 IL	40-43
13. Edith E. Gould Flora Alice Gould	1871 IL-1960 IL 1875 IL-1926 IL	44-45
14. Etta J. Campbell m. Harvey Marshall	1877 IL-1952 TX 1876 KS-1946 LA	46-47

15. Leo F. Campbell m. Fleeta M. Cantwell	1892-1962 IL 1898 IL-1976 MO	**48-49**
16. Edith L. Thrall	1874 IL-1950 IL	
17. Victor W. Thrall m. Carrie F. Jones	1877 KS-1963 TN 1877 IL-1952 TN	**50-52**
18. Wm. Flint Thrall m. Enola L. Keisling	1880 IL-1941 NC 1878 IL-1950 OH	**53**
19. Charles H. Thrall m. Gertrude Gerking	1883 IL-1968 IL 1881 IL-1950 IL	**54**
20. Harold L. Thrall m. Elizabeth Schriber	1885 IL-1966 IL 1884 IL-1979 IL	**55-57**
21. Mary V. Thrall m. David S. Cover	1902 IL-1976 IL 1899 IL-1970 IL	**58-59**
Gen. 10 1875-2018		**Presidents Grant-Trump**
22. Edgar A. Morgan m. Addie Gould	1875 IL-1925 IN 1878 IL-1963 IN	+
23. Myrtle Morgan m. Christopher Collins	1884 NE-1965 CA 1874 CA-1949 CA	+
24. Raymond Morgan m. Ada Pearl Vensel	1890 NE-1936 CA 1892 AZ-1920 AZ	+
25. Ezra Lon Morgan m. Mary F. Flint	1879 IL-1937 MO 1881 IL-1945 MO	+
26. Earl A. Morgan m. Effie G. Bankston	1890 IL-1960 IL 1891 IL-1987 IL	+
27. Evart W. Morgan m1. Elsie P. Drury m2. Eva Brines	1892 IL-1979 CO 1889 IL-1914 IL 1889 IL-1981	
28. Hale E. Morgan m. Edna B. Wheeler	1886 IL-1954 CA 1889 IL-1979 CA	+
29. Glen W. Morgan m1. Mina Lois Sims m2. Ava B. [-?-]	1890 IL-1957 CA 1891 IL-1979 CA 1913? IL?-1957+	+
30. Willard Morgan m. Wilma Ann Snider	1898 IL-1948 CA 1906 CA-2001 CA	+
31. William Britton m1. Sarah M. Castile m2. Helen G. Ross	1887 IL-1965 CA 1885 IL-1966 CA 1901 MN-1957 CA	+
32. Floyd E. Britton m1. Gladys Gaunt m2. Hazel Thorsness	1890 IL-1982 WI 1891 IL-1961 IL 1897 IL-1978 WI	+
33. Lucille Britton m. Timothy McKnight	1892 IL-1975 IL 1891 IL-1973 IL	+

34. Vivian Britton m. Harry I. Hannah	1894 MO-1991 IL 1890 IL-1973 IL	+
35. Waldo V. Britton	1897 MO-1926 MO	
36. Elsie M. Britton m. Verla C. Crawley	1899 MO-1997 IL 1896 IN-1964 IL	+
37. Ethel L. Britton m. Milton Hartman	1893 IL-1984 MO 1892-1964	+
38. Ernest R. Britton m. Martha L. Hughes	1903 IL-1983 MI 1902 IL-1993 MI	+
39. Kathleen V. Pifer m. Hugh J. McNelly	1914 VA-1980 NJ 1911 IL-1997 NJ	+
40. Edwin M. Gould m. Rhodean Purdue	1894 IL-1993 FL 1903 IL-1992 FL	+
41. Victor L. Gould m1. Ella Lippert m2. Geraldine Hacke	1898 IL-1983 CA 1895 MO-1988 MO 1912 MO-2000 CA	+
42. Paul G. Gould m1. Ada L. Shaffer m2. Rosa Germanini	1901 IL-1998 FL 1905 IL-1985 FL 1909 GA-1993 FL	+
43. Areta H. Gould m. Emery H. Martin	1907 IL-1998 IL 1906 IL-1987 IL	+
44. M. Lucille Pifer m. George Y. King	1911 VA-1983 AZ 1904 IL-2003 AZ	+
45. Cecil Melvin Pifer m1. Rosalie Galeener m2. Kathryn Sande	1915 VA-1995 AZ 1919 IL-2008 WI 1917 IL-1994 AZ	+
46. Carrie E. Marshall m. H. L. Daughenbaugh	1900 LA-1977 1898 LA-1983 LA	+
47. Beulah Marshall	1904 LA-1983 LA	
48. Leona Campbell m. Chester Pearson	1920 IL-1999 1915 IL-1995 IL	+
49. Mary A. Campbell m. Edward Kohler	1931 IL-2013 KY 1928 IL-2016 KY	+
50. Edith F. Thrall m. George A. Mooers	1904 IL-1989 OH 1899 TN-1987 OH	+
51. Evelyn G. Thrall m. Jess Jennings Bird	1904 IL-1989 OH 1903 IRE-1982 TN	+
52. Victor W. Thrall Jr. m. Donna M. Brown	1918 IL-2000 IL 1917 IL-2013 IL	+
53. E. Rosalie Thrall m. Colin Carmichael	1907 IL-1999 FL 1905 SCOT-1978 FL	+

54. Robert M. Thrall m. Natalie Hunter	1914 IL-2006 PA 1913 IL-2004 PA	+
55. Elizabeth Thrall m. Ronald Henderson	1918 IL-2008 IN 1914 IL-2002 IL	+
56. Miriam R. Thrall m. George N. Foster	1921 IL-2010 IL 1918 IL-1999 IL	+
57. H. James Thrall m. Joan E. Walker	1925 IL-2018 IN 1924 IL-2006 IL	+
58. William H. Cover m. Ruth Alice Palmer	1923 IL-1986 MO 1927 OH-2013 OH	+
59. David L. Cover m1. Billie J. Taake m2. Ava M. Goddard	1925 IL-1990 IL 1929 IL-2014 MO 1926 IL-2010 IL	+

+ = children in Generation 11

Introduction

This book is a cross between a reference work and a collection of stories. It seeks be more interesting than a reference book, and more accurate than family legend. The chapters trace each family's descendants "downstream." This arrangement gives equal importance to all the descendants and cousins, and places the families in the context of their friends and relations and times. Readers can use it to climb their ancestral tree as well.

This book also strives to meet genealogy standards—research thoroughly, cite accurately, analyze and correlate evidence, resolve conflicts when possible, and write clearly.[1] Previous accounts of the family said little about adopted or fostered children. They and their descendants are included here, as are those who lived to grow up but did not marry or have children.

Readers may pause when reading and ask, "How do we know that?" Because they deserve a prompt answer, this book includes footnotes (all intended to be complete in themselves, with minimal abbreviations). Finding aids include table of contents, family finder, people finder (all at the front of the book), and index (at the back).

This book could not exist without the kindness and thoughtfulness of family members and distant relatives who over the years shared information and ideas. They helped preserve the information—records and letters and artifacts—that allow us glimpse our ancestors' thoughts and deeds, flickering in the strobe light of history. Lisa Alzo's skills helped make the dream of a book feasible.

Many questions are left unanswered here, but an imperfect book is better than none at all. Living people are not included. Additional information, improved sources, and documented corrections are welcome.

---

[1] Board for Certification of Genealogists, *Genealogy Standards* (Nashville, Tennessee: Ancestry Imprint, Turner Publishing, 2014), 1–3.

Family Overview

The children, grandchildren, and great-grandchildren of Hannah James and Worthy Thrall were the eighth, ninth, and tenth generations from Connecticut immigrant William Thrall and his wife (whose name is not known). Of these three generations, Mary Elizabeth (Thrall) Morgan was the first, born in 1833, and Harold James Thrall, who died in 2018, was the last. In those 185 years the seventh, eighth, and ninth generations did many things:

- farmed and gardened, mostly by necessity and sometimes with distinction;
- attended, preached, and served in mostly Methodist churches;
- played, sang, and taught music;
- taught art, law, literature, mathematics, and mechanical engineering;
- practiced teaching at all levels, nursing, medicine, law, and traffic engineering;
- adopted or fostered children;
- held local offices and occasionally sought higher ones;
- advocated Prohibition;
- taught black children and freedmen to read;
- helped organize a special train from Alabama to the 1938 Rose Bowl; and
- ran businesses including the Bone Gap general store; the Brown Valve and Manufacturing Company in Alhambra, California; and an international food corporation.

The family took part in several American migrations. Worthy's Thrall ancestors lived in Connecticut for five generations. As the colony and then state filled up, they began moving on:

- Worthy's grandfather Samuel^5 in the 1700s moved north twice, to western Massachusetts and to southern Vermont.

- Worthy's father Eliphas^6 moved north to Underhill, Vermont, and then southwest to Licking County, Ohio.
- Once grown and married, Worthy^7 himself moved southwest into Wabash and Edwards counties, Illinois.

Born in Vermont in 1809, Worthy came to Granville, Ohio, with his birth family in 1815. There he met and married Hannah James, the daughter of Welsh Baptist immigrants; most if not all Thralls before him had married New Englanders. In 1834 the couple joined at least two of Worthy's brothers in southeastern Illinois.

Most of Worthy and Hannah's grandchildren and spouses died in Illinois (Generation 9, chapters 6–21). Most of their great-grandchildren and spouses died in Illinois, California, Florida, and Missouri (Generation 10, chapters 22–59).

A few of their descendants (or spouses) spoke against war, and many participated:

- Solon Gould (Chapter 3) took up arms for the Union in the Civil War;
- in World War I Earl Amos Morgan (Chapter 26), Harry Ingalls Hannah (Chapter 34), and Verla C. Crawley (Chapter 36) served; and
- in World War II Francis E. Morgan (Chapter 22, child iv), Dale Sims (Chapter 22, child xii), Victor L. Gould (Chapter 41), Cecil Melvin Pifer (Chapter 45), Beulah Marshall (Chapter 47), Chester "Jackie" Pearson (Chapter 48), George A. Mooers (Chapter 50), Victor Thrall Jr. (Chapter 52), George Foster (Chapter 56), H. James Thrall (Chapter 57), William H. Cover (Chapter 58), and David L. Cover (Chapter 59) served.

As a group, the great-grandchildren's lives spanned multiple states over more than a century. Hannah did not live to know any of them: her first great-grandchild, Edgar A.^{10} Morgan, was born four months after she died in 1875. The last great-grandchild, Harold James "Jim"^{10} Thrall, was born in 1925—two months after Edgar's death—and died in 2018. When

Edgar was born there were 45 million Americans;[2] when Jim died there were 328 million.[3]

MIGRATION STORIES

Thomas S. Hinde—an experienced observer probably known to the Thralls as a writer, Methodist preacher, Ohio settler, and a founder of Mount Carmel, Wabash County, Illinois—recommended that westering families move in two stages. The "less incumbered," he wrote, should travel early in the year, descending the Ohio River with the spring flood. The rest (presumably including women and children) should travel by land in the fall when the waters were low, "bringing only their beds and bedding, and clothing, and such necessary articles as may be immediately wanted, and can be transported with little expense."[4] Actual migrants varied: the unrelated Holton family of Vermont traveled together to western Illinois in the fall of 1835, a fourteen-week overland trek by wagon.[5]

The Thrall and Gould accounts that have survived were terse and after-the-fact, but they apparently did follow some of Hinde's advice.

---

[2] US Bureau of the Census, "Annual Population Estimates for the United States: 1790 to 1970," *Historical Statistics of the United States, Colonial Times to 1970*, Bicentennial Edition, part 1 (Washington, D.C.: Government Printing Office, 1970), 8.

[3] US Census Bureau, "US and World Population Clock," which read just over 330,000,000 on 16 August 2020 (https://www.census.gov/popclock).

[4] Thomas S. Hinde, "Circular," *Mount Carmel Sentinel* (Illinois), Wednesday 19 November 1834, p. 2, col. 5; microfilm, "Miscellaneous Illinois Newspapers" M-22B, Abraham Lincoln Presidential Library, Springfield.

[5] Joan A. Hunter, "An Overland Journey from Vermont to Illinois as Recollected by Mary Holton (1793–1874) with a Genealogical Summary," *Vermont Genealogy* 10 (October 2005):183–90. Later installments: vols. 12 (July and October 2007) and 13 (April, July, and October 2008).

Map 1. Thrall and Gould migrations

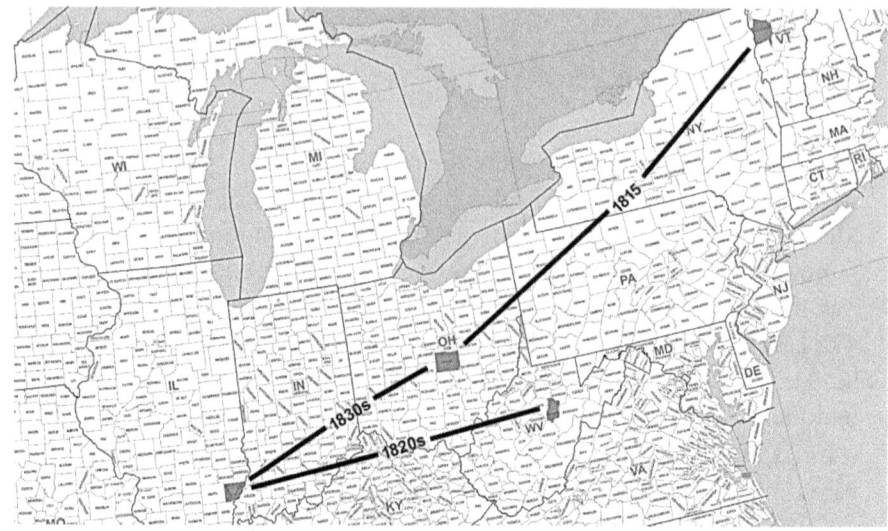

Map 1. *Migration points: 1815 Thralls from Chittenden County, Vermont, to Licking County, Ohio; 1820s and 1830s Thralls from Licking County, Ohio, to Wabash and Edwards counties, Illinois; 1820s Goulds from Upshur County, then Virginia, to Wabash and Edwards. Not shown: earlier Thralls north from Connecticut to Massachusetts and Vermont; Simon James's family from Wales to Philadelphia, western Pennsylvania, and Licking County, Ohio.*[6]

A typewritten text attributed to Worthy's first cousin Walter Thrall (1794–1885)[7] of Rutland, Vermont, outlined the Thralls' first trip from Vermont to Ohio:

---

[6] Map adapted from US Census Bureau (www2.census.gov/geo/maps/general_ref/us_base/stco2003/stco2003.pdf).

[7] "Thrall," *Old Northwest Genealogical Quarterly* 9 (April 1906):179. Walter, later a probate judge and genealogist in Pickaway County, Ohio, was the son of Eliphas's brother Jesse.

> On June 15, 1815 in company with two cousins, I started for Granville, Ohio, as I had a large circle of relatives in that township.[8] My two cousins, Joel and Oliver Thrall [Worthy's older brothers], and myself fitted out a two-horse wagon, in which we put our chests and the few articles which we thought the most necessary in a new country. We could travel upon an average about 25 miles per day . . . and about the 20th of July we got to Granville.[9]

On this trip Joel would have been 23 years old, Walter 21, and Oliver 18. Worthy, himself only a week short of six years old, may have envied their adventure.[10] And there was more to the story: Joel was jumping bail on a charge of forgery in Vermont.[11]

A 1960 obituary described Freeman and Dorcas Gould's early family trip from Virginia to Illinois:

---

[8] Ten years earlier, in 1805, residents of Granville, Massachusetts, including some Thralls, had organized a group migration to what became Granville, Licking County, Ohio: William T. Utter, *Granville: The Story of an Ohio Village* (Granville, Ohio: Granville Historical Society and Denison University, 1956), 18–55.

[9] "Some Notes Left by Mr. Walter Thrall," brief typescript pasted into the back of *Genealogy of the Thrall Family: Also of the Rose Family to the Year 1862* (Poultney, Vermont: Randall Brothers, 1890), Ohio Genealogical Society library, Bellville. Also, Henry Bushnell, *History of Granville, Licking County, Ohio* (Columbus: Press of Hann and Adair, 1889), 105.

[10] Walter's birth 2 May 1794: "Thrall," *Old Northwest Genealogical Quarterly* (April 1906):179. Oliver's birth 29 July 1796: Ridge Cemetery, Lick Prairie Precinct, Wabash County, Illinois, grave marker readings at Interment.net. Joel's birth summer 1792: Harold Henderson, "'Faultless Could I Love Him Less?': Joel S. Thrall and His Descendants in Vermont, Quebec, Ohio, and Texas," Part 2, *New England Historical and Genealogical Register* 172 (Fall 2018):341–53, specifically 346.

[11] For details, Harold Henderson, "'Faultless Could I Love Him Less?': Joel S. Thrall and His Descendants in Vermont, Quebec, Ohio, and Texas," Part 1, *New England Historical and Genealogical Register* 172 (Summer 2018):248–256, specifically 249–51.

The parents of this pioneer Gould family migrated to Edwards county in the early 1830's with their sons Calvin, Charles and Solon [who later married Laura Thrall] from French Creek, West Virginia [then Virginia]. They floated on a raft on the Fox River into the Monongahela up to Pittsburg, then into the Ohio River to the mouth of the Wabash River where they turned north to locate in Edwards county [Illinois] southwest of Bone Gap. With them on the raft they brought their household goods and domesticated animals.[12]

HOME TOWN, HOME COLLEGE

McKendree College (now McKendree University), in southwestern Illinois' St. Clair County, long remained a family gathering point. At least 31 of Worthy and Hannah's descendants and spouses studied there. In 1928 the college's centennial commencement drew many family members of the ninth and tenth generations (Chapter 5);[13] a contingent of the tenth, eleventh, and twelfth generations attended the installation of a new McKendree president 67 years later, 29 April 1995.[14]

In 1870 Worthy's future daughter-in-law Edith Marie Flint became the first woman to receive a degree from McKendree who had attended classes there. (The year before, Mary Julia Jewett received a degree based on examination.)[15]

---

[12] "Edith Evelyn Gould Graveside Services Held Sunday," clipping from unnamed newspaper dated "11-16-60," in author's possession. Obviously an oft-told family tale, it was likely put in print for remembrance, as Edith was the last of her siblings.

[13] "Many Attend Commencement at Lebanon," *Belleville Daily News-Democrat* (Illinois) Thursday 21 June 1928, p. 7, col. 4.

[14] Program, McKendree College, "The Inauguration of James M. Dennis, The Thirty-Second President of McKendree College," 29 April 1995; in author's possession, tub 8, folder 232.

[15] *Centennial McKendree College with St. Clair County History* (Lebanon, Illinois: McKendree College, 1928), 234–36.

Some overly exuberant stories have Edith the first woman college graduate west of the Appalachians. This would have come as a surprise to Ohio's Oberlin College, which first admitted women in 1837.

Peoria, Decatur, and Evansville

Worthy and Hannah's children grew up in or near the rural Edwards County village of Bone Gap, enmeshed in a network of family and friends. When the Peoria, Decatur, and Evansville Railroad came through prior to 1883,[16] the village moved itself half a mile west in order to be connected and have a station. (Worthy's grandson Wilbur^9 Morgan [Chapter 8] had a part in this and built a new store.)[17] In 1891 the railroad ran south from Olney through tiny towns—Calhoun, Parkersburg, West Salem, Bone Gap, Browns, Seigert or Seigert Station, and Grayville—before crossing the Wabash River into Indiana.[18]

At this time it was possible to claim that "anything could be bought in Bone Gap that could be bought anywhere." Nevertheless few grandchildren and no great-grandchildren chose to remain.

---

[16] *Combined History of Lawrence, Edwards, and Wabash Counties, Illinois, 1682–1883* (Philadelphia: J. L. McDonough, 1883), 164.
[17] "Communities . . . Bone Gap Precinct," *History of Edwards County, Illinois* (Albion: Edwards County Historical Society, 1980) 1:9.
[18] Illinois Railroad and Warehouse Commissioners, "Railroad Map of Illinois, 1891"; Illinois Digital Archives > Railroad Maps of Illinois (idaillinois.org/cdm/singleitem/collection/p16614coll7/id/10). Seigert is absent from Edward Callary, *Place Names of Illinois* (Urbana and Chicago: University of Illinois Press, 2009) and topozone map of the area (topozone.com/illinois/edwards-il/locale/seigert-station-historical). Between Browns and Grayville the only feature today is Fortney Church.

Map 2. 1891 Bone Gap and railroads

Map 2. *Towns and railroads in 1891 in the Bone Gap area of southeastern Illinois, featuring Richland, Edwards, and Wabash counties. The Peoria, Decatur, and Evansville line served Bone Gap.*

METHODISTS AND THEIR MESSAGE

Worthy himself was not a Methodist minister, but a "class leader." A key part of the denomination's early organization, the class leader kept its many small and isolated congregations connected, especially in the early days when ministers were scarce and circuit riders appeared irregularly.

Eleven of Worthy and Hannah's descendants over three generations became what one might call professional Methodists:

- one of Worthy and Hannah's children (Leonidas Worthy[8] Thrall) and the spouse of another (Charles Wesley Campbell);
- five of their grandchildren (Virgil Nathan[9] Gould, Victor Worthy[9] Thrall, Charles Haven[9] Thrall, and Harold Leonidas[9] Thrall) and the spouse of a sixth (Joseph Walter Britton);
- one more grandchild (Edith Laura[9] Thrall), a deaconess who could have been a minister and an excellent one, had the times allowed; and
- one great-grandchild (Charles[10] Mooers) and one spouse of an adopted great-grandchild (Hugh McNelly).

These preachers and their faithful did not necessarily support the early 20th-century status quo. In 1908 the Methodist Episcopal Church, then the largest US Protestant denomination,[19] stood publicly in favor of:

- "the protection of the worker from dangerous machinery, occupational disease, injuries, and mortality,"
- "a living wage in every industry," and
- "the highest wage that each industry can afford and . . . the most equitable division of the products of industry that can ultimately be devised."[20]

In a 1915 baccalaureate sermon delivered prior to US intervention, Leonidas Thrall described World War I as "wicked and needless," and looked forward to arbitration taking the place of war.[21] He lived long enough to note the local boys who were joining or being

---

[19] Bureau of the Census, *Religious Bodies 1906* (Washington, DC: Government Printing Office, 1910), Bulletin 103, 2nd edition, 17–21.

[20] Harry F. Ward, editor, *A Year Book of the Church and Social Service in the United States* (New York: Missionary Education Movement, 1916), 197–98.

[21] "The True Aristocracy," delivered 30 May 1915; *Harrisburg Chronicle* (Illinois).

conscripted into World War I after all.[22] His descendants in the eleventh, twelfth, and thirteenth generations have yet to see his hope fulfilled.

More than forty of Worthy and Hannah's descendants and spouses were full- or part-time teachers. They included collegians like Carrie[8] (Thrall) Campbell, who would face a few dozen rural school pupils for a few weeks at a time, often in winter; small-town high-school teachers like Emery H. Martin, who climbed the 20th-century ladder from sports coach to principal; and numerous college and university professors. Music, instrumental and vocal, was a common thread among the descendants.

Three of Worthy and Hannah's great-grandchildren, and the spouse of a fourth, achieved the distinction of being listed in *Who's Who*: William Everett[10] Britton (Chapter 31), Timothy Irle McKnight (Chapter 33), Ethel Lucretia[10] (Britton) Hartman (Chapter 37), and Robert McDowell[10] Thrall (Chapter 54).[23] It is arguable that grandchild William Flint[9] Thrall (Chapter 18), co-author of the classic *Handbook to Literature*, did not miss the cut by much.[24]

---

[22] Postcard from Leonidas 4 April 1917 (in author's possession, tub 13, binder item 326.21).

[23] William Everett Britton entry, *Who Was Who in America* (Wilmette, Illinois: Marquis Who's Who, 1989), 9:48 (1985–1989). Also, Timothy Irle McKnight entry, 243. Also, Ethel Lucretia Britton Hartman entry, *Who's Who of American Women 1977–1978* (Chicago: Marquis Who's Who, 1977), 374–75. Also, Robert McDowell Thrall entry, *Who Was Who in America 2006–2007*, 18:241 (New Providence, New Jersey: Marquis Who's Who, 2007).

[24] "William Flint Thrall," in Winfield Scott Downs, editor, *Encyclopedia of American Biography*, new series, 16:63–65 (New York City: The American Historical Company, 1943).

Chapter 1

Seventh Generation

Worthy Thrall–Hannah James Family

"And now Lizzie the worst of it, we have no dinner and in debt 13 dollars"

---

1. WORTHY[7] **THRALL** (*Eliphas*[6], *Samuel*[5], *John*[4-3], *Timothy*[2], *William*[1])[25]
Birth: 22 June 1809 in Underhill, Chittenden County, Vermont
Death: 3 January 1852 in Bone Gap, Edwards County, Illinois
Burial: Bone Gap Cemetery[26]
Spouse: **HANNAH JAMES**, married 15 November 1832,[27] likely in Granville, Licking County, Ohio

---

[25] For Eliphas[6] son of Samuel[5]: *Massachusetts Vital Records*, Granville, 1732–1902, microfiche #2 (Oxford: Holbrook Research Institute, 1988), original p. 114. For Samuel[5] son of John[4]: John of Windsor's 29 August 1748 will naming wife Mary and son Samuel (*Digest of the Early Connecticut Probate Records, Hartford District, 1729–1750*, 3:668–69); and Samuel's 11 July 1737 birth to John and Mary (*Connecticut Vital Records to 1870 [Barbour Collection]*), Windsor, 277 (americanancestors.com). For John[4] son of John[3]: John of Windsor's 1732 will, naming wife Mindwell and son John (*Early Connecticut Probate 1729–1750*, 3:120); and Henry R. Stiles, *History and Genealogies of Ancient Windsor 1635–1891* (1892–93; reprinted 1992), 2:761–62. For John[3] husband of Mindwell and son of Timothy[2] and for Timothy[2] son of William[1]: Mary Walton Ferris, "Thrall Family," *Dawes-Gates Ancestral Lines*, vol. 2, *Gates and Allied Families* (privately printed, 1931), 792–97. The immigrant William[1] Thrall remains a mystery. Many dubious assertions have been made, but no evidence of him has been found prior to his 1637 Connecticut land grant.

[26] Photograph of Rosalie (Thrall) Carmichael about 1974 between the standing and legible gravestones of Worthy and Hannah Thrall; in author's possession. For place of birth, Morthy [Worthy] Thrall household, 1850 US census, Edwards County, Illinois, p. 256 (stamped, *verso*), dwelling 84, family 85. Also, Worthy Thrall burial #281, Duane Smith, compiler, "Old Part of [Bone Gap] Cemetery," handwritten list of 380 numbered burials with names, birth dates, and death dates; photocopy in author's possession. Worthy's dates are erroneously given as 12 June 1809 and 2 January 1852.

[27] Rosalie (Thrall) Carmichael, "Thrall Genealogy" (17-page typescript on onion skin in red binder, by Rosalie although no author is named), 3; in author's possession, tub 2, item 34. This booklet was the hard-won product of diligent old-school genealogy: visits with relatives, letters requesting information, and reproduction of copies by manual typewriter using onion-skin and carbon paper.

Spouse's parents: Simon and Elizabeth [–?–] James of Wales[28]
Spouse's birth: 11 April 1809 in Licking County, Ohio
Spouse's death: 27 March 1875 in Illinois
Spouse's burial: Bone Gap Cemetery[29]

Worthy, the youngest child of Eliphas and Mary (Mead) Thrall, was six years old in 1815, when he and most of his family left Underhill, Vermont, for Granville, Ohio.[30] Having no word from him, and few words about him, we must squeeze the available facts hard.

Growing up in Granville during the 1820s, Worthy needed few sermons to make him conscious of mortality. He was 13 years old when sister Orilla (Thrall) Brown died back in Vermont;[31] seventeen when sister Caroline H. (Thrall) Cooper died in Wabash County, Illinois, leaving

---

[28] For Hannah's parents and siblings, Harold Henderson, "Licking County Pioneers Simon and Elizabeth James and Their Children," *Ohio Genealogical Society Quarterly* 57(4), 2017: 353–63.

[29] For dates, Hannah's grave marker as viewed during author's visit 24–25 May 2001. Inscription: "Thanks be to God who giveth us the victory through our Lord Jesus Christ." For birthplace, Morthy [Worthy] Thrall household for Hannah, 1850 US census, Edwards County, Illinois, p. 256 (stamped, *verso*), dwelling 84, family 85. For Hannah wife of Worthy, Duane Smith, compiler, "Old Part of [Bone Gap] Cemetery," handwritten list of 380 numbered burials with names, birth dates, and death dates; photocopy in author's possession.

[30] For a concise summary of the reasons many Vermonters went west, Charles T. Morrissey, *Vermont: A Bicentennial History* (New York: W.W. Norton, 1981), 109–110. For a Thrall-specific reason to do so (brother Joel's bail-jumping on a forgery charge in June 1815): Harold Henderson, "'Faultless Could I Love Him Less?': Joel S. Thrall and His Descendants in Vermont, Quebec, Ohio, and Texas," Part 1, *New England Historical and Genealogical Register* 172 (Summer 2018):248–256, specifically 249–50.

[31] Joyce Anne White, *Descendants of Joseph and Hannah (Johnson) Brown of Jericho, Vermont* (Richmond, Vermont: privately printed, 2006), 12–13, a thorough account of the Brown family, including the descendants of Orilla (Thrall) Brown, Worthy's older sister.

four young children;[32] and eighteen when brother Joel, a doctor, died in nearby Franklin County, Ohio.[33] Caroline was the sister closest to Worthy in age; when they were young she is most likely to have been a stand-in mother figure in the family of ten children. Worthy and Hannah gave her name to a daughter.

Gone to Illinois

In 1831 the Granville Methodist Church's Sunday School "stuard's book" (recording attendance and offerings to the church) listed Elizabeth James and Hannah James (mother and daughter) on the same page as Eliphas and Worthy Thrall. In 1832 the same names appeared, except that Hannah's last name was scratched out and "Thrall" written over it in a different hand. In 1833, Hannah and Worthy were listed side by side like other married couples.[34] In 1834 they left for good after paying their taxes: 31.2 cents on one horse (valued at $40) and one head of cattle ($8).[35]

---

[32] Caroline H. Cooper grave marker, died 24 August 1826, Sand Hill Cemetery, Mount Carmel, Wabash County, Illinois, image, memorial #72,661,409 for Caroline H. Thrall Cooper by Robert (findagrave.com). Also, author's visit 14 October 2011. Worthy might well have known the inscription by heart: "My flesh shall slumber in the ground/Till the last joyfull trump shall sound/Then burst the bands with sweet surprise/And in my Saviour's image rise." The full hymn, of which this is the sixth stanza, draws on Psalm 17, under the heading, "The Sinner's Portion and Saint's Hope" in Paul Henkel, editor, *Church Hymn Book: consisting of newly composed hymns with the addition of hymns and psalms, from other authors, carefully adapted for the use of public worship, and many other occasions*, 1st edition (New Market, Virginia: Solomon Henkel, 1816), 352–53 (hymnary.org). Caroline's epitaph substituted "bands" for "chains;" another hymn version, perhaps of Calvinistic bent, had "awfull" for "joyfull."

[33] Harold Henderson, "'Faultless Could I Love Him Less?': Joel S. Thrall and His Descendants in Vermont, Quebec, Ohio, and Texas," *New England Historical and Genealogical Register* 172 (Summer 2018):248–256 (Part 1) and (Fall 2018):341–52 (Part 2), specifically 346.

[34] Thrall and James entries in Sunday School steward's record of contributions, beginning in 1831, Granville Centenary Methodist Church, Granville, Licking County, Ohio, viewed by author Thursday 12 April 2001, courtesy of Ken and Sandra Nihiser.

[35] Worthy Thrall entry, "Tax Record Licking County 1834 Auditor of State," Granville Township, p. 246; absent 1835, pp. 147–48; "Tax Records, 1834–1835," images 268 and 596–97 of 776, FHL 545,115, DGS 4,849,368 (familysearch.org).

They traveled that year with baby Elizabeth "in the old prairie schooner,"[36] headed for Wabash County in southeastern Illinois. The 350-mile trip linked them in a chain migration, following tracks first laid down by sister Caroline and her husband Samuel Cooper, and later at various times by brothers Oliver, Lyman, and Aaron.

Land and farming

On 13 January 1837 Worthy paid the US government $100 for 80 acres immediately adjacent to his brothers' properties in Wabash County, Illinois.[37] Over the next few years he purchased a total of 260 acres there, and then sold parcels to Guy Lockwood and John White [Whyde?] in 1842–43.[38] Wabash County records—decimated by an 1857 courthouse fire and an 1877 courthouse tornado—leave an incomplete record of the brothers' land transactions.[39]

---

[36] Letter from Caroline (Thrall) Campbell, transcribed by her grand-niece genealogist Rosalie (Thrall) Carmichael in "Thrall Genealogy" (17-page typescript on onion skin in red binder, by Rosalie Thrall Carmichael although no author is named), 3; in author's possession, tub 2, item 34. Pagination could differ in other versions; there were many updates over the years and no definitive publication.

[37] The patent arrived 28 July 1838: Bureau of Land Management, "Land Patent Search," database, *General Land Office Records* [GLO] (glorecords.blm.gov/PatentSearch), Wabash County entry #4644 for Worthy Thrall. For original purchase date and amount, "Illinois Public Domain Land Sales Database" 110:85, Illinois State Archives (cyberdriveillinois.com/departments/archives/databases/data_lan.html).

[38] Worthy and Hannah Thrall to Guy Lockwood (180 acres), Wabash (?) County Deeds B:256, 10 August 1842, recorded 11 Oct 1858. Also, Worthy and Hannah Thrall to John Whide (80 acres), Wabash (?) County Deeds E:608, 27 January 1843, recorded 8 May 1843.

[39] Illinois State Archives, "Documented Records Losses," *Wabash County Fact Sheet* (cyberdriveillinois.com/departments/archives/irad/wabash.html) mentions the fire but not the tornado. Also, Wabash County, Illinois, Commissioners Court Proceedings 1825–1832, pp. 1, 102; Eastern Illinois University Regional Archives Depository, Charleston. For the tornado, Sgt. Henry Calver, Paper 41 [report on Mount Carmel tornado of 4 June 1877], 517–27 (courthouse at 521), in *Report of the Secretary of War*, volume 4, Signal Office (Washington DC: Government Printing Office, 1877); 45th Congress, Second Session, House of Representatives Executive Document 1, Part 2.

In the early 1840s[40] Worthy and family moved about four miles west into Bone Gap Precinct in Edwards County. There he first patented 80 acres, dividing and selling it,[41] then buying another 80 acres (the west half of the northwest quarter of Section 17, Township 1 South, Range 14 West), which remained in the family.[42] In 1872 Hannah and her four surviving children (Mary, Laura, Carrie, and Leonidas) and son-in-law Solon Gould sold 36 acres off the south end to Jacob Harms for $875.[43]

In 1850 Worthy's 80-acre farm was valued at $500.[44] It ranked average or a little below compared to neighboring farms, with his 40 "improved" acres, $500 cash value of farm, $150 value of livestock, and 600 bushels of "Indian corn" harvested in the past year. In contrast, his investment of $100 in machinery placed him above the neighborhood

---

[40] Reportedly "since the age of nine years her [Mary Elizabeth's] home has been in Edwards county," implying that the family moved in 1841 or 1842. Rev. G. A. Seed, "Obituary" for Mary Elizabeth Thrall Morgan, *Albion Journal-Register* (Illinois), Thursday 15 January 1903, p. 3, col. 3.

[41] Edwards County entry #9863 for Worthy Thrall (40 acres, NE ¼ SE ¼ Section 9 Township 1S Range 14W), patent dated 1 August 1844; Bureau of Land Management, "Land Patent Search," database, General Land Office Records [GLO] (glorecords.blm.gov/PatentSearch). Also, Worthy Thrall to Charles J. Root 6 February 1845, recorded 24 September 1846 (20 acres), F:68, Edwards County, Illinois, Grantee Index 1; image 166 of 726, FHL 1,401,783, DGS 8,117,694 (familysearch.org). Similarly, to David Benson 25 September 1845, recorded 9 December 1845 (20 acres), E:511; image 166 of 726. Original deeds not viewed.

[42] David S. Rude to Worthy Thrall 10 June 1847, recorded 24 June, F:199, Edwards County, Illinois, FHL 1,401,782 item 3, DGS 7,625,301; image 402 of 726, FHL 1,401,783, DGS 8,117,694 (familysearch.org). Index entry.

[43] Hannah Thrall, Mary E. Morgan, Solon H. Gould, Laura L. Gould, Hannah C. Thrall, and Leonidas W. Thrall to Jacob Harms for $875 (part SW ¼ NW ¼ Section 17, T1S, R14W), Edwards County, Illinois, Deeds W:626, 28 September 1872, recorded 6 January 1881. The disposition of the northern 44 acres has not been determined.

[44] Morthy [Worthy] Thrall household, 1850 US census, Edwards County, Illinois, p. 256 (stamped, *verso*), dwelling 84, family 85. The $500 figure for "real estate" is identical to the "cash value of farm" given in the agriculture schedule (following note).

average[45] and his farmland and buildings, at $6.25 per acre, were well above the county average of $5 per acre.[46]

Methodist class leader

Like many of his siblings, Worthy was an ardent Methodist. The first Methodist society in Bone Gap was organized in the summer of 1835 by Rev. Richard Haney of Mount Vernon, with Worthy as class leader. They met in the home of John Brown and were accordingly known as the "John Brown Class": John Brown, Lydia Brown, Worthy Thrall, Hannah Thrall, John Hocking, Susanna Hocking, James Hocking, Lucinda Hocking, and Pertam[i]a Rude.

"Circuit preaching was on week-days at intervals of four weeks," it was recalled in 1908. "At this time much depended upon the Class Leader[,] Local Preachers[,] and Exhorters who held services every Sunday. . . . For eight or ten years [the class] met at private houses, and then it began to meet regularly at the Stanley School House and had preaching every two weeks on Wednesday."[47] After thirteen years, in 1848 it merged with the "Mills Prairie Class," led by Ansel Gould Sr. and Luther Morgan (families later variously related to Worthy by marriage). Under the ministry of John Thatcher and his assistant Thomas Parker,

---

[45] Worthy Thrall entry, 1850 US census, agriculture schedule, Edwards County, Illinois, pp. 885–86, line 24 (ancestry.com). This schedule included much additional information about the farm and its products. "Neighborhood" in this case refers to those farms, usually about forty, enumerated on one page of the schedule.

[46] Charles H. Barnard and John Jones, *Farm Real Estate Values in the United States by Counties, 1850–1982*, Statistical Bulletin #751, Economic Research Service, US Department of Agriculture (Washington, DC: US Government Printing Office, 1987), Table 1, p. 3 for states, and Table 2, pp. 24–29 for Illinois counties (hathitrust.org). Unfortunately, these numbers do not distinguish between improved and unimproved land, as the 1850 agriculture schedule did, so I have conservatively assumed that the acreage discussed includes both (thus Worthy's 80 total acres valued at $500 = $6.25 per acre). If only improved land were considered, his farm would exceed both the Illinois and US figures in value. Illinois farmland value statewide averaged $8 per acre; the US national average was $11. Land values per acre in Illinois counties in 1850 ranged from a low of $3 in Franklin, Saline, and Wayne counties (southern Illinois) to a high of $14 per acre in Vermilion County (east-central Illinois).

[47] M. E. Shurtleff, recording steward, "History First M.E. [Methodist Episcopal] Church, Bone Gap, Illinois." Handwritten text prepared about 1908, photocopy in author's possession.

a church building was erected and dedicated in August 1849, then called Salem Methodist Episcopal Church.[48] (Thomas Parker was Worthy's nephew—the son of Thomas and Mary [Thrall] Parker of Granville, Ohio, and a grandson of Eliphas and Mary [Mead] Thrall.)[49]

The Lawrenceville Circuit of the church included Bone Gap, and held conferences quarterly. Worthy attended these gatherings 21 July 1849 and 4 May, 20 July, and 2 November in 1850. On 20 July 1850, "Brother Danl B. Leech" was recommended by the "Society at Salem" (later Bone Gap), examined on doctrine and discipline, and was by vote licensed to preach.[50]

At work

Preacher Daniel "Leech" may well have been one of the neighbors with whom Worthy traded work. In addition to farming, Worthy was a wheelwright, cabinet maker, and wagon maker. "In his boyhood days or young manhood he had learned also the blacksmith's [trade,]" wrote daughter Carrie many years later, "but I think never worked very much at that as it hurt him but did the carpenter work more, made bureaus, bedsteads, tables—always kept a man in the shop for the blacksmith and helped him."[51]

---

[48] *History of Edwards County, Illinois* (Albion: Edwards County Historical Society, 1980), 32.

[49] "Memoir of Thomas Parker," *Minutes of the Central Ohio Conference of the Methodist Episcopal Church, Upper Sandusky, 9–14 September 1853* (Cincinnati: Methodist Book Concern, 1863), 38–39, which does not name his parents but identifies him as born in Newark, Licking County, Ohio, 25 December 1827, corresponding to the following census entry: Thomas Parker [Sr.] household for Thomas Parker [Jr.] age 23 born Ohio, "M.E. [Methodist Episcopal] Clergyman," 1850 US census, Etna Township, Licking County, Ohio, pp. 608–609, dwelling 1905, family 1937. His story is beyond our scope.

[50] "A Continuation of the Records of the Minutes of Quarterly Meeting Conferences held on Lawrenceville Circuit, Illinois Conference of the Methodist Episcopal Church," 28 October 1848, 20 January 1849, 28 April 1849, 21 July 1849, 10 November 1849, 26 January 1850, 4 May 1850, 20 July 1850, 2 November 1850, handwritten meeting reports, McKendree College, Lebanon, St. Clair County, Illinois.

[51] Letter from Caroline (Thrall) Campbell, transcribed and typed by her grand-niece genealogist Rosalie (Thrall) Carmichael in "Thrall Genealogy" (17-page typescript on onion skin in red binder, by Rosalie although no author is named), 3; in author's possession, tub 2, item 34.

Fragmentary information on Worthy's work between 19 May 1840 and 1 February 1850 can be glimpsed in handwritten entries on four fragile sheets, separated from a printed account book that once held at least 67 pages. They mention almost entirely blacksmithing work, but the sample is tiny and woodworking might have occupied a separate book. Named customers and therefore neighbors were:

* George Lough/Low in 1841 and 1843–45;
* Robert Lee in 1841 and 1843;
* Charles Root in 1841;
* John S. Kitchen in 1840, 1843, and 1848;
* Daniel and William S. Leach in 1841 and 1843;
* S./H. Crowder in 1849;
* C. T. (?) Hendricks in 1847;
* Alpheus Rude in 1849; and
* apparently Guy Crooks.

Most accounts were kept in quarters (25 cents) and fractions thereof. Each job of work, credit or debit, was briefly noted. The commonest task was "to sharp[en] [plow]shares" for 12½ cents. These and other farm-related jobs were concentrated in the spring.

Sometimes labor was traded: it appears that Worthy did "part of days work" valued at 25 cents 18 July 1844 and supplied 2½ bushels of wheat valued at $1.25 (50 cents a bushel) 21 August, and included those amounts when he and George Lough settled up 24 January 1845. "Shoeing [horses]" was not as common as one might expect, and cost 50 cents.

The most expensive jobs were "35 lbs of plow irons" ($7.00, name and date torn off); "31 lbs of plough laid with steel" ($5.66, 27 June 1842, for Charles Root), and "22 lbs of plough irons" ($3.66, 6 June 1848, customer not visible). Other jobs included:

- "shoeing and repair coffee mill" (56¼ cents, 25 December 1845 for George Lough);
- "make teakettle bail" (18¾ cents, 10 July 1840, customer not visible);

- "mend hoes drawing knife & bell" (25 cents, 8 June 1843 for George Low);
- "one iron pitch fork" (37½ cents, 27 June 1843 for Daniel Leach);
- "one scratch awl" (6¼ cents—the least expensive job on record—10 July 1843 for Daniel Leach);
- "repair waggon" (50 cents, 2 January 1841 for Daniel Leach);
- "one hoe one set of loom irons . . . &c" ($1.62½, 20 May 1843 for William S. Leach);
- "mend brush cythe make grass nail & put hinge to stove door" (37½ cents, 1 September 1841 for Charles Root); and
- "set tire [?] & mend fire shovel" (87½ cents, 31 July 1841 for Daniel Leach).[52]

Historian Fred Anderson describes a similar rural economy in western Massachusetts, where Worthy's grandfather Samuel Thrall lived two generations earlier, in the late 1700s:

> Any rural householder at any given time would owe and be owed by dozens of his neighbors. Moreover, few men possessed liquid assets sufficient to settle all, or even many, of their debts on demand. . . . For them, economic survival meant not being called on to settle their obligations frequently (or worst of all, unexpectedly). The way to succeed within these cash-starved town economies was not to get ahead, but to be a patient creditor and a faithful debtor . . . not the sort of man who would increase his estate at his townsmen's expense.[53]

Worthy's early death created no known record beyond his grave marker. A family story has it that he was cutting wood for the minister in very cold weather, became sick, and died at age 35. The age is wrong, and Bone Gap had no resident minister at the time. Perhaps Daniel Leach was

---

[52] Worthy Thrall account books, images and transcription from delicate originals—four sheets or partial sheets out of a total of at least 67—arbitrarily designated A1, A2, B1, B2, C1, C2, D1, and D2; images in author's possession.

[53] Fred Anderson, *A People's Army: Massachusetts Soldiers and Society in the Seven Years' War* (Chapel Hill: University of North Carolina Press, 1984), 30. Also, Fernand Braudel, *The Structures of Everyday Life: Civilization & Capitalism 15th–18th Century* (New York: Harper & Row, 1981) 1:446–48.

the preacher in question, or perhaps the circuit rider was then living near Bone Gap. Worthy left no will; his estate was administered by son-in-law Amos B. Morgan with a bond of $200.[54]

Hannah

Like Worthy, Hannah was the youngest child in her family. She lived almost a quarter-century as Worthy's widow, and saw her son Leonidas through McKendree College, combining her earnings from weaving with help from her two older daughters.[55] In 1860, eight years after Worthy's death, the farm still had 40 improved acres (by then, below average for the neighborhood) and was worth about $1200 (average for the neighborhood). It was the only farm in the neighborhood with no horses, and one of twelve farms there that raised no hay. Perhaps Hannah was hiring help and buying feed for the two "milch cows."[56]

Daughter Hannah Caroline "Carrie" was about seven years old when Worthy died. She left the only record that hints how bleak the family's world must have been, as father Worthy's 1852 death was followed by that of daughter Rachel in 1857.

"Dear, grand old Uncle Oliver," Carrie wrote years later. "My heart is in my throat and eyes whenever I think of him. While he was much older than father, he lived many years after father was gone and was so good to come and see us and encourage and cheer us up." The older

---

[54] Worthy Thrall probate, Edwards County, Illinois, 1 May 1854 administration; "Illinois, Wills and Probate Records, 1772–1999" > Edwards > Probate Court files, box 10 > images 1673–77 of 2101 (ancestry.com).

[55] Rosalie (Thrall) Carmichael in "Thrall Genealogy" (17-page typescript on onion skin in red binder, by Rosalie although no author is named), 3; in author's possession, tub 2, item 34.

[56] Hannah Thrall farm entry, 1860 US census, agriculture schedule, Albion P.O., Edwards County, Illinois, pp. 11–12, line 13. Near neighbors are defined as the 39 other farms enumerated on the same page. Ancestry.com's image is much less readable than the NARA microfilm.

Oliver survived Worthy by only 6 ½ years, but the gift of his presence lasted longer in her memory.[57]

In May 1870 mother Hannah was living in Lebanon where son Leonidas attended McKendree College. His older sisters helped make his education possible, as the following letter from Hannah shows. From family circumstances—mother Hannah and her oldest daughter Mary Elizabeth Morgan both being widows—it seems likely that Laura and Solon Gould were significant contributors. That month Hannah wrote to daughters "Lizzie" Morgan and Laura Gould in Bone Gap:[58]

> We were all glad to get a letter from you we are all well at present. Call and Wog [not identified] are so busy I must answer your letter. They have some fine times in college and trust profitable. We still have good Tuesday evening prayer meetings. Lonny [Leonidas] goes to every meeting of late. If sinners will go to hell from Lebanon, I do not believe this praying band will have to answer for their sins any more than Noah, Elijah, or Daniel of old would have to answer for the sins of the unbelieving stubborn sinners in their time. When they are solemnly warned by precept and example having the eyes of their understanding inlighted and they see what is for their eternal good and refuse to yield to the gospels' plan for salvation they will be condemned but God's people will be clear of their guilt.
>
> I must confess there are some cold professors [who] to all appearance go after the world and fashion and vanity more than after God. It costs ten dollars to get a dress made in the fashion so much trimming and flouncing. How vain it does look and how displeasing to Him who suffered so much to redeem a lost and ruined

---

[57] Rosalie (Thrall) Carmichael in "Thrall Genealogy" (17-page typescript on onion skin in red binder, by Rosalie although no author is named), 3; in author's possession, tub 2, item 34. For Oliver's dates, 29 July 1796 to 15 August 1858: Charles Koenig's 1988 reading of Ridge Cemetery, Lick Prairie Precinct, Wabash County, Illinois (http://www.interment.net/data/us/il/wabash/ridge.htm).

[58] Hannah James Thrall in Lebanon to daughters Elizabeth Morgan and Laura Gould in or near Bone Gap, May 1870, letter #1 in Flint/Thrall letters and the only known letter from her hand.

world from sin and death and to bring us back to happiness and favor with himself.

Hannah went on to ask after her four Morgan grandchildren:

> How is Milton doing, is he still serving Jesus as his best friend. I hope he is. I am glad Crete can write so well. Think she will make a good writer. I am so glad Allen can write, which hand does he write with? Tell Willie to write [illegible]. Why don't Milton ever write? I hope to see you all soon.

From Lebanon east to Olney by train was about 100 miles, with another 25 miles' travel south to Bone Gap by horse and wagon (the railroad reached Bone Gap later). Travel arrangements could be tricky and had to be made in advance by letter:

> Who and when will it be convenient to meet us at the depot the 3 or 4 of June. Let us know, we will meet you at Olney Friday or Saturday noon. Write and let us know when it will suit the best. You better come with the big wagon for us, we want to bring our trunks and chest with us, what we put [send as] freight will not come to Olney the same day that we do [thus requiring an extra fifty-mile round trip by wagon to retrieve their luggage] and now Lizzie the worst of it, we have no dinner and in debt 13 dollars. We want you to send some soon. Tell Laura and Solon we will want forty dollars. If you can't get it no other way, get it off Mr. Bride. Send some right soon.

The back of the letter included a note to Laura:

> You said if we would stay through spring term you would see that we would have money to take us through. I guess you will find it [illegible line] tried to be saving. Lonny feels so bad about it but we all come out right if we do the best we can and leave the rest with God, that is all we can do. Do you know of any school Call could get [a job teaching in]? Write and let [us] know.

Children of Worthy[7] and Hannah (James) Thrall: (a proposed eighth child, Nancy, said to be born in 1834, seems unlikely as there were only 23 months between the births of Mary and Laura)[59]

2 i. MARY ELIZABETH[8] THRALL (*Worthy[7], Eliphas[6], Samuel[5], John[4-3], Timothy[2], William[1]*) was born 15 November 1833 in Granville, Licking County, Ohio, and died 6 January 1903 in Bone Gap, Edwards County, Illinois. She married 24 January 1852 in Edwards County AMOS B. MORGAN.

3 ii. LAURA LUCINA[8] THRALL (*Worthy[7], Eliphas[6], Samuel[5], John[4-3], Timothy[2], William[1]*) was born 3 October 1835 in Illinois and died 12 February 1898. She married 3 April 1862 SOLON HARPER GOULD.

 iii. CYRUS[8] THRALL (*Worthy[7], Eliphas[6], Samuel[5], John[4-3], Timothy[2], William[1]*) was born 23 July 1838 in Illinois, and died there 3 July 1841.[60]

 iv. RACHEL EMELINE[8] THRALL (*Worthy[7], Eliphas[6], Samuel[5], John[4-3], Timothy[2], William[1]*) was born 17 September 1841 (calculated) in Illinois, and died in Bone Gap 23 January 1857.[61] Eight-year-old "Emaline" was attending school in 1850.[62]

---

[59] D. Stephen Thrall and Grant Leslie Thrall, *Thrall Genealogy 1630–1965: Descendants of William Thrall* (privately printed, 1965), 69. No other source is known for this child.

[60] Worthy Thrall household for boy under age 5, 1840 US census, Wabash County, Illinois, p. 157, line 18. For name, Rosalie (Thrall) Carmichael, "Thrall Genealogy" (17-page typescript on onion skin in red binder, by Rosalie Thrall Carmichael although no author is named), 3; in author's possession, tub 2, item 34.

[61] Morthy [Worthy] Thrall household for apparent daughter "Emaline" age 8 born Illinois, 1850 US census, Edwards County, Illinois, p. 256 (stamped, *verso*), dwelling 84, family 85. Also, Rosalie (Thrall) Carmichael, "Thrall Genealogy" (17-page typescript on onion skin in red binder, by Rosalie Thrall Carmichael although no author is named), p. 3; in author's possession, tub 2, item 34. Also, "Rachel Dau. of W. & H. Thrall, 15 yrs. 4 mo. 6 days," implying birth about 17 September 1841: Duane Smith, compiler, "Old Part of [Bone Gap] Cemetery," handwritten list of 380 numbered burials with names, birth dates, and death dates; photocopy in author's possession.

[62] Morthy [Worthy] Thrall household for Emaline, 1850 US census, Edwards County, Illinois, p. 256 (stamped, *verso*), dwelling 84, family 85.

v. RIGDON/ROYDON/BRYDEN⁸ THRALL (*Worthy⁷, Eliphas⁶, Samuel⁵, John⁴⁻³, Timothy², William¹*) was born 1842–43 in Edwards County, and died after the 1850 census, when he was age seven and attending school.⁶³

4 vi. HANNAH CAROLINE "CARRIE" ⁸ THRALL (*Worthy⁷, Eliphas⁶, Samuel⁵, John⁴⁻³, Timothy², William¹*) was born 18 January 1845 in Edwards County, and died 31 December 1924 (the last of the children) at Lake Charles, Calcasieu Parish, Louisiana. She married 2 September 1875 CHARLES WESLEY CAMPBELL.

5 vii. LEONIDAS WORTHY⁸ THRALL (*Worthy⁷, Eliphas⁶, Samuel⁵, John⁴⁻³, Timothy², William¹*) was born 21 February 1850 in Bone Gap, and died 21 May 1918 in Du Quoin, Perry County, Illinois. He married first 29 September 1873 EDITH MARIE FLINT, and second 27 December 1900 EMILY MARTHA JONES.

---

⁶³ Three variants appear. For Rigdon: Morthy [Worthy] Thrall household for apparent son Rigdon (author's reading) age 7 born Illinois, 1850 US census, Edwards County, Illinois, p. 256 (stamped, *verso*), dwelling 84, family 85. For Bryden: D. Stephen Thrall and Grant Leslie Thrall, *Thrall Genealogy 1630–1965: Descendants of William Thrall* (privately printed, 1965), 69. For Roydon: Morthy [Worthy] Thrall household for apparent son Roydon (Ancestry.com's reading) age 7 born Illinois, 1850 US census, Edwards County, Illinois, p. 256 (stamped, *verso*), dwelling 84, family 85.

Chapter 2

Eighth Generation

Mary Thrall–Amos Morgan Family
parents at chapter 1

"Prepared for the change"

2. **Mary Elizabeth**^{8} **Thrall** (*Worthy^7, Eliphas^6, Samuel^5, John$^{4-3}$, Timothy^2, William^1*)
Birth: 15 November 1833 in Licking County, Ohio
Death: 6 January 1903 in Bone Gap, Edwards County
Burial: 7 January 1903 at the Bone Gap Methodist Cemetery^{64}
Spouse: **Amos B. Morgan,** married 24 January 1852 in Edwards County^{65}
Spouse's parents: Theodore and Lydia Haskell (?) (Rude) Morgan^{66}
Spouse's birth: about 22 January 1827 (calculated) in Virginia

---

^{64} Rev. G. A. Seed, "Obituary" for Mary Elizabeth Thrall Morgan, *Albion Journal-Register* (Illinois), Thursday 15 January 1903, p. 3, col. 3. She had been ill for two years. For gravestone, author's visit, 24–25 May 2001, when it was partially legible. Age at death 69 [??] years, 1 month, 22 days, implying birth about 15 November 1833. Inscription on her grave marker: "Servant of God well done / Thy glorious warfare's past / The battles fought the victory won / And thou are crowned at last!"

^{65} Amos B. Morgan–Mary E. Thrall licensed 17 January, married 24 January 1852, Edwards County, Illinois, Marriage Book B:139. Norman Allyn, MG [minister of the gospel], officiated. (His surname may have been given to their second son.) Mary's obituary gives the 23rd: Rev. G. A. Seed, "Obituary" for Mary Elizabeth Thrall Morgan, *Albion Journal-Register* (Illinois), Thursday 15 January 1903, p. 3, col. 3.

^{66} Rev. G. A. Seed, "Obituary" for Mary Elizabeth Thrall Morgan, *Albion Journal-Register* (Illinois), Thursday 15 January 1903, p. 3, col. 3.

Spouse's death: 11 October 1865, said to be age 38 years, 8 months, 19 days
Spouse's burial: Bone Gap Cemetery[67]

Mary Elizabeth was no doubt the girl aged 5–10 in Worthy Thrall's 1840 household.[68] She lived in Edwards County "since the age of nine years," or 1842–43, suggesting that was when the family moved from neighboring Wabash County. She was "converted [to Methodism] when she was 14 years of age" (about 1847–48).[69] In 1850 she was age 16 and not attending school.[70] Two years later her father was dead and she was married.

In 1860 her husband Amos was a farmer with $1700 in real estate and $600 in personal property; the household included Milton age 7, "Allan" age 4, "Wilber" age 2, and Virginia-born schoolteacher Rebecca Morgan.[71] Amos had 100 improved acres; his machinery was worth $100, livestock $600, and the farm as a whole $1700. In the previous year he had raised 1000 bushels of "Indian corn" and four tons of hay. In all these categories he was in the top half or quarter of his

---

[67] Amos B. Morgan grave marker inscription, Bone Gap Cemetery, viewed by author 24–25 May 2001: "His sun went down in cloudless skies / Assured upon the morn to rise / In lovelier array / Does he forget? O no; / For memory's golden chain / Still binds his heart to friends below / Until we meet again." Death date October 11, 1865, age 38 years, 8 months, 19 days, from grave marker—implying birth about 22 January 1827. Almost all such calculations involve a degree of uncertainty: see Barbara Levergood, "Calculating and Using Dates and Date Ranges," *National Genealogical Society Quarterly* 102 (March 2014): 51–75. Also, Rev. G. A. Seed, "Obituary" for Mary Elizabeth Thrall Morgan, *Albion Journal-Register* (Illinois), Thursday 15 January 1903, p. 3, col. 3. For birth state Virginia, Amos B. Morgan household, 1860 US census, Edwards County, Illinois, pp. 868–69, dwelling/family 474.

[68] Worthy Thrall household for girl age 5–10, 1840 US census, Wabash County, Illinois, p. 157, line 18.

[69] Rev. G. A. Seed, "Obituary" for Mary Elizabeth Thrall Morgan, *Albion Journal-Register* (Illinois), Thursday 15 January 1903, p. 3, col. 3.

[70] Morthy [Worthy] Thrall household for Mary, 1850 US census, Edwards County, Illinois, p. 256 (stamped, *verso*), dwelling 84, family 85.

[71] Amos B. Morgan household, 1860 US census, Edwards County, Illinois, pp. 868–69, dwelling/family 474. Rebecca has not been identified.

neighbors.[72] In 1860 Edwards County land averaged about $11 per acre; with either 140 or 160 total acres, Amos's farm was average or a little above.[73]

Amos owned parcels of land in three different sections of Township 1 South, Range 14 West in Edwards County, but much of his land ownership history is obscure:

- In Section 9: When the Shurtliff family defaulted on their mortgage, Amos purchased the 80 acres in question 14 June 1851: the southeast quarter of the northwest quarter, and the northwest quarter of the southwest quarter.[74] On 4 November 1859 he and wife Mary sold about an acre of the southwest quarter of the southwest quarter to Edwin D. Rude for $5.[75] When and how Amos purchased that small parcel is not known.
- In Section 6 (about a mile to the northwest), on 5 January 1854 Amos received a federal government patent for 80 acres, the south half of the SE quarter. By the time he received the patent, he and wife Mary had already sold half of the land (the southwest quarter of the southeast quarter) for $40 to Julius Stanley 18 February 1853.[76] Later, on 11 February 1860, he sold 20 more acres (the

---

[72] Annie [Amos] Morgan farm entry, 1860 US census, agriculture schedule, Albion P.O., Edwards County, Illinois, p. 11, line 21. Near neighbors are defined as the 39 other farms enumerated on the same page. The image at Ancestry.com is much less readable than the microfilm version.

[73] Charles H. Barnard and John Jones, *Farm Real Estate Values in the United States by Counties, 1850–1982*, Statistical Bulletin #751, Economic Research Service, US Dept. of Agriculture (Washington, DC: US Government Printing Office, 1987), Table 1, p. 3 for states, and Table 2, pp. 24–29 for Illinois counties (hathitrust.org).

[74] Amos B. Morgan from Commissioner, Edwards County, Illinois, deeds H:361–63, 14 June 1851, recorded 24 September 1852; Edwards County Recorder, Albion.

[75] Amos B. Morgan to Edwin D. Rude, Edwards County, Illinois, deeds L:705-6, 4 November 1859, recorded 10 March 1860; Edwards County Recorder, Albion. L. P. Rude and L. S. [?] Thrall witnessed.

[76] Edwards County entry #16371 for Amos B. Morgan (40 acres, S ½ SE ¼ Section 6, Township 1S Range 14W), patent dated 5 January 1854; Bureau of Land Management, "Land Patent Search," database, *General Land Office Records* [GLO] (glorecords.blm.gov/PatentSearch). Also, Amos B. Morgan to Julius Stanley, Edwards County, Illinois, deeds I:23, 18 February 1853, recorded 28 May (SW ¼ SE ¼ Section 6, Township 1S Range 14W); Edwards County Recorder, Albion.

south half of the northeast quarter of the southeast quarter) to Maxwell W. Morgan (relationship not known) for $80, leaving Amos with 20 acres there.[77]

- In Section 3 (to the northeast) Amos bought 20 acres from Robert Thread Jr. 1 May 1857, the south half of the southeast quarter of the southwest quarter, for $145, close to Amos's other properties in Section 9.[78]

At some point—perhaps after Amos's death in 1865—all four children appeared in a guardianship proceeding.[79]

In 1870, eighteen-year-old Milton was the farmer and had $1200 in real estate.[80] In 1880 he was in Nebraska (Chapter 6); his young son Edgar Morgan remained in grandmother Elizabeth Morgan's household, along with Milton's as yet unmarried sister Lucretia. A separate household in the same building included Amos's son "Alan T.," daughter-in-law Rosina A., and infant grandson Ezra L. (Chapter 25)[81]

In that year, Elizabeth Morgan sold her undivided interest in land in Section 17 to her sister Laura L. Gould for $250.[82] In 1881 Mary E. Morgan and others sold about 40 acres to Winfield S. Bare for $140—part

---

[77] Amos B. Morgan to Maxwell W. Morgan, Edwards County, Illinois, deeds O:553-4, 7 February. 1864, recorded 18 May 1864; Edwards County Recorder, Albion. Witnesses were G. L. Rude and L. T. Rude.

[78] Amos B. Morgan from Robert Thread Jr., Edwards County, Illinois, deeds K:351–52, recorded 19 March 1868; Edwards County Recorder, Albion.

[79] Entries for Milton W. Morgan, Alan T. Morgan, Wilber Morgan, Lucretia Morgan, Edwards County Historical Society, *Guardian Index to Files, Albion, Illinois—Includes Insolvents, Adoption, and Insane Persons* (Albion, Illinois: Edwards County Historical Society, no date), 13. Original reportedly in Edwards County Circuit Clerk, Box 26, no. 81, not viewed.

[80] Mary E. Thrall [*sic*] household, 1870 US census, Albion Precinct, Edwards County, Illinois, p. 300, dwelling 329, family 328.

[81] Elizabeth Morgan household, 1880 US census, Albion, Edwards County, Illinois, ED 7, p. 424D, dwelling 565, family 574.

[82] Mary E. Morgan to Laura L. Gould, Edwards County, Illinois, Deeds W:615 (NW ¼ NW ¼ and part of SW ¼ NW ¼ [thus somewhat under 80 acres], Section 17, Township 1S, Range 14W), 1 February 1880, recorded 27 October; Edwards County Recorder's Office, Albion. William Stanley and son Wilbur Morgan witnessed.

of the land Amos had bought in 1851, in the northwest quarter of the southwest quarter of Section 9, Township 1 South, Range 14 West.[83]

In 1900 Mary Elizabeth was in her 60s, living with daughter Lucretia and son-in-law Joseph Walter Britton in Glenwood, Schuyler County, Missouri—some 375 miles northwest of Bone Gap.[84] About 1901 "she was stricken with the disease which finally proved fatal. She gradually grew worse and during the last two weeks the end seemed very near. She was prepared for the change."[85]

Children of Mary Elizabeth[8] (Thrall) and Amos B. Morgan, all born in Edwards County:

6   i. MILTON WORTHY[9] MORGAN (*Mary Elizabeth Thrall[8], Worthy[7], Eliphas[6], Samuel[5], John[4-3], Timothy[2], William[1]*) was born 12 December 1852 and died 30 September 1899 in Edwards County. He married first 5 January 1871 CLEMENTINE CLARK, and second 14 May 1882 AMANDA MARIE TEACHOUT.

7   ii. ALLYN THEODORE[9] MORGAN (*Mary Elizabeth Thrall[8], Worthy[7], Eliphas[6], Samuel[5], John[4-3], Timothy[2], William[1]*) was born 15 August 1856 near Bone Gap, and died there 29 November 1931. He married first 10 January 1878 ROSINA ABIGAIL SMITH, second 14 July 1881 as her second husband LOUISA A. (THRALL) GASH, and third 9 November 1886 MARY CATHERINE SCHOFIELD.

---

[83] Mary E. Morgan et al. to Winfield S. Bare, Edwards County, Illinois, Deeds Y:231 (pt. NW ¼ SW ¼ Section 9, Township 1S, Range 14W); Grantor Index D–Z, FHL 1,401,783, DGS 8,117,694, image 335 of 726 (familysearch.org).

[84] James [Joseph] W. Britton household, 1900 US census, Glenwood, Schuyler County, Missouri, ED 132, sheet 4B, dwelling/family 76.

[85] Rev. G. A. Seed, "Obituary" for Mary Elizabeth Thrall Morgan, *Albion Journal-Register* (Illinois), Thursday 15 January 1903, p. 3, col. 3.

8   iii. WILBUR AMOS^9 MORGAN (*Mary Elizabeth Thrall^8, Worthy^7, Eliphas^6, Samuel^5, John$^{4-3}$, Timothy^2, William^1*) was born 22 February 1858 and died 4 August 1945. He married 7 January 1884 ELIZA JANE SMITH.

9   iv. LUCRETIA ADA "CRETIE"^{9} MORGAN (*Mary Elizabeth Thrall^8, Worthy^7, Eliphas^6, Samuel^5, John$^{4-3}$, Timothy^2, William^1*) was born 21 September 1863 and died July 1906 in Edwards County. She married 17 December 1885 REV. JOSEPH WALTER BRITTON.

Chapter 3

Eighth Generation

Laura Lucina Thrall–Solon Harper Gould Family
parents at chapter 1

"The amount of work done by her would shame most of the healthy people by whom we are surrounded"

3. LAURA LUCINA⁸ THRALL (*Worthy⁷, Eliphas⁶, Samuel⁵, John⁴⁻³, Timothy², William¹*)
Birth: 3 October 1835 in Bone Gap, Edwards County, Illinois
Death: 12 February 1898, Bone Gap
Burial: Bone Gap Cemetery
Spouse: **SOLON HARPER GOULD,** married 3 April 1862 "near Bone Gap"[86]
Spouse's parents: Freeman and Dorcas (Ward) Gould
Spouse's birth: 17 April 1837 in Bone Gap
Spouse's death: 3 or 4 February 1914 in Bone Gap
Spouse's burial: Bone Gap Cemetery[87]

---

[86] Family questionnaire 15 June 1899, Solon H. Gould pension file 743,817 (service of Solon H. Gould, Company B, 18th Illinois Infantry and Company 90, Battalion 2, Veteran Reserve Corps), Case Files of Approved Pension Applications..., 1861–1934; Civil War and Later Pension Files, Record Group 15, Department of Veterans Affairs, National Archives and Records Administration [NARA], Washington, DC. Levi English officiated at the marriage.

[87] Solon H. Gould entry #284, aged "62 yrs. 4 mo. 9 Days," Duane Smith, compiler, "Old Part of [Bone Gap] Cemetery," handwritten list of 380 numbered burials with names, birth dates, and death dates; photocopy in author's possession. For 4 February, Dennis Northcott and Thomas Brooks, *Grand Army of the Republic Department of Illinois, Transcription of the Death Rolls, 1879–1947* (St. Louis, Missouri: Northcott, 2005), 176.

Laura

Laura was no doubt the girl under age five in Worthy Thrall's 1840 Wabash County household.[88] In 1850 she was thirteen and attending school.[89] She was among those instrumental in supporting Leonidas through his education at McKendree and ministry career. After Laura's death at age 62, Edith (Flint) Thrall wrote to her husband Leonidas:

> I was not surprised to hear your news. After a long life of suffering bravely borne she rests. Her life of pain is not the most prominent thought that remains. Her great energy and the amount of work done by her would shame most of the healthy people by whom we are surrounded. She was a christian and to one of her temperament this meant no idle dream. She was earnest in everything. As I think of her this morning I think of her as a strong character and capable of deep and lasting affections. Those whom she loved so well know this is the uttermost. It is one more tie on the other side. I am so glad Victor went with you. I believe it will be a comfort to the folks [Goulds] for he was always something of a favorite with her.[90]

---

[88] Worthy Thrall household for girl age 5–10, 1840 US census, Wabash County, Illinois, p. 157, line 18.

[89] Morthy [Worthy] Thrall household for Laura, 1850 US census, Edwards County, Illinois, p. 256 (stamped, *verso*), dwelling 84, family 85.

[90] Edith Flint Thrall in Lebanon to Leonidas in Bone Gap, 14 February 1898; Flint–Thrall letter 89, in author's possession. Edith herself died within the year.

Sol's youth

Aside from four years in the Civil War and two years thereafter logging five miles south of Rochester Mills in Wabash County, Solon spent his whole life farming in Edwards County a mile and a half southwest of Bone Gap.[91]

At age nine, "I was chopping wood in the door yard, and struck my shin with the corner of the ax blade, and splintered the bone." Rather surprisingly, this had no obvious ill effects then or later. Ten years later he "had the ague pretty bad—terribly bad;" afterwards he and his brother Stephen noticed a few small blue "knots" on his left leg, but thought little of them.[92]

Sol's Civil War

Following President Lincoln's 3 May 1861 call for three-year volunteers, Solon enlisted in the US Army on the 28th in Anna, Union County, Illinois. He was 24 years old, 5 feet 9 inches tall, with dark hair, gray eyes, and a dark complexion.[93] Later on, the circumstances of his mustering-in became a matter of contention.

---

[91] Solon H. Gould, claimant's statement, deposition A, 10 December 1890, p. 10 of special examiner's report; Solon H. Gould pension file 743,817 (service of Solon H. Gould, Company B, 18th Illinois Infantry and Company 90, Battalion 2, Veteran Reserve Corps), Case Files of Approved Pension Applications..., 1861–1934; Civil War and Later Pension Files, Record Group 15, Department of Veterans Affairs, National Archives and Records Administration [NARA], Washington, DC.

[92] S. B. Gould, deposition B, pp. 13–14 of special examiner's report; Solon H. Gould pension file 743,817 (service of Solon H. Gould, Company B, 18th Illinois Infantry and Company 90, Battalion 2, Veteran Reserve Corps), Case Files of Approved Pension Applications..., 1861–1934; Civil War and Later Pension Files, Record Group 15, Department of Veterans Affairs, National Archives and Records Administration [NARA], Washington, DC.

[93] James M. McPherson, *Battle Cry of Freedom: The Civil War Era* (New York: Oxford University Press, 1988), 322. Also, Solon H. Gould entry, "Illinois Civil War Muster and Descriptive Rolls Detail Report," Illinois State Archives (ilsos.gov/isaveterans/civilMusterSearch.doc).

Solon first served as a private in Company B, 18th Illinois Infantry. For a rank-and-file soldier his record is surprisingly eventful. In September 1861 he was absent from duty and in the regimental hospital.[94] In December 1861 he was assigned 28 days of extra duty as a carpenter. In March and April 1862 he was "absent sick,"[95] but the hospital muster roll had him on duty there as a "nurse" as of 17 February.[96] For most of the first half of 1862 he was on "detached service" as a hospital nurse; perhaps inconsistently, he is also said to have been involved in the battles of Fort Donelson (13–15 February) and Shiloh (6–7 April).[97] He was home on "sick furlough" after Fort Donelson, when Dr. Schaefer gave him medicine for a "torpid liver."[98]

That summer came the turning point. As Solon told it four years later, "he was attacked with varicose veins in left leg and at the knee joint caused by overdrilling through Corn fields disabling him . . . .

---

[94] Solon H. Gould entries, Company B, 18th Illinois infantry, list of returns on various dates, Combined Military Service Record cards; National Archives and Records Administration, Washington, DC.

[95] Solon H. Gould entry, Company B, 18th Illinois infantry, Combined Military Service Record card for November–December 1861; National Archives and Records Administration, Washington, DC.

[96] Solon H. Gould entry, Hospital muster roll, 18th Illinois infantry, Combined Military Service Record card for March–April 1862; National Archives and Records Administration, Washington, DC.

[97] Solon H. Gould entries, Company B, 18th Illinois infantry, Combined Military Service Record cards for January–February and March–April 1862. Also, "Remarks" on Solon H. Gould Combined Military Service Record card, created 1894 based on muster-out roll 18 June 1864; National Archives and Records Administration, Washington, DC. The card is keyed to his being in the 90th Company, 2nd Battalion, of the Veterans Reserve Corps, but includes information on his earlier service.

[98] Solon H. Gould deposition 10 December 1890, Special Examiner's report, p. 29; Solon H. Gould pension file 743,817 (service of Solon H. Gould, Company B, 18th Illinois Infantry and Company 90, Battalion 2, Veteran Reserve Corps), Case Files of Approved Pension Applications..., 1861–1934; Civil War and Later Pension Files, Record Group 15, Department of Veterans Affairs, National Archives and Records Administration, Washington, DC.

[and preventing] him from doing full duty for the remainder of the term of service."[99] Two sergeants from Solon's company later testified that

> Said Soldier continued to do full service until . . . Aug. 1st 1862. While at Jackson Tenn. he became lame and Dr. Henry W. Davis the Sen. Surgeon of said Regt. Said that he was attacked with varicose veins . . . disabling him in such a manner as to prevent him from doing full duty and about Aug. 1863 he was sent to the invalid corps. That the said soldier was supposed to be in good health at the time he entered the service.[100]

For reasons not given, sometime in the last two months of 1862, Sol was court-martialed and had ten days of pay stopped.[101] In November he was also "Co. woodchopper."[102] On 18 April 1863 he was "absent on Detachment with Capt. Davis," and from May through August that year he was "absent on a Detachment to Recruit Negroes."[103] (Did his younger brother-in-law Leonidas Thrall [Chapter 5] ever chat with Sol about those experiences?)

---

[99] Solon H. Gould claim for invalid pension, 29 August 1866, Solon H. Gould pension file 743,817 (service of Solon H. Gould, Company B, 18th Illinois Infantry and Company 90, Battalion 2, Veteran Reserve Corps), Case Files of Approved Pension Applications..., 1861–1934; Civil War and Later Pension Files, Record Group 15, Department of Veterans Affairs, National Archives and Records Administration, Washington, DC.

[100] Sergeant's Affidavit to Disability of Soldier, George McMurchy and Daniel Kinsall, 13 March 1869, Gallatin County, Illinois; Solon H. Gould pension file 743,817 (service of Solon H. Gould, Company B, 18th Illinois Infantry and Company 90, Battalion 2, Veteran Reserve Corps), Case Files of Approved Pension Applications..., 1861–1934; Civil War and Later Pension Files, Record Group 15, Department of Veterans Affairs, National Archives and Records Administration [NARA], Washington, DC.

[101] Solon H. Gould entry, Company B, 18th Illinois infantry, Combined Military Service Record cards for November–December 1862; National Archives and Records Administration, Washington, DC.

[102] Solon H. Gould entries, Company B, 18th Illinois infantry, list of returns on various dates, Combined Military Service Record card; National Archives and Records Administration, Washington, DC.

[103] Solon H. Gould entries, Company B, 18th Illinois infantry, Combined Military Service Record cards for May–June and July–August 1863; National Archives and Records Administration, Washington, DC.

As of 1 August 1863 Solon had been disabled for 12 months and in hospital for two. Deemed "unfit for active field service," he was placed in a "provisional encampment" at Fort Pickering in Memphis.[104] In October he was transferred to the "invalid corps," eventually the 90th Company, 2nd Battalion, Veterans Reserve Corps (VRC). Perplexingly, "the military records do not show cause of transfer to Invalid Corps."[105]

Despite his invalid status, on 7 December 1863 Solon was promoted from private to corporal,[106] and after Memphis was stationed in St. Louis and then Rock Island (Illinois), where he spent the first few months of 1864 "on daily duty making coffins" and interring deceased prisoners of war. He was discharged 18 June.[107]

Henry Wilson's Postwar Vendetta

Early on, Solon somehow provoked the wrath of Company B's adjutant Henry S. Wilson, later promoted to captain and then to major. Nevertheless, in 1868, Solon started to build his case for a disability pension due to his service. He traveled some 60 miles to Shawneetown, Gallatin County, Illinois, where he called on Wilson. Sol recalled that he "respectfully asked [Wilson] for a certificate to the facts of the contracting disability in the service, and was roughly and profanely answered that he

---

[104] Solon H. Gould entry, Company B, 18th Illinois infantry, Combined Military Service Record card for 1 August 1863; National Archives and Records Administration, Washington, DC.

[105] J. C. Ainsworth, Captain and Assistant Surgeon, US Army, War Department, Record and Pension Division, 3 June 1890, responding to a 28 May query from the Interior Department Bureau of Pensions; Solon H. Gould pension file 743,817 (service of Solon H. Gould, Company B, 18th Illinois Infantry, Company 90, Battalion 2, Veteran Reserve Corps), Case Files of Approved Pension Applications..., 1861–1934; Civil War and Later Pension Files, Record Group 15, Department of Veterans Affairs, National Archives and Records Administration, Washington, DC.

[106] Solon H. Gould entries, 90th Company, 2nd Battalion (and predecessor units), Veteran Reserve Corps, Combined Military Service Record card, citing Company Muster and Descriptive Roll, National Archives and Records Administration, Washington, DC.

[107] Solon H. Gould entries, 90th Company, 2nd Battalion (and predecessor units), Veteran Reserve Corps, Combined Military Service Record cards for November–December 1863, January–February 1864, March–April 1864, and May–June 1864. Cards from the Illinois unit and the VRC date his changes of status variously.

(the said Henry S. Wilson) would not give him a certificate for anything."[108]

On 12 March 1869 Major Wilson followed up by writing directly to the commissioner of pensions. In his capacity as a former officer, he warned the commissioner that Solon was likely to apply for a pension he did not deserve, because he was an "imposter . . . a big stout Healthy man." Wilson denied holding any ill will, and then added that a pension for him would be "a great imposition upon the Govt."

Their disagreement went all the way back to Solon's 1861 mustering-in. Solon later called that physical examination a sham: "My legs were not examined. There was no objection to taking me."[109] Wilson, however, remembered "some dispute regarding some kind of disease in [Solon's] legs. He asserted that it did not injure him in the least and on his assertion was finally mustered in."[110]

About the time Wilson characterized Solon as hale and hearty, Dr. L. W. Low of Albion, Edwards County, estimated he was half disabled. In 1871 examining surgeon Dr. John J. Lescher of Mount Carmel, Wabash County, called him one-third disabled. Dr. Herman Schaefer of Edwards County, the Gould family physician, stated in 1870 that "from his knowledge of said Gould he would have known it if [Solon] had been

---

[108] Solon H. Gould affidavit, Grayville, Illinois, 23 March 1870; Solon H. Gould pension file 743,817 (service of Solon H. Gould, Company B, 18th Illinois Infantry and Company 90, Battalion 2, Veteran Reserve Corps), Case Files of Approved Pension Applications..., 1861–1934; Civil War and Later Pension Files, Record Group 15, Department of Veterans Affairs, National Archives and Records Administration, Washington, DC.

[109] Solon H. Gould, claimant's statement, deposition A, 10 December 1890, p. 8 of special examiner's report; Solon H. Gould pension file 743,817 (service of Solon H. Gould, Company B, 18th Illinois Infantry and Company 90, Battalion 2, Veteran Reserve Corps), Case Files of Approved Pension Applications..., 1861–1934; Civil War and Later Pension Files, Record Group 15, Department of Veterans Affairs, National Archives and Records Administration, Washington, DC.

[110] H. S. Wilson in Shawneetown, Illinois, letter to [Commissioner of Pensions] J. H. Barret, Washington DC; Solon H. Gould pension file 743,817 (service of Solon H. Gould, Company B, 18th Illinois Infantry and Company 90, Battalion 2, Veteran Reserve Corps), Case Files of Approved Pension Applications..., 1861–1934; Civil War and Later Pension Files, Record Group 15, Department of Veterans Affairs, National Archives and Records Administration, Washington, DC.

afflicted with Varicose veins at the time of his enlistment,"[111] the implicit conclusion being that his health issues originated in the service.

Wilson's letter to the pension commissioner lacked the promised medical documentation, and contradicted itself by enthusiastically claiming that Solon was ineligible for a pension both because he had been "diseased" upon mustering in *and* because three years of soldiering had restored him to robust health.

Solon's claim was rejected 22 April 1869 following an examination.[112] Fearing that the well had been poisoned, the following spring he asked for reconsideration, saying that during his service in Company B he had "incurred the displeasure of Captain Henry S. Wilson, who swore vengeance against this declarant."[113]

Years later, as pension requirements were relaxed and new depositions taken, Solon did receive a pension. In 1895, nephew Allyn T. Morgan swore that he had known Solon "personaly for 23 years and have worked for him Some nearly every Summer Since 1872. I never knew him

---

[111] Examining Surgeon's Certificate, Dr. L. W. Low, 4 May 1867; Solon H. Gould pension file 743,817 (service of Solon H. Gould, Company B, 18th Illinois Infantry and Company 90, Battalion 2, Veteran Reserve Corps), Case Files of Approved Pension Applications..., 1861–1934; Civil War and Later Pension Files, Record Group 15, Department of Veterans Affairs, National Archives and Records Administration, Washington, DC. Similarly, Examining Surgeon's Certificate, Dr. John J. Lescher, 23 March 1871. Similarly, affidavit by Dr. Herman Schaefer, 17 January 1870.

[112] Special Examiner's report, p. 23; Solon H. Gould pension file 743,817 (service of Solon H. Gould, Company B, 18th Illinois Infantry, Company 90, Battalion 2, Veteran Reserve Corps), Case Files of Approved Pension Applications..., 1861–1934; Civil War and Later Pension Files, Record Group 15, Department of Veterans Affairs, National Archives and Records Administration, Washington, DC.

[113] Solon H. Gould affidavit, Grayville, Illinois, 23 March 1870; Solon H. Gould pension file 743,817 (service of Solon H. Gould, Company B, 18th Illinois Infantry and Company 90, Battalion 2, Veteran Reserve Corps), Case Files of Approved Pension Applications..., 1861–1934; Civil War and Later Pension Files, Record Group 15, Department of Veterans Affairs, National Archives and Records Administration, Washington, DC.

when he could do any thing like a days work."[114] In 1886 Solon was an officer in the Bone Gap Post 224 of the Grand Army of the Republic.[115]

10 December 1890

Land—and books

In 1870 Solon had $240 in real estate and $500 in personal property.[116] Ten years later his household in Albion included his widowed mother Dorcas, age 72.[117] His sisters Edith and Alice were also in the household in 1880, 1900, and 1910.[118]

---

[114] Allyn T. Morgan affidavit 26 January 1895; Solon H. Gould pension file 743,817 (service of Solon H. Gould, Company B, 18th Illinois Infantry and Company 90, Battalion 2, Veteran Reserve Corps), Case Files of Approved Pension Applications..., 1861–1934; Civil War and Later Pension Files, Record Group 15, Department of Veterans Affairs, National Archives and Records Administration, Washington, DC. Original spelling retained.

[115] "The Veteran's Corner ... Organized for the New Year," *Daily Inter Ocean* (Chicago), Saturday 2 January 1886, p. 16, cols. 5–6.

[116] Solon H. Gould household, 1870 US census, Albion Precinct, Edwards County, Illinois, p. 283, dwelling 59, family 60. For brother Stephen, Freeman Gould will 12 September 1872 naming him as a son, Edwards County Will Record A:14; "Illinois, Wills and Probate Records, 1772–1999" > Edwards > Will records 1815–1922 > image 182 of 649 (ancestry.com).

[117] Solon H. Gould household, 1880 US census, Albion Precinct, Edwards County, Illinois, ED 7, p. 426C, dwelling 589, family 600.

[118] Solon H. Gould household, 1880 US census, Albion Precinct, Edwards County, Illinois, ED 7, p. 426C, dwelling 589, family 600. Similarly, 1900, Bone Gap village, ED 16, sheet 4B, dwelling/family 74. Similarly, 1910, Bone Gap village, sheet 3B, dwelling/family 77.

Father Freeman Gould died 4 January 1873, leaving Solon about 157½ acres. The four brothers each received one-sixth of Freeman's personal property after debts were paid; mother Dorcas received the remaining third as well as a 2½-acre lot.[119]

In 1880 Solon's farm of 250 acres was above average (among ten near neighbors) in improved acreage, woodland acreage, and cash value of the farm ($3750). It was valued at $15 per acre, below the county average of $18.[120] Only one neighbor equaled his machinery; his corn crop was a bit above average but yield per acre was among the lowest; his three-acre orchard was the largest.[121] That same year his wife Laura bought 45 acres from her sister Mary Morgan for $250.[122]

Mother Dorcas's will, written 14 October 1882, made Solon her executor and bequeathed him 40 additional acres if he "shall furnish me with fuel and a sufficient amount of farm produce to feed me, and one servant (or more if sickness shall make it necessary for me to keep more than one servant) and pay me the sum of Sixty-five Dollars per annum during the term of my natural life." He was also to sell her 2½-acre lot, cow, horse, buggy, harness, and kitchen furniture, dividing the proceeds equally among the brothers.

But Dorcas was no ordinary farm wife. She left special instructions for the household library:

---

[119] Freeman Gould will 12 September 1872, Edwards County Will Record A:14; "Illinois, Wills and Probate Records, 1772–1999" > Edwards > Will records 1815–1922 > image 182 of 649 (ancestry.com). Solon's inheritance was the N½ NW, Section 18, Township 1S, Range 14W, less Dorcas's lot, and the E½ NE Section 7. The two eighties are about half a mile apart. Freeman received federal patents 2063, 2343, and 7435 for them in 1838 and 1840 (glorecords.blm.gov).

[120] Charles H. Barnard and John Jones, *Farm Real Estate Values in the United States by Counties, 1850–1982*, Statistical Bulletin #751, Economic Research Service, US Department of Agriculture (Washington, DC: US Government Printing Office, 1987), Table 1, p. 3 for states, and Table 2, pp. 24–29 for Illinois counties (hathitrust.org).

[121] Solon H. Gould farm, 1880 US census, agriculture schedule, Albion Precinct, Edwards County, Illinois, p. 37, line 5.

[122] Mary E. Morgan to Laura L. Gould, Edwards County, Illinois, Deeds W:615 (NW ¼ NW ¼ and part of SW ¼ NW ¼, Section 17, Township 1S, Range 14W), 1 February 1880, recorded 27 October; Edwards County Recorder's Office, Albion. William Stanley and son Wilbur Morgan witnessed.

It is my will and desire that my sons Calvin C. Charles F. Solon H. and Stephen B. Gould shall severally be entitled to all the books now in the library on which their names are attached to the covers and that the remainder be equally divided between my four sons above named by the appraisers of my Estate.[123]

In the fall of 1887 Solon was "quite sick with his rheumatism."[124] Soon thereafter Solon and Laura deeded each of their children some land to start with: 40 acres to Alta 2 June 1888;[125] 35 acres to Virgil 24 October 1893;[126] 45 acres to Edith the same day;[127] and 60 acres to Alice 4 January 1895.[128]

Children of Laura Lucina[8] (Thrall) and Solon Harper Gould:

10   i. ALTA ARETA[9] GOULD (*Laura Lucina Thrall[8], Worthy[7], Eliphas[6], Samuel[5], John[4-3], Timothy[2], William[1]*) was born 15 September 1865 in Bone Gap, and died 6 June 1957. She married 23 April 1890 EDWARD G. BRITTON.

11   The Leighton-Pifer-Gould Connection.

---

[123] Dorcas Gould will, Edwards County Will Record A:116; "Illinois, Wills and Probate Records, 1772–1999" > Edwards > Will records 1815–1922 > image 284 of 649 (ancestry.com). This time Solon's land was the NW quarter of the SE quarter of Section 7.

[124] Edith Thrall in Bone Gap to Lonnie [Leonidas], letter, Friday 7 October 1887; Flint-Thrall letter #23, in author' possession.

[125] Solon H. Gould and wife to Alta Gould, 2 June 1888, recorded same day, Edwards County, Illinois, deeds 1:419 (NE SE Section 7, Township 1 South Range 14 West); Edwards County Recorder's Office, Albion.

[126] Solon H. Gould and wife to Virgil Gould, 24 October 1893, Edwards County, Illinois, deeds 5:507 (NE NW Section 18, Township 1 South, Range 14 West); Edwards County Recorder's Office, Albion.

[127] Laura L. Gould et ux to Edith E. Gould, 24 October 1893, recorded 4 November, Edwards County, Illinois, deeds 5:508; Edwards County Recorder's Office, Albion.

[128] Solon H. Gould et ux to Alice F. Gould, 4 January 1895, recorded 15 January 1896, Edwards County, Illinois, deeds 6:246; Edwards County Recorder's Office, Albion.

12   ii. Rev. Virgil Nathan⁹ Gould (*Laura Lucina Thrall⁸, Worthy⁷, Eliphas⁶, Samuel⁵, John⁴⁻³, Timothy², William¹*) was born 5 August 1868 in Bone Gap, and died 16 November 1959 in Chula Vista, San Diego County, California. He married 11 May 1893 Dora Sophia Leighton.

13   iii. Edith Evelyn⁹ Gould (*Laura Lucina Thrall⁸, Worthy⁷, Eliphas⁶, Samuel⁵, John⁴⁻³, Timothy², William¹*) was born August 1871 at Bone Gap and died 11 November 1960.

13   iv. Alice Flora⁹ Gould (*Laura Lucina Thrall⁸, Worthy⁷, Eliphas⁶, Samuel⁵, John⁴⁻³, Timothy², William¹*) was born 1 June 1875 and died 19 October 1926 in Bone Gap.

Tree 1. Allied Gould–Thrall Families

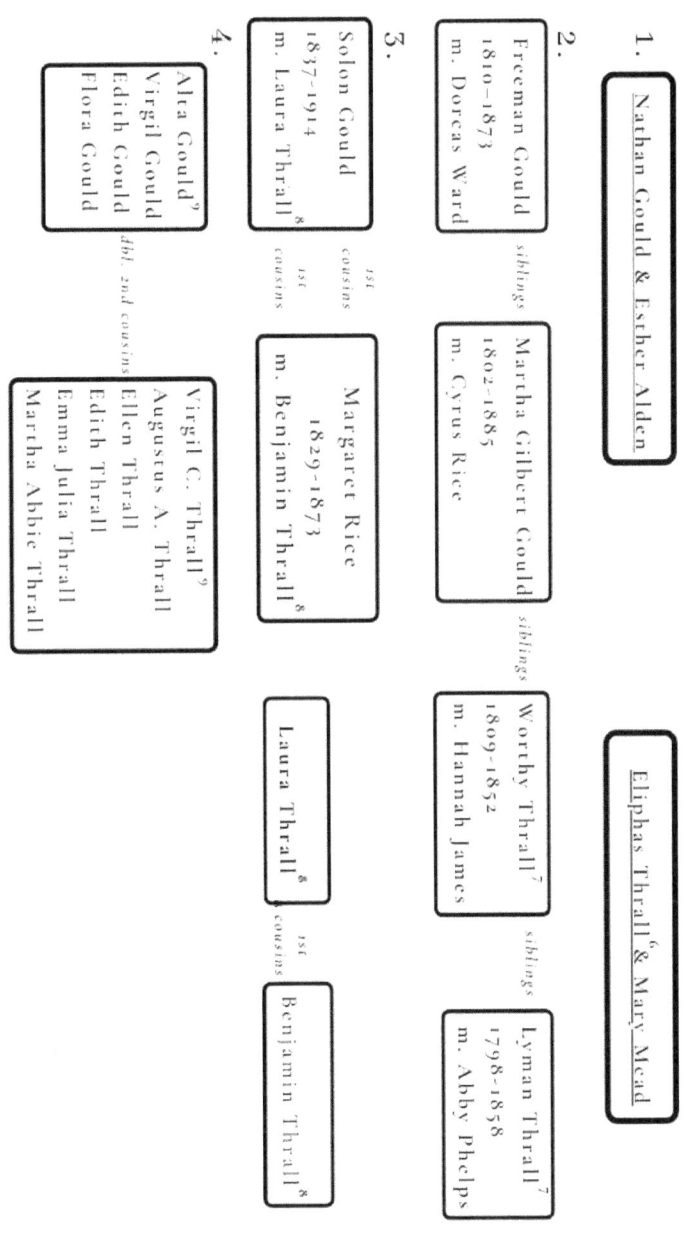

Tree 1. Allied Gould-Thrall Families with four generations entwined

1. Nathan Gould & Esther Alden — Eliphas Thrall[6] & Mary Mead

2. Freeman Gould
   1810–1873
   m. Dorcas Ward

   siblings

   Martha Gilbert Gould
   1802–1885
   m. Cyrus Rice

   siblings

   Worthy Thrall[7]
   1809–1852
   m. Hannah James

   siblings

   Lyman Thrall[7]
   1798–1858
   m. Abby Phelps

3. Solon Gould
   1837–1914
   m. Laura Thrall[8]

   1st cousins

   Margaret Rice
   1829–1873
   m. Benjamin Thrall[8]

   Laura Thrall[8] *1st cousins* Benjamin Thrall[8]

4. Alta Gould[9]
   Virgil Gould
   Edith Gould
   Flora Gould

   dbl. 2nd cousins

   Virgil C. Thrall[9]
   Augustus A. Thrall
   Ellen Thrall
   Edith Thrall
   Emma Julia Thrall
   Martha Abbie Thrall

Solon and Margaret were first cousins; his father Freeman and her mother Martha were siblings. Laura and Benjamin were also first cousins; her father Worthy and Benjamin's father Lyman were brothers.

So the *offspring of those two unions are double second cousins*. They share two sets of great-grandparents: Nathan Gould and his wife Esther Alden, and Eliphas Thrall and his wife Mary Mead.

Story #1: A walk in the orchard

Late one summer or fall, probably in the 1890s, "Uncle Sol" was walking in the Goulds' orchard with his young grand-nephew Harold Thrall:

> Uncle Sol was a big guy who could pop a whole apple into his mouth at once. Young Hallie would pick up an apple and try it, then throw it down.
>
> One of Hallie's apples had a worm in it; Uncle Sol picked it up and popped it in his mouth.
>
> Young Harold exclaimed, "Uncle Sol, Uncle Sol, that apple has a worm in it!"
>
> Uncle Sol kept chewing, finally swallowed, and spoke: "Dead now."[129]

---

[129] Recollection of Harold Thrall's daughter Elizabeth, written in the 1990s, in author's possession.

Chapter 4

Eighth Generation

Hannah Caroline "Carrie" Thrall–Charles Campbell Family

parents at chapter 1

"The word 'impossible' was not in his religious vocabulary"

4. HANNAH CAROLINE "CARRIE"^{8} THRALL (*Worthy^7, Eliphas^6, Samuel^5, John$^{4-3}$, Timothy^2, William^1*)
Birth: 18 January 1845 or 1846 in Bone Gap, Edwards County
Death: 31 December 1924 in Lake Charles, Calcasieu Parish, Louisiana[130]
Burial: Orange Grove Cemetery, Lake Charles, Calcasieu Parish, Louisiana[131]
Spouse: REV. CHARLES WESLEY CAMPBELL, married 2 September 1875 in Bone Gap[132]

---

[130] Rosalie (Thrall) Carmichael, "Thrall Genealogy" (17-page typescript on onion skin in red binder, by Rosalie Thrall Carmichael although no author is named), 6; in author's possession, tub 2, item 34, giving 18 January 1845 and 31 December 1925. These dates are not cited, but the birth date might be from Carrie herself. However, her grave marker says 1846–1924: "Carrie H. Thrall Wife of Rev. C. W. Campbell" grave marker (image), Orange Grove Cemetery, Lake Charles, Calcasieu Parish, Louisiana, memorial #65,266,731 for Carrie H. Thrall Campbell by Melissa Daigle (findagrave.com). The grave marker is correct as to her death date, as she was memorialized in September 1925: "Mrs. C. W. Campbell," *Minutes of the Seventy-fourth Annual Session, Southern Illinois Conference, Methodist Episcopal Church, Centralia, Illinois, 22–27 September 1925*, 180.

[131] "Rev. C. W. Campbell of the Southern Illinois Conference 1851–1922 Veteran of the cross," grave marker, Orange Grove Cemetery, Lake Charles, Calcasieu Parish, Louisiana, image, memorial #65,266,710 by Melissa Daigle (findagrave.com).

[132] "Mrs. C. W. Campbell," *Minutes of the Seventy-fourth Annual Session, Southern Illinois Conference, Methodist Episcopal Church, Centralia, Illinois, 22–27 September 1925*, 180.

Spouse's parents: Silas C. and Phoebe (Young) Campbell[133]
Spouse's birth: 15 January 1851 in Newport, Vermillion County, Indiana
Spouse's death: 1 December 1922 at Lake Charles[134]
Spouse's burial: Orange Grove Cemetery, Lake Charles, Calcasieu Parish, Louisiana[135]

In 1860 young Charles Campbell and his family were in paradise—Paradise Township, Coles County, Illinois, that is—about 80 miles southwest of his Newport, Vermillion County, Indiana, birthplace. They had $1700 in real estate and $900 in personal property.[136] The farm's cash value in 1860 was about average compared to the neighbors; its production of 2000 bushels of "Indian corn" was well above average.[137] At $11.33 per acre, the land was below the county's average value that year of $19.[138]

---

[133] Silas Campbell household for apparent wife Phoebe age 46 born Tennessee and apparent son Charles W. age 9 born Indiana, 1860 US census, Paradise Township, Coles County, Illinois, p. 132, dwelling/family 916. For Phoebe's birth surname, *Centennial McKendree College with St. Clair County History* (Lebanon, Illinois: McKendree College, 1928), 365.

[134] "Rev. Charles W. Campbell," *Minutes of the Seventy-second Annual Session, Southern Illinois Conference, Methodist Episcopal Church*, Benton, Illinois, 26–30 September 1923, 72–73. The Louisiana Statewide Death Index (1819–1964) has him dying 2 December 1922 (ancestry.com).

[135] Carrie H. Thrall wife of Rev. C. W. Campbell grave marker, Orange Grove Cemetery, Lake Charles, Calcasieu Parish, Louisiana, image, memorial #65,266,731 for Carrie H. Thrall Campbell by Melissa Daigle (findagrave.com). Her grave marker gives dates 1846–1924, each one year off from other records.

[136] Silas Campbell household 1860 US census, Paradise Township, Coles County, Illinois, p. 132, dwelling/family 916. If the children's ages and birthplaces are accurate, Silas and family left Tennessee in the late 1840s.

[137] S. C. Campbell, 1860 US agriculture census, Paradise Township, Coles County, Illinois, p. 35, line 29, compared to the other 38 farms on that page.

[138] Charles H. Barnard and John Jones, *Farm Real Estate Values in the United States by Counties, 1850–1982*, Statistical Bulletin #751, Economic Research Service, US Dept. of Agriculture (Washington, DC: US Government Printing Office, 1987), Table 1, p. 3 for states, and Table 2, pp. 24–29 for Illinois counties (hathitrust.org).

In 1870–71 Charles enrolled at McKendree College, but not the following year.[139] Later on,

> he completed a course at Illinois Wesleyan University [in Bloomington, McLean County, Illinois] where his brother-in-law William Henry Harrison Adams was president] and received the degree of Ph.B. in 1880. He took a graduate course in McKendree and received the degree of Ph.M. in 1898. . . .
>
> Mr. Campbell became a member of the Methodist Church while a student at McKendree during the pastorate of Dr. G. W. Hughey at Lebanon. He did not enter the ministry until some years later. He was a teacher for a number of years. He was principal of the Houston (Tex.) Seminary from 1882 to 1886. Since entering the ministry he has been a member of the Austin, Missouri, Gulf Mission, Arkansas, and Southern Illinois Conferences.[140]

Hannah Caroline became a Methodist in 1854, and began attending McKendree College in the fall of 1869, when she joined future sister-in-law Edith Flint as a founding member of the women's Clionian literary society. She withdrew from the college after two years for health reasons.[141]

Carrie and Charles married in 1875, and may have gone to Texas soon after, perhaps in part for Charles's health. Either then or at a later date he became president of the Methodist School for Negroes in

---

[139] Charles W. Campbell (of Lebanon), p. 7, 37th *Catalogue of M'Kendree College 1870–71* (St. Louis: R.P. Studley, 1870). Absent from student list, p. 6, 38th Catalogue of M'Kendree College 1871–72 (similarly), images 215 and 243 of 336 (archive.org). Several years are bound or photographed together starting with 1864–65.

[140] *Centennial McKendree College with St. Clair County History* (Lebanon, Illinois: McKendree College, 1928), 365.

[141] "Mrs. C. W. Campbell," *Minutes of the Seventy-fourth Annual Session, Southern Illinois Conference, Methodist Episcopal Church* (1925), 180. Also, Edith Flint in Lebanon to Lonnie (Leonidas), 12 April 1871, Flint–Thrall letter #3, in author's possession: "I was disappointed in the news from Carrie. I had so hoped to hear that she was much better."

Houston, also known as the "Houston Seminary." She taught there for "several years."[142]

Back in Illinois by 1880, Charles was teaching school in Edwards County; young Etta was a "boarder" in their household[143] (Chapter 14). Carrie taught a month in Yankeetown School there; the class included young relatives, among them "Cretie" Morgan and Alta Gould.[144] Returning to McKendree, Carrie graduated in 1882 with an M.S. degree.[145]

Thereafter Charles and Caroline traveled farther afield than many other family members:

- 1881: Charles was licensed to preach in Olney, Richland County, in the Southern Illinois Conference of the Methodist Episcopal Church.

- 1882–86: Houston, Texas, despite an 1882 family letter saying, "Charlie expects to teach either at Alma [?] or Ofallon this winter. I don't much think they will go south."[146] But it appears they did so. When Carrie received her M.S. degree from McKendree in

---

[142] "Mrs. C. W. Campbell," *Minutes of the Seventy-fourth Annual Session, Southern Illinois Conference, Methodist Episcopal Church* (1925), 180.

[143] Charles W. Campbell household, 1880 US census, Albion, Edwards County, Illinois, ED 7, p. 415B, dwelling 416, family 423.

[144] "Miscellaneous School Records, Edwards County, Illinois, 1865, 1873–1875, 1878–1880, 1883 and 1888," Yankeetown month ending 10 January 1880, typescript evidently transcribed from a standard "Schedule of a Common School," 7–8; Edwards County Historical Society, Albion, Illinois.

[145] *Centennial McKendree College with St. Clair County History* (Lebanon, Illinois: McKendree College, 1928), 279. Also, McKendree College Alumni Record, pp. 38–52, evidently published about 1893, where the listing ends (https://mckendree.libguides.com/ld.php?content_id=50070180).

[146] Edith Flint Thrall in Lebanon to Leonidas, letter dated only 1882 (possibly in the fall, as she refers to "this winter" and the potential of cold weather); Flint–Thrall letter 23, in author's possession.

1882 she was identified as a teacher living in Houston.[147] And the following photograph and writing on the back suggest that Etta would have been young at the time of the picture, strengthening the early 1880s date. The writer has not been identified, but references to "Uncle Charlie" and "Aunt Carrie" suggests someone in generation 9 or a spouse.[148]

---

[147] McKendree College Alumni Record, p. 49, part of a larger book evidently published about 1893, where the listing ends (mckendree.libguides.com/ld.php?content_id=50070180).

[148] Image in author's possession; original photo at Foster's house in Urbana, Illinois.

The Campbells' charges after Houston:

- 1886: Charles was first brought into connection with the Austin Conference[149]
- 1888: Atlanta, Macon County, Missouri[150]
- 1889–90: Novelty, Knox County, Missouri[151]
- 1891: Kirksville circuit, Adair County, Missouri[152]
- 1892–93: Glenwood, Schuyler County, Missouri[153]
- 1894–95: Vandalia and Laddonia, Audrain County, Missouri.[154] In July 1895 they spent a few days in East St. Louis, Illinois, and were expected "home" in Lebanon 29 July.[155]

---

[149] *Minutes of the Fifty-Fifth Session of the Southern Illinois Conference of the Methodist Episcopal Church held at Vandalia, Illinois, September 19—24, 1906* (St. Louis: Press of Perrin & Smith, [1906]), 77.

[150] *Minutes of the Missouri Annual Conference of the Methodist Episcopal Church held in Hannibal, Missouri, March 28th to April 2nd, 1888* (Kirksville: Journal Printing House, 1888), "Conference Appointments," 178.

[151] *Minutes of the Missouri Annual Conference of the Methodist Episcopal Church held in Cameron, Missouri, March 20th to 25th, 1889* (Kirksville: Journal Printing House, 1889), "Conference Appointments," 32. Also, *Minutes of the Seventy-Second Session of the Missouri Annual Conference of the Methodist Episcopal Church held in Maryville, Missouri, March 12th to 17th, 1889* [*sic*, 1890] (Hannibal: Standard Printing, 1890), "Conference Appointments," 82.

[152] *Minutes of the Seventy-Third Session of the Missouri Annual Conference of the Methodist Episcopal Church held at Brookfield, Missouri, March 4th to 9th, 1891* (St. Joseph: Posegate Printing and Lithographing, 1891), "Appointments," 117.

[153] *Minutes of the Seventy-Fourth Session of the Missouri Annual Conference of the Methodist Episcopal Church held at Chillicothe, Missouri, March 2 to 7, 1892* (Kirksville: Journal Printing, 1892), "Conference Roll," 199. Also, Edith (Flint) Thrall in Greenville to Edith Laura Thrall, letter postmarked 7 November 1892; #31 of Flint–Thrall letters, in author's possession. Also, *Minutes of the Seventy-Fifth Session of the Missouri Annual Conference of the Methodist Episcopal Church held at Kirksville, Missouri, March 29 to April 3, 1893* (Kirksville: Journal Printing, 1893), "Appointments," 17.

[154] *Minutes of the Seventy-Sixth Session of the Missouri Annual Conference of the Methodist Episcopal Church held at Memphis, Missouri, March 28 to April 2, 1894* (Kirksville: Journal Printing Co, 1894), "Appointments," 64. Also, *Minutes of the Seventy-Seventh Session of the Missouri Annual Conference of the Methodist Episcopal Church held at Stanberry, Mo., March 27 to April 1, 1895* (Monroe City: F.L. Link, [1895]), "Appointments," 110.

[155] Edith Flint Thrall in Lebanon to Edith Laura Thrall, letter 28 July 1895; Flint–Thrall letter 64, in author's possession.

- 1896: Green City, Sullivan County, Missouri[156]
- 1897: Hamilton circuit, Caldwell County, Missouri[157]
- 1898–1900: Crowley, Acadia Parish, Louisiana,[158] in the Gulf Mission Conference. In 1900 eight-year-old Leo W. Dodd was in their household as a lodger[159] (Chapter 15). At some point Charles also helped "to organize the work at Houston Heights."[160]
- 1901: Welsh, Jefferson Davis Parish, Louisiana, where Charles also served as secretary of the Gulf Mission Methodist Conference[161]
- 1903: Alvin, Brazoria County, Texas, where his charge was the "Winnie Circuit"[162] (Winnie and Alvin are 75 miles apart).

---

[156] *Minutes of the Seventy-Eighth Session of the Missouri Annual Conference of the Methodist Episcopal Church held at Trenton, Missouri, April 1–6, 1896* (Kirksville: Democrat Publishing, 1896), "Appointments," 158.

[157] *Minutes of the Seventy-Ninth Session of the Missouri Annual Conference of the Methodist Episcopal Church held at Bethany, Missouri, March 24–29, 1897* (Chillicothe: Johnson & Kiergan, [1897]), "Appointments," 15.

[158] *Minutes of the Eightieth Session of the Missouri Annual Conference of the Methodist Episcopal Church held at Hannibal, Missouri, March 16–21, 1898* (Chillicothe: Johnson & Kiergan, [1898]), 54 (where he was called "supernumerary") and "Conference Roll," 76 (where he was reported transferred to Crowley). Also, *Journal of the Second Annual Session of the Gulf Mission Conference of the Methodist Episcopal Church held at Crowley, Louisiana, Feb. 3–7, 1898* (Jennings: Times Printing House, 1898), "Appointments," [3], 9, where he was introduced to the conference. Also, *Journal of the Third Annual Session of the Gulf Mission Conference of the Methodist Episcopal Church held in Lake Charles, Louisiana, Feb. 25, 1899* (Jennings: Times Printing House, 1899), "Appointments," [3]. Also, *Journal of the Fourth Annual Session of the Gulf Mission Conference of the Methodist Episcopal Church held in Marshall, Texas, February 1st to 5th, 1900* (Jennings: Record Print, [1900]), "Appointments," [21].

[159] Charles W. Campbell household, 1900 US census, Crowley, Acadia Parish, Louisiana, ED 9, sheet 5B, dwelling/family 88.

[160] "Rev. Charles W. Campbell," *Minutes of the Seventy-second Annual Session, Southern Illinois Conference, Methodist Episcopal Church* (1923), 72–73.

[161] *Journal of the Fifth Annual Session of the Gulf Mission Conference of the Methodist Episcopal Church held at Jennings, La., Jan. 17 to 21, 1901* (Crowley: Rice Belt News Print, 1901), 2, 5. Several pulpits were not filled.

[162] *Journal of the Seventh Annual Session of the Gulf Mission Conference of the Methodist Episcopal Church held at Port Arthur, Texas, February 5–9, 1903* (Crowley, Louisiana: Signal Printing, 1903), 67, 69.

- 1904: transferred to the Arkansas conference[163]
- 1906–7: Villa Ridge, Pulaski County, Illinois,[164] Southern Illinois Conference, where "he spent the remainder of his ministerial life. He organized classes and built churches at Mounds and Christopher. His last work was that of reviving the work at Villa Ridge and restoring it to the list of regular appointments. This he did after he was on the retired list. . . . The word 'impossible' was not in his religious vocabulary."[165]
- 1908: Villa Ridge and Mounds, Pulaski County, Illinois.[166] At the 1909 conference, Rev. J. W. McNeill reported that while Charles had "suffered a few weeks affliction," he deserved much credit: "At Mounds, a rapidly growing town located on the I. C. R. R. [Illinois Central Railroad], nine miles north of Cairo, a . . . church building was dedicated by Dr. J. F. Harmon on the fourth Sunday in July. Cost, $3,000. Rev. C. W. Campbell, the pastor, is entitled to much credit for untiring energy in pushing this enterprise to completion. The building will comfortably accommodate 300 people."[167]

---

[163] *Official Journal of the Gulf Annual Conference of the Methodist Episcopal Church held at Hughes Springs, Texas, February 4–9, 1904, Twelfth Annual Session* (Louisville, Kentucky: Pentecostal Publishing House, [1904]), 108.

[164] *Minutes of the Fifty-Fifth Session of the Southern Illinois Conference of the Methodist Episcopal Church held at Vandalia, Illinois, September 19–24, 1906* (St. Louis: Press of Perrin & Smith, [1906]), "Appointments," 18. Also, *Minutes of the Fifty-Sixth Session of the Southern Illinois Conference of the Methodist Episcopal Church held at Mount Carmel, Illinois, from September 18th to 23rd, 1907* (St. Louis: Perrin & Smith, [1907]), "Appointments," 26.

[165] "Rev. Charles W. Campbell," *Minutes of the Seventy-second Annual Session, Southern Illinois Conference, Methodist Episcopal Church* (1923), 72–73.

[166] *Minutes of the Fifty-Seventh Session of the Southern Illinois Annual Conference of the Methodist Episcopal Church held at McLeansboro, Illinois, September 16–21, 1908* (St. Louis: Perrin & Smith, [1908]), "Appointments," 28.

[167] *Minutes of the Fifty-Eighth Session of the Southern Illinois Annual Conference of the Methodist Episcopal Church held at Centralia, Illinois, September 22–27, 1909* (St. Louis: Perrin & Smith, [1909]), 82, 85.

- 1909–10: Johnston City, Williamson County, Illinois[168]
- 1910–11: O'Fallon, St. Clair County, Illinois[169]
- 1912: Olive Branch, Alexander County, Illinois[170]

In 1916, the Southern Illinois conference listed him as a "retired minister."[171] But his retirement was active, serving as pastor in Reevesville, Johnson County, Illinois, in 1918.[172] At last, at Villa Ridge, Pulaski County, in 1920, his occupation was simply "beekeeper."[173]

Children (adopted) of Hannah Caroline[8] (Thrall) and Charles W. Campbell:

14   i. ETTA J.^{9} CAMPBELL (*Hannah Caroline Thrall^8, Worthy^7, Eliphas^6, Samuel^5, John$^{4-3}$, Timothy^2, William^1*) was born February 1877 in Illinois and died 7 December 1952 in Wichita Falls, Texas. She married 24 January 1900 HARVEY C. MARSHALL.

---

[168] *Minutes of the Fifty-Eighth Session of the Southern Illinois Annual Conference of the Methodist Episcopal Church held at Centralia, Illinois, September 22–27, 1909* (St. Louis: Perrin & Smith, [1909]), "Conference Appointments," 26. Also, Charles W. Capbell [Campbell] household, 1910 US census, Johnston City, Williamson County, Illinois, ED 165, sheet 23B, dwelling 574, family 580. Unlike 1900, Leo's middle initial was F and his parents were born in Indiana and Illinois.

[169] *Minutes of the Fifty-Ninth Session of the Southern Illinois Annual Conference of the Methodist Episcopal Church held at Olney, Illinois, Sept. 28 to Oct. 3, 1910*, "Conference Appointments," 25. Also, *Minutes of the Sixtieth Session of the Southern Illinois Conference, Methodist Episcopal Church, held at East St. Louis, Illinois, September 20–25, 1911* (Marion, Illinois: Stafford Publishing, [1911]), "Conference Appointments," 23.

[170] *Minutes of the Southern Illinois Annual Conference of the Methodist Episcopal Church held at Cairo, Illinois, September 25–30, 1912* (Marion: Stafford Print, [1912]), "Conference Appointments," 23.

[171] *Minutes of the Southern Illinois Annual Conference of the Methodist Episcopal Church held at Robinson, Illinois, October 4–8, 1916* (Eldorado, Illinois: Zelah J. Farmer, [1916]), "Disciplinary Questions," 11.

[172] Rev. J. W. Flint, "Memoir and Reminiscence of the Late L. W. Thrall," clipping from unidentified newspaper, probably DuQuoin, May 1918.

[173] C. W. Campbell household, 1920 US census, Villa Ridge Precinct, Pulaski County, Illinois, ED 102, sheet 3A, dwelling 60, family 61.

15 ii. LEO F.^{9} CAMPBELL (*Hannah Caroline Thrall^8, Worthy^7, Eliphas^6, Samuel^5, John$^{4-3}$, Timothy^2, William^1*) was born 2 April 1892 in Texas or Louisiana, and died 21 February 1962 in Anna, Union County, Illinois. He married 21 September 1915 FLEETA M. CANTWELL.

Chapter 5

Eighth Generation

Leonidas W. Thrall–Edith M. Flint–Emily Jones Family
parents at chapter 1

"The idea suddenly dawned upon me that if it was not a crime to be born a girl it was at least a misfortune."

5. LEONIDAS WORTHY^8 THRALL (*Worthy^7, Eliphas^6, Samuel^5, John$^{4-3}$, Timothy^2, William^1*)
Birth: 21 February 1850 in Bone Gap[174]
Death: 21 May 1918 in Du Quoin, Perry County[175]
Burial: College Hill Cemetery, Lebanon, St. Clair County[176]
Spouse #1: **EDITH MARIE FLINT,** married 29 September 1873[177]
Spouse #1 parents: William and Mary (Gedney) Flint[178]
Spouse #1 birth: 16 February 1845 near Lebanon, St. Clair County, Illinois

---

[174] 21 February 1850: Leonidas Worthy Thrall grave marker, image, College Hill Cemetery, Lebanon, Illinois, memorial #12,068,902 by Alberta Daniels Withrow (findagrave.com). 2 February 1850: "Rev. L. W. Thrall," *Minutes of the Southern Illinois Annual Conference of the Methodist Episcopal Church, Greenville, 2–6 October 1918*, pp. 60–62.

[175] "Rev. L. W. Thrall," *Minutes of the Southern Illinois Annual Conference of the Methodist Episcopal Church, Greenville, 2–6 October 1918*, pp. 60–62.

[176] Leonidas Worthy Thrall grave marker, image, College Hill Cemetery, Lebanon, Illinois, memorial #12,068,902 by Alberta Daniels Withrow (findagrave.com).

[177] "Rev. L. W. Thrall," *Minutes of the Southern Illinois Annual Conference of the Methodist Episcopal Church, Greenville, 2–6 October 1918*, pp. 60–62.

[178] William Flint household for apparent wife Mary age 38 and daughter Edith age 5, 1850 US census, St. Clair County, Illinois, District #3, pp. 41-42, dwelling/family 323. Also, *Centennial McKendree College with St. Clair County History* (Lebanon, Illinois: McKendree College, 1928), 213. For mother's birth surname, William Flint–Mary Gedney marriage #23, 21 March 1842, Cowbit Parish Church, Lincolnshire. William Hughes officiated. Certified copy in author's possession.

Spouse #1 death: 10 November 1898 in Lebanon
Spouse #1 burial: College Hill Cemetery, Lebanon[179]
Spouse #2: **EMILY MARTHA JONES,** married in Ingraham, Clay County, 27 December 1900
Spouse #2 parents: Robert H. and Emily E. (Hammer) Jones[180]
Spouse #2 birth: June 1865 in Rose Hill, Jasper County[181]
Spouse #2 death: 8 November 1957 at Methodist Home for the Aged, Quincy, Adams County[182]
Spouse #2 burial: College Hill Cemetery, Lebanon, St. Clair County[183]

Edith

Edith taught art classes in and around Lebanon. "Her future husband [Leonidas] used to say that he enrolled in the art class for the sole purpose of getting to know the teacher better."[184] The story is told that as a child her night-time reading was rationed by the size of the candle she had.

---

[179] Edith Flint Thrall grave marker, image, College Hill Cemetery, Lebanon, Illinois, memorial #12,068,897 for Edith Marie Flint Thrall by Alberta Daniels Withrow (findagrave.com).

[180] Leonidas Worthy Thrall–Emily M. Jones marriage license #956, 18 December 1900, marriage 27 December; Clay County, Illinois, Marriage Record 2:74; FHL 1,008,793, DGS 4,539,325, image 372 of 601 (familysearch.org). Rev. John W. Flint (Edith Marie Flint Thrall's sister) presided; witnesses were Gertrude Gerking and Cameron Harmon. For Emily's middle name, Clay County, Illinois, Marriage Record G (1896–1905):285; FHL 1,008,796, DGS 4,539,328, image 178 of 678 (familysearch.org).

[181] For June 1865, Robert H. Jones household for daughter Emily M. age 35, 1900 US census, Pixley Township, Clay County, Illinois, sheet 5A, dwelling 100, family 101. For place of birth, Leonidas Worthy Thrall–Emily M. Jones marriage license marriage #956, 18 December 1900, marriage 27 December; Clay County, Illinois, Marriage Record 2:74; FHL 1,008,793, DGS 4,539,325, image 372 of 601 (familysearch.org).

[182] "Emily Jones Thrall," *Pantagraph* (Bloomington, Illinois), Saturday 9 November 1957, p. 6, col. 8.

[183] Emily Jones Thrall grave marker, image, College Hill Cemetery, Lebanon, Illinois, memorial #12,068,899 by Alberta Daniel Withrow (findagrave.com).

[184] Rosalie (Thrall) Carmichael, "Thrall Genealogy" (17-page typescript on onion skin in red binder, by Rosalie Thrall Carmichael although no author is named), 6; in author's possession, tub 2, item 34.

She graduated from McKendree in the class of 1870, receiving the degree of B.S., and in 1873, M.S. She was one of the founders of the Clionian Literary Society there, and was the first woman to graduate from McKendree as a regular student,[185] as opposed to by examination.

In the early 1870s, Edith wrote to her future husband, counting the cost of marrying a Methodist minister:

> The trials you bade me look at I have reviewed and now will set them in order before me just as they present themselves to me. A life of voluntary renunciation of all the vanities of riches when wealth is the end and aim of life for many. A way farer's tent and friends of brief acquaintance[,] ties made and broken until the heart's love for friends is scattered among hundreds instead of concentrated on few—all this when . . . the associations that cling around one spot of earth, one round of familiar faces, seem the one thing dear next to life. All this—and this is all.[186]

A few months before they were married they also corresponded on women's suffrage. Edith wrote:

> I am not ultra, but on the question of social and legal equality between man and woman I am radical and have been since my tenth year. At that time a scene was enacted in which I . . . was made to take the place McChamberlain spoke of when he said the sister was compelled to give in to her brother because he was a boy and she only a girl. For the first time in my life the idea suddenly dawned upon me that if it was not a crime to be born a girl it was at least a misfortune.

---

[185] *Centennial McKendree College with St. Clair County History* (Lebanon, Illinois: McKendree College, 1928), 213.

[186] Edith Marie Flint to Leonidas W. Thrall, letter # TK, undated but clearly prior to marriage so early 1870s; in author's possession.

> I do not imagine that the ballot is a panacea for all of wrongs or of evils. How can I when I see those who enjoy the privilege often wronged and cruelly oppressed. . . .
>
> Like yourself I consider the matter fated to succeed and I also agree with you in thinking that in God's good time it will be settled and that in the best way. As for Miss Anthony, we need a 'John Brown' perhaps and I guess the country can spare her as well as any other unless it be Woodhull/Claflin.[187]

As a pastor's wife and on her own account, Edith was active "in the work of the Woman's Christian Temperance Union, Womans Foreign Missionary Society, Sunday-school and Epworth League, and exerted a great influence upon every Church with which she was connected. Her gentle wisdom, her sweet humility, and her broad and tender sympathies made her a successful leader in all departments of Church work."[188]

She rarely described her health struggles, but they were many. In the fall of 1894 she visited Muncie, Delaware County, Indiana, where the locals were burning a seemingly inexhaustible supply of natural gas:

> I had a cold when I went to Muncie and the first house I went to they burned the natural gas without any stove pipes. A stove stood within two feet of my bed and a fire burned in it all night. It inflamed my lungs and Wed. night I had to go to a doctor. He relieved me but said I must not go back to the open stove. I thought then that I would have to go right home but Mrs. Hypes came to the rescue and took me home with her. I staid there until eight o clock Fri night. A few minutes after nine that night we started home and traveled all night. I did not sleep any and

---

[187] Edith M. Flint in Lebanon to Leonidas W. Thrall, Flint–Thrall letter 13, 10 July 1873; in author's possession. Victoria Claflin Woodhull was a feminist who ran for President in 1872: "Victoria Woodhull," *Wikipedia* (en.wikipedia.org/wiki/Victoria_Woodhull) and the references cited therein.

[188] "Mrs. Edith Flint Thrall," *Minutes of the 48th Session of the Southern Illinois Conference of the Methodist Episcopal Church, Mount Carmel, 27 September–2 October, 1899*, 38–39.

> took fresh cold so I got home pretty badly under the weather. Nelly was sick and I had to walk home from the depot. Papa [Leonidas] was gone and oh dear there was so much to do and I was so poorly. I had not eaten as much as one good meal for four days and my appetite did not return for several days . . . . Have done no ironing for two weeks until today. Willie tried so hard to cook something I could eat and he got up some nice meals but you know how it is.[189]

After graduating, Edith helped preserve the institutional memory of Clio (of which she was the first president) in a paper for an 1888 reunion, where she mentioned Thecla Bernays (who did not graduate but received an honorary degree in 1902) and Elizabeth Holding, a graduate who was first a foreign missionary and later active in the Deaconess Home in Chicago.[190]

Edith wrote to Leonidas when he attended the Methodists' nationwide general conference in Cleveland in 1896:

> We heard something about the little breeze [dispute?] in regard Y.P.S.C.E. It seems there are some men in the conference who grow excited over trifles. You know when a vessel is full it runs over whether it holds a hogshead or a gill.[191]

Edith's intermittent weakness and sickness did not prevent her from accompanying Leonidas to Toronto in the summer of 1897.[192] That summer she also wrote to son Will about the family's 1898 Fourth of July in Lebanon—her last, as it turned out:

---

[189] Edith Flint Thrall in Salem to Edith Laura Thrall in Lebanon, 22 October 1894, Flint–Thrall letter 57, in author's possession.

[190] *Centennial McKendree College with St. Clair County History* (Lebanon, Illinois: McKendree College, 1928), 316.

[191] Edith Flint Thrall in Lebanon to Leonidas W. Thrall at Hawley House in Cleveland, 15 May 1896, Flint–Thrall letter 73, in author's possession.

[192] Edith Flint Thrall in Toronto, postcard to "Children" in Lebanon, 17 July 1897, Flint–Thrall letter 85, in author's possession.

> Early in the day Faith Watts came over to see if we did not want to go into partnership with them in making ice cream. That suited very well and soon after Mand Watts Bust came to see if we were fixed so we could go over and put our provisions with theirs and have a picnic dinner in their yard. We called the roll at the cupboard door and concluded to join forces. They had a chicken and we had a beef steak. I made some *sataned* eggs (as Victor called them) and Edie mashed some potatoes. I sent Mand two cans of oysters and she made some oyster salad and also salmon salad.
>
> We had a dish of lemon cake and Mr. Watts bought some sponge cake. After a while he came in and announced to the family that he had invited [McKendree] Pres. Chamberlain's folks and Bro Leoy and his two daughters. Then I saw Prof. Walton coming slowly along the street looking lonely so we invited him and we had a very pleasant crowd.[193]

Edith was long a sufferer from asthma; the birth of her third child nearly killed her (Chapter 18); after other brushes with the Grim Reaper, she died at the age of 53. Letters written a decade later by her youngest and oldest sons reflect the power of her mind and convictions, and their sense of a profound loss. Harold was a student in Chicago visiting friends when he remembered what day it was:

> It was . . . just ten years since Mama was taken away from us and I tho't what those ten years might have meant to us if God had seen fit to spare her to us; He knows best and I know that she is happy now. If I did not know that it would be a much harder thing for me to understand why she should have been taken away from us so soon.[194]

---

[193] Edith (Flint) Thrall in Lebanon to William F. Thrall in Vincennes, Indiana, 6 July 1898, Flint–Thrall letter #68, in author's possession.

[194] Harold L. Thrall in Chicago to an unknown family member, letter about November 1908; in author's possession, tub 13, binder 325.

Victor, the eldest son and then pastor at Lebanon, recalled the family's sojourn there in the 1890s:

> I have many memories that different places bring to my mind when I am out in town. So often I pass the house where mamma died and many times I live over her last days and long for her. What would it mean for her to visit us here in the parsonage?
>
> The cemetery has filled up far beyond her grave. I like the spot. I think we have a choice lot there. I have been out a number of times. Nine years from the day she left us I buried a Mrs. Whitaker on a lot just east of where we laid Mamma. It was cold and cloudy, within & without.[195]

Emily

> Dr. Thrall's second wife, Emily Jones Thrall, was a fine looking woman with a wonderful store of humorous and entertaining stories. She was a graduate trained nurse. Her husband [Leonidas] was fond of saying that his first wife was the first woman graduate of McKendree College and his second wife was the first trained nurse in Illinois.
>
> She took her training in Bethlehem, Penna. And wore a large round nurse's pin. This training was very useful caring for a diabetic husband and helping at the births of grandchildren.[196]

Emily attended school through the 8th grade.[197] In 1900 she was 35, unmarried, and living in her father Robert's household in Pixley, Clay County, Illinois, as a trained nurse. His occupation was recorded as

---

[195] Victor W. Thrall in Lebanon, Illinois, to Edith L. Thrall in Aurora, letter 18 February 1908; in author's possession, tub 13, binder 325.

[196] Rosalie (Thrall) Carmichael, "Thrall Genealogy" (17-page typescript on onion skin in red binder, by Rosalie Thrall Carmichael although no author is named), 6; in author's possession, tub 2, item 34.

[197] D. S. Cover household for mother-in-law Emily M. Thrall, 1940 US census, Tunnel Hill Township, Johnson County, Illinois, ED 44-14, sheet 11B, dwelling 210.

"invalid," and a second trained nurse, listed as "visitor," was also present.[198] After Emily was widowed in 1918, she was the nurse at Jennings Seminary in Aurora, Kane County, Illinois.[199]

Known affectionately as "Grandma Thrall," Emily was also a pioneer, having "entered the nursing profession when it was still frowned upon for the girl with a gentle upbringing." She also served for a number of years as "superintendent of nurses at the Quincy home [Methodist Home for the Aged] where she spent the last 12 years of her life as a resident."[200] As a housewife in 1916, she wrote to her daughter and stepdaughter, "I did some needed cleaning in the pantry today—separating sheep from goats. I have a pile of goats in the alley ready to burn."[201]

In 1926 she visited her sister, Mrs. George Gerking (formerly Kate Jones), in Lebanon,[202] and stepson Harold Thrall and family in Mansfield, Piatt County.[203] In 1935 she was with her niece Gertrude (Gerking) Thrall and stepson/nephew-in-law Rev. Charles Thrall at 126 Barker Avenue in Peoria, Peoria County, where he was pastor at St. John's Methodist.[204]

---

[198] Robert H. Jones household, 1900 US census, Pixley Township, Clay County, Illinois, sheet 5A, dwelling 100, family 101.

[199] Rosalie (Thrall) Carmichael, "Thrall Genealogy" (17-page typescript on onion skin in red binder, by Rosalie Thrall Carmichael although no author is named), 6; in author's possession, tub 2, item 34.

[200] "Emily Jones Thrall," *Pantagraph* (Bloomington, Illinois), Saturday 9 November 1957, p. 6, col. 8.

[201] In author's possession, tub 13, binder 325, letter 81.

[202] "Lebanon," *News-Democrat* (Belleville, Illinois), Thursday 13 May 1926, p. 8, col. 5.

[203] "Live News of Central Illinois Towns," *Daily Pantagraph* (Bloomington, Illinois), Saturday 6 September 1924, p. 12, col. 3.

[204] Emma [Emily] J. Thrall entry, *Polk's Peoria City Directory 1935* (Peoria, Illinois: R.L. Polk, 1935), p. 579, image 280 of 466 (ancestry.com, which labeled the 1935 directory as 1933 and the 1933 directory as 1935). No related Thralls were in Peoria in 1933.

Before going to Quincy in 1945 or 1946, she again lived with Charles and Gertrude[205] at 1101 Fell Avenue in Bloomington, McLean County.[206]

Leonidas

Leonidas may have owed his given name to Leonidas Lent Hamline, a lawyer and later a spellbinding Methodist circuit rider around Newark and Granville, Licking County, Ohio, in the early 1830s— just the time and place when Worthy and Hannah were courting and marrying.[207]

Worthy died so young that Leonidas never knew him, and grew up a poor farm boy—the only boy in the household. Uncle Oliver visited; mother Hannah took in weaving to support herself and the children. She wove the cloth for a "suit of jeans" for Leonidas to wear to Northwestern University's academy before he entered McKendree. One of his ambitions was to make life easier for his mother so that she would not have to work such long hours at her weaving.[208]

At age 19 he came home "& put in corn crop & hired out to neighbors & sold corn in field."[209] With her and his sisters' support, Leonidas developed his gift for reasoned oratory, attended first the academy and then McKendree College, graduating in three years and receiving a master's degree in 1875.

"His unusual scholarship and brilliant oratory attracted much attention and gave no uncertain promise of the great pulpit and platform ability which so strongly marked his entire Conference career. He was

---

[205] "Emily Jones Thrall," *Pantagraph* (Bloomington, Illinois), Saturday 9 November 1957, p. 6, col. 8.

[206] Emily J. Thrall entry, *Polk's Bloomington (McLean County, Ill.) City Directory 1946* (St. Louis, Missouri: R. L. Polk, 1946), p. 357, image 178 of 331 (ancestry.com). Her 1957 obituary placed her departure for Quincy in 1945.

[207] Walter C. Palmer, *Life and Letters of Leonidas L. Hamline* (New York: Carlton & Porter, 1866), 76–77 (babel.hathitrust.org).

[208] Rosalie (Thrall) Carmichael, "Thrall Genealogy" (17-page typescript on onion skin in red binder, by Rosalie Thrall Carmichael although no author is named), 3; in author's possession, tub 2, item 34.

[209] Handwritten note by son Harold L. Thrall, in author's possession, binder 514C.

frequently in demand for baccalaureate sermons and class day addresses, in which kind of work he peculiarly excelled."[210]

It was not all hard labor. McKendree classmate W. A. Kelsoe told of dropping by Leonidas's room on his way to Greek class sometime in the 1870s: "If I didn't know the lessons, Thrall did, and he had been taught to help the needy."[211]

According to both his McKendree biography and family tradition, "before his graduation he taught a school for colored children at Lebanon."[212] Apparently Leonidas ran a school and taught freedmen to read and write. A generation later, one of his students' sons protected Charles Thrall from a threshing-crew bully.[213] Leonidas's graduation oration was on "the Negro's place in American life."[214]

Leonidas wrote to his future wife, perhaps in 1873:

> Whisky was "all the go" on the train last night. The train was loaded with Dutchmen returning from the Singerfest. Nearly everyone in my car had a bottle which he occasionally drew, sipped, and handed to his neighbor. When my turn would come I had "thanks" for them. I will not touch it, for I see hell in it. An old lady sat near me who, when the train stopped for supper, unrolled from a paper a piece of bread which the remains of her teeth were just sufficient to enable her to masticate. God bless her came involuntarily to my lips. While I have been writing the above in the store here a drunken man assaulted me and cursing me of being a Catholic Joe. He said he "knew 'em by kind o'

---

[210] "Rev. L. W. Thrall," *Minutes of the Southern Illinois Annual Conference of the Methodist Episcopal Church, Greenville, Illinois, 2–6 October 1918*, p. 60.

[211] W. A. Kelsoe, "Reminiscence" of L. W. Thrall, *Southern Illinois Methodist* 4(2):5, col.1, (unpaginated), July 1918.

[212] *Centennial McKendree College with St. Clair County History* (Lebanon, Illinois: McKendree College, 1928), 225.

[213] Elizabeth S. Thrall, handwritten account circa 1968, transcribed 11 August 2003, in author's possession, binder 514E. Also an earlier set of notes by her husband, pre-1966.

[214] Handwritten note by son Harold L. Thrall, in author's possession, binder 514C.

insight." I paid little attention to him and at last he has left me.[215]

In October 1872 he was admitted "on trial" to the Southern Illinois Conference, Methodist Episcopal Church.[216] His early pastorates were at Liberty, White County (1872), and Freeburg, St. Clair County (1873). On 27 September 1874 he was ordained as a deacon, admitted to "full connection," and sent to Pinckneyville, Perry County (1874–75).[217] In 1876 he was ordained an elder.

That fall he was transferred to the South Kansas Conference, "having been elected president of Hartford Collegiate Institute at Hartford, Lyon County, Kansas."[218] Dividing his time between preaching and teaching, he was "very active in the exciting campaign in that State which resulted in constitutional prohibition in 1890."[219] While in Kansas he served churches at Hartford (Lyon County), Columbus (Cherokee County), and Independence (Montgomery County) in the southeastern part of the state.[220]

Kansas did not improve Edith's asthma and they returned to Illinois, where for the next 39 years they were stationed at:

- Ashley, Washington County (1879–82).

---

[215] Leonidas W. Thrall in Olney to Edith M. Flint, Flint–Thrall letter #14, perhaps 1873; in author's possession.

[216] *Journal and Minutes of the Twenty-First Session of the Southern Illinois Conference [Methodist Episcopal Church], Mount Vernon, Illinois, 2–7 October 1872* (St. Louis: R. P. Studley, 1872), 21.

[217] *Journal and Minutes of the Twenty-Third Session of the Southern Illinois Conference [Methodist Episcopal Church], Mount Carmel, Illinois, 23–26 September 1874* (St. Louis: Barns & Beynon, [1874?]), 138, 150.

[218] "Rev. L. W. Thrall," *Minutes of the Southern Illinois Annual Conference of the Methodist Episcopal Church, Greenville, Illinois, 2–6 October 1918*, pp. 60–62.

[219] "Biographical Sketch read at Funeral Service," *Du Quoin Tribune* (Illinois), 24 May 1918, p. 12, in author's possession, item 504 (oversize brown envelope).

[220] *Centennial McKendree College with St. Clair County History* (Lebanon, Illinois: McKendree College, 1928), 225.

- Grayville, White County (1882–83), where toddler son Will "kept begging to go back to Ashley saying with his sobs, 'Take Lilly home.'"[221]
- Metropolis, Massac County (1884–86), their first parsonage with an upstairs. "The boys played in the big yard," wrote older sister Edith Laura later, "but sometimes they quarreled as boys will. Father divided the yard into fourths and each had his own little corner to play in. That settled things for a while."[222]
- Salem, Marion County (1887–88). In the fall of 1887, Leonidas and Edith carried on a lengthy discussion by letter as to the needed purchases (maybe a rug, not a wood stove) and furnishing of the parsonage.[223]
- Greenville, Bond County (1889–93). "We had a family in the church named Murdock. One time Mother was out in the yard helping dig up burdocks. A caller came and Will told the caller that mother was out in the yard digging up the murdocks."[224]
- Vandalia District, presiding elder (1893–98).
- Lebanon, St. Clair County (1899–1903).
- Flora, Clay County (1903–12), "the longest pastorate ever served in the Southern Illinois Conference."
- Harrisburg, Saline County (1912–16).
- DuQuoin, Perry County (1916–18), where "while suffering under great physical afflictions"—mainly diabetes, for which there was little help—Leonidas "still continued to do the whole work of a

---

[221] Edith Laura Thrall, "Will's Childhood," typescript of family memories written probably shortly after his death 15 October 1941 and certainly prior to hers 14 June 1950.

[222] Edith Laura Thrall, "Will's Childhood," typescript of family memories written probably shortly after his death 15 October 1941 and certainly prior to hers 14 June 1950.

[223] Edith Thrall in Bone Gap to Lonnie [Leonidas], Flint–Thrall letter #23, Friday 7 October 1887; in author's possession.

[224] Edith Laura Thrall, "Will's Childhood," typescript of family memories written probably shortly after his death 15 October 1941 and prior to hers 14 June 1950.

Methodist preacher, many times preaching from his chair when unable to stand in the pulpit."[225]

A McKendree trustee for more than 30 years, he was elected to the Methodist General Conferences in 1896 (Cleveland) and 1900 (Chicago).[226] The McKendree College board wrote in memory of his thirty years of service there:

> He was clear in thought, constant in devotion and active and self-sacrificing in service. . . . he keenly felt the need of high standards for its student attainment. He was therefore an advocate of recognized standards, and the fact that we now have a favorable rating with standardizing agencies, is in no small sense due to his influence on this board.[227]

His baccalaureate sermon at Harrisburg 30 May 1915 looked forward optimistically to the twentieth century:

> Let us continue to hope and pray that the present wicked and needless war [World War I] shall prove to be, as has been predicted, 'the twilight of the kings.' Let us pray that it may be followed by the awakening and renaissance . . . .
>
> We may expect to see the morning glow of a Federation of Nations, the international policing of all lands and all seas, the final enthronement of peaceable arbitration as a substitute for the sword.[228]

---

[225] "Rev. L. W. Thrall," *Minutes of the Southern Illinois Annual Conference of the Methodist Episcopal Church, Greenville, Illinois, 2–6 October 1918*, pp. 60–62.
[226] Ibid.
[227] "In Memory of Dr. L. W. Thrall," McKendree College Joint Board of Trustees, 7 June 1918. Copy in author's possession.
[228] "The True Aristocracy," delivered 30 May 1915, published in the *Harrisburg Chronicle* (Illinois).

Ten years after Leonidas's death, in June 1928 many family members converged at the McKendree College commencement:

- from Aurora, Kane County, Illinois, Deaconess Edith Thrall (chapter 16);
- from Albion, Calhoun County, Michigan, Rev. Victor W. Thrall, wife Carrie, and children Victor Jr. and Evelyn (chapter 17);
- from Quincy, Adams County, Illinois, Rev. Charles H. Thrall, wife Gertrude, son Robert, and mother-in-law Kate Gerking (chapter 19);
- from Newman, Douglas County, Illinois, Rev. Harold L. Thrall, wife Elizabeth, and children Elizabeth, Miriam, and Harold J. (chapter 20);
- from Tunnel Hill, Johnson County, Illinois, Mrs. David Cover (Mary Virginia), sons Billie and Leon, and her mother Emily (Jones) Thrall (chapter 21); and
- from Reading, Hillsdale County, Michigan, Rev. Charles Mooers and wife Edith (chapter 17).[229]

The four brothers (Victor, Will, Charles, and Harold) all married college graduates who were older than they were. Three of the brothers became Methodist ministers; the fourth married a Methodist minister's daughter.

Children of Leonidas Worthy^8 and Edith Marie (Flint) Thrall:

16 i. EDITH LAURA^9 THRALL (*Leonidas Worthy^8, Worthy^7, Eliphas^6, Samuel^5, John$^{4-3}$, Timothy^2, William^1*) was born 1 July 1874 in Freeburg, St. Clair County, Illinois, and died 14 June 1950 in Galva, Henry County, Illinois.

17 ii. VICTOR WORTHY^9 THRALL (*Leonidas Worthy^8, Worthy^7, Eliphas^6, Samuel^5, John$^{4-3}$, Timothy^2, William^1*) was born 19 April 1877 in Hartford, Lyon County, Kansas; and died 21 August 1963 in

---

[229] "Many Attend Commencement at Lebanon," *Belleville Daily News-Dispatch* (Illinois), p. 7, col. 4, Thursday 21 June 1928.

Knoxville, Knox County, Tennessee. He married 25 December 1903 CARRIE FRANCES JONES.

18   iii. WILLIAM FLINT^9 THRALL (*Leonidas Worthy^8, Worthy^7, Eliphas^6, Samuel^5, John$^{4-3}$, Timothy^2, William^1*) was born 15 December 1880 in Ashley, Washington County, Illinois, and died 15 October 1941 in Chapel Hill, Madison County, North Carolina. He married 6 January 1906 ENOLA LOUDICY KEISLING.

19   iv. CHARLES HAVEN^9 THRALL (*Leonidas Worthy^8, Worthy^7, Eliphas^6, Samuel^5, John$^{4-3}$, Timothy^2, William^1*) was born 20 October 1883 in Grayville, White County, Illinois, and died 18 January 1968, in Pontiac, Livingston County, Illinois, the last of the siblings. He married 27 August 1907 GERTRUDE GERKING.

20   v. HAROLD LEONIDAS^9 THRALL (*Leonidas Worthy^8, Worthy^7, Eliphas^6, Samuel^5, John$^{4-3}$, Timothy^2, William^1*) was born 13 November 1885 in Metropolis, Massac County, Illinois, and died in Galva, Henry County, Illinois, 8 April 1966. He married 9 May 1911 ELIZABETH SCHRIBER.

Child of Leonidas Worthy^8 and Emily (Jones) Thrall:

21   vi. MARY VIRGINIA^9 THRALL (*Leonidas Worthy^8, Worthy^7, Eliphas^6, Samuel^5, John$^{4-3}$, Timothy^2, William^1*) was born 17 March 1902 in Lebanon, St. Clair County, Illinois, and died 9 March 1970 in Metropolis, Massac County, Illinois. She married 31 July 1922 DAVID COVER.

Tree 2. Allied Jones–Thrall Families[230]

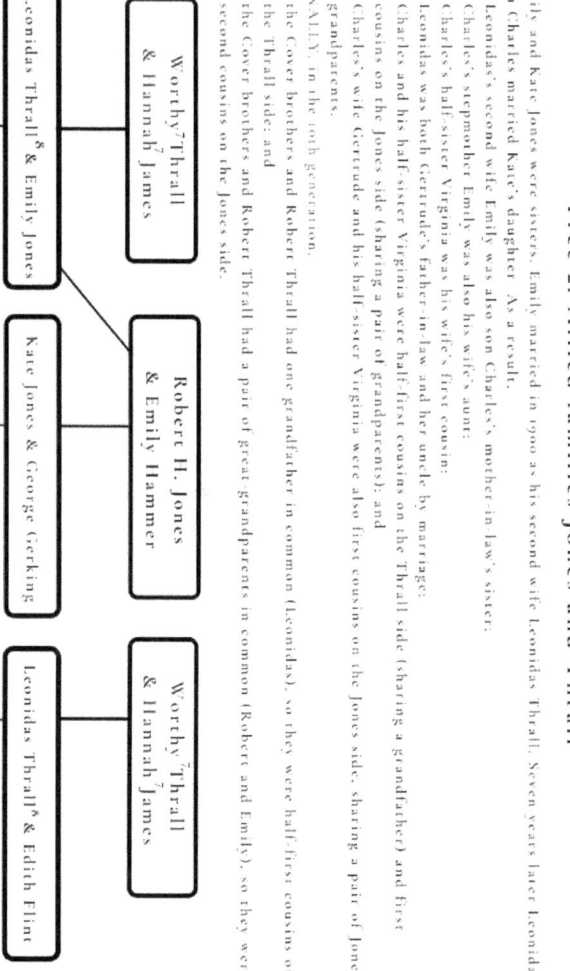

---

[230] George W. Gerking–Kate Jones marriage #529, Ingraham, Clay County, Illinois, 17 October 1880, Register of Marriages 1(1878–1895):41, naming her parents Robert H. Jones and Emily Hammer; FHL 1,008,793, DGS 4,539,325, image 89 of 601 (familysearch.org).

Story 2: Housework in Kansas, 1878

In December 1878 Edith (Flint) Thrall wrote to sister Mary (Flint0 Nelson, describing their domestic round in Kansas:

> We manage to do our own work except the washing and ironing. I guess you laugh at my saying 'we.' Well I can assure you Lonnie does a great deal.
>
> When we get up he makes a fire and then gets breakfast while I dress the children [Edith Laura and Victor] and get them washed and ready for breakfast. We usually make coffee and fry meat and I keep light bread on hand. This makes a very comfortable breakfast. Then while I wash the dishes he makes a fire in the sitting room and sweeps the floor.
>
> Then we have prayers and I set the bedroom in order, while he goes to his studies till two oclock when he goes out to visit the people.
>
> Now you see how we manage to do without a girl. Our washing is done away from home and by a first-class laundress.[231]

---

[231] Edith Marie (Flint) Thrall letter from Columbus, Kansas, to Mary (very probably sister Mary [Flint] Nelson), 20 December 1878; Flint–Thrall letter #18, in author's possession. In this time and place laundry involved major physical labor.

Chapter 6

Ninth Generation

Milton Morgan–Clementine Clark–Amanda Teachout Family

parents at chapter 2

"One of the old Edwards County boys who stood true"

6. **Milton Worthy**^{9} **Morgan** (*Mary E. Thrall^8, Worthy^7, Eliphas^6, Samuel^5, John$^{4-3}$, Timothy^2, William^1*)
Birth: 12 December 1852 in Edwards County
Death: 30 September 1899 in Edwards County
Burial: Bone Gap Cemetery, Edwards County[232]
Spouse #1: **Martha Clementine Clark**, married in Edwards County 5 January 1871[233]
Spouse #1's parents: perhaps Robert and Mary [–?–] Clark[234]

---

[232] Milton W. Morgan grave marker, Bone Gap Cemetery, Bone Gap, Illinois, image, memorial #42,652,807 for Milton Worthy Morgan by David Kaspareit (findagrave.com). Memorial includes a photo said to be of him. Also, "S. A. McL," obituary for "M. W. Morgan," clipped from an unidentified and undated newspaper, likely Albion, in author's possession. Also, author's visit, 24–25 May 2001. Age at death 46 years 9 months 18 days, consistent with the dates given.

[233] Milton W. Morgan–Clementine Clark marriage #146, 5 January 1871, Edwards County, Illinois, Marriage Record D:30 (1869–1915); "Illinois, County Marriages, 1810–1940" > FHL 1,401,779, DGS 4,661,396 > image 595 of 787 (familysearch.org).

[234] Robert Clark (age 43) household for apparent wife Mary (age 34) and apparent daughter Clementine (age 11), 1860 US census, Marion Township, Decatur County, Indiana, p. 189, dwelling/family 1404, but that family is not close to Edwards County, Illinois. There is also a Robert Clark who married Mary F. Britton in White County, Illinois, 12 March 1844 (White County marriages, p. 156; "Illinois County Marriages, 1810–1940" > FHL 977,068, DGS 5,204,400 > image 144 of 573 [familysearch.org].) But their Clementine may have married someone else.

Spouse #1's birth: about 1849 in Indiana

Spouse #1's death: 1875–80,[235] possibly in Columbus, Platte County, Nebraska[236]

Spouse #2: **AMANDA MARIE TEACHOUT**, married 14 May 1882 in Antelope County, Nebraska[237]

Spouse #2's parents: William and Ruth Ann (Marr) (Bisbee) Teachout

Spouse #2 birth: 17 September 1863[238] in Michigan (possibly in Bethel/Ovid, Branch County)

Spouse #2 death: 1946 (possibly 2 December) in Los Angeles

Spouse #2 burial: Whittier, Los Angeles County, California[239]

---

[235] Clementine Morgan might have been buried in Columbus Cemetery, Platte County, Nebraska, but the evidence is thin. It consists of an isolated small stone labeled "Morgan," said to be in a lot purchased by M.W. Morgan in 1879. Death is said without sourcing to be 19 December 1875; burial reportedly in Space 1, Lot 80, Section 11, Row 9. Clementine Morgan, memorial #41,318,705, by Shirley (Bruhn) Martys and CarolJJ (findagrave.com).

[236] "Ancestors of Addie Claudia Morgan," family tree, by Carol Ann Lyle, 11 June 1997; copy in author's possession. The tree was sourced but the sources have become separated from it.

[237] Amanda Isachant [Teachout]–M. W. Morgan marriage application 12 May 1882 and certificate #98, 14 May 1882, Marriage Record, Antelope County, Nebraska, p. 179; "Nebraska, Marriage Records 1855–1908" > Antelope > 1876–1888 > image 512 of 1036. The form was incompletely filled out; E. M. Blackford officiated. Amanda was said to be age 20, Milton 29, both residents of (adjacent) Madison County.

[238] "Application of Children to complete claim of soldier and his deceased widow, their mother," and notes on jacket of minors' pension file 746,961, within Ruth A. Teachout pension file 248,399 (service of William F. Teachout, Company L, 5th Michigan Cavalry), Case Files of Approved Pension Applications..., 1861–1934; Civil War and Later Pension Files, Record Group 15, Department of Veterans Affairs, National Archives and Records Administration, Washington, DC.

[239] For possible exact birth date and place, Amanda M. Morgan grave marker, Rose Hills Memorial Park, Whittier, Los Angeles County, California (Myrtle Lane, Section 3, Lot 1338, Entrance Gate 14), image, memorial #117,529,913 for Amanda Marie Teachout Morgan by Stuart Strout Woodside Skolfield (ancestry.com).

Milton

On 27 September 1875, Milton and his wife Martha sold 19 acres to George W. Shannon.[240] All were then residents of Edwards County. The following month they sold the remaining acre for $100 to John H. Clark.[241] For reasons unknown, the family soon left Bone Gap for Madison County, Nebraska, where Milton taught school for more than twenty years.

Although the record is very incomplete, Milton's children seem to have spent much time with their Illinois grandparents. Young Edgar, Milton's only surviving child with Martha, was with his grandmother in Bone Gap in 1880.[242] Edgar was not present in Milton and second wife Amanda's Nebraska household in 1885.[243] Milton's brief obituary named neither of his wives and none of his children.[244]

Although Milton grew up in a religious household, he reportedly first joined "the Christian church" at age 29 (about 1882) in Madison, Madison County, Nebraska.[245] (It's not clear which denomination was meant.) Milton was apparently in Bennett village, Jefferson precinct, Madison County, Nebraska, in March 1884 when he wrote an undated

---

[240] Milton W. and Martha C. Morgan to George W. Shannon, Edwards County, Illinois deeds W:62, 27 September 1875, recorded 20 October 1875; Edwards County Recorder's Office, Albion. This was the east half of the SE quarter of the NW quarter in Section 9, Township 1 South Range 14 West, excepting one acre in the northwest corner. David S. Rude and Maria Stanley witnessed.

[241] Milton W. and Clementine Morgan to John H. Clark, Edwards County, Illinois, deeds V:611, 16 October 1875, recorded 23 October; Edwards County Recorder's Office, Albion.

[242] Elizabeth Morgan household for "son" [grandson] Edgar age 4, 1880 US census, Albion, Edwards County, Illinois, ED 7, p. 424D, dwelling 565, family 574.

[243] M. W. Morgan household for Amanda age 21 and Myrtle age 1, 1885 Nebraska state census, Burnett Village, Jefferson Precinct, Madison County, Nebraska, p. 4, dwelling/family 33. Amanda's father was reportedly born in New York state, her mother in Canada.

[244] "S. A. McL," obituary for "M. W. Morgan," clipped from an unidentified and undated newspaper, likely Albion, in author's possession.

[245] Ibid.

letter on behalf of Amanda's mother, "Mrs. Anna Teachout," who was in "very destitute Circumstances."[246] He was teaching school there and living with wife Amanda (age 21) and daughter Myrtle (age 1).[247] In 1885 in Dry Creek, Nebraska (close to if not within Madison County), he was one of the signing witnesses when Anna gave her power of attorney to George E. Lemon.[248]

On 3 June 1892 Milton wrote another letter from Tilden, Madison County, Nebraska, on behalf of his mother-in-law ("surely a needy and deserving case") to Green Berry Raum. Raum had distinguished himself in the Civil War, served a term in Congress from southeastern Illinois 1867–69, and was pension commissioner 1889–93 under President Benjamin Harrison. Milton identified himself to Raum as "one of the old

---

[246] M. W. Morgan to Wm. W. Dudley Esq., undated handwritten letter from Bennett (Burnett?), Nebraska, received in pension office 25 March 1884; Ruth A. Teachout pension file 248,399 (service of William F. Teachout, Company L, 5th Michigan Cavalry), Case Files of Approved Pension Applications..., 1861–1934; Civil War and Later Pension Files, Record Group 15, Department of Veterans Affairs, National Archives and Records Administration, Washington, DC.

[247] M. W. Morgan household for Amanda age 21 and Myrtle age 1, 1885 Nebraska state census, Burnett Village, Jefferson Precinct, Madison County, Nebraska, p. 4, dwelling/family 33. Amanda's father was reportedly born in New York state, her mother in Canada.

[248] Anna Teachout power of attorney to George E. Lemon, 20 July 1885, Dry Creek (Pierce or Madison County), Nebraska; Ruth A. Teachout pension file 248,399 (service of William F. Teachout, Company L, 5th Michigan Cavalry), Case Files of Approved Pension Applications..., 1861–1934; Civil War and Later Pension Files, Record Group 15, Department of Veterans Affairs, National Archives and Records Administration, Washington, DC.

Edwards County boys who stood true to you in three campaigns for congress."[249]

Later in 1892 Milton and family reportedly moved to Pilger, Stanton County, Nebraska (immediately east of Madison County), where he is said to have joined the Methodist Church and the M.W.A. (probably the fraternal group Modern Woodmen of America).[250] They were still there in 1895.[251]

Milton returned to Bone Gap about 1898 with health problems serious enough that he had to undergo surgery twice: first in Olney, and later in St. Louis. "He said it was not without an appreciation of the fact that he might never rise from there alive, but he was ready to go."[252] He remains an enigmatic figure.

---

[249] M. W. Morgan in Tilden, Nebraska, to Hon. G. B. Raum, commissioner of pensions, Washington, DC, 3 June 1892; Ruth A. Teachout pension file 248,399 (service of William F. Teachout, Company L, 5th Michigan Cavalry), Case Files of Approved Pension Applications..., 1861–1934; Civil War and Later Pension Files, Record Group 15, Department of Veterans Affairs, National Archives and Records Administration, Washington, DC. For biographical information on Raum (1829–1909), *Biographical Directory of the United States Congress* (http://bioguide.congress.gov/scripts/biodisplay.pl?index=R000071) and Arlington National Cemetery (http://www.arlingtoncemetery.net/gbraum.htm). His Wikipedia entry is more detailed and mentions his book, *The Existing Conflict between Republican Government and Southern Oligarchy* (1884, reprint, New York: Negro Universities Press, 1969).

[250] "M. W. Morgan," obituary by "S. A. McL," clipped from an unidentified and undated newspaper, likely Albion, in author's possession.

[251] Ruth A. Teachout deposition 19 April 1885 in Battle Creek, Madison County, Nebraska; Ruth A. Teachout pension file 248,399 (service of William F. Teachout, Company L, 5th Michigan Cavalry), Case Files of Approved Pension Applications..., 1861–1934; Civil War and Later Pension Files, Record Group 15, Dept. of Veterans Affairs, National Archives and Records Administration [NARA], Washington, DC.

[252] "M. W. Morgan," obituary by "S. A. McL," clipped from an unidentified and undated newspaper, likely Albion, in author's possession.

Amanda

Amanda was six years old in 1870, living with her parents William and Ann (Bisbee) (Marr) Teachout in Monroe Township, Benton County, Iowa, one county west of Cedar Rapids.[253] Most likely during the 1870s she completed eight years of schooling.[254] In 1880 she was in neighboring Jackson Township, where her half-brother Lawson Bisbee headed a large household.[255] Two years later she became Milton Morgan's second wife.

Amanda was 31 years old 13 July 1894 in Battle Creek, Madison County, Nebraska, when she vouched for her widowed mother's marriage to William F. Teachout.[256] Four years later Amanda herself was widowed.

Many things are unclear about Amanda and Milton's time in Nebraska, including even whether Amanda and the children accompanied Milton back to Bone Gap in the late 1890s. But in 1900 Amanda and

---

[253] William Teachout household, 1870 US census, Monroe Township, Benton County, Iowa, p. 4, dwelling/family 25. Amanda and Nellie were called sisters in Nellie's 1945 death notice: "Deaths and Funerals…Spangler," *Arizona Republic*, Thursday 21 June 1945, p. 11, col. 1.

[254] Findley MacDonald household for mother-in-law "Lamanda" [grandmother-in-law Amanda] Morgan, 1940 US census, Montebello Township, Los Angeles County, California, ED 19-420, sheet 11A, dwelling 247. The turbulent Marr/Bisbee/Teachout families are a stern reminder to beginners that census surnames may not be all they seem.

[255] Lawson Bisbee household for Amanda "Bisbee" (actually Teachout), age 16, 1880 US census, Jackson Township, Benton County, Iowa, ED 32, p. 10, dwelling 84, family 86.

[256] General Affidavit of A. Case and A. M. Morgan 13 July 1894, Battle Creek, Madison County, Nebraska; Ruth A. Teachout pension file 248,399 (service of William F. Teachout, Company L, 5th Michigan Cavalry), Case Files of Approved Pension Applications…, 1861–1934; Civil War and Later Pension Files, Record Group 15, Department of Veterans Affairs, National Archives and Records Administration, Washington, DC.

Myrtle and Raymond were living in Bone Gap next door to Milton's brother Willard.[257]

The family soon returned west. In 1901 Amanda was in University Place, Lancaster County, Nebraska (since annexed by Lincoln). She and her siblings Franklin and Nellie were seeking to "complete" her father William's Civil War pension in applications made 30 July and 23 August.[258] Amanda (no occupation given) and the children lived at three different addresses in Lincoln in 1901, 1903, and 1905.[259] From there they moved to Maricopa County, Arizona.

On 17 February 1905 Amanda paid $500 for lot 21 in Block N of the University Addition to Phoenix for $500, subject to a $900 (!) mortgage to Nels and Bertha Burkey.[260] In 1910 Amanda was a homeowner and dressmaker at 1304 West Polk in Phoenix.[261] In 1912 son Raymond was living there and working as a clerk at Talbot & Hubbard, a seller of hardware, paints, oils, glass, and blacksmith

---

[257] Amanda Morgan household, 1900 US census, Bone Gap, Edwards County, Illinois, ED 16, sheet 9A, dwelling 167, family 170. "William" at dwelling 168, family 171.

[258] "Application of Children to complete claim of soldier and his deceased widow, their mother," and notes on jacket of minors' pension file 746,961, within Ruth A. Teachout pension file 248,399 (service of William F. Teachout, Company L, 5th Michigan Cavalry), Case Files of Approved Pension Applications..., 1861–1934; Civil War and Later Pension Files, Record Group 15, Department of Veterans Affairs, National Archives and Records Administration, Washington, DC. The grown Teachout children's claim appears to have foundered on the Pension Bureau's insistence on proof of Ebenezer Bisbee's death, without which Ruth Ann would not have been legally married to the soldier William F. Teachout.

[259] Amanda Morgan "wid. M. W." lived on the north side of Miller, first east of Warren (1901); on the northwest corner of College and Fowler (1903); and at 302 East Adams (1905); *Hoye's City Directory of Lincoln* (Lincoln: Hoye Directory, 1901), p. 384, image 191 of 351 (ancestry.com). Similarly, 1903, p. 438, image 225 of 445; and 1905, p. 143, image 73 of 485. The Morgans were not found in 1906 or 1907. In 1905 University Place was enumerated separately within the Lincoln directory.

[260] Ira E. and Ida M. Stanford to Amanda M. Morgan, Maricopa County, Arizona, deeds 64:593, 17 February 1905; FHL 2,196,935, DGS 8,593,883, image 1692 of 1754 (familysearch.org).

[261] Amanda Morgan household, 1910 US census, Phoenix, Maricopa County, Arizona, Ward 2, ED 60, sheet 13A, dwelling 287, family 302. It is possible that she received a death benefit from Milton's membership in the MWA, enabling her to afford a house.

supplies.²⁶² The following year Raymond was a salesman at E. L. Shaw (Shaws Smoke House) and living at 154 11th Avenue North; Amanda was not listed.²⁶³ In 1920 she was a nurse, living with son Ray and family at 720 East McKinley. Ray and E. S. Bittman were running the Nitrolene Sales Company at the northeast corner of West Adams and 4th Avenue.²⁶⁴

At some point in the 1920s Amanda moved on to California. In 1930 she was a "housekeeper" and homeowner in Compton, Los Angeles County (the house was valued at $2500).²⁶⁵ In 1935 and 1940 she was "mother-in-law" (actually grandmother-in-law) in the household of Findley and "Marjori" MacDonald in Montebello Township, East Los Angeles.²⁶⁶ Amanda was still in Los Angeles on 20 June 1945, when her sister Nellie Ann Spangler (wife of Henry W.) died in Phoenix.²⁶⁷

---

²⁶² Amanda M. and Raymond L. Morgan entries, *Phoenix City and Salt River Valley Directory 1912* (Los Angeles: Arizona Directory Company, 1911), 171–72. For Talbot & Hubbard, p. 229, image 118 of 216 (ancestry.com).

²⁶³ Raymond L. Morgan and Edwd. L. Shaw entries, *Phoenix City and Salt River Valley Directory 1913* (Los Angeles: Arizona Directory Company, 1912), 230 and 276.

²⁶⁴ Ray L. Morgan household for mother Amanda age 55, 1920 US census, Phoenix, Maricopa County, Arizona, ED 64, sheet 8B, dwelling 159, family 189. Also, Ray L., Ada P., and Mrs. Amanda M. Morgan, 720 East McKinley, *Phoenix City and Salt River Valley Directory 1920* (Los Angeles: Arizona Directory Company, 1920), pp. 380 and 390, images 330 and 340 of 763 (ancestry.com).

²⁶⁵ Amanda Morgan household, 1930 US census, Compton, Los Angeles County, California, ED 871, sheet 6A, dwelling 147, family 180. She was reported age 66, first married at age 18 (approximately 1882).

²⁶⁶ Findley MacDonald household for mother-in-law Lamanda [grandmother-in-law Amanda] Morgan, 1940 US census, Montebello Township, Los Angeles County, California, ED 19-420, sheet 11A, dwelling 247.

²⁶⁷ "Deaths and Funerals…Spangler," *Arizona Republic*, Thursday 21 June 1945, p. 11, col. 1.

Children of Milton Worthy⁹ and Clementine (Clark) Morgan:

    i. (possibly) ALICE¹⁰ MORGAN (*Milton W. Morgan⁹, Mary E. Thrall⁸, Worthy⁷, Eliphas⁶, Samuel⁵, John⁴⁻³, Timothy², William¹*) is rumored to have been born about 1873 or 1877, and apparently died young.²⁶⁸

22   ii. EDGAR ALSINIUS¹⁰ MORGAN (*Milton W. Morgan⁹, Mary E. Thrall⁸, Worthy⁷, Eliphas⁶, Samuel⁵, John⁴⁻³, Timothy², William¹*) was born 2 August 1875 in Bone Gap, Edwards County, Illinois; died 17 April 1925 at 2213 East Virginia Street, Evansville, Vanderburgh County, Indiana; and was buried in Bone Gap Cemetery. He married 28 January 1897 ADELE "ADDIE" GOULD.

Children of Milton Worthy and Amanda Marie (Teachout) Morgan:

23   iii. MYRTLE BELL¹⁰ MORGAN (*Milton W. Morgan⁹, Mary E. Thrall⁸, Worthy⁷, Eliphas⁶, Samuel⁵, John⁴⁻³, Timothy², William¹*) was born 29 January 1884 in Nebraska and died 15 June 1965 in San Bernardino, California. She married as his second wife 10 May 1910 in Phoenix, Maricopa County, Arizona Territory, CHRISTOPHER COLUMBUS COLLINS.

    iv. UNKNOWN¹⁰ MORGAN (*Milton W. Morgan⁹, Mary E. Thrall⁸, Worthy⁷, Eliphas⁶, Samuel⁵, John⁴⁻³, Timothy², William¹*) was born say 1887 and died before 1900.²⁶⁹

24   v. RAYMOND LEE¹⁰ MORGAN SR. (*Milton W. Morgan⁹, Mary E. Thrall⁸, Worthy⁷, Eliphas⁶, Samuel⁵, John⁴⁻³, Timothy², William¹*) was born 14 May 1890 in Meadow Grove, Madison County, Nebraska; died 27 March 1936 in Los Angeles; and was buried with his mother in Whittier, Los Angeles County, California. He married first 16 February 1913 in Maricopa County, Arizona, ADA PEARL VENSEL.

---

268 Unsourced family trees are the only evidence for her existence.
269 Amanda Morgan household, 1900 US census, Bone Gap, Edwards County, Illinois, ED 16, sheet 9A, dwelling 167, family 170; she had 3 children, 2 living.

Genealogical puzzle 1:

Milton probably spent more than half his life in Nebraska.

Starting with the sketchy account in the preceding chapter, how much more of Milton's life in Nebraska can be rediscovered and reconstructed?

Chapter 7

Ninth Generation

Allyn Morgan–Rosina Smith–Louisa (Thrall) Gash–Mary Schofield Family
parents at chapter 2

Edwards County commissioners "see after the burials of Paupers but not Soldiers widows"

7. ALLYN THEODORE^9 MORGAN (*Mary E. Thrall^8, Worthy^7, Eliphas^6, Samuel^5, John$^{4-3}$, Timothy^2, William^1*)
Birth: 15 August 1856 near Bone Gap, Edwards County, Illinois
Death: 29 November 1931 in Bone Gap after an eight weeks' illness and a stroke
Burial: 2 December 1931 in Bone Gap Cemetery[270]
Spouse #1: **ROSINA ABIGAIL SMITH**, married 10 January 1878 at William Stanley's in Edwards County
Spouse #1 parents: Clark B. and Sarah (Winchel) Smith [271]

---

[270] "A.T. Morgan, One of County's Leading Residents, Is Dead," *Albion Journal-Register* (Illinois), Thursday 3 December 1931, p. 1, col. 8. Also, Allyn T. Morgan burial #99, Duane Smith, compiler, "Old Part of [Bone Gap] Cemetery," handwritten list of 380 numbered burials with names, birth dates, and death dates; photocopy in author's possession. For illness, "A. T. Morgan of Bone Gap Dies Sunday Night," *Mt. Carmel Daily Republican-Register* (Illinois), Monday 30 November 1931, p. 1, col. 6.

[271] Allyn Theodore Morgan–Rosina Abigail Smith, license #781, 8 January 1878, marriage 10 January, Edwards County, Illinois, Register of Marriages 1:1; "Illinois, County Marriages, 1810–1940" > FHL 1,401,780, DGS 4,661,397 > image 210 of 654 (familysearch.org). They were both age 21. William Stanley, J.P., officiated, and Randle Rude was the only witness. Her parents were named. For her father's reported birth in New York 8 June 1831, see Roger C. Moe's unsourced pedigree chart dated 22 December 1996 from Columbia, Missouri, in author's possession.

Spouse #1 birth: 1856, possibly 1 December, in Allegany County, New York[272]
Spouse #1 death: 1880, possibly 13 December[273]
Spouse #1 burial: Bone Gap Cemetery[274]
Spouse #2: LOUISA A. (THRALL) GASH, married as her second husband 14 July 1881 in Barnhill Township, Wayne County, Illinois[275]
Spouse #2 parents: Homer G. and Mary (Sutton) Thrall
Spouse #2 birth: about 1861 in Illinois (perhaps Edwards County)[276]
Spouse #2 death: not known; perhaps before 9 November 1886
Spouse #2 burial: not known
Spouse #3: Mary Catherine Schofield, married 9 November 1886[277]

---

[272] Exact date, unsourced, from 22 December 1996 pedigree chart by family member Roger C. Moe. For Rosina's place of birth, Allyn Theodore Morgan–Rosina Abigail Smith, license #781, 8 January 1878, marriage 10 January, Edwards County, Illinois, Register of Marriages 1:1; "Illinois, County Marriages, 1810–1940" > FHL 1,401,780, DGS 4,661,397 > image 210 of 654 (familysearch.org).

[273] Reportedly died "two years" after the 1878 marriage: "A.T. Morgan, One of County's Leading Residents, Is Dead," *Albion Journal-Register* (Illinois), Thursday 3 December 1931, p. 1, col. 8. Exact date, unsourced, from 22 December 1996 pedigree chart by family member Roger C. Moe.

[274] Rosina wife of Allyn, 1856–1880, in Duane Smith, compiler, "Old Part of [Bone Gap] Cemetery," handwritten list of 380 numbered burials with names, birth dates, and death dates; photocopy in author's possession.

[275] Allyn S. [T.] Morgan–Louisa A. Gast [Gash] marriage entry, Wayne County, Illinois, license #115, 9 July 1881, marriage register C:172, 14 July 1881; FHL 1,391,820, DGS 7,730,774 (familysearch.org). The marriage register called for ages, parents' names, previous marriages, and other information, none of which was provided.

[276] Homer G. Terrall [Thrall] household for apparent daughter Lonza [Louisa] A., age 9, 1870 US census, Barnhill Township, Wayne County, Illinois, p. 24, dwelling/family 17. For possible place of Louisa's birth around 1861: Homer G. Thrall household, 1860 US census, Edwards County, Illinois, p. 64, dwelling 487, family 485. For Homer's wife's birth surname, "Mary Goodwin," *Wayne County Press* (Illinois), 1 March 1888, p. 6, col. 3.

[277] "A.T. Morgan, One of County's Leading Residents, Is Dead," *Albion Journal-Register* (Illinois), Thursday 3 December 1931, p. 1, col. 8. The date of 8 November 1886 is also seen (partially sourced tree, Descendants of Joseph Schofield, prepared in the early 2000s by "Brenda" Bperk930@aol.com, in author's possession).

Spouse #3 parents: William Bobbitt and Hannah Mariah (Doty) Schofield[278]
Spouse #3 birth: 29 April 1862 in Albion, Edwards County
Spouse #3 death: 1 August 1932 in Olney, Richland County sanitarium[279]
Spouse #3 burial: Bone Gap Cemetery[280]

Allyn may well have been given the unusually spelled surname of the minister who married his parents.[281] He himself was converted to Methodism at age fifteen (about 1871) and remained a member "for more than sixty years." A local leader, he was elected justice of the peace for seven consecutive terms.

> For three terms he was appointed by the circuit judge to the office of county parole and mothers' pension officer of Edwards county. Mr. Morgan was of that somewhat rare combination of loyalty to the traditions of the past and an aggressive participant in the civic and religious affairs of the present, in all of which he assumed a progressive, optimistic attitude, with a profound belief that the affairs of men

---

[278] Middle names are given in a partially sourced tree, Descendants of Joseph Schofield, prepared in the early 2000s by "Brenda" Bperk930@aol.com, in author's possession. She also reports that William B. Schofield served in Company F, 152nd Regular Volunteers, February–November 1865. Reportedly died November 1919, Edwards County. Supposedly Hannah Maria Doty's parents were John H. Doty and Abigail Wade of New Jersey and Ohio: Ethan Allen Doty, *The Doty–Doten Family in America: Descendants of Edward Doty, an Emigrant by the Mayflower, 1620* (Brooklyn, New York: privately printed, 1897), 459(?).

[279] "Obituary of Mrs. Mary C. Morgan" [corner torn off], clipping from unknown newspaper, possibly Albion, in author's possession. Hannah's surname from Allyn T. Morgan–Mary C. Schofield marriage license #1607, 8 November 1886, Edwards County Marriage Record 9 November 1886, 1:67; "Illinois County Marriages, 1810–1940" > FHL 1,401,780, DGS 4,661,397 > image 279 of 654 (familysearch.org).

[280] Mary C. Morgan 1862–1932 grave marker with husband Allyn, image, Bone Gap Cemetery, Edwards County, Illinois, memorial #143,882,412 for Mary Catherine Schofield Morgan by Janice (Teel) Crites (findagrave.com).

[281] Amos B. Morgan–Mary E. Thrall licensed 17 January, married 24 January 1852, Edwards County, Illinois, Marriage Book B:139. Norman Allyn, M.G., officiated.

are gradually being worked out by the golden rule and the principles of the Christian religion.[282]

A. T. MORGAN,
Probation Officer of Edwards County. Insurance Agent, Justice of the Peace

But sometimes even a lengthy obituary says much less than it could. This is a relatively peaceful and public account of a man who was married three times and who went to bat for his first wife's stepmother and daughter in their dispute with the Pension Bureau.

Rosina Smith (wife #1)

In 1860 Rosina was four years old, living in her family's household in New Hudson, Allegany County, New York.[283] But she soon lost her mother and younger brother. Father Clark B. Smith moved west to Wisconsin, where he married a young Civil War widow, Julia (Whittaker) Henshaw, in Marquette County there, and became guardian of her three Henshaw children.[284]

---

[282] "A.T. Morgan, One of County's Leading Residents, Is Dead," *Albion Journal-Register* (Illinois), Thursday 3 December 1931, p. 1, col. 8.

[283] Clark B. Smith household for apparent daughter Rosina, 1860 US census, New Hudson, Allegany County, New York, p. 789, dwelling [blank], family 467. Clark, a "farm hand," had $100 in real estate and $150 in personal estate.

[284] Andrew Jackson Henshaw–Julia Whitaker marriage 1 January 1857, Town of Princeton, Marquette County, Wisconsin, JP J.M. Fish presiding; official manuscript copy of original, in Julia Smith minors' pension file 19130 (service of Andrew Jackson Henshaw, Company H., 18th Wisconsin Infantry), Case Files of Approved Pension Applications..., 1861–1934; Civil War and Later Pension Files, Record Group 15, Department of Veterans Affairs, National Archives and Records Administration, Washington, DC; p. 10 (fold3.com). Andrew died in a Confederate prison in August 1862; p. 18 (fold3.com). Julia married second Clark B. Smith 27 October 1864 in the Town of Shields, Marquette County, Wisconsin; official manuscript copy of original, pp 23–24 (fold3.com).

The blended family moved south to Salem Precinct, Edwards County, Illinois. In 1870 Rosina was 13, living with:

father Clark B.,
stepmother Julia,
three Henshaw step-siblings (Oliver H., 12; Anderson, 11; Ada, 8; and her sister Clarinda, 3).[285]

The fall of 1879 may have been hard times for newlywed Allyn: he gave a $63.10 "chattel mortgage" to John Randolph 5 November 1879; it was recorded the following spring (5 April 1880), when perhaps the financial crisis had passed.[286]

In 1880, Allyn, Rosina, and ten-month-old Ezra were enumerated as a separate household in the same building as his mother Mary Elizabeth, his 16-year-old sister Lucretia (attending school), and four-year-old "son" Edgar (actually Elizabeth's grandson, Milton's son, and Allyn's nephew.)[287]

Allyn was a farmer working 60 acres on shares, with eighteen acres in corn and seventeen in wheat. Compared to the nearest nine farms the acreage, machinery, and livestock values were a little below average.[288] With a value of $20 per acre, Allyn's farm was a bit above the Edwards

---

[285] Clark B. Smith household, 1870 US census, Salem Precinct, Edwards County, Illinois, p. 345, dwelling/family 113. The enumerator erroneously used the surname Shaw for the last four children, and compounded the error by applying it to Clarinda Smith as well. Apparent wife Julia, age 33, was reported unable to write.

[286] Allyn T. Morgan to John Randolph, 5 November 1879, recorded 5 April 1880, Edwards County, Illinois, chattel mortgage G:62; Grantor Index D–Z, FHL 1,401,783, DGS 8,117,694, image 333 of 726 (familysearch.org). Original not viewed.

[287] Elizabeth Morgan household for "son" [grandson] Edgar age 4, 1880 US census, Albion, Edwards County, Illinois, ED 7, p. 424D, dwelling 565, family 574. Similarly, Alan [Allyn] T. Morgan household, dwelling 565, family 575.

[288] Alan [Allyn] Morgan farm, 1880 US census, agriculture schedule, Albion Precinct, Edwards County, Illinois, p. 45, line 1. Of the 192 farms enumerated in that precinct, less than one-sixth (31) were being farmed on shares.

County average of $18 and below the Illinois statewide average of $32.[289] A farmer in 1900 and 1910, he was an insurance agent in 1920 and 1930.[290] In 1930 the family lived in a $200 house in Bone Gap.[291]

More than half a century after the Civil War and more than a quarter century after Rosina's early decease, Allyn still did his best to advocate for Clarinda Frauli, who he described as his sister-in-law (a reasonable shorthand: she was his first wife's half-sister). Clarinda had cared for her aged widowed mother Julia; within days of Julia's death, Clarinda filed for reimbursement of $66.75 in care, funeral, and cemetery expenses from the unpaid portion of the pension (roughly, more than $1000 in 2018). Three years of correspondence and dispute ensued, but it appears that the claim was never paid.[292]

In November 1918 Allyn addressed the US pension commissioner in a handwritten letter, using language that might have been considerably saltier had he not been a Methodist:

> Clarinda Frauli . . . wants to know what Evidence you have that her mother Julia Smith left an acre of land when she died. I will go to county seat and get certificates from the County Clerk and Recorder of Deeds soon to show that she owned no real estate at death. She had ¼ acre but deeded [it] to her daughter Clarinda McKrell, now Frauli, to pay one hundred and fifteen dollars that she was owing some months before she died. The tax valuation shows the

---

[289] Charles H. Barnard and John Jones, *Farm Real Estate Values in the United States by Counties, 1850–1982*, Statistical Bulletin #751, Economic Research Service, US Department of Agriculture (Washington, DC.: US Government Printing Office, 1987), Table 1, p. 3 for states, and Table 2, pp. 24–29 for Illinois counties (hathitrust.org).

[290] Allan [Allyn] T. Morgan household, 1900 US census, Bone Gap, Edwards County, Illinois, ED 16, sheet 2A, dwelling/family 24. Similarly, 1910, ED 16, sheet 2B, dwelling/family 49; 1920, ED 20, sheet 4B, dwelling 188, family 139; and 1930, ED 3, sheet 2A, dwelling/family 35.

[291] Allyn T. Morgan household, 1930 US census, Bone Gap, Edwards County, Illinois, ED 3, sheet 2A, dwelling/family 35.

[292] Application for Reimbursement, 22 June 1918, Julia Smith pension file 19130, pp. 99–101 (fold3.com). For a thorough explanation: *Measuring Worth* (https://www.measuringworth.com/calculators/uscompare).

land to be worth $100.00. If they fail to get this back pension the debts will not all be paid. We have no board of supervisors in Bone Gap Vill[age] nor in the county. We have three county Commissioners for the whole county who see after the burial of Paupers but not Soldiers widows. Please let us know where the Evidence came from that Julia Smith owned one acre of land at her death.

Respectfully, A. T. Morgan J.P.

P.S. Clarinda Frauli has taken care [of] her mother for years without any Pay at all and there is no one wishes to take any advantage of the Government at all. Yours ATM[293]

Allied Families Flint-Morgan

The Flint and Thrall families intermarried twice in different generations. In 1873, Leonidas[8] Thrall married Edith Flint. In 1906 Mary Fletcher Flint (daughter of Edith's brother John Wesley Flint) married Ezra Leonidas[10] Morgan (great-grandson of Leonidas's father Worthy Thrall). As a result, the four children of Mary and Ezra were both grandchildren and great-grandchildren of the immigrants William Flint and Mary Gedney,[294] and great-grandchildren of Worthy Thrall and Hannah James in two different lines.

---

[293] A. T. Morgan to Hon. A. M. Saltzgaber, Commissioner of Pensions, letter 21 November 1918, Julia Smith pension file 19130, pp. 122–23 (fold3.com).

[294] For the marriage, William Flint–Mary Gedney marriage #23, 21 March 1842, Cowbit, Lincolnshire. "Edith F. Thrall," *Belleville Weekly Advocate* (Illinois), 18 November 1898, back page, col. 2. Also, "Memoirs—John Wesley Flint, D.D.," in *Southern Illinois Conference Methodist Episcopal Church, Minutes of the Seventy-Fifth Annual Session* (1926), 53–54.

Louisa (Thrall) Gash (Wife #2)

The 1870 household of Homer "Terrall" (Thrall) in Wayne County, Illinois, included apparent daughter "Lonza" (Louisa) A., age 9.[295] Two doors down, as the enumerator traveled, was a Frazier household with three Gash children including 13-year-old Andrew S.[296] Louisa married 7 March 1878 Andrew Langston Gash.[297] Their son Homer was born September 1879;[298] in 1880 the family lived with her widowed mother Mary.[299] Little Homer died 23 October 1880, age 1 year and 1 month,[300] and his father did not last much longer: Andrew L. Gash, born 24 March 1857, died of "a long and lingering suffering with consumption" 1 December 1880, age 23 years and 8 months.[301]

The recently widowed Allyn T. Morgan, resident one county east, married second 14 July 1881 in Wayne County, Louisa A. Gash, who was born in Barnhill, Wayne County. They were married "at res. of Mary A. Thrall" (Louisa's widowed mother) by J. P. Yungling, minister of the

---

[295] Homer G. Terrall [Thrall] household for apparent daughter Lonza [Louisa] A., 1870 US census, Barnhill Township, Wayne County, Illinois, p. 24, dwelling/family 17.

[296] William Frazier household for apparent son Andrew S. [probably L.] Gash, 1870 US census, Barnhill Township, Wayne County, Illinois, p. 24, dwelling/family 19.

[297] "In Barnhill, March 7th, by Rev. James Crews, Mr. Andrew L. Gash to Miss Louisa A. Thrall," abstracted from *Wayne County Press*, 21 March 1878; Doris Ellen Witter Bland, compiler, *Wayne County, Illinois Newspaper Gleanings, 1876–1879* (Fairfield, Illinois: Bland Books, April 1989), 45.

[298] "Births . . . Mrs. Andrew L. Gash, Barnhill, Sept. 23, boy," *Fairfield Register* (Illinois), 30 October 1879, in Doris Ellen Witter Bland, compiler, *Wayne County, Illinois Newspaper Gleanings, 1876–1879* (Fairfield, Illinois: Bland Books, 1989), 102.

[299] Mary Thrall household, 1880 U.S census, Barnhill Township, Wayne County, Illinois, p. 22, dwelling/family 16. Similarly, A. L. Gash household, dwelling 16, family 17.

[300] Homer M. Gash, Ebenezer Cemetery, Barnhill Township, Wayne County, Illinois, grave marker read by Michael J. Von Gebel, September 2007; Wayne County Trails: History and Genealogy (genealogytrails.com/ill/wayne/cem_ebenezer.html).

[301] For marriage: "In Barnhill, March 7th, by Rev. James Crews, Mr. Andrew L. Gash to Miss Louisa A. Thrall," abstracted from *Wayne County Press*, 21 March 1878; Doris Ellen Witter Bland, compiler, *Wayne County, Illinois Newspaper Gleanings, 1876–1879* (Fairfield, Illinois: Bland Books, April 1989), 45. Few marriages seem to have been recorded in Wayne County before 1879. Also, "Deaths . . . Andrew Lankston Gash," *Wayne County Press* (Illinois), 9 December 1880, p. 2, col. 3.

gospel.[302] (Allyn's 1886 marriage to Mary C. Schofield was said at the time to be his third.)[303]

Thrall-Morgan allied families

Allyn and Louisa were second cousins, sharing one set of great-grandparents. Eliphas[6] and Mary (Mead) Thrall were both:

parents of Lyman[7] Thrall, grandparents of Homer G.[8] Thrall,[304] and great-grandparents of Louisa[9] Thrall;[305] and

parents of Worthy[7] Thrall, grandparents of Mary Elizabeth[8] (Thrall) Morgan,[306] and great-grandparents of Allyn Theodore[9] Morgan.

---

[302] Allyn S. [T.] Morgan–Louisa A. Gast [Gash] marriage entry, Wayne County, Illinois, license #115, 9 July 1881, marriage register C:172, 14 July 1881; FHL 1,391,820, DGS 7,730,774 (familysearch.org). The marriage register called for ages, parents' names, previous marriages, and other information, none of which was provided. This was also the case with the few other 1879–1881 marriages, placed together in this book out of chronology. Most entries from 1887 and later are complete.

[303] Allyn T. Morgan–Mary C. Schofield marriage license #1607, 8 November 1886, Edwards County, Illinois, Marriage Record 9 November 1886, 1:67; "Illinois County Marriages, 1810–1940" > FHL 1,401,780, DGS 4,661,397 > image 279 of 654 (familysearch.org).

[304] D. Stephen Thrall and Grant Leslie Thrall, *Thrall Genealogy 1630–1965: Descendants of William Thrall* (privately printed, 1965), 39–40, 66–67.

[305] Homer G. Terrall [Thrall] household for apparent daughter Lonza [Louisa] A., age 9, 1870 US census, Barnhill Township, Wayne County, Illinois, p. 24, dwelling/family 17.

[306] D. Stephen Thrall and Grant Leslie Thrall, *Thrall Genealogy 1630–1965: Descendants of William Thrall* (privately printed, 1965), 39–40, 69.

Mary Catherine Schofield (wife #3)

Allyn married third 9 November 1886 Mary Catherine Schofield,[307] the daughter of William B. and Hannah M. (Doty) Schofield.[308]

"Lodger" Leslie A. Stone was living in Allyn and Mary C.'s household in 1910 (about ten years old) and 1920 (when he was about nineteen, not related, and a farm laborer); it seems likely that he was at least partly raised and supported by them. Leslie and his parents were all born in Kentucky.[309] He was born 27 February 1898 in Bone Gap or January 1900 in Shelby Precinct, Edwards County.[310] In 1900 he lived in the household of John Will and Minnie Stone and five older children in

---

[307] "A.T. Morgan, One of County's Leading Residents, Is Dead," *Albion Journal-Register* (Illinois), Thursday 3 December 1931, p. 1, col. 8.

[308] "Obituary of Mrs. Mary C. Morgan [corner torn off]," clipping from unknown newspaper, possibly Albion, in author's possession. Hannah's birth surname from Allyn T. Morgan–Mary C. Schofield marriage license #1607, 8 November 1886, Edwards County, Illinois, Marriage Record 9 November 1886, 1:67; "Illinois County Marriages, 1810–1940" > FHL 1,401,780, DGS 4,661,397 > image 279 of 654 (familysearch.org).

[309] For 27 February 1898: Allan [Allyn] T. Morgan household for Leslie A. Hone [Stone] age 10, 1900 US census, Bone Gap, Edwards County, Illinois, ED 16, sheet 2A, dwelling/family 24. Similarly, Leslie A. Stone age 19, 1910, ED 16, sheet 2B, dwelling/family 49. For January 1900: John Will Stone household for son Leslie Stone, age 5 months, 1900 US census, Shelby Precinct, Edwards County, Illinois, ED 21, sheet 15B, dwelling 306, family 310. Leslie may have aged himself some to get his seaman's certificate.

[310] Leslie Stone signature, photo, description, and thumbprint on undated but evidently 1918 Form S-5 (Rev), Hillsborough County, Florida; "United States, Applications for Seaman's Protection Certificates, 1916–1940" > Florida > 002-Tampa > images 107–8 of 701 (ancestry.com).

Shelby Precinct.[311] Minnie's death in January 1901[312] may have caused his birth family to disperse. In 1918 Leslie was described as having blue eyes and brown hair, standing 5 feet 6 inches tall, and weighing 135 pounds.[313]

He left Bone Gap soon after the 1920 census and was living in Wilton, Muscatine County, Iowa, when he married Matilda Elizabeth Meeks (age 19) there 15 June 1921, the daughter of B. F. and Mary (Beggs) Meeks.[314] Evidently there was no happy ending: In 1925 Matilda Meeks was divorced and living in Washington Township, Buchanan County, Iowa;[315] and in 1930 a right-age Illinois-born Leslie A. Stone was a single farm laborer lodging in Cedar County, Nebraska.[316]

"A very bad occurrence happened" in Bone Gap 19 June 1929, when Mary Catherine (in her late 60s) suffered a dislocated and doubly fractured hip while feeding her chickens in the back yard. She "caught her foot in some wire netting which caused her to fall. . . . Her cries were

---

[311] John Will Stone household for Leslie Stone, son age 5 months, 1900 US census, Shelby Precinct, Edwards County, Illinois, ED 21, sheet 15B, dwelling 306, family 310.

[312] Minerva C. Stone death notice, EXPR newspaper, p. 7, 20 January 1901, as identified by Vigo County, Indiana, public library. This record gave her death as 16 January 1901 and her father as O. W. Stone; she was said to have lived in Sullivan County, Indiana, prior to being in Monroe County, Indiana. Her death certificate gives 17 January, adding that she died of "la grippe" and was buried in Bloomington, Monroe County, Indiana, on the 19th. However, there is also a grave in Illinois: Minnie Stone (1872–1901) grave marker, Shiloh Cemetery, Samsville, Edwards County, Illinois, image, memorial #132,390,582 for Minnie Clark [?] Stone by Elaine Michels (findagrave.com).

[313] Leslie Stone signature, photo, description, and thumbprint; "United States, Applications for Seaman's Protection Certificates, 1916–1940" > Florida > 002-Tampa > images 107–8 of 701 (ancestry.com).

[314] Leslie A. Stone–Matilda Elizabeth Meeks marriage 15 June 1921, Muscatine County, Iowa, return of marriages for fiscal year ending 30 June 1921, p. 192; "Iowa, Marriage Records, 1880–1940" > 1920–21 > 494 Madison–Pocahontas > image 196 of 403 (ancestry.com).

[315] Matilda Meeks, 1925 Iowa state census, Washington Township, Buchanan County, Iowa, unpaginated, line 9; "Iowa, State Census Collection, 1836–1925" > 1925 > Buchanan > Washington > image 117 of 122 (ancestry.com).

[316] Elmer J. Ayer household for Leslie A. Stone age 30 born Illinois, parents born United States, 1930 US census, Precinct 20, Cedar County, Nebraska, ED 28, sheet 4A, dwelling [blank], family 80.

heard by neighbors nearby" and she was soon moved by ambulance to the Weber sanitarium in Olney,[317] 25 miles north.

The hospital evidently became a local place of pilgrimage. More than two dozen people, including the three Pifer children (Chapters 39, 44, 45), reportedly visited Mary C. ("Mrs. A. T. Morgan") at the Olney Sanitarium during the first week of August 1929.

> Mrs. Morgan was very glad to see all these people. She is slowly gaining and hopes to be home in two or three weeks, as her limb is now out of the cast. [Evidently all readers at the time knew the backstory.] But she is so tired lying there as it has now been fifty days since she has been able to turn over. All her friends will be glad when she is able to return to her home again.[318]

She survived the immobility treatment and on 20 August 1929 she came home in King's Ambulance. "Mrs. Morgan stood the trip home very well."[319] During the following week she had visitors from as far away as northern Indiana.[320]

Two years later the local news was lighter: "Mrs. [A.T.] Morgan and the following three sisters were together Saturday for the first time in ten years: Mrs. J. W. Moss and Mrs. Albert Horton of Albion and Mrs. Abbie Blackard of Dalton City. Their ages total 283 years."[321]

---

[317] "Bone Gap Woman Painfully Hurt When She Falls," *Daily Republican-Register* (Mount Carmel, Illinois), Wednesday 26 June 1919, p. 4, col. 1.

[318] "Many People Visit Woman in Sanitarium," *Daily Republican-Register* (Mount Carmel, Illinois), Wednesday 7 August 1929, p. 4, col. 2.

[319] "Annual Chowder Will Be Held" (Bone Gap locals), *Daily Republican-Register* (Mount Carmel, Illinois), Wednesday 21 August 1929, p. 5, col. 3.

[320] "News Notes of Interest from the Bone Gap Area," *Daily Republican-Register* (Mount Carmel, Illinois), Wednesday 28 August 1929, p. 6, col. 2. The list could be a valuable search option for researchers seeking to track dispersed families and friends from Bone Gap.

[321] "Senior Play Is to Be Presented" (Bone Gap locals), *Daily Republican-Register* (Mount Carmel, Illinois), Thursday 14 May 1931, p. 7, col. 3.

Allied families Schofield, Thrall, Morgan

English immigrant Charles Schofield had numerous children, including sons John Naylor Schofield and William Bobbitt Schofield.[322] The two brothers married Thrall daughters who were first cousins once removed. John married Lucy Croker Thrall, a daughter of Lyman Thrall. William's daughter Mary Catherine married Allyn Theodore Morgan as his third wife. Allyn was a grandson of Lyman's brother Worthy. The descendants of these two marriages are all connected to both families.

Mary Catherine's father William B. Schofield was born at "Yorkshire, Brathwait, England," 27 March 1828, and came to the U.S. with his parents, settling in Albion and marrying 28 December 1852 Hannah M. Doty. They had nine children, who as of his death at age 91 in November 1919 were:

Henry O. Schofield of Chicago;
Lydia M. Moss of Albion;
Anna M., who died in infancy;
Abigail C. Blackard of Dalton City, Moultrie County, Illinois;
Geo. E., who died in infancy;
Mary C. Morgan of Bone Gap;
Ralph D. who died in 1883 at age 19;
Agnes A. Horton; and
Eunice B. Adrian of Albion.[323]

John N. Schofield (son of Charles) was born 12 October 1826 in Braithwaite, Yorkshire, England, died 5 October 1893 in Albion, Edwards

---

[322] Charles Schofield household, 1850 US census, Albion, Edwards County, Illinois, p. 246 (stamped)/491 (penned) verso, dwelling/family 9.

[323] "Charter Member of Masonic Lodge: Squire Wm. B. Schofield, of Albion, Is Called By Death," *Mount Carmel Daily Republican-Register* (Illinois), Thursday 20 November 1919, p. 3, col. 1. William was a Civil War veteran; his obituary (evidently cribbed from the Albion newspaper) says that he had eight grandsons and four great-grandsons in World War I.

County, Illinois, and married Lucy C. Thrall 23 February 1860.[324] The daughter of Worthy's brother Lyman,[325] she was born 1 May 1839, died 19 July 1891, and was buried at Old Albion Cemetery the following day.[326] John and Lucy's daughter Lenora Schofield married Nathan E. Smith as his second wife, and Ina Smith was their only child.[327]

Mary Catherine[3] Schofield (granddaughter of Charles, daughter of William B.) was born 27 March 1828 in Braithwaite, Yorkshire, England, and died 15 November 1919 in Albion.[328] She married as his third wife Allyn Theodore Morgan, grandson of Worthy Thrall.[329]

---

[324] John N. Schofield–Lucy C. Thrall license and marriage 23 February 1860, Edwards County, Illinois, Marriage Record C (1855–1869):163; FHL 1,401,779, DGS 4,661,396, image 407 of 787 (familysearch.org). A partially sourced family tree, "Descendants of Joseph Schofield," from Brenda (Bperk930@aol.com) gives Naylor and Croker as their respective middle names.

[325] Lyman Thrall household for apparent daughter Lucy age 10, 1850 US census, Wabash County, Illinois, p. 405 *recto* and *verso*, dwelling 212, family 206. Also, D. Stephen Thrall and Grant Leslie Thrall, *Thrall Genealogy 1630–1965: Descendants of William Thrall* (privately printed, 1965), 384–85, Lyman Thrall entry, naming a daughter Lucy who married a Schofield.

[326] Lucy C. Thrall entry, *Old Albion Cemetery* (Albion, Illinois: Edwards County Historical Society, no date, 23. She was said to be 53 years, 2 months, 19 days old.

[327] "Smith Funeral Services Held," *Daily Republican-Register* (Mount Carmel, Illinois), p. 3, cols. 5–6. Nathan E. Smith served four years as state senator from Albion, and worked there as an undertaker for more than 65 years.

[328] "Obituary of Mrs. Mary C. Morgan Give [corner torn off]," clipping from unknown newspaper, possibly Albion, in author's possession. Also, Mary C. Morgan grave marker (image, 1862–1932), Bone Gap Cemetery, Bone Gap, Illinois, memorial #143,882,412 for Mary Catherine Schofield Morgan by Janice (Teel) Crites (findagrave.com).

[329] "A.T. Morgan, One of County's Leading Residents, Is Dead," *Albion Journal-Register* (Illinois), Thursday 3 December 1931, p. 1, col. 8.

Child of Allyn Theodore⁹ and Rosina (Smith) Morgan:

25 i. EZRA LEONIDAS "LON"*¹⁰* MORGAN (*Allyn Theodore Morgan⁹, Mary Elizabeth Thrall⁸, Worthy⁷, Eliphas⁶, Samuel⁵, John⁴⁻³, Timothy², William¹*) was born 22 August 1879 in Bone Gap, and died 9 October 1937 in St. Louis. He married 26 June 1906 in Murphysboro, Jackson County, Illinois, MARY FLETCHER FLINT.

Probable child of Allyn Theodore⁹ and Louisa/Ida (Thrall)(Gash) Morgan:

ii. MINNIE L.*¹⁰* MORGAN (*Allyn T. Morgan⁹, Mary E. Thrall⁸, Worthy⁷, Eliphas⁶, Samuel⁵, John⁴⁻³, Timothy², William¹*) lived 1 year, 2 months, and 10 days—conjecturally, from July 1882 to September 1883. She is known only from a reading of a worn and unphotographed stone in Ebenezer Cemetery, Wayne County: "(date illegible) aged 1 yr, 2 mo. 10 days dau. of A. P. and L. A. Morgan, budded on earth to bloom in heaven."[330] There is plenty of time between their known marriage 14 July 1881 and Allyn's third marriage in 1886; indeed, it would be unusual in this time and place for a marriage not to produce at least one child. (And Louisa had already had one child with her first husband.) It is not known how the marriage ended, or what became of Louisa (Thrall) (Gash) Morgan.

Children of Allyn Theodore⁹ and Mary Catherine (Schofield) Morgan:

iii. ROSCOE RALPH*¹⁰* MORGAN (*Allyn T. Morgan⁹, Mary E. Thrall⁸, Worthy⁷, Eliphas⁶, Samuel⁵, John⁴⁻³, Timothy², William¹*) was born about 30 November 1887 and died 29 July 1888, when he was said to be 8 months and 29 days old.[331]

---

[330] Minnie L. Morgan grave marker, no image, Ebenezer Cemetery, Wayne County, Illinois, memorial #34,713,446 by David Shelton (findagrave.com).
[331] "Little Roscoe," misdated clipping (7/2/88) from unnamed newspaper, possibly Albion, in author's possession.

26   iv. EARL AMOS[10] MORGAN (*Allyn T. Morgan*[9], *Mary E. Thrall*[8], *Worthy*[7], *Eliphas*[6], *Samuel*[5], *John*[4-3], *Timothy*[2], *William*[1]) was born 10 June 1890 in Bone Gap, Edwards County; died 17 March 1960 in Illinois Central Hospital, Cook County; and was buried at Spencer Heights Memorial Cemetery, Mounds, Pulaski County, Illinois. He married 10 June 1920 in Mounds EFFIE GERTRUDE BANKSTON.

27   v. EVART/EVERETT WILLIAM[10] MORGAN (*Allyn T. Morgan*[9], *Mary E. Thrall*[8], *Worthy*[7], *Eliphas*[6], *Samuel*[5], *John*[4-3], *Timothy*[2], *William*[1]) was born 19 March 1892 in Bone Gap, Edwards County;[332] died 2 March 1979 in Pueblo, Pueblo County, Colorado; and was buried in Imperial Memorial Gardens there on the 6th. He married first 20 March 1912 in Bone Gap ELSIE P. DRURY. He married second before 1920 EVA BRINES.

---

[332] Everett [Evart] William Morgan WWI draft card #595/6, Bone Gap, Illinois; "US, World War I, Draft Registration Cards, 1917–1918" > Illinois > Edwards County > Draft Card M > image 187 of 210 (ancestry.com).

Tree 3. Allied Schofield–Thrall–Morgan Families

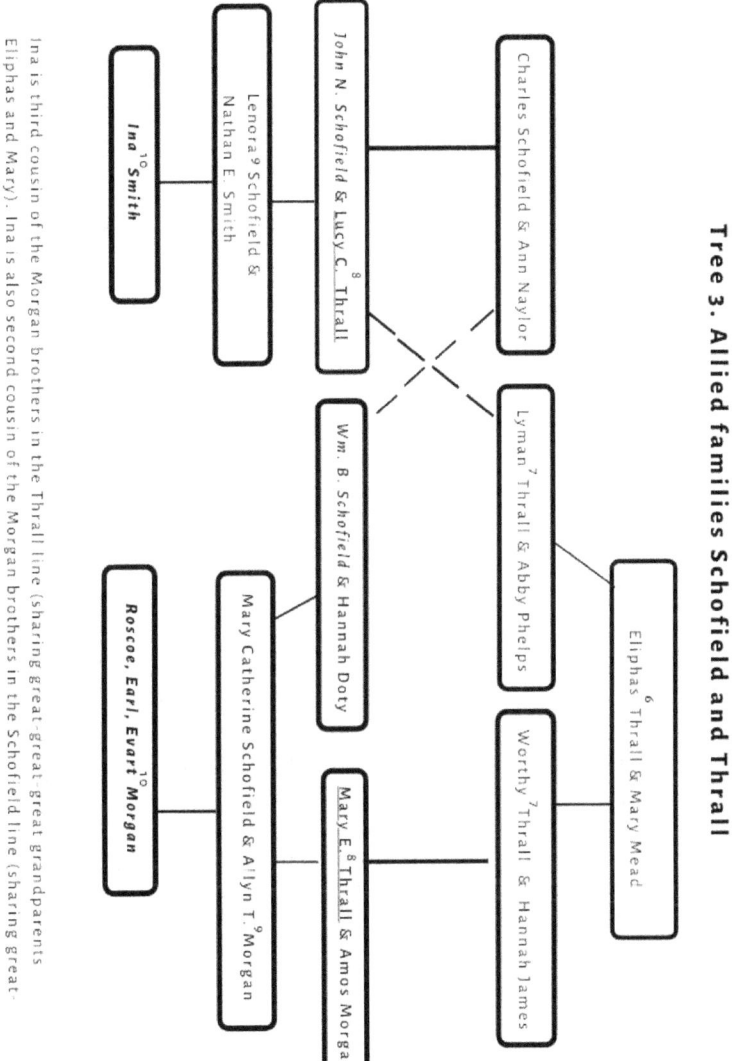

Tree 3. Allied families Schofield and Thrall

Ina is third cousin of the Morgan brothers in the Thrall line (sharing great-great-great grandparents Eliphas and Mary). Ina is also second cousin of the Morgan brothers in the Schofield line (sharing great-great grandparents Charles and Ann).

Tree 4. Allied Flint-Morgan Families

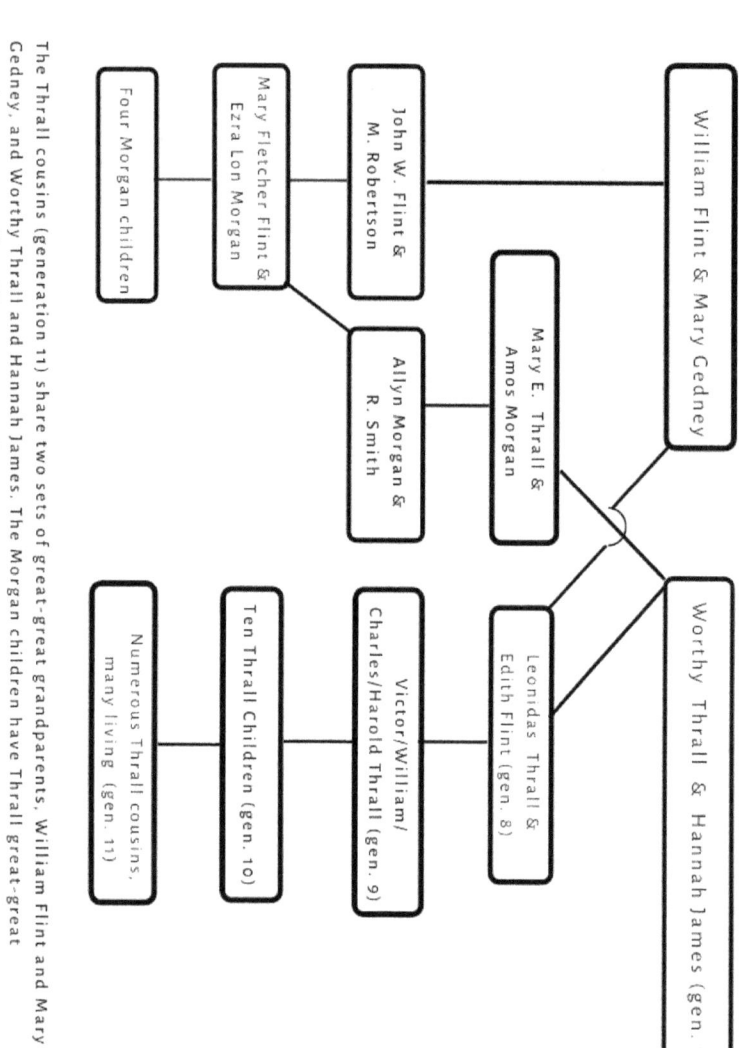

The Thrall cousins (generation 11) share two sets of great-great grandparents, William Flint and Mary Cedney, and Worthy Thrall and Hannah James. The Morgan children have Thrall great-great grandparents as well as Flint great-grandparents

Genealogical puzzle 2:
Who were the parents of Lulu Irene Geoffroy?

After her second marriage, the trail of Louisa (Thrall) (Lankston) Morgan grows steadily colder. It is not out of the question that she may have had a third child with a third husband. Several records connect a cryptic Wayne County birth to long-lived Kansan Lulu Irene (Morgan) Geoffroy:

(1) An unnamed daughter was born in Merriam, Wayne County, 25 October 1887 to William Turham Morgan and Ida Morgan, (her birth surname given as Thrall). William Turham was a 21-year-old farmer; the word "Morgan" was written after his name in another hand. Ida was 27 years old; her parents were both "American" and born in Illinois. The baby was female and the mother's third child. The mother's surnames, age, and the baby being her third birth all point to Louisa. No other record of William Turham Morgan has been found. Targeted autosomal DNA testing could focus on and compare Lulu's descendants with Louise's siblings' and potential cousins' descendants.

(2) Lulu Irene Hooper, born October 1887, appeared in 1900 as a 12-year-old "niece" in the household of Louisa's sister Florence (Thrall) Hooper. Florence was reported as having had one child -- then one living and present in that household-- namely Mary.[333]

(3) Lulu Irene Morgan was age 19, born in Fairfield, Wayne County, on 26 December 1906, when she made an affidavit to marry Frank Geoffroy of Abilene, Dickinson County, Kansas, in Kansas City,

---

[333] Flo Hooper household, 1900 US census, Fairfield, Wayne County, Illinois, ED 98, sheet 19A, dwelling 110, family 421. Flo kept a boardinghouse; had one child, one living (Mary in this household); and was divorced. Lulu's last name was given as Hooper, birth October 1887.

Missouri.[334] Neither the affidavit nor the license named her parents.

(4) In 1909 Lulu was called a cousin of A. H. Thrall.[335] This is very probably Albert Homer Thrall, son of Henry Clay Thrall, Louisa's older brother.[336] If Louisa was indeed Lulu's mother, then Lulu and and Albert would have been first cousins.

(5) In 1923 the obituary of Florence's daughter Mary Cynthia (Hooper) Kirby called Lulu Geoffrey her sister.[337] This does not square with the 1900 household.[338] Mary and Lulu may well have grown up together, and calling her "sister" at a later date raised no difficult questions.

(6) Lulu Geoffroy's birthday was given as 25 October 1887,[339] corresponding exactly to the Wayne County birth record of the unnamed daughter at the time.

---

[334] Frank Geoffroy–Lulu Irene Morgan affidavits, marriage application #36738, 26 December 1906, Kansas City, Jackson County, Missouri; "Missouri, Jackson County, Marriage Records, 1840–1985," image 612,592 of 695672 (ancestry.com). Also, unnumbered marriage license and return, 26 December 1906, for Frank Geoffroy and Lulu Irane [Irene] Morgan, Jackson County Recorder of Deeds; "Missouri, Marriage Records, 1805–2002" > Jackson > Record Images for Jackson > 1896–1907 > image 2637 of 2751. Minister R. R. Mason officiated. Lulu was said to be of Wayne County, Illinois.

[335] [Untitled local notes], *Marysville Advocate-Democrat* (Kansas), Thursday 13 October 1909, p. 5, col. 1: "Mr. and Mrs. A. H. Thrall are in the city the guests at the Frank Geoffroy home. They expect to remain here a month or six weeks. Mr. Thrall, who is a cousin of Mrs. Geoffroy, is connected with the International Conservatory of Music."

[336] Henry Thrall household for Albert H. age 3, 1880 US census, Barnhill Township, Wayne County, Illinois, ED 144, p. 153B, dwelling/family 13.

[337] Transcribed obituary for Mary Cynthia Hooper Kirby, born 28 March 1878 at Fairfield, Wayne County, Illinois, and died in Beatrice, Gage County, Nebraska, 30 January 1923, reportedly from a Fairfield newspaper in Mr. K. Verdaine Hooper's grandmother's collection.

[338] Flo Hooper household, 1900 US census, Fairfield, Wayne County, Illinois, ED 98, sheet 19A, dwelling 110, family 421. Flo kept a boardinghouse; had one child, one living (Mary in this household); and was divorced. Lulu's last name was given as Hooper, birth October 1887.

[339] Lulu Geoffroy index entry, US Social Security Death Index.

(7) In 1940, Frank "Geoffrey" and wife "Mary" were living at 1849 Pembroke in Topeka, Shawnee County, Kansas. Frank had completed eight years of schooling, "Mary" three years of high school.[340] This is the same address given for Frank Geoffroy and wife Lulu I. in Topeka in 1942.[341]

(8) In 1947, Lulu Irene Geoffroy filed for Social Security, giving her birth date as 25 October 1888, birth place Fairfield, parents John M. Morgan and Idella Thrall. Preliminary searching does not turn up any such couple.

---

[340] Frank Geoffrey [Geoffroy] household for wife Mary [Lulu], 1940 US census, Topeka, Shawnee County, Kansas, ED 89-47, sheet 10B, dwelling 205.
[341] Frank Geoffroy (Lulu I.) entry, *Polk's Topeka (Shawnee County, Kans.) City Directory 1942* (Kansas City, Missouri: R. L. Polk, 1942), p. 140, image 67 of 345 (ancestry.com).

Chapter 8

Ninth Generation

Wilbur Morgan–Jennie Smith Family

parents at chapter 2

"A firm believer in prohibition"

8. **WILBUR AMOS^9 MORGAN** (*Mary E. Thrall^8, Worthy^7, Eliphas^6, Samuel^5, John$^{4-3}$, Timothy^2, William^1*)
Birth: 22 February 1858 in Edwards County, Illinois
Death: 4 August 1945
Burial: Bone Gap Cemetery^{342}
Spouse: **ELIZA JANE "JENNIE" SMITH,** married 7 January 1884 in Olney, Richland County, Illinois
Spouse's parents: Abner Turner and Deanna (Saunders) (Honchin/Houchin) Smith
Spouse's birth: 12 February 1862 near Parkersburg, Richland County
Spouse's death: 2 December 1945 in Pasadena, Los Angeles County, California
Spouse's burial: Bone Gap Cemetery^{343}

---

^{342} "Life Sketch of W. A. Morgan, Bone Gap Pioneer," unnamed newspaper clipping (likely Albion) dated "Aug 16 45," in author's possession, binder 511, Morgans. Also, Wilbur A. and Eliza J. Morgan joint grave marker, image, Bone Gap Cemetery, Bone Gap, Illinois, memorial #138,327,564 by Janice (Teel) Crites (findagrave.com). Also, author's visit to the area, 24–25 May 2001.

^{343} Wilbur A. Morgan–Eliza J. Smith marriage license #3, 7 January 1884, Register of Marriages 3A (1878–1893):90; "Illinois County Marriages, 1810–1940" > FHL 1,221,093, DGS 5,202,988 > image 989 of 1098 (familysearch.org). County Judge F. D. Preston officiated. Also, Wilbur A. and Eliza J. Morgan joint grave marker, image, Bone Gap Cemetery, Bone Gap, Illinois, memorial #138,327,564 by Janice (Teel) Crites (findagrave.com). Also, "Death Occurs in California," *Daily Republican-Register* (Mount Carmel, Illinois), Thursday 13 December 1945, p. 3, col. 3.

Jennie's mother died before she was seven, and her father died when she was fifteen, leaving her in the care of multiple step-parents; she reportedly came to Bone Gap in the early 1880s.[344] The following sequence of events describes a 20-year household transformation involving three wives and two husbands, giving Jennie a tumultuous childhood:

- 1859 (19 March): Diana Sanders married William Anderson Houchin/Honchin;[345]

- 1861 (8 January): Diana (Saunders) Honchin married second Abner T. Smith;[346]

- 1862 (12 February): **Eliza Jane "Jennie" Smith** born;[347]

- 1868 (reportedly 29 November): Diana (Saunders) (Honchin) Smith died in Richland County, Illinois, reportedly age 25 years, 9 months, 15 days;[348]

- before 1870: widower Abner T. Smith evidently married second Eliza [–?–], born 1844;

---

[344] "Death Occurs in California," *Daily Republican-Register* (Mount Carmel, Illinois), Thursday 13 December 1945, p. 3, col. 3.

[345] William Anderson Honchin–Dianah Sanders marriage register, 19 March 1859, Edmonson County, Kentucky, p. 27; Kentucky, County Marriage Records, 1783–1965 > Edmonson > 1833–1870 > image 12 of 28 (ancestry.com).

[346] Abner T. Smith–Diana Honchin [Houchin?] marriage, license and certificate, 8 January 1861, Edwards County, Illinois, p. 193; FHL 1,401,779, DGS 4,661,396; "Illinois, County Marriages, 1810–1940," image 424 of 787 (familysearch.org).

[347] "Death Occurs in California," *Daily Republican-Register* (Mount Carmel, Illinois), Thursday 13 December 1945, p. 3, col. 3.

[348] Dianna Houchins Smith, no image of grave marker, Ridgely Cemetery, Parkersburg, Richland County, Illinois, memorial #38,278,791 by BjJ (findagrave.com).

- 1870: Abner Smith household in Madison Township, Richland County, Illinois, included Abner age 40, Eliza 26, **Eliza J. 8**, Benjamin F. 7; Pinkney Hill 3, Thomas C. Hill 2;[349]

- 1870 Snyder household, also in Madison Township, included William Snyder, 38 years old; Elizabeth, 39; Mary, 13; William, 4; Fanny J., 2; William Dodds, 13; and Samuel F. Dodds, 9;[350]

- 1878 (January 8) Abner T. Smith died leaving an estate of $680,[351] leaving **Eliza J.** an orphan;

- 1879 Widow Eliza [-?-] Smith married second as his second wife William Snyder; and

- 1880 household (all born in Illinois): William Snider, 49 years old; Elisa [Eliza], 37; William, 14; Fanny, 12; Charley, 9; James I., 11/12; **Eliza J. Smith, 18, stepchild**; William H., 9; Mary E., 7; Lewis E., 5; Pinkney S. Hill, 14, stepchild; Thomas C. Hill, 12; Rebecca Armstrong, 28, sister-in-law; Grisom Lee 24, no relation, married.[352]

In 1878 Wilbur, age 20, attended seven days at Yankeetown School in Edwards County with his younger sister Cretie. Later the same

---

[349] Abner Smith household, 1870 US census, Madison Township, Richland County, Illinois (Fairview Post Office), sheet 13, dwelling/family 97.

[350] William Snyder household, 1870 US census, Madison Township, Richland County, Illinois (Fairview Post Office), sheet 18, dwelling/family 142.

[351] Abner T. Smith probate, Richland County, Illinois, probate court hearing 29 January 1878, death date 8 January; "Illinois, Wills and Probate Records, 1772–1999" > Richland > Will and Guardian Records > Administrator Record, Book B, 1866–1882 > image 529 of 564 (ancestry.com).

[352] William Snider household, 1880 US census, Madison Township, Richland County, Illinois, ED 173, p. 77C, dwelling 99, family 101.

winter, in 1879, they both attended 22 days.[353] In 1880 he was a laborer in the John W. Bircket household in Albion.[354]

> The country grade schools around Bone Gap furnished his early education in the days when it was felt a four month term yearly was all that could be spared to children whose help was needed with the farm work. It was necessary for Mr. Morgan to miss two entire years of school since his father's [Amos Morgan] death at the age of 39 placed the duty of maintaining the home on the sons. In addition to helping with the farm work, he secured a contract at the age of 16 to cut and haul wood at $1.00 per cord for the nearby country schools. By the fall of 1879 he had accumulated funds enough to enable him to enter Illinois Wesleyan University at Bloomington for a year of study there. . . . In November of 1880 he travelled to Nebraska to visit his brother Milton who was employed as a school teacher.[355]

Returning to Bone Gap, Wilbur purchased a small grocery store, and moved it nearer to the railroad when the Peoria, Decatur, and Evansville Railroad came along. "W. Morgan was a leader in the movement to the new site where he constructed the first building, a general store which was one of the finest in the county."[356] Willard was town postmaster from 11 February 1881 to 2 November 1886.[357] He aided in the incorporation of Bone Gap in 1892 and served as police

---

[353] "Miscellaneous School Records, Edwards County, Illinois, 1865, 1873–1875, 1878–1880, 1883 and 1888," Yankeetown 20 November 1878, typescript evidently transcribed from a standard "Schedule of a Common School," 3–6; copy in author's possession, likely from Edwards County Historical Society, Albion, Illinois. Teacher Alice Pickering was paid $20 the first time and $30 the second.

[354] John W. Bircket household for Wilbur Morgan, 1880 US census, Albion, Edwards County, Illinois, ED 7, p. 424C, dwelling 555, family 564.

[355] "Life Sketch of W. A. Morgan, Bone Gap Pioneer," unnamed newspaper clipping (likely Albion) dated "Aug 16 45," in author's possession, binder 511, Morgans.

[356] "Communities . . . Bone Gap Precinct," *History of Edwards County, Illinois* (Albion: Edwards County Historical Society, 1980) 1:9.

[357] Wilbur A. Morgan entry, *Record of Appointment of Postmasters 1832–September 30, 1971*, National Archives Microfilm Publication M841, Roll 28, Illinois, Du Page–Johnson Counties, vol. 53 (1878–93):64–5, Bone Gap, Edwards County, Illinois; "US, Appointments of US Postmasters, 1832–1971" > Illinois > Du Page–Johnson > image 76 of 597 (ancestry.com).

magistrate from 1894 to 1900. From 1890 to 1910 he was school treasurer for the district and from 1906 to 1910 was president of the town board of trustees.

Meanwhile he became radicalized. "In 1879, on hearing a number of addresses on the subject, he became a firm believer in prohibition" and joined the Prohibition Party in 1903, running unsuccessfully on its ticket for Congress in 1904 and the state legislature in 1906.[358] In 1914 he was the party's candidate for clerk of the Illinois Supreme Court.[359]

In 1904 he was involved in the National Good Roads Association, a popular rural cause around that time and one of which he gained first-hand knowledge over the years,[360] having visited Nebraska in 1880 and 1894; Oklahoma in 1901; the northern tier of states to the Pacific northwest in 1906, 1907, 1909, and 1910; and California in 1924, 1926, 1927, 1928, 1936, and 1940. "On these visits he and Mrs. Morgan resided in California for periods of a few months up to two years. . . . however, he never wavered in his affection for and loyalty to the community where he was born."[361] In the summer of 1915 he and J. T. Drury were organizing a private "first class" railroad car to travel from Bone Gap to the exposition in San Francisco.[362]

He had one year of college; Jennie completed eight years of school.[363] In 1930 they lived with widowed sister-in-law Nora Smith in Salem Precinct near Bone Gap in a $1200 house she owned.[364] Jennie

---

[358] "Life Sketch of W. A. Morgan, Bone Gap Pioneer," unnamed newspaper clipping (likely Albion) dated "Aug 16 45," in author's possession, binder 511, Morgans.

[359] "Bone Gap Man Named," *Mt. Carmel Evening Register* (Illinois), Friday 10 July 1914, p. 1, col. 5.

[360] "The Good Roads," *Evening Register* (Mount Carmel, Illinois), Saturday 24 September 1904, p. 2, col. 3.

[361] "Life Sketch of W. A. Morgan, Bone Gap Pioneer," unidentified newspaper clipping (likely Albion) dated "Aug 16 45," in author's possession, binder 511, Morgans.

[362] "Going to Exposition?" *Daily Republican-Register* (Mount Carmel, Illinois), Tuesday 27 July 1915, p. 4, col. 4.

[363] William [Wilbur A.] Morgan household, 1940 US census, Bone Gap, Edwards County, Illinois, ED 24-3, sheet 2B, dwelling 45. Their house was valued at $300.

[364] Nora Smith household for Wilbur A. and Eliza J. Morgan, 1930 US census, Salem Precinct, Edwards County, Illinois, ED 12, sheet 2A, dwelling/family 31.

became a member of the Methodist Episcopal church and the W.C.T.U. [Women's Christian Temperance Union] . . . Her husband was ever ready to say that her work was equal to his as they went forward together in the upbuilding of home and community. . . . To the last she aided him as she read to him from the Bible they both loved when his failing eyesight made it no longer possible for him to see.[365]

In the late 1930s and early 1940s, all three of Wilbur and Jennie's sons were working at the Brown Valve and Manufacturing Company in Alhambra, Los Angeles County, California.[366] In 1941, Glen was president and Willard treasurer; the business address was 2020 Lemon.[367]

Children of Wilbur Amos^9 and Eliza Jane "Jennie" (Smith) Morgan (all buried at Mountain View Cemetery and Mausoleum in Altadena, Los Angeles County):

28   i. HALE EUGENE^{10} MORGAN (*Wilbur A. Morgan^9, Mary E. Thrall^8, Worthy^7, Eliphas^6, Samuel^5, John$^{4-3}$, Timothy^2, William^1*) was born 4 June 1886 in Bone Gap, and died 28 December 1954 in Los Angeles County, California. He married EDNA BLANCHE WHEELER.

29   ii. GLEN WILBUR^{10} MORGAN (*Wilbur A. Morgan^9, Mary E. Thrall^8, Worthy^7, Eliphas^6, Samuel^5, John$^{4-3}$, Timothy^2, William^1*) was born 25 June 1890, and died 27 November 1957 in Victorville, San

---

[365] "Funeral of Mrs. W. A. Morgan Sunday," unnamed newspaper clipping (likely Albion) in author's possession.

[366] Hale Eugene Morgan, WW2 draft card, serial #484, order #189; "US, World War II, Draft Registration Cards, 1942" > California > Lother–Zwanzig > image 481 of 2392 (ancestry.com). Glen W. Morgan entry (vice-president and manager), *Alhambra (California) City Directory 1935* (Los Angeles: Los Angeles Directory, 1935), p. 108, image 107 of 463 (ancestry.com). Willard A. Morgan entry, *San Marino City Directory, Season 1936–1937* (South Pasadena, California: California Directory, 1936), p. 54, image 53 of 101 (ancestry.com).

[367] Brown Valve & Manufacturing entry, *Alhambra (California) City Directory 1941* (Los Angeles, California: Los Angeles Directory, 1941), p. 73, image 40 of 233 (ancestry.com).

Bernardino County, California. He married 1 September 1915 in Evansville, Vanderburgh County, Indiana, MINA LOIS SIMS. He married second between 1950 and 1952, AVA B. [–?–].

30 iii. WILLARD AMOS^{10} MORGAN (*Wilbur A. Morgan^9, Mary E. Thrall^8, Worthy^7, Eliphas^6, Samuel^5, John^{4,3}, Timothy^2, William^1*) was born 20 November 1898, probably in Bone Gap, and died 13 September 1948. He married 24 October 1929 in Los Angeles, California, WILMA ANN SNIDER.

Chapter 9

Ninth Generation
parents at chapter 2

Maria Lucretia Ada "Crete" Morgan– Joseph W. Britton Family

Subdivision sales and minister's wife

9. MARIA LUCRETIA ADA[9] "CRETE" MORGAN (*Mary E. Thrall[8], Worthy[7], Eliphas[6], Samuel[5], John[4-3], Timothy[2], William[1]*)
Birth: about September 1863 in Bone Gap, Edwards County[368]
Death: 22 July 1906
Burial: Bone Gap Cemetery[369]
Spouse: **REV. JOSEPH W. BRITTON,** married 17 December 1885 in Edwards County[370]
Spouse's parents: John and Harriet (Beeney) Britton[371]
Spouse's birth: 15 January 1855 in Mount Vernon, Knox County, Ohio

---

[368] John W. Britton–Lucretia A. Morgan marriage license #1530, 16 December 1885, married 17 December at Bone Gap, Edwards County, Illinois, marriage record 1:61; FHL 1,401,780, DGS 4,661,397, image 273 of 654 (familysearch.org). For birth month and year, James [Joseph] W. Britten [Britton] household, 1900 US census, Glenwood, Schuyler County, Missouri, ED 132, sheet 4B, dwelling/family 76. For birth year 1864, note below.

[369] "*Memoir of Sister Britton,*" *Minutes of the 55th Session of the Southern Illinois Conference, Methodist Episcopal Church, Vandalia,* 19–24 September 1906, pp. 71–72. Lucretia M. Britton (1864–1906) grave marker, Bone Gap Cemetery, Bone Gap, Edwards County, Illinois, image, memorial #141,241,523 for Lucretia Morgan Britton by Janice (Teel) Crites (findagrave.com).

[370] John W. Britton–Lucretia A. Morgan marriage license #1530, 16 December 1885, married 17 December at Bone Gap, Edwards County, Illinois, marriage record 1:61; FHL 1,401,780, DGS 4,661,397, image 273 of 654 (familysearch.org). Witnesses were D. B. [Daniel Bassett?] Leach, W. A. Morgan, "et al." Rev. M. N. Powers officiated.

[371] John W. Britton–Lucretia A. Morgan marriage license #1530, 16 December 1885, married 17 December at Bone Gap, Edwards County, Illinois, marriage record 1:61; FHL 1,401,780, DGS 4,661,397, image 273 of 654 (familysearch.org).

Spouse's death: 30 March 1925 in Mattoon, Coles County
Spouse's burial: Bone Gap Cemetery[372]

Maria Lucretia's first cousin Alta Areta Gould married Joseph's brother Edward (chapter 10).

At age 15 "Cretie" attended Yankeetown School (near Bone Gap) in November 1878 in Edwards County (all 22 days) sometimes with her older brother Wilber, age 20 (7 days). They attended again in 1879 (the same winter), both for 22 days.[373] In the month ending 10 January 1880, Cretie and her first cousin Alta Gould spent 21 days and 8 days respectively in Yankeetown School, this time taught by Mrs. C. T. Campbell, their aunt.[374]

In the early 1880s up until her 1885 marriage, Lucretia sold lots in Morgan's Addition to Bone Gap—nine transactions totaling $575 (very

---

[372] "Rev. J. W. Britton," *Minutes of the 74th Session of the Southern Illinois Conference, Methodist Episcopal Church, Centralia, 22–27 September 1925*, p. 177. Also, Rev. Joseph W. Britton grave marker (1855–1925), Bone Gap Cemetery, Bone Gap, Edwards County, Illinois, exact birth and death dates and burial place undocumented, memorial #141,241,451 by Janice (Teel) Crites (findagrave.com). Also, John W. Britton–Lucretia A. Morgan marriage license 1530, 16 December 1885, married 17 December at Bone Gap, Edwards County, Illinois, marriage record 1:61; FHL 1,401,780, DGS 4,661,397, image 273 of 654 (familysearch.org). For month and year, James [Joseph] W. Britten [Britton] household, 1900 US census, Glenwood, Schuyler County, Missouri, ED 132, sheet 4B, dwelling/family 76.

[373] "Miscellaneous School Records, Edwards County, Illinois, 1865, 1873–1875, 1878–1880, 1883 and 1888," Yankeetown 20 November 1878, typescript evidently transcribed from a standard "Schedule of a Common School," 3–6; copy in author's possession, likely from Edwards County Historical Society, Albion, Illinois. Teacher Alice Pickering was paid $20 the first term and $30 the second.

[374] "Miscellaneous School Records, Edwards County, Illinois, 1865, 1873–1875, 1878–1880, 1883 and 1888," Yankeetown, month ending 10 January 1880, typescript evidently transcribed from a standard "Schedule of a Common School," 7–8; copy in author's possession, likely from Edwards County Historical Society, Albion, Illinois.

roughly $15,800 in 2019).³⁷⁵ She also sold 20 acres to Howell C. Porter 26 April 1884.³⁷⁶ How she came into possession of these properties is not known. Late in October 1887 she was traveling from Bone Gap north to Evanston.³⁷⁷

Following Lucretia's death, Rev. Joseph married second as her first husband in 1908 Mary Bailey, who was born about November 1853 in Illinois; ³⁷⁸ died possibly 9 September 1939 in Fredonia, Wilson County, Kansas; and was reportedly buried at Fredonia City Cemetery there,³⁷⁹ the daughter of James H. and Ann E. [–?–] Bailey.³⁸⁰

In the mid-1870s Joseph joined the Methodist Church in West Union, Clark County, Illinois, taught school, attended Knox College (Galesburg, Knox County, Illinois) and State Normal (Lebanon, Ohio), and graduated from Garrett Seminary (Evanston, Cook County, Illinois)

---

³⁷⁵ All in Edwards County, Illinois, from Lucretia A. Morgan, in Grantor Index D–Z, FHL 1,401,783, DGS 8,117,694 (familysearch.org): (1) to Ephraim Carter, 23 December 1881, $70, Y:207, image 335 of 726; (2) to Elijah G. Phillips, 11 October 1881, $15, Y:235, image 335 of 726; (3) to Mary Rude, 10 December 1881, $15, Y:249, image 336 of 726; (4) to Peter Hocking 28 January 1882, $45, Y:412, image 337 of 726; (5) to Elizabeth Morgan [not identified] 18 September 1882, $375, Y:420, image 337 of 726; (6) to [brother] Wilbur A. Morgan 11 October 1881, $30, Y:421, image 337 of 726; (7) to Maggie D. Rice, 29 March 1884, $4, 1:69, image 339 of 726; (8) to Elijah G. Phillips [again] 16 December 1885, $35, 1:194, image 341 of 726; and (9) to J. W. Birckett 20 September 1884, $8, 2:194, image 343 of 726. For the conversion, *Measuring Worth* (measuringworth.com/calculators/uscompare).

³⁷⁶ Lucretia A. Morgan to Howell C. Porter, 26 April 1884, recorded 8 May (part of S ½ SE ¼ NW ¼ Section 8, Township 1S, Range 14W), 1:61; Grantor Index D–Z, FHL 1,401,783, DGS 8,117,694, image 339 of 726 (familysearch.org).

³⁷⁷ Edith Thrall in Bone Gap to Lonnie [Leonidas], Flint–Thrall letter #23, Friday 7 October 1887; in author's possession.

³⁷⁸ J. W. Bitton [Britton] household for wife Mary (married two years), 1910 US census, Mount Olive, Macoupin County, Illinois, ED 59, sheet 5A, dwelling 104, family 109. Marriage year also from "Rev. J. W. Britton," *Minutes of the 74th Session of the Southern Illinois Conference, Methodist Episcopal Church, Centralia, 22–27 September 1925*, p. 177.

³⁷⁹ Mary E. Britton memorial #64,604,681 by Judy Mayfield, no image of grave marker, Fredonia City Cemetery, Fredonia, Kansas (findagrave.com).

³⁸⁰ J. H. Bailey household for daughter Mary, 1900 US census, Fredonia, Wilson County, Kansas, ED 162, sheet 8B, dwelling 180, family 185. Also, James Bailey household for child Mary age 3, 1860 US census, T6 R5 E, Effingham County, Illinois, p. 22, dwelling/family 152.

He received an exhorter's license in 1875 and served more than thirty years as an ordained minister in Illinois and Missouri.[381] Among his charges were (dates may overlap, as Illinois held its annual conferences in the fall and Missouri in the spring):

- Albion, Edwards County, Illinois, on trial (1883)[382]
- Oblong, Crawford County, Illinois, on trial (1884)[383]
- Bible Grove, Clay County, Illinois (1885-86)
- At school (1887-89)
- Marion, Williamson County, Illinois (1890)
- Anna, Union County, Illinois (1891)
- Benton, Franklin County, Illinois (1892)[384]
- Novelty, Knox County, Missouri (1893-94)[385]
- Green Castle, Sullivan County, Missouri (1895–1897)[386]

---

[381] "Rev. J. W. Britton," *Minutes of the 74th Session of the Southern Illinois Conference, Methodist Episcopal Church, Centralia, 22–27 September 1925*, p. 177. Elsewhere he is said to have entered the "traveling ministry" in 1885: "Chronological Roll of the Southern Illinois Conference," *Minutes of the 58th Session of the Southern Illinois Conference, Methodist Episcopal Church, Centralia, 22–27 September 1909*, p. 17.

[382] "Record of Members," *Minutes of the 51st Session of the Southern Illinois Conference, Methodist Episcopal Church, Fairfield, 24–29 September 1902*, p. 85, image 84 of 166 (archive.org).

[383] "List of Appointments," *Minutes of the 33rd Session of the Southern Illinois Conference, Methodist Episcopal Church, Fairfield, 22–29 September 1884*, p. 8.

[384] "Record of Members," *Minutes of the 51st Session of the Southern Illinois Conference, Methodist Episcopal Church, Fairfield, 24–29 September 1902*, p. 85, image 84 of 166 (archive.org).

[385] "Appointments," *Minutes of the 76th Session of the Missouri Conference, Methodist Episcopal Church, Memphis, 28 March–2 April 1894*, J. W. Britton for his second year at Novelty, p. 64, image 332 of 552, Missouri conferences 1888–99 (babel.hathitrust.org). Also, at the previous conference, Novelty was "to be supplied" (image 281 of 552). Also, "Vivian B. Hannah" (born there), *Journal Gazette* (Mattoon, Illinois), Friday 18 October 1991, p. B4, col. 4.

[386] "Appointments," *Minutes of the 77th Session of the Missouri Conference, Methodist Episcopal Church, Stanberry, 27 March–1 April 1895*, p. 111, image 379 of 552, Missouri conferences 1888–99 (babel.hathitrust.org). Similarly, *78th Session, Trenton, 1–6 April 1896*, p. 158, image 428 of 552. Similarly, *79th Session, Bethany, 24–29 March 1897*, p. 15, image 473 of 552.

- Greentop, Schuyler County, Missouri (1898)[387]
- Glenwood, Schuyler County, Missouri (1900), where he started a new church building, finished by a successor;[388] thirteen-year-old son William attended eight months of school that year, but none of the other children did; Lucretia's mother Elizabeth (Thrall) Morgan, aged 66, was with them[389]
- Memphis, Scotland County, Missouri (1901–2)[390]
- Huey, Clinton County, Illinois (1902–3)[391]
- Beaver Creek, Bond County, Illinois (1904)
- Troy, Madison County, Illinois (1905–6)[392]
- Medora, Macoupin County, Illinois (1907)[393]
- Mount Olive, Macoupin County, Illinois (1908–9),[394] where in 1910 the family included four children (Lucile 17, Vivian 15,

---

[387] "Appointments," *Minutes of the 80th Session of the Missouri Conference, Methodist Episcopal Church, Hannibal, 16–21 March 1898*, p. 55, image 513 of 552.

[388] "Appointments" (his second year there), *Minutes of the 82nd Session of the Missouri Conference, Methodist Episcopal Church, Kirksville, 14–19 March 1900*, unpaginated, image 20 of 706 (babel.hathi.trust, per University of Illinois, 1900–1909). Similarly, "Reports," 1902, Brookfield, p. 91.

[389] James [Joseph] W. Britten [Britton] household, 1900 US census, Glenwood village, Schuyler County, Missouri, ED 132, sheet 4B, dwelling/family 76. Schuyler is in the northernmost tier of Missouri counties; Glenwood's population that year was 434.

[390] "Appointments," *Minutes of the 81st Session, of the Missouri Conference, Methodist Episcopal Church, Maryville, 1901*, p. 17, image 73 of 706. Similarly, "Appointments," *82nd Session, Brookfield, 1902, Brookfield*, image 107 of 706 (babel.hathitrust.org). The first year was "Memphis circuit," the second "Memphis."

[391] "Appointments," *Minutes of the 51st Session of the Southern Illinois Conference, Methodist Episcopal Church, Fairfield, 24–29 September 1902*, p. 18, image 122 of 408 (archive.org). Similarly, "Appointments" (third year), *52nd Session, Mount Vernon, 23–28 September 1903*, p. 12, image 12 of 166 (archive.org).

[392] "Conference Appointments 1905," *54th Session, East St. Louis, 22 September–2 October 1905*, p. 14, image 20 of 478 (babel.hathitrust.org). Similarly, 1906, *55th Session, Vandalia, 19–24 September 1906*, p. 16, image 136 of 478.

[393] "Conference Appointments 1907," *Minutes of the 56th Session of the Southern Illinois Conference, Methodist Episcopal Church, Mount Carmel, 18–23 September 1907*, p. 26, image 255 of 578 (babel.hathitrust.org).

[394] "Appointments" (first year), *Minutes of the 57th Session of the Southern Illinois Conference, Methodist Episcopal Church, McLeansboro, 16–21 September 1908*, p. 26. Similarly (second year), *58th Session, Centralia, 22–27 September 1909*, p. 24.

Waldo 12, and Elsie 10) all of whom were in school, and second wife Mary[395]
- Vergennes, Jackson County, Illinois (1910)[396]
- Mount Vernon, Wesley Church, Jefferson County, Illinois (1911–12)[397]
- Farina, Fayette County, Illinois (1913–16), where he later retired[398]
- Ashley, Washington County, Illinois (1917–19)[399]
- Tilden, Randolph County, Illinois (1920–21)[400]
- Brighton, Macoupin County, Illinois (1922)[401]

"On every charge they served . . . [Lucretia] left a multitude of friends sorrowing because of her departure."[402]

---

[395] J. W. Bitton [Britton] household, 1910 US census, Mouth [Mount] Olive, Macoupin County, Illinois, ED 59, sheet 5A, dwelling 104, family 109.

[396] "Appointments," *Minutes of the 59th Session of the Southern Illinois Conference, Methodist Episcopal Church, Olney, 28 September–3 October 1910*, p. 27.

[397] "Appointments," *Minutes of the 60th Session of the Southern Illinois Conference, Methodist Episcopal Church, East St. Louis, 22–25 September 1911*, p. 24. Also, "Appointments," *Minutes of the Southern Illinois Conference, Methodist Episcopal Church, Cairo, 25–30 September 1912*, p. 21.

[398] For Troy and Farina, "Rev. J. W. Britton," *Minutes of the 74th Session of the Southern Illinois Conference, Methodist Episcopal Church, Centralia, 22–27 September 1925*, p. 177.

[399] "Appointments," third year, *Minutes of the 67th Session of the Southern Illinois Conference, Methodist Episcopal Church, Greenville, 2–6 October 1918*, p. 19, image 20 of 600 (archive.org). Similarly, fourth year, *68th Session, Mount Carmel, 1–5 October 1919*, p. 19, image 144 of 600.

[400] "Appointments," first year, *Minutes of the 69th Session of the Southern Illinois Conference, Methodist Episcopal Church, Metropolis, 29 September–3 October 1920*, p. 21, image 264 of 600 (archive.org). Similarly, second year, *70th Session, Mount Vernon, 21–26 September 1921*, p. 22, image 286 of 600.

[401] "Appointments," first year, *Minutes of the 71st Session of the Southern Illinois Conference, Methodist Episcopal Church, Alton, 27 September–1 October 1922*, p. 25, image 24 of 109 (archive.org). Similarly, second year (handwritten notation: "retired"), *72nd Session, Benton, 27–30 September 1922*, p. 27, image 26 of 128.

[402] "Memoir of Sister Britton," *Minutes of the 55th Session of the Southern Illinois Conference, Methodist Episcopal Church, Vandalia, 19–24 September 1906*, pp. 71–72.

Joseph's second wife Mary, identified as Mrs. J. W. Britton, stepmother of Mrs. Harry I. Hannah (Vivian [Britton] Hannah) died in Fredonia, Wilson County, Kansas, 10 September 1939.[403]

Their children remained close even after the parents were gone. In the spring of 1948 there gathered in Mattoon for a weekend "Prof. and Mrs. W. E. Britton of Urbana, Mr. and Mrs. Floyd E. Britton and Mr. and Mrs. V. Crawley of East St. Louis . . . with Attorney and Mrs. Harry I. Hannah."[404]

Children of Maria Lucretia "Cretie"^{9} (Morgan) and Joseph Walter Britton:

31   i. WILLIAM EVERETT^{10} BRITTON (*Maria Lucretia "Cretie" Morgan^9, Mary E. Thrall^8, Worthy^7, Eliphas^6, Samuel^5, John$^{4-3}$, Timothy^2, William^1*) was born 23 March 1887 in Bible Grove, Clay County; died reportedly 6 November 1965 in Los Angeles County, California; and was buried in Bone Gap. He married first 28 July 1916 SARAH MYRTLE CASTILE, and second, reportedly in Cook County, 23 or 30 July 1949 HELEN GLADYS ROSS.

32   ii. FLOYD EVANSTON^{10} BRITTON (*Maria Lucretia "Cretie" Morgan^9, Mary E. Thrall^8, Worthy^7, Eliphas^6, Samuel^5, John$^{4-3}$, Timothy^2, William^1*) was born 24 December 1890 in Marion, Williamson County; died 3 June 1982 in Spread Eagle, Florence County, Wisconsin; and was interred at Memorial Park Cemetery and Crematorium there. He married first 25 December 1912 in Mound City, Pulaski County, GLADYS GAUNT. He married second as her third husband before 6 January 1963 HAZEL C. (RECK) (CROCKER) THORSNESS.

33   iii. LUCILE EVANGELINE^{10} BRITTON (*Maria Lucretia "Cretie" Morgan^9, Mary E. Thrall^8, Worthy^7, Eliphas^6, Samuel^5, John$^{4-3}$, Timothy^2, William^1*) was born 2 September 1892 in Anna, Union County, and

---

[403] "Mattoon Woman's Stepmother Dies," *Journal-Gazette* (Mattoon, Illinois), Thursday 14 September 1939, p. 12, col. 1.

[404] "Personals," *Daily Journal-Gazette and Commercial-Star* (Mattoon, Illinois), Tuesday 23 March 1948, p. 10, col. 4.

died 15 March 1975 at the Homestead Hotel in Evanston, Cook County. She married 25 December 1912 in Mound City, Pulaski County, TIMOTHY IRLE MCKNIGHT.

34   iv. VIVIAN^{10} BRITTON (*Maria Lucretia "Cretie" Morgan^9, Mary E. Thrall^8, Worthy^7, Eliphas^6, Samuel^5, John$^{4-3}$, Timothy^2, William^1*) was born 7 September 1894 in Novelty, Knox County, Missouri; died 17 October 1991 in Mattoon, Coles County, Illinois; and was buried at Dodge Grove Cemetery there. She married 29 June 1917 in Ashley, Washington County, Illinois, HARRY INGALLS HANNAH.

35   v. WALDO VINCENT^{10} BRITTON (*Maria Lucretia "Cretie" Morgan^9, Mary E. Thrall^8, Worthy^7, Eliphas^6, Samuel^5, John$^{4-3}$, Timothy^2, William^1*) was born 21 September 1897 in Greencastle, Sullivan County, Missouri; died 13 February 1926 in St. Louis, Missouri; and was buried at Bone Gap on the 16th.

36   vi. ELSIE MAE "PEG"^{10} BRITTON (*Maria Lucretia "Cretie" Morgan^9, Mary E. Thrall^8, Worthy^7, Eliphas^6, Samuel^5, John$^{4-3}$, Timothy^2, William^1*) was born October 1899 in Missouri; died 1997; and was buried with her husband. She married in 1930 VERLA C. CRAWLEY.

Tree 5. Allied Thrall–Morgan–Gould–Britton Families

Tree 5. Allied Families Thrall-Morgan-Gould-Britton

Two Britton brothers married Thrall first cousins. The children of the two marriages were second cousins on the Thrall side, and first cousins on the Britton side.

- John Britton & Dorothy Chugg
  - John E. Britton & Harriet H. Beeny
    - Edward G. Britton & Alta A. Gould (Ch. 10)
      - Henry[10] Britton
      - Ethel L.[10] Britton
      - Ralph[10] Britton
      - Virgil[10] Britton
      - Ernest[10] Britton
  - Worthy[7] Thrall & Hannah James
    - Solon Gould & Laura L.[8] Thrall
    - Amos B.[8] Morgan & Mary E. Thrall
      - Joseph W. Britton & Lucretia[9] Morgan (Ch. 9)
        - William E.[10] Britton
        - Floyd E.[10] Britton
        - Lucile E.[10] Britton
        - Vivian B.[10] Britton
        - Waldo V.[10] Britton
        - Elsie M.[10] Britton
        - Hannah[10] Britton

The children of Ed and Alta and the children of Joseph and Lucretia are first cousins on the Britton side (sharing grandparents John and Harriet), and second cousins on the Thrall side (sharing great-grandparents Worthy and Hannah).

Chapter 10

Ninth Generation
parents at chapter 3

Alta Areta Gould–Edward George Britton Family
parents at chapter 3

First silo in Pulaski County

10. ALTA ARETA⁹ GOULD (*Laura L. Thrall⁸, Worthy⁷, Eliphas⁶, Samuel⁵, John⁴⁻³, Timothy², William¹*)
Birth: 15 September 1865 in Bone Gap, Edwards County
Death: 6 June 1957
Burial: Cairo City Cemetery, Village Ridge, Pulaski County[405]
Spouse: **EDWARD GEORGE BRITTON**, married 23 April 1890[406]
Spouse's parents: John Edward and Harriet Hannah (Beeney) Britton[407]
Spouse's birth: 5 January 1862 in Ohio
Spouse's death: 9 April 1953

---

[405] For exact dates, Alta A. Britton grave marker, Cairo City Cemetery (also Villa Ridge Cemetery), image, memorial #103,801,393 for Alta Areta Gould Britton by Linda Knowlton (findagrave.com).

[406] "Golden Wedding Day Observed," *Daily Republican-Register* (Mount Carmel, Illinois), Monday 29 April 1940, p. 5, cols. 4–5.

[407] John Britton household for son Edward, age 18, 1880 US census, Mason Township, Effingham County, Illinois, ED 141, sheet 17A, no family numbers, dwelling 105. Britton family (including information from 1870, p. 33, dwelling 257, family 260): John born England about 1821, Harriet born Ohio 1826–27, Joseph born Ohio 1855–56, William born Ohio 1857, Sarah born Ohio 1857–58, Ida born Ohio 1859–1860, Edmond/Edward born Ohio 1861–62, Charles born Illinois 1864, Richard/Richmond born Illinois 1866–67, and Benson born Illinois 1870. Also, John W. Britton–Lucretia A. Morgan marriage license #1530, 16 December 1885, married 17 December at Bone Gap, Edwards County, Illinois, marriage record 1:61; FHL 1,401,780, DGS 4,661,397, image 273 of 654 (familysearch.org). For Joseph's parents' middle names, unsourced family tree by Michael S. Britton, 3 August 2006, in author's possession.

Spouse's burial: with his wife[408]

Growing up in rural Edwards County, Alta Gould and first cousin Cretie Morgan attended Yankeetown School in the winter of 1879–1880 (eight days for Alta, 21 for Cretie), taught by their aunt Caroline Campbell.[409]

In 1930 Edward was selected as one of ten Illinois "master farmers."[410]

> Mr. Britton's parents came from Effingham county to Pulaski county in 1883. In 1895 Mr. and Mrs. Britton purchased an 80 acre farm . . . north of Mounds. On this rough worn out hill land they built their home nestled among great beech trees centuries old. From time to time as their business grew they added more land until now the farm consists of nearly 400 acres. In 1905 they built the large modern dairy barn which was then and continues to be one of the most modern structures of its kind in Southern Illinois. At the time of the construction of the barn, the Brittons brought to Pulaski county the first silos. Many people came to see the large round structures and to predict what would happen to the green corn 'canned' in such a manner. Since then ensilage and alfalfa hay have been the basic feeds for the [Holstein] dairy herd. . . . When the Brittons started on a rented farm with rented livestock they began gradually to buy and improve a herd for themselves.

---

[408] For exact dates, Edward G. Britton grave marker, Cairo City Cemetery (also Villa Ridge Cemetery), image, memorial #55,829,168 by Lisa Caponetto (findagrave.com). For Edward's birth state, Edward G. Britton household, 1930 US census, Mounds Precinct, Pulaski County, Illinois, ED 9, sheet 5B, dwelling/family 134.

[409] "Miscellaneous School Records, Edwards County, Illinois, 1865, 1873–1875, 1878–1880, 1883 and 1888," Yankeetown month ending 10 January 1880, typescript evidently transcribed from a standard "Schedule of a Common School," 7–8; copy in author's possession, likely from Edwards County Historical Society, Albion, Illinois.

[410] "He Is Named Master Farmer," *Mt. Carmel Republican-Register* (Illinois), Thursday 11 December 1930, p. 5, col. 1.

They had 85 head of cattle in 1940.[411] Edward completed eight years of schooling, Alta three years of college.[412]

> The Beechwood Dairy wagon was a familiar sight on the streets of Mounds making its deliveries of bottled milk from house to house until 1927 when the Brittons entered into a contract with the Midwest Corporation of Cairo for the sale of their milk. Now [1940] each morning at 6:30 a large truck calls at the dairy and takes the entire output of milk to Cairo, where it is pasteurized, bottled, and distributed. For many years they took or sent milk and butter to Cairo, first by making the trip twice each week by wagon, then they shipped by the 'suburban,' an Illinois Central special train from Cairo to Mounds and return for men from Cairo to work in the yards [at Mounds], then later the milk was sent by the 'interurban' traction line.

The Brittons credited the University of Illinois Extension, the Farm Bureau, and two magazines—*Hoard's Dairyman* for livestock breeding methods and *Prairie Farmer* for general farm management.[413]

Alta Areta's first cousin Lucretia Morgan married Edward Britton's brother Joseph (Chapter 9). Their children were thus paternal first cousins and maternal second cousins of the children of Maria Lucretia "Cretie"[9] (Morgan) and Joseph Walter Britton (tree #5).

---

[411] "Golden Wedding Day Observed," *Daily Republican-Register* (Mount Carmel, Illinois), Monday 29 April 1940, p. 5, cols. 4–5.
[412] Ed G. Britton household, 1940 US census, Mounds, Pulaski County, Illinois, ED 27-10, sheet 17A, dwelling 355.
[413] "Celebrating Their Golden Wedding Today," *Cairo Evening Citizen and Bulletin* (Illinois), lengthy undated clipping, likely 23 April 1940.

Children of Alta Areta⁹ (Gould) and Edward George Britton:

i. HENRY E.*¹⁰* BRITTON⁴¹⁴ (*Alta A. Gould⁸, Laura L. Thrall⁸, Worthy⁷, Eliphas⁶, Samuel⁵, John⁴⁻³, Timothy², William¹*) was born about February 1891, and died 19 January 1892, age 10 months and 27 days.⁴¹⁵

37 ii. ETHEL LUCRETIA*¹⁰* BRITTON (*Alta A. Gould⁸, Laura L. Thrall⁸, Worthy⁷, Eliphas⁶, Samuel⁵, John⁴⁻³, Timothy², William¹*) was born January 1894 or 5 November 1893 in Mounds, Pulaski County; died 13 August 1984 in Sikeston, Scott/New Madrid County, Missouri; and was buried at Cairo City Cemetery in Villa Ridge, Pulaski County. She married 6 October or 23 December 1913 MILTON MILES HARTMAN.

iii. RALPH H.*¹⁰* BRITTON (*Alta A. Gould⁸, Laura L. Thrall⁸, Worthy⁷, Eliphas⁶, Samuel⁵, John⁴⁻³, Timothy², William¹*) was born probably late April 1896,⁴¹⁶ and died 16 September 1907, age "11-4-19."⁴¹⁷

---

⁴¹⁴ "Golden Wedding Day Observed," *Daily Republican-Register* (Mount Carmel, Illinois), Monday 29 April 1940, p. 5, cols. 4–5. All five children named; Henry is the only one who never appeared in a census. Placement in the family is speculative.

⁴¹⁵ Edward G. Britton household for wife "Altie," 1900 US census, Burkville Precinct, Pulaski County, Illinois, ED 68, sheet 16B, dwelling 350, family 378. She had had four children, of whom three were living. Age at death from Wanda L. Atherton, Glenna Conant Badgley, and Martha W. McMunn, *"Where They Sleep": Cemetery Inscriptions of Pulaski County, Illinois* (Carterville, Illinois: Genealogy Society of Southern Illinois, 1993), 3:22. The reading evidently includes a typographical error, with infant Henry E. Britton, "s/ E. G. & A.A. Britton," dying 19 January 1882, eight years prior to his parents' marriage, at a time when his mother would have been 15 years old.

⁴¹⁶ Edward Britton household for son Ralph age 4 (born April 1896), 1900 US census, Burkville Precinct, Pulaski County, Illinois, ED 68, sheet 16B, dwelling 350, family 378.

⁴¹⁷ Ralph H. Britton entry, Wanda L. Atherton, Glenna Conant Badgley, and Martha W. McMunn, *"Where They Sleep": Cemetery Inscriptions of Pulaski County, Illinois* (Carterville, Illinois: Genealogy Society of Southern Illinois, 1993), 3:22. Two unsourced online memorials lacking images vary on minor points, but agree that Ralph H. Britton died 16 September 1907, age 11, with parents "E.G. & A.A.," and was buried in Cairo City Cemetery, Villa Ridge, Pulaski County, Illinois: Ralph H. Britton memorial #55,829,148 by Lisa Caporetto; and Ralph H. Britton memorial #143,117,803 by BjJ (findagrave.com). Complicating the picture is that the 1900 census reported that Alta had had 4 children, 3 living (preceding note), and that the 1910 census reported she had had 5 children, 3 living (Edward G. Britton household for wife "Allie A.," 1910 US census, Burkville Precinct, Pulaski County, Illinois, ED 86, sheet 7B, dwelling 146, family 148)—yet both Ralph and Virgil were present in 1900 and absent in 1910 and thereafter. Perhaps the 1910 enumerator erred and should have written 5 children, 2 living.

iv. VIRGIL C.¹⁰ BRITTON (*Alta A. Gould⁹, Laura L. Thrall⁸, Worthy⁷, Eliphas⁶, Samuel⁵, John⁴⁻³, Timothy², William¹*) was born in Illinois probably late May 1898⁴¹⁸ and probably died 14 October 1900, aged 2 years, 4 months, and 28 days.⁴¹⁹

38 v. ERNEST RAYMOND¹⁰ BRITTON (*Alta A. Gould⁹, Laura L. Thrall⁸, Worthy⁷, Eliphas⁶, Samuel⁵, John⁴⁻³, Timothy², William¹*) was born 23 March 1903 in Illinois and died November 1983, last residence in Midland, Midland County, Michigan. He married about 1925 MARTHA E. HUGHES.

39 vi. KATHLEEN VIRGINIA¹⁰ PIFER (*Alta A. Gould⁹, Laura L. Thrall⁸, Worthy⁷, Eliphas⁶, Samuel⁵, John⁴⁻³, Timothy², William¹*), foster child of Ed and Alta, was born 11 February 1914 in Covington, Alleghany County, Virginia, and died 13 October 1980 following a "long illness" involving diabetes and heart disease, last residence Lake Hopatcong, Morris County, New Jersey. She married 20 August 1935 near Mounds, Pulaski County, REV. HUGH JOHN MCNELLY.

---

⁴¹⁸ Edward Britton household for son Virgil age 2 (born May 1898), 1900 US census, Burkville Precinct, Pulaski County, Illinois, ED 68, sheet 16B, dwelling 350, family 378.

⁴¹⁹ Virgie C. Britton entry, in Wanda L. Atherton, Glenna Conant Badgley, and Martha W. McMunn, *"Where They Sleep": Cemetery Inscriptions of Pulaski County, Illinois* (Carterville, Illinois: Genealogy Society of Southern Illinois, 1993), 3:22. This reading also (see note above) evidently includes a typographical error of "1890" for "1900." The typed death date and age at death would place his birth two years prior to his parents' marriage, and there is a right-age Virgil in the household in the 1900 census. Also, preceding note.

Chapter 11

Ninth Generation

The Leighton–Pifer–Gould Connection

parents at chapters 3, 13

From western Virginia to southern Illinois

In 1981, more than half a century after the events, Rev. Hugh John McNelly wrote a brief sketch of this family connection (chapter 39):

> Kathleen Virginia Pifer was born in Covington [Alleghany County], Virginia, on February 11, 1914. Her family was broken up when she was 2 years old, and her mother had to place her in a series of foster homes. Her 'deliverance' came this way—Rev. Virgil Gould, a Methodist Minister in Illinois, had married Kathleen's aunt [Dora Sophia Leighton]. Kathleen was sent north to them, but Rev. Gould could not afford to keep her, so his sister 'Aunt Alta' Britton, took Kathleen into her home at Mounds, Illinois. At the age of 7, a new life began for the rebellious little redhead. She was a part of a loving Christian family! There she found Christ as her personal Savior. Piano lessons were provided for her. After High School the Brittons sent her to the same college their son and daughter had attended—McKendree. She graduated with a major in piano and a minor in pipe organ, plus the State Public School Music Certificate.[420]

Scattered records fill out and complicate this account. It appears that three siblings came "north" to Bone Gap (which is more west than north of Covington): Lucille before 1920, Kathleen about 1921, and Cecil

---

[420] "Kathleen Virginia McNelly," *Journal and Yearbook of the Northern New Jersey Annual Conference, The United Methodist Church, 124tht Session, Madison, New Jersey, 31 May–3 June 1981*, pp. 333–34.

not long after 1920. Dora (Leighton) Gould was their aunt by virtue of being Kathleen's mother's older sister.

The family below is numbered separately from other chapters; more detailed information on the three children adopted or fostered is in the noted chapters, where they are numbered the same as biological children.

1. WILLIAM H.^{2} LEIGHTON (*Daniel^1*) was born 24 December 1845 in Botetourt County, Virginia, son of Daniel and Louisa (Reynolds) Leighton, and died of gangrene in Covington, Alleghany County, Virginia, 2 September 1919.[421] William, a blacksmith, married 22 October 1868 in Alleghany County **VIRGINIA SUSAN BROWN**, daughter of M. D. and Mary Brown.[422] Virginia was born 26 July 1851 in Alleghany County, died there 31 March 1930, and was buried at Mount Pleasant Cemetery there the following day.[423]

Children of William H.^{2} and Virginia Susan (Brown) Leighton:[424]

2   i. DORA SOPHIA^3 LEIGHTON (*William H. Leighton^2, Daniel^1*) was born 2 August 1871 in Alleghany County, Virginia; died at the Methodist Home 3 December 1957; and was buried at Bone Gap Cemetery.[425] She married 11 May

---

[421] Wm. H. Leighton death 2 September 1919, Virginia certificate #22634; "Virginia, Death Records, 1912–2014" > 1919 > 22534–23032 > image 104 of 544 (ancestry.com).

[422] W. H. Leighton–J. S. Brown marriage 22 Oct 1868, Alleghany County, Virginia, Register of Marriages, p. 11, line 58; FHL 30,523, DGS 7,578,829, image 84 of 206 (familysearch.org). Bride's parents were M. D. and [blank] Brown.

[423] Virginia Susan Leighton death 31 March 1930, Virginia certificate #5210; "Virginia Death Records, 1912–2014" > 1930 > 05075–05625 > image 161 of 625 (ancestry.com).

[424] Virginia was reported to have had five children with five living in 1900, and five with four living in 1910. Wm. Leighton household for wife Virginia, 1900 US census, Covington, Alleghany County, Virginia, ED 5, sheet 33B, dwelling 525, family 556; similarly, 1910, ED 5, sheet 12A, dwelling/family 224.

[425] "Mrs. Dora Gould died at Lawrenceville," clipping from unknown newspaper (quite possibly the *Albion Journal*) labeled "Dec 57," in author's possession. For exact date, "Central Illinois Deaths…Mrs. Virgil Gould," *Daily Illinois State Journal* (Springfield), Wednesday 4 December 1957, p. 26, col. 2.

1893 in Alleghany County, Virginia, REV. VIRGIL NATHAN GOULD (chapter 12).[426]

ii. HOPE G.[3] LEIGHTON (*William H. Leighton², Daniel¹*) was born in Virginia about February 1875.[427]

iii. ROBERT CHARLES[3] LEIGHTON (*William H. Leighton², Daniel¹*) was born in Virginia about 1877,[428] and died as a widower 5 October 1945 in Fayetteville, Fayette County, West Virginia.[429] He was in his uncle Rev. Virgil Gould's household in 1900.[430]

iv. OLLIE LEIGHTON[3] (*William H. Leighton², Daniel¹*) was born about 1879 in Virginia.[431]

3   v. WILLIE GENEVA[3] LEIGHTON (*William H. Leighton², Daniel¹*) was born 22 April 1885 and died 28 December 1936. She married first LEO WILLIAM PIFER and second FRANK STUPLE.

     2. **DORA SOPHIA[3] LEIGHTON** (*William H. Leighton², Daniel¹*)was born 2 August 1871 in Alleghany County, Virginia; died at the Methodist Home 3 December 1957;

---

[426] Dora S. Leighton–Virgil N. Gould marriage 11 May 1893, p. 48, line 30; FHL 30,523, DGS 7,578,829, image 122 of 206 (familysearch.org).

[427] Wm. Leighton household for son Hope G. age 25, 1900 US census, Covington, Alleghany County, Virginia, ED 5, sheet 33B, dwelling 525, family 556. Also, William Leighton household for daughter Hope G. age 7, 1880 US census, Covington Township, Alleghany County, Virginia, ED 3, p. 121D, dwelling/family 106.

[428] William Leighton household for son Robert age 3, 1880 US census, Covington Township, Alleghany County, Virginia, ED 3, p. 121D, dwelling/family 106.

[429] Robert Charles Leighton death, 5 October 1945, Fayette County, West Virginia Register of Deaths from January 1, 1945, p. 31, #5; FHL 584,754, DGS 4,226,923 (familysearch.org), from West Virginia Department of Arts, Culture and History (wvculture.org/vrr).

[430] Virgil N. Gould household for Robert Leighton, 1900 US census, Bone Gap, Edwards County, Illinois, ED 16, sheet 4B, dwelling/family 73.

[431] William Leighton household for son Ollie age 1, 1880 US census, Covington Township, Alleghany County, Virginia, ED 3, p. 121D, dwelling/family 106.

and was buried at Bone Gap Cemetery.[432] She married 11 May 1893 in Alleghany County, Virginia, **REV. VIRGIL NATHAN GOULD**.[433] They had six children between 1894 and 1907 (chapter 12).

3. **WILLIE GENEVA³ LEIGHTON** (*William H. Leighton², Daniel¹*) was born 22 April 1885 in Alleghany County, Virginia; died there of "pelvic inflammatory disease with abscess and peritonitis" 28 December 1936; and was buried at Mount Pleasant Cemetery there.[434] She married first 23 June 1907 in Alleghany County, Virginia, likely as his second wife, **WILLIAM LEE PIFER**; they had five children by the time she divorced him for desertion in January 1919. (The divorce record appears confused: it noted four children; there appear to have been five, but only three were then living.) William Pifer was born in Shenandoah County, Virginia, about 1881.[435] In 1910 he was employed as a "helper beater" in the paper mill, and they owned their home with a mortgage.[436] Willie married second in the early 1920s an older man, **JOHN FRANKLIN "FRANK" STUPLE**, son of Jacob and Laura (Jackson) Stuple. He was born 8 March 1873 in Augusta County, Virginia, and died at the county district home there 10 March 1946.[437]

---

[432] "Mrs. Dora Gould died at Lawrenceville," clipping from unknown newspaper (quite possibly the *Albion Journal*) labeled "Dec 57," in author's possession. For exact date, "Central Illinois Deaths...Mrs. Virgil Gould," *Daily Illinois State Journal* (Springfield), Wednesday 4 December 1957, p. 26, col. 2.

[433] Dora S. Leighton–Virgil N. Gould marriage 11 May 1893, p. 48, line 30; FHL 30,523, DGS 7,578,829, image 122 of 206 (familysearch.org).

[434] For 22 April 1885, Willie Virginia Stuple death, Virginia state certificate 29966; "Virginia, Death Records, 1912–2014" > 1936 > 29830–30283 > image 157 of 505 (ancestry.com). For May 1886, Wm. Leighton household for son Millie [daughter Willie] age 14, 1900 US census, Covington, Alleghany County, Virginia, ED 5, sheet 33B, dwelling 525, family 556. This conflict has not been resolved.

[435] "Record of Divorce Granted," Alleghany County, Virginia, January 1919 term, William Lee Pifer and Willie Geneva Leaghlan [Leighton]; "Virginia, Divorce Records, 1918–2014" > 1919 > 00001–00500 > image 118 of 508.

[436] William Pifer household, 1910 US census, Covington, Alleghany County, Virginia, ED 5, sheet 11A, dwelling/family 207. He was reportedly 28, she 23.

[437] J. Frank Stuple death 10 March 1946, Virginia certificate #6230; "Virginia, Death Records, 1912–2014" > 1946 > 06062–06428 > image 185 of 403 (ancestry.com).

Children of Willie Geneva³ (Leighton) and William Lee Pifer:

i. JOSEPHINE H.⁴ PIFER (twin) (*Willie Geneva Pifer³, William H. Leighton², Daniel¹*) was born 18 May 1908, died 8 July 1908, and was buried in Mount Pleasant Cemetery, Alleghany County, Virginia.⁴³⁸

ii. LORINE M.⁴ PIFER (twin) (*Willie Geneva Pifer³, William H. Leighton², Daniel¹*) was born 18 May 1908, died 14 August 1908, and was buried in Mount Pleasant Cemetery.⁴³⁹

iii. LUCILLE⁴ PIFER (*Willie Geneva Pifer³, William H. Leighton², Daniel¹*) was born about 1912 in Virginia and died 12 March 1983 in Sun City, Maricopa County, Arizona. She married GEORGE Y. KING. In 1920 Lucille was an "adopted child" living with Edith and Alice Gould in Bone Gap (adoptive/social parents, chapters 13 and 44).

iv. KATHLEEN VIRGINIA⁴ PIFER (*Willie Geneva Pifer³, William H. Leighton², Daniel¹*) was born 11 February 1914 in Covington, Alleghany County, Virginia, and died in Morris County, New Jersey, 13 October 1980 following a "long illness" involving diabetes and heart disease. She married 20 August 1935 near Mounds, Pulaski County, Illinois, REV. HUGH JOHN MCNELLY. After spending time in several foster homes she went to Edward

---

⁴³⁸ Josephine H. Piper grave marker #232, row 14, Mount Pleasant Cemetery, Jackson River Road, Alleghany County, Virginia, image, memorial #144,098,963 by j stockwell (findagrave.com). Note: Findagrave.com calls this place Mount Pleasant United Methodist Church Cemetery, but this is anachronistic as no denomination by that name existed until 1968. The name given in Robert Stover's 1937 survey (Library of Virginia Digital Collection) is more plausible, and accords with the 1848 deed from Adam Dressler to the trustees of the Methodist and Presbyterian churches (http://files.usgwarchives.net/va/alleghany/cemeteries/mtplesnt01.txt).

⁴³⁹ Lorine M. Piper grave marker #231, row 14, Mount Pleasant Cemetery, Jackson River Road, Alleghany County, Virginia, image, memorial #144,098,935 by j stockwell (findagrave.com). Also, William Pifer household, 1910 US census, Covington, Alleghany County, Virginia, ED 5, sheet 11A, dwelling/family 203. Wife Willie was reported to have had two children, but they were not listed in the household, and the box for number of living children was left blank. Similar situations appear on the following census page, suggesting that the enumerator chose to refrain from writing a zero in that column.

and Alta Gould about 1921 (adoptive/social parents, chapters 10 and 39).

v. Cecil Melvin[4] Pifer ($Willie\ Geneva\ Pifer^3$, $William\ H.\ Leighton^2$, $Daniel^1$) was born 14 July 1915 in Covington, Alleghany County, Virginia, and died 15 June 1995 in Phoenix, Maricopa County, Arizona. In 1920 he was living with his mother and grandmother in Covington, Alleghany County, Virginia. Although evidence for a date is lacking, he likely came to Bone Gap soon thereafter. Cecil married first 17 June 1938 Rosalie F. Galleener. He married second as her second husband 23 July 1950 in Great Falls, Cascade County, Montana, Kathryn Inez (Williams) Sande (adoptive/social parents, chapters 13 and 45).

Child of Willie Geneva (Leighton) (Pifer) and John Franklin Stuple:

vi. Mary Louise[4] Stuple ($Willie\ Geneva\ Pifer\ Stuple^3$, $William\ H.\ Leighton^2$, $Daniel^1$) was born 24 March 1927 in Virginia and died 6 May 2001 at 206 Redwood Court in Lorain, Lorain County, Ohio.[440] She married first 26 October 1946 in Covington, Virginia, Richard Edgar Haynes, who was born about 1926, the son of Edgar J. and Maud (Thompson) Haynes.[441] She may have married second about April 1969 [–?–] Brown, and married third about June 1991 [–?–] Clausen.[442]

---

[440] Mary Louise Clausen, Ohio death index entry, citing certificate #38494, Lorain County; "Ohio Death Index, 1908–1932, 1938–1944, 1958–2007" (familysearch.org).

[441] Mary Louise Stuple–Richard Edgar Haynes marriage 26 October 1946, #36458, Covington, Alleghany County, Virginia; "Virginia, Marriage Records, 1936–2014" > 1946 > 36412–36762 > image 49 of 356 (ancestry.com). Southern Baptist minister Ray R. McCulloch officiated.

[442] Mary Louise Stuple entries, US Social Security Applications and Claims Index, 1936–2007 (ancestry.com).

Chapter 12

Ninth Generation

Virgil Gould–Dora Leighton Family
parents at chapter 3

"In politics you played the game / No fiend would stoop to do"

12. VIRGIL NATHAN^9 GOULD (*Laura L. Thrall^8, Worthy^7, Eliphas^6, Samuel^5, John$^{4-3}$, Timothy^2, William^1*)
Birth: 5 August 1868[443] near Bone Gap
Death: 16 November 1959, Lawrenceville Methodist Old Folks Home, Lawrence County, Illinois
Burial: Bone Gap Cemetery[444]
Spouse: **DORA SOPHIA LEIGHTON**, married 11 May 1893 in Alleghany County, Virginia[445]
Spouse's parents: William and Virginia Susan (Brown) Leighton[446]
Spouse's birth: 2 August 1871 in Virginia (probably Covington, Alleghany County)
Spouse's death: 3 December 1957 at the Methodist Home in Lawrenceville, Illinois
Spouse's burial: Bone Gap Cemetery

---

[443] Family questionnaire 15 June 1899, Solon H. Gould pension file 743,817 (service of Solon H. Gould, Company B, 18th Illinois Infantry and Company 90, Battalion 2, Veteran Reserve Corps), Case Files of Approved Pension Applications..., 1861–1934; Civil War and Later Pension Files, Record Group 15, Department of Veterans Affairs, National Archives and Records Administration, Washington, DC.

[444] "Retired Minister; Former Bone Gap Resident is Dead" (Rev. Virgil Gould), *Albion Journal Register* (Illinois), Wednesday 18 November 1959, p. 1, col. 1.

[445] Dora S. Leighton–Virgil N. Gould marriage 11 May 1893, Alleghany County, Virginia, register of marriages, p. 48, line 30; FHL 30,523, DGS 7,578,829, image 122 of 206 (familysearch.org). Also, "Retired Minister; Former Bone Gap Resident is Dead," *Albion Journal* (Illinois), Wednesday 18 November 1959, p. 1, col. 1.

[446] "Mrs. Dora Gould died at Lawrenceville," clipping from unknown newspaper (likely the *Albion Journal*) labeled "Dec 57," in author's possession. For exact date, "Central Illinois Deaths...Mrs. Virgil Gould," *Daily Illinois State Journal* (Springfield), Wednesday 4 December 1957, p. 26, col. 2.

In the winter of December–January 1877–1878, ten-year-old Virgil attended 22 days of school at College Hill, Edwards County.[447] Both he and Dora completed four years of high school.[448]

Around the time of their 1893 marriage, Virgil appeared to be settling into farming. In February he bought about three acres near his parents from Lewis and Julia Schafer of Mount Carmel for $800, and in October his parents deeded him about 35 acres for $1, reserving about 5 acres for themselves, "to be occupied by either or both of them for a home . . . and for no other purpose."[449] In 1900 Virgil was farming in Bone Gap and the family lived next to his father Solon and sisters Edith and Flora; also in the household was painter Robert Leighton, Dora's brother.[450]

Later, in 1907, Virgil made another move into farming, signing a detailed five-year agreement with Sol Miller for another parcel adjacent to him and his parents. Virgil was to pay Miller $72 a year for each of the next five years (payable in money or crops or stock), and then to pay $1200 at the end of five years, and receive a deed to the 40 acres—all this, provided that he maintain the fences; trim hedges at least once a year; use "first class fertilizer" when plowing; cut no hedge trees now growing unless necessary; make no oil, gas, or coal lease; and pay all taxes and assessments.[451]

Curiously this was also the year Virgil took up the Methodist ministry, joined the Southern Illinois Conference of the Methodist Episcopal

---

[447] "Miscellaneous School Records, Edwards County, Illinois, 1865, 1873–1875, 1878–1880, 1883 and 1888," College Hill "18 December–January 17th 1878," typescript evidently transcribed from a standard "Schedule of a Common School," 12; copy in author's possession, likely from Edwards County Historical Society, Albion, Illinois. Teacher D. M. Dean was paid $37.50.

[448] Virgil Gould household, 1940 US census, Lemay Township, St. Louis County, Missouri, ED 95-183, sheet 9B, dwelling 238.

[449] Solon H. Gould and wife to Virgil N. Gould, Edwards County, Illinois, Deeds, 5:507, 24 October 1893; Edwards County Recorder's Office, Albion.

[450] Virgil N. Gould household, 1900 US census, Bone Gap, Edwards County, Illinois, ED 16, sheet 4B, dwelling/family 73.

[451] Virgil N. Gould and Sol Miller agreement, 1907, Edwards County, Illinois, Deeds 18:118; Edwards County Recorder's Office, Albion.

Church, and began to be stationed in other counties as needed (see below). It remains unclear what became of the agreements with Miller or the implicit agreement with his parents.[452]

Virgil and Dora served various charges. (Conference years usually began in the autumn, leading to occasional ambiguity.)[453]

- Jeffersonville ("Geff"), Wayne County (1907)[454]
- Sumner Circuit, Lawrence County (1908–9)[455]; in 1910 he was in Sumner[456]
- Wheeler, Jasper County (1910);[457]
- Noble, Richland County (1911–12);[458]
- Steeleville, Randolph County (1913);
- Jonesboro, Union County (1914–15);
- Elkville, Jackson County (1916–17); [459]

---

[452] *Centennial McKendree College with St. Clair County History* (Lebanon, Illinois: McKendree College, 1928), 617.

[453] "Pastoral Record," *Journal and Year Book, The Sixth Session of the Southern Illinois Conference of the Methodist Church*, East St. Louis, 138, covers his full career. Additional information on some charges or sources in the notes.

[454] "Areta H. Martin," *State Journal-Register* (Springfield, Illinois), 17 December 1998, p. 38, col. 4.

[455] "Appointments," *Minutes of the 57th Session of the Southern Illinois Conference, Methodist Episcopal Church, McLeansboro, 16–21 September 1908*, p. 29. Also, "Illinois Methodist Conference Ends," *Paducah Evening Sun* (Kentucky), Wednesday 29 September 1909, p. 6, cols. 3–4. Also in the Olney district of the Southern Illinois Conference that year were L. W. Thrall at Flora, H. L. Thrall at Noble, and J. W. Flint at Lawrenceville.

[456] Virgil Gould household, 1910 US census, Sumner, Lawrence County, Illinois, Ward 3, ED 123, sheet 8B, dwelling 193, family 212.

[457] "Appointments," *Minutes of the 59th Session of the Southern Illinois Conference, Methodist Episcopal Church, Olney, 28 September–3 October 1910*, p. 27. This year Wheeler apparently had its largest population—255: "Wheeler, Illinois" (en.wikipedia.org/wiki/Wheeler, Illinois), citing "Census of Population" (census.gov).

[458] "Appointments," *Minutes of the 60th Session of the Southern Illinois Conference, Methodist Episcopal Church, East St. Louis, 22–25 September 1911*, p. 24. Also, "Appointments," *Minutes of the 61st Session of the Southern Illinois Conference, Methodist Episcopal Church, Cairo, 25–30 September 1912*, p. 24.

[459] "Appointments," *Minutes of the Southern Illinois Conference, Methodist Episcopal Church, Robinson, 4–8 October 1916*, p. 13.

- Trenton, Sugar Creek Township, Clinton County (1918–20);[460]
- Cisne, Wayne County (1921);[461]
- Waltonville, Jefferson County (1922–23);[462]
- Freeburg and New Athens, St. Clair County (1924–29);[463]
- Orient and Zeigler, Franklin County (1929–1933);[464] in 1930 they were living next door to daughter Areta and family, renting but with a radio;[465]
- Settlement House, East St. Louis, St. Clair County (1934–5); in 1935 he officiated at adoptive niece Kathleen Pifer's wedding (chapter 39);[466]
- Dewey Avenue, Granite City, Madison County (1936).

In 1926, while stationed in St. Clair County, Virgil published a poem, "Inferno Up-to-Date," in which a deceased Congressman found himself in hell, even though he had lived a virtuous life and voted "dry" (for Prohibition). Satan explained to him that "In politics you played the game / No fiend would stoop to do."[467]

---

[460] Virgil N. Gould household, 1920 US census, Sugar Creek Township, Clinton County, Illinois, Ward 1, ED 21, sheet 3A, dwelling/family 75.

[461] "Society," *Belleville News-Democrat* (Illinois), Monday 26 December 1921, p. 2, col. 4. Edwin's father officiated.

[462] "Appointments," *Minutes of the 72nd Session of the Southern Illinois Conference, Methodist Episcopal Church, Benton, 26–30 September 1923*, p. 28.

[463] "Freeburg," *Belleville News-Democrat* (Illinois), Tuesday 6 October 1925, p. 12, col. 4; similarly, Saturday 24 September 1927, p. 8, col. 6. Also, *Centennial McKendree College with St. Clair County History* (Lebanon, Illinois: McKendree College, 1928), 617.

[464] Lizzie A. Roth, "Freeburg," *Belleville News-Democrat* (Illinois), Tuesday 8 October 1929, p. 5, col. 5. Also, "Southern Illinois Pastors Assigned at Methodist Episcopal Meeting," *Evansville Courier and Press* (Indiana), Wednesday 7 October 1931, p. 5, col. 2. Also, "Pifer–King," *Daily Republican-Register* (Mount Carmel, Illinois), Thursday 29 March 1934, p. 3, cols. 5–6. Rev. Virgil Gould of Zeigler officiated at niece Lucille's wedding.

[465] Augie Fowld [Virgil Gould] household, 1930 US census, Zeigler, Franklin County, Illinois, ED 37, sheet 8A, dwelling/family 187.

[466] "Bone Gap News," *Mt. Carmel Republican-Register* (Illinois), Wednesday 4 September 1935, p. 6, col. 5.

[467] "A Poem A Day," *Belleville News-Democrat* (Illinois), Wednesday 30 June 1926, p. 8, col. 1.

Virgil retired in 1937.[468] In 1940 he and Dora were across the Mississippi River, living in a $6000 house they owned on Telegraph Road in Lemay Township, St. Louis County, Missouri. (That year an average Missouri dwelling was valued at $2392.) Neither had an occupation listed.[469]

In 1949 and 1952 he and Dora were living in Gillespie, Macoupin County.[470] In 1953, both in their 80s, they renewed their wedding vows and celebrated their 60th anniversary with son Victor in Chula Vista, San Diego County, California.[471] They stayed there until December 1956, when they decided "to join friends and relatives at the rest home" back in Lawrenceville.[472]

Children of Virgil Nathan^9 and Dora Sophia (Leighton) Gould:

40 i. EDWIN "EDWY" MALCOLM^{10} GOULD (*Virgil Nathan Gould^9, Laura Lucina Thrall^8, Worthy^7, Eliphas^6, Samuel^5, John$^{4-3}$, Timothy^2, William^1*) was born 11 September 1894 in Bone Gap, and died 15 February 1993 in Palm Beach County, Florida. He married 26 December 1921 in Marissa, St. Clair County, RHODEAN ALICE PERDUE.

ii. UNKNOWN^{10} GOULD (*Virgil Nathan Gould^9, Laura Lucina Thrall^8, Worthy^7, Eliphas^6, Samuel^5, John$^{4-3}$, Timothy^2, William^1*) was born

---

[468] "Pastoral Record," *Journal and Year Book, The Sixth Session of the Southern Illinois Conference of the Methodist Church, East St. Louis*, 138.

[469] Virgil Gould household, 1940 US census, Lemay Township, St. Louis County, Missouri, ED 95-183, sheet 9B, dwelling 238. Statewide figures from United States Census Bureau, Census of Housing, Historical Census of Housing Tables, Median Home Values Unadjusted 1940 (census.gov/hhes/www/housing/ census/historic/ values.html).

[470] "Gillespie To Hold Homecoming," *Daily Illinois State Journal* (Springfield), Saturday 28 May 1949, p. 7, col. 4. Also, similarly, "Midstate Happenings," Tuesday 20 May 1952, p. 6, col. 1.

[471] "Rev., Mrs. Virgil Gould Mark 60th Wedding Anniversary," *Chula Vista Star* (California), Thursday 21 May 1953, p. 3, cols. 3-4.

[472] "Dora S. Gould, Mother of CV Doctor, Dies," *Chula Vista Star-News* (California), Thursday 5 December 1957, p. 8A, col. 3.

perhaps 1896 and died before 1900 (when Dora was reported to have had three children, two living).[473]

41   iii. Dr. Victor Leighton[10] Gould (*Virgil Nathan Gould[9], Laura Lucina Thrall[8], Worthy[7], Eliphas[6], Samuel[5], John[4-3], Timothy[2], William[1]*) was born 23 November 1898 in Bone Gap, and died 11 July 1983 in Los Banos, Merced County, California. He married first about 1920 Ella Lippert, and married second 12 September 1933 in De Soto, Jefferson County, Missouri, Geraldine Ernestine Hacke.

42   iv. Paul Glenwood[10] Gould (*Virgil Nathan Gould[9], Laura Lucina Thrall[8], Worthy[7], Eliphas[6], Samuel[5], John[4-3], Timothy[2], William[1]*) was born 21 February 1901; died 2 December 1998 in Lake Worth, Palm Beach County, Florida; and was buried at Lake Worth Memory Gardens Cemetery. He married in the early 1930s Ada L. Shaffer.

    v. Unknown[10] Gould (*Virgil Nathan Gould[9], Laura Lucina Thrall[8], Worthy[7], Eliphas[6], Samuel[5], John[4-3], Timothy[2], William[1]*) was born perhaps 1904 and died before 1910 (when Dora was reported to have had six children, four living).[474]

43   vi. Areta Hope[10] Gould (*Virgil Nathan Gould[9], Laura Lucina Thrall[8], Worthy[7], Eliphas[6], Samuel[5], John[4-3], Timothy[2], William[1]*) was born 18 October 1907 in Geff (Jeffersonville), Wayne County; died 15 December 1998 in Urbana, Champaign County; and was buried the 19th in Woodlawn Cemetery there. She married 23 December 1928 in Freeburg, St. Clair County, Emery H. Martin.

---

[473] Virgil N. Gould household, 1900 US census, Bone Gap, Edwards County, Illinois, ED 16, sheet 4B, dwelling/family 73. Also, "Mrs. Dora Gould died at Lawrenceville," unidentified December 57 newspaper clipping, which also states, "One child died in infancy."

[474] Virgil Gould household, 1910 US census, Sumner, Lawrence County, Illinois, Ward 3, ED 123, sheet 8B, dwelling 193, family 212.

Chapter 13

Ninth Generation

Edith Evelyn Gould and Flora Alice Gould Family
<u>parents at chapter 3</u>

"A primary teacher in the Bone Gap school for 22 years"

13. EDITH EVELYN^9 **GOULD** (*Laura L. Thrall^8, Worthy^7, Eliphas^6, Samuel^5, John$^{4-3}$, Timothy^2, William^1*)
Birth: 21 September 1871 at Bone Gap, Edwards County[475]
Death: 11 November 1960 at the Methodist Old Folks Home at Lawrenceville, Lawrence County
Burial: Bone Gap Cemetery[476]

ALICE FLORA "FLO"^{9} **GOULD** (*Laura L. Thrall^8, Worthy^7, Eliphas^6, Samuel^5, John$^{4-3}$, Timothy^2, William^1*)
Birth: 1 June 1875[477]

---

[475] Family questionnaire 15 June 1899, Solon H. Gould pension file 743,817 (service of Solon H. Gould, Company B, 18th Illinois Infantry and Company 90, Battalion 2, Veteran Reserve Corps), Case Files of Approved Pension Applications..., 1861–1934; Civil War and Later Pension Files, Record Group 15, Department of Veterans Affairs, National Archives and Records Administration, Washington, DC. For August 21 instead, Edith E. Gould listing #324, Duane Smith, compiler, "Old Part of [Bone Gap] Cemetery," handwritten list of 380 numbered burials with names, birth dates, and death dates; photocopy in author's possession.

[476] "Edith Evelyn Gould Graveside Services Held Sunday," clipping from unknown newspaper (likely the *Albion Journal*) dated 16 November 1960, in author's possession.

[477] Family questionnaire 15 June 1899, Solon H. Gould pension file 743,817 (service of Solon H. Gould, Company B, 18th Illinois Infantry and Company 90, Battalion 2, Veteran Reserve Corps), Case Files of Approved Pension Applications..., 1861–1934; Civil War and Later Pension Files, Record Group 15, Department of Veterans Affairs, National Archives and Records Administration, Washington, DC. Also, Solon Gould household for daughter Flora born June 1875, 1900 US census, Bone Gap, Edwards County, Illinois, ED 16, sheet 4B, dwelling/family 74.

Death: 19 October 1926 in Bone Gap after "an illness of several months"[478]

Burial: Bone Gap Cemetery [479]

In February 1896 Edith and Flora Gould, in their twenties, visited with their similar-age first cousin Edith Laura Thrall (Chapter 16) in Salem, Marion County,[480] about 70 miles west of Bone Gap.

"Miss Edith [Gould], as she was locally known, was educated at College Hill rural school, McKendree College in Lebanon and the Methodist Deaconess Training School, Northwestern University, Evanston. She was a primary teacher in the Bone Gap school for 22 years, and active in community affairs." From about 1935 to 1953 she lived with her sister Alta A. Britton in Mounds, Pulaski County; thereafter she moved to the Old Folks Home. She completed three years of college.[481]

In 1898 Edith (Flint) Thrall, the sisters' aunt by marriage, relayed some cryptic news: "A letter from Edith Gould that came Saturday brought word that after so long a fight with death Flo. has begun to get better. She is still with [sister] Alta. They don't think it best to bring her [evidently Flo] home for a while yet. They fear the effect of old association if she should come back before she has recovered a good degree of strength."[482]

---

[478] "Music Teacher Is Summoned at Bone Gap," *Daily Republican-Register* (Mount Carmel, Illinois), Friday 22 October 1926, p. 4, col. 5.

[479] Flo Gould listing #323, Duane Smith, compiler, "Old Part of [Bone Gap] Cemetery," handwritten list of 380 numbered burials with names, birth dates, and death dates; photocopy in author's possession.

[480] "Local and General," *Marion County Republican* (Salem, Illinois), Thursday 27 February 1896, p. 5, col. 4.

[481] "Edith Evelyn Gould Graveside Services Held Sunday," clipping from unknown newspaper (likely the *Albion Journal*) dated 16 November 1960, in author's possession. Also, Ed G. Britton household for sister-in-law Edith, 1940 US census, Mounds, Pulaski County, Illinois, ED 27-10, sheet 17A, dwelling 355.

[482] Edith Flint Thrall in Lebanon to son William Flint Thrall in Vincennes, Indiana, 4 July 1898, letter; Flint–Thrall letter 93, in author's possession.

The sisters lived in their father Solon's household in 1880, 1900, and 1910. In 1910 Edith was a public-school teacher and Alice a music teacher.[483]

In 1918 the sisters signed an affidavit on behalf of their cousin Allyn T. Morgan's sister-in-law Clarinda Frauli's claim that Clarinda's mother Julia, widow of a Civil War soldier, had no income other than her pension and that the government should pay Julia's end-of-life expenses from the unpaid portion of her pension (chapter 7).[484]

In 1920 Flo was teaching music.[485] She was elected vice-president of the Bone Gap cemetery association in 1922;[486] the following year she visited the Olney sanitarium where she "was operated on for a cancer."[487] Perhaps this was the illness that ended her life at the age of 51.

Shopping in Mount Carmel 9 October 1926 were Edith and foster children Lucille and Melvin Pifer.[488] In 1933 an area newspaper called Edith the aunt of the three Pifer siblings;[489] an adequate approximation,

---

[483] Solon H. Gould household for daughters Edith and Alice, 1880 US census, Albion Precinct, Edwards County, Illinois, ED 7, p. 426C, dwelling 589, family 600. Similarly, 1900, Bone Gap village, ED 16, sheet 4B, dwelling/family 74. Similarly, 1910, Bone Gap village, sheet 3B, dwelling/family 77.

[484] Application for Reimbursement 23 July 1918 by Clarinda E. Frauli, Julia Smith minors' pension file 19130 (service of Andrew Jackson Henshaw, Company H, 18th Wisconsin Infantry), Case Files of Approved Pension Applications..., 1861–1934; Civil War and Later Pension Files, Record Group 15, Department of Veterans Affairs, National Archives and Records Administration, Washington, DC; pp. 99–101 (fold3.com).

[485] Edith E. Gould household for sister "Alice F." and "adopted child" Lucille Pifer, 1920 US census, Bone Gap, Edwards County, Illinois, ED 20, sheet 1A, dwelling/family 11.

[486] "Albion Licked By Bone Gap" (Bone Gap locals), *Daily Republican-Register* (Mount Carmel, Illinois), Wednesday 11 January 1922, p. 2, col. 2.

[487] "Operators Named by Telephone Co." (Bone Gap locals), *Daily Republican-Register* (Mount Carmel, Illinois), Wednesday 28 March 1923, p. 5, col. 3.

[488] "Mrs. Jack Is Hostess to Country Club" (Bone Gap locals), *Daily Republican-Register* (Mount Carmel, Illinois), Wednesday 12 October 1927, p. 4, col. 2.

[489] "Bone Gap News," *Daily Republican-Register* (Mount Carmel, Illinois), Thursday 6 July 1933, p. 6, col. 3.

but actually Edith's sister-in-law Dora (Leighton) Gould was their aunt; Edith was the sister of Rev. Virgil Gould, the children's uncle by marriage.

As the years went by, Edith spent more time with relatives and especially her sister Alta Britton in Mounds. By 1939 an area newspaper put it this way: "Miss Edith Gould of Mounds is spending a few days at her home here [Bone Gap]."[490] In 1954 she spent several weeks with foster children Melvin and Lucille and their families in Peoria before returning to her sister's at Mounds.[491] In 1958 visitors to the Methodist Home in Lawrenceville found her in "excellent spirits and fairly good health."[492]

Biological children of William Leo and Willie Geneva (Leighton) Pifer (chapters 11, 39, 44, 45), fostered and reared by Edith and Flora Gould (Table 6, Chapter 11):[493]

44 i. LUCILLE[10] PIFER was born about 1912 in Virginia; died 12 March 1983 in Sun City, Maricopa County, Arizona; and was buried at Sunland Memorial Park there. She married 18 March 1934 GEORGE Y. KING.

45 ii. CECIL MELVIN[10] PIFER was born 14 July 1915 in Covington, Alleghany County, Virginia, and died 15 June 1995 in Phoenix, Maricopa County, Arizona, a retired Air Force lieutenant colonel. He married first 17 June 1938 ROSALIE F. GALEENER, and second, as her second husband, 23 July 1950 in Great Falls, Cascade County, Montana, KATHRYN INEZ (WILLIAMS) SANDE.

---

[490] "Bone Gap Personals," *Daily Republican-Register* (Mount Carmel, Illinois), Friday 14 April 1939, p. 5, col. 5.

[491] "Bone Gap News," *Daily Republican-Register* (Mount Carmel, Illinois), Wednesday 23 June 1954, p. 6, col. 6.

[492] "Bone Gap News," *Daily Republican-Register* (Mount Carmel, Illinois), Friday 22 August 1958, p. 6, col. 5.

[493] "Edith Evelyn Gould Graveside Services Held Sunday," clipping from unknown newspaper (likely the *Albion Journal*) dated 16 November 1960, in author's possession.

Chapter 14

Ninth Generation

Etta Campbell–Harvey Marshall Family
parents at chapter 4

"A prominent planter of this parish . . . active in church and civic affairs"

14. ETTA JANE "ETTIE"^{9} **CAMPBELL** (*Hannah Caroline Thrall*^{8}, *Worthy*^{7}, *Eliphas*^{6}, *Samuel*^{5}, *John*$^{4-3}$, *Timothy*^{2}, *William*^{1})
Birth: February 1877 in Illinois[494]
Death: 7 December 1952 in Wichita Falls, Wichita County, Texas, of cancer of the pancreas
Burial: Jennings, Jefferson Davis Parish, Louisiana[495]
Spouse: **HARVEY CENTENNIAL MARSHALL,** married 24 January 1900 in Crowley, Louisiana[496]
Spouse's parents: Robert N. and Eleanor "Ellen" (Milton) Marshall[497]

---

[494] Harvey Marshall household for wife "Eda," married zero years, 1900 US census, Acadia Parish, Police Jury Ward 5, Louisiana, Ward 5, ED 7, sheet 8A, dwelling 118, family 119. They were next door to his older brother Adelbert "Dell" Marshall.

[495] Elta [Etta] Campbell, Texas death certificate #53703, 7 December 1952, Wichita Falls; "Texas, Death Certificates, 1903–1982" > Wichita > 1952 > Oct–Dec > image 170 of 240. Daughter Bullah [Beulah] Marshall was the informant.

[496] "Were Wedded," *Crowley Signal* (Louisiana), Saturday 27 January 1900, p. 8, cols. 2–3. Her adoptive father, Rev. Charles W. Campbell, officiated.

[497] Robert N. Marshall household for Harvey C. age 4, 1880 US census, Newton Township, Harvey County, Kansas, ED 234, p. 457A, dwelling/family 3. If the children's birthplaces are correct, the Marshall family was in Illinois until about 1866, then Iowa until about 1874, and then in Kansas. Harvey was at least the seventh child. (Was he named after their new county of residence?) For Ellen's birth surname, see Robert N. Marshall–Eleanor Milton marriage 2035, 16 December 1860, Registry of Marriages in Ogle County, Illinois, C:35; "Illinois, County Marriages, 1810–1940" > 5,204,725 > image 644 of 864 (familysearch.org). For Robert's middle name, see unsourced assertion, Robert N. Marshall grave marker, South Crowley Cemetery, Acadia Parish, Louisiana, memorial #108,430,731 for Robert Newton Marshall by Melanie Perry (findagrave.com).

Spouse's birth: 15 April 1876 in Abilene, Dickinson County, Kansas[498]
Spouse's death: 27 September 1946 at Lake Charles, Calcasieu Parish, Louisiana[499]
Spouse's burial: Not known

Charles and Caroline had no biological children. In 1880, the 30something couple's household included a three-year-old Illinois-born Etta J., listed as a "boarder" in their Albion household.[500] Harvey C. was the four-year-old son of Robert N. Marshall and Ellen [–?–] Marshall, living in Newton, Harvey County, Kansas.[501]

Clues as to Etta's biological parents are scarce. Censuses inconsistently recorded her and her parents' birthplaces.

---

[498] Harvey Marshall household for "Eda," 1900 US census, Acadia Parish, Police Jury Ward 5, Louisiana, Ward 5, ED 7, sheet 8A, dwelling 118, family 119. For specific birthplace, note below.

[499] Harvey C. Marshall death 27 September 1946, Louisiana certificate 10284, vol. 10 (1946), Caddo–St. Landry parishes; image 44 of 2174, FHL 1,221,812, item 1, DGS 4,215,530 (familysearch.org). Also, "Service at Jennings Planned on Saturday," *Beaumont Journal* (Texas), Saturday 24 September 1946, p. 2, col. 1. Etta outlived Harvey.

[500] Charles W. Campbell household for "boarder" Etta, 1880 US census, Albion, Edwards County, Illinois, ED 7, p. 46B, dwelling 416, family 423.

[501] Robert N. Marshall household for Harvey C. age 4, 1880 US census, Newton Township, Harvey County, Kansas, ED 234, p. 457A, dwelling/family 3.

Table 1. Etta's and parents' stated birthplaces

Census year	Etta's birthplace	Father's birthplace	Mother's birthplace
1880	Illinois	_	_
1900	Illinois	Indiana	Illinois
1910	Indiana	Indiana	Indiana
1920	Missouri	Missouri	Missouri
1930	Indiana	Ireland	Scotland
1940	Indiana	_	_

1880: Charles W. Campbell household for "boarder" Etta, 1880 US census, Albion, Edwards County, Illinois, ED 7, p. 46B, dwelling 416, family 423. **1900:** Harvey Marshall household for wife "Eda," married zero years, 1900 US census, Acadia Parish, Police Jury Ward 5, Louisiana, Ward 5, ED 7, sheet 8A, dwelling 118, family 119. **1910:** Harvey Marshall household, 1910 US census, Calcasieu Parish, Police Jury Ward 10, ED 51, sheet 23B, dwelling 450, family 402. **1920:** Harvey C. Marshall household, 1920 US census, Lake Charles, Calcasieu Parish, Ward 3, ED 42, sheet 8A, dwelling 144, family 149. **1930:** Howard L. Daughenbaugh household, 1930 US census, New Iberia City, Iberia Parish, Ward 6, ED 8, sheet 2A, dwelling 27, family 32. **1940:** Similarly, 1940, Lake Charles, Calcasieu Parish, ED 10-15, sheet 23 B, dwelling 555.

The 1900 census accurately reported the birth states of her social/adoptive parents. Her 1952 death certificate, for which their daughter Beulah was the informant, named neither Charles nor Caroline's birth states.[502] An unsourced tree claims a 22 February 1877 birth date in South Bend, St. Joseph County, Indiana.[503] Absent well-planned DNA testing and analysis among potential relatives, the only conclusion seems to be that the answers to these questions was not a family priority.

Harvey came to Crowley, Acadia Parish, in 1894 and to Jennings, Jefferson Davis Parish, in 1907. He was a rice planter; they settled on his farm "near Estherwood."[504] In 1910 they were in Calcasieu Parish where he rented a rice farm and Etta's brother Leo was a laborer.[505]

---

[502] Harvey C. Marshall death 27 September 1946, Louisiana certificate #10284, Vol. 10 (1946), Caddo–St. Landry parishes; image 44 of 2174, FHL 1,221,812, item 1, DGS 4,215,530 (familysearch.org).

[503] https://www.ancestry.com/familytree/person/tree/18739353/person/704807707/facts?_phsrc=beD1513&_phstart=successSource

[504] "Were Wedded," *Crowley Signal* (Louisiana), Saturday 27 January 1900, p. 8, cols. 2–3.

[505] Harvey Marshall household, 1910 US census, Calcasieu Parish, Police Jury Ward 10, ED 51, sheet 23B, dwelling 450, family 402.

In 1918 Harvey was of medium height and stout build, with red hair and gray eyes; the family lived on Rural Route 27.[506] "For many years Mr. Marshall was a prominent planter of this parish and had always been active in church and civic affairs. Ill health forced his retirement from active work in 1926."[507]

In 1930 and 1940 Harvey and Etta lived in their daughter and son-in-law's household, first in New Iberia and then in Lake Charles.[508] After Harvey's death in 1946, Etta moved to 3309 Barratt in Wichita Falls, Texas, probably to be near daughter Beulah, who was the informant on her 1952 death certificate.[509]

Children of Etta Jane^9 (Campbell) and Harvey Centennial Marshall:

46 i. CARRIE ELEANOR^{10} MARSHALL (*Etta Jane Campbell^9, Hannah Caroline Thrall^8, Worthy^7, Eliphas^6, Samuel^5, John$^{4-3}$, Timothy^2, William^1*) was born 1 November 1900 in Louisiana, died 31 January 1977, and was buried in Greenwood Cemetery, Jennings, Jefferson Davis Parish, Louisiana. She married 17 December 1919 in Calcasieu Parish HOWARD LEE DAUGHENBAUGH.

47 ii. BEULAH^{10} MARSHALL (*Etta Jane Campbell^9, Hannah Caroline Thrall^8, Worthy^7, Eliphas^6, Samuel^5, John$^{4-3}$, Timothy^2, William^1*) was born 11 August 1904 in Louisiana and died 29 December 1983 in Louisiana.

---

[506] Harvey "Centenial" Marshall WWI draft card, serial #2828, order #2822, 12 September 1918, Lake Charles, Louisiana, local board; "US, World War I Draft Registration Cards, 1917–1918" > Louisiana > Calcasieu County > Draft Card M > image 235 of 753 (ancestry.com).

[507] "Service at Jennings Planned on Saturday," *Beaumont Journal* (Texas), Saturday 24 September 1946, p. 2, col. 1.

[508] Howard L. Daughenbaugh household, 1930 US census, New Iberia City, Iberia Parish, Ward 6, ED 8, sheet 2A, dwelling 27, family 32. Similarly, 1940, Lake Charles, Calcasieu Parish, ED 10-15, sheet 23B, dwelling 555.

[509] Elta [Etta] Campbell, Texas death certificate #53703, 7 December 1952, Wichita Falls; "Texas, Death Certificates, 1903–1982" > Wichita > 1952 > Oct–Dec > image 170 of 240.

Chapter 15

Ninth Generation

Leo Campbell–Fleeta Cantwell Family
parents at chapter 4

"Used her musical talents as a soloist, piano teacher, choir director, and church organist and pianist"

15. LEO FRANK^9 CAMPBELL (*Hannah C. Thrall^8, Worthy^7, Eliphas^6, Samuel^5, John$^{4-3}$, Timothy^2, William^1*)
Birth: 2 April 1892 in Louisiana or Texas (see table)
Death: 21 February 1962 at Union County Hospital, Anna, Union County, Illinois[510]
Burial: Cobden Cemetery, Cobden, Union County, Illinois[511]
Spouse: **FLEETA M. CANTWELL**, married 21 September 1915 in Benton, Franklin County, Illinois[512]
Spouse's parents: John and Annie (Payne) Cantwell[513]
Spouse's birth: 2 December 1898 in St. John, Perry County, Illinois

---

[510] "Leo F. Campbell, Father of Paducah Resident, Dies," *Paducah Sun-Democrat* (Kentucky), 23 February 1962, p. 16A, col. 1.

[511] Leo Frank Campbell grave marker, Cobden Cemetery, Cobden, Illinois, image, memorial #101,879,325 by Alethea England (findagrave.com).

[512] Leo F. Campbell–Fleeta Cantwell marriage 21 September 1915, Franklin County, Illinois, marriage record I:586, license #279; FHL 1,005,312, DGS 4,661,326, image 670 of 676 (familysearch.org). At the time both were living in Christopher, Franklin County. Also, "Deaths...Fleeta Campbell," *Southern Illinoisan* (Carbondale), Thursday 22 April 1976, p. 30, col. 5.

[513] Leo F. Campbell–Fleeta Cantwell marriage 21 September 1915, Franklin County, Illinois, marriage return, Register of Marriages 3:407, license #279; FHL 1,005,308, DGS 4,661,322, image 216 of 336 (familysearch.org). Fleeta was not yet 17 years old. Witnesses were J. T. Campbell (Fleeta's father) and Connie T. Campbell (Carrie Thrall Campbell?).

Spouse's death: 21 April 1976 in St. Louis, Missouri[514]
Spouse's burial: Cobden Cemetery, Cobden, Union County, Illinois[515]

Charles and Caroline had no biological children. In 1900 Leo was called "Leo W. Dodd."[516] Leo's 1915 marriage register named Charles W. Campbell as his father and left his mother's name blank.[517] Relevant records in the table below leave Leo's biological/genetic ancestry mysterious.

---

[514] "Deaths…Fleeta Campbell," *Southern Illinoisan* (Carbondale), Thursday 22 April 1976, p. 30, col. 5. Also, John Cantwell household for Fleeta age 1, 1900 US census, Du Quoin, Perry County, Illinois, ED 48, sheet 5B, dwelling 98, family 99. For exact place of birth, Leo F. Campbell–Fleeta Campbell marriage 21 September 1915, Franklin County, Illinois, marriage return, Register of Marriages 3:407, license #279; FHL 1,005,308, DGS 4,661,322, image 216 of 336 (familysearch.org).

[515] Fleeta M. Campbell grave marker, Cobden Cemetery, Cobden, Illinois, image, memorial #45,536,724 for Fleeta M. Cantwell Campbell by Alethea England (findagrave.com).

[516] Charles W. Campbell household for Leo W. Dodd, age 8, lodger, 1900 US census, Crowley, Acadia Parish, Louisiana, ED 9, dwelling/family 88.

[517] Leo F. Campbell–Fleeta Campbell marriage 21 September 1915, Franklin County, Illinois, register of marriages 3:407 (1907–16), license 279; FHL 1,005,308, DGS 4,661,322, image 216 of 336 (familysearch.org).

Table 2. Leo's and parents' stated birth places

Year	Leo's birth state	Father's birth state	Mother's birth state
1900	Louisiana (as "Leo W. Dodd, lodger")	Wisconsin	Louisiana
1910A	Louisiana	Indiana	Illinois
1910B	Louisiana	Indiana	Indiana
1915	West Point, Fayette County, Texas	–	–
1917	Lake Charles, Calcasieu Parish, Louisiana	–	–
1920	Louisiana	Louisiana	Texas
1930	Louisiana	Indiana	Illinois
1940	Texas	–	–
1942	Giddings, Lee County, Texas	–	–

Giddings and West Point are about 30 miles apart, two counties west of Houston. **Sources. 1900:** Charles W. Campbell household for Leo W. Dodd, age 8, lodger, 1900 US census, Crowley, Acadia Parish, Louisiana, ED 9, dwelling/family 88. **1910A:** Charles W. Capbell [Campbell] household for Leo F. Capbell [Campbell], enumerated 13 May, 1910 US census, Johnston City, Williamson County, Illinois, ED 165, sheet 23B, dwelling 574, family 580. **1910B:** Harvey Marshall household for "son" Leo Campbell, 1910 US census, Police Jury Ward 10, Calcasieu Parish, Louisiana, ED 51, sheet 23B, dwelling 450, family 402. The double enumeration probably reflects confusion as to Leo's regular "place of abode" as of 15 April 1910. **1915:** Leo F. Campbell–Fleeta Campbell marriage 21 September 1915, Franklin County, Illinois, register of marriages 3:407 (1907–16), license #279; FHL 1,005,308, DGS 4,661,322, image 216 of 336 (familysearch.org). **1917:** Leo F. Campbell, WWI draft card #44, Precinct 1, Cobden, Union County, Illinois, 5 June 1917; "US, World War I, Draft Registration Cards, 1917–1918" > Illinois > Union County > Draft Card C > image 14 of 343 (ancestry.com). **1920:** Leo F. Campbell household, 1920 US census, Cobden, Union County, Illinois, ED 138, sheet 9A, dwelling 64, family 65. **1930:** similarly, 1930 US census, ED 9, sheet 13B, dwelling/family 95. **1940:** Leo Campbell household, 1940 US census, Cobden, Union County, Illinois, ED 91-9, sheet 6A, dwelling 122. **1942:** Leo Frank Campbell, WWII draft card serial #787; "US, World War II, Draft Registration Cards, 1942" > Camp–Campbell > image 1730 of 2042 (ancestry.com).

In 1910 Leo was with his sister Etta and brother-in-law Harvey, working on their rice farm in Calcasieu Parish, Louisiana.[518] Leo's adoptive father, Rev. C. W. Campbell, officiated at Leo and Fleeta's

---

[518] Harvey Marshall household for son [brother-in-law] Leo Campbell, 1910 US census, Police Jury Ward 10, Calcasieu Parish, Louisiana, ED 51, sheet 23B, dwelling 450, family 402.

marriage.[519] In 1917 Leo was clerking in the general store of H. A. DuBois and Sons in Cobden, Union County. He was described as short, with blue eyes and light brown hair.[520]

Leo and Fleeta stayed in Cobden for at least twenty-five years; in 1920 he was in "merchandise sales"[521] and in 1930 clerk in a general store there.[522] In 1940 they were renting for $10 a month; he earned $1014 as a bookkeeper in a box mill, and she earned $1200 as a social worker for the State of Illinois. He completed two years of college (possibly at McKendree) and Fleeta four years of high school.[523] In 1942 he was working at the DuBois and Sons store.[524]

During the 1950s Fleeta was matron of the IOOF (Odd Fellows) Home in Mattoon, Coles County, Illinois, and Leo was superintendent. They lived at 1 East Lafayette Heights there.[525] She was a member of Cobden's First Baptist Church, Women's Club, and Rebekah Lodge.[526]

---

[519] Leo F. Campbell–Fleeta Campbell marriage 21 September 1915, Franklin County, Illinois, marriage record I:586, license #279; FHL 1,005,312, DGS 4,661,326, image 670 of 676 (familysearch.org).

[520] Leo F. Campbell, WWI draft card #44, Precinct 1, Cobden, Union County, Illinois, 5 June 1917; "US, World War I, Draft Registration Cards, 1917–1918" > Illinois > Union County > Draft Card C > image 14 of 343 (ancestry.com).

[521] Leo F. Campbell household, 1920 US census, Cobden, Union County, Illinois, ED 138, sheet 9A, dwelling 64, family 65.

[522] Leo F. Campbell household, 1930 US census, Cobden, Union County, Illinois, ED 9, sheet 13B, dwelling/family 95.

[523] Leo Campbell household, 1940 US census, Cobden, Union County, Illinois, ED 91-9, sheet 6A, dwelling 122.

[524] Leo Frank Campbell, WWII draft card serial #787; "US, World War II, Draft Registration Cards, 1942" > Camp–Campbell > image 1730 of 2042 (ancestry.com).

[525] Leo F. Campbell and Fleeta M./F. Campbell entries, *Polk's Mattoon City Directory 1950* (St. Louis: R. L. Polk, 1950), p. 61, image 32; similarly, 1953, p. 58, image 30; 1955, p. 52, image 29 (ancestry.com).

[526] "Deaths…Fleeta Campbell," *Southern Illinoisan* (Carbondale), Thursday 22 April 1976, p. 30, col. 5.

Children of Leo Frank^9 and Fleeta M. (Cantwell) Campbell:

48   i. LEONA "LENA" MAE^{10} CAMPBELL (*Leo Frank Campbell^9, Hannah Caroline Thrall^8, Worthy^7, Eliphas^6, Samuel^5, John$^{4\text{-}3}$, Timothy^2, William^1*) was born 1920 (possibly 13 September) in Illinois; died in 1999 (possibly 31 July); and was buried at Block 10, lot 2D, grave 5 in Cobden Cemetery, Cobden, Union County. She married at Jackson, Cape Girardeau County, Missouri, 19 August 1938 CHESTER EDWARD "JACKIE" PEARSON.

    ii. HELEN MARIE^{10} CAMPBELL (*Leo Frank Campbell^9, Hannah Caroline Thrall^8, Worthy^7, Eliphas^6, Samuel^5, John$^{4\text{-}3}$, Timothy^2, William^1*) was born about 1922 (possibly 26 November) in Illinois; died in 1938 (possibly 1 February, of pneumonia); and was buried at Cobden Cemetery.^{527}

49   iii. MARY ANNA^{10} CAMPBELL (*Leo Frank Campbell^9, Hannah Caroline Thrall^8, Worthy^7, Eliphas^6, Samuel^5, John$^{4\text{-}3}$, Timothy^2, William^1*) was born about 1932 (possibly 17 August 1931) in Illinois; died 30 October 2013 in Paducah, McCracken County, Kentucky; and was buried at Mount Kenton Cemetery there three days later. She married about 1951 EDWARD AUGUST KOHLER.

---

^{527} Leo F. Campbell household for daughter Helen Marie age 8, 1930 US census, Cobden, Union County, Illinois, ED 9, sheet 13B, dwelling/family 95. Also, Helen Marie Campbell grave marker, image, Cobden Cemetery, Cobden, Illinois, memorial #45,429,616 by Althea England (findagrave.com).

Chapter 16

Ninth Generation

Edith Laura Thrall Family
parents at chapter 5

Keepers of houses of ill fame were more afraid of Methodist deaconess Lucy Hall than of the police

16. EDITH LAURA^9 THRALL (*Leonidas^8, Worthy^7, Eliphas^6, Samuel^5, John$^{4-3}$, Timothy^2, William^1*)
Birth: 1 July 1874 in Freeburg, St. Clair County, Illinois
Death: 13 June 1950 in Kewanee, Henry County, Illinois[528]
Burial: College Hill Cemetery, Lebanon, St. Clair County, Illinois[529]

Leonidas wrote to his mother and sister 7 July 1874,

Wednesday—July 1st—was a day of rejoicing in our little household. Of course the little cherub is pretty and from her mouth upwards—including her ears—she resembles Carrie more nearly than any other of her relations. Her eyes are blue; her mouth is Edith's exactly. She is twenty two inches long and has been generally reckoned to weigh about nine pounds though she has not been weighed.[530]

---

[528] "Edith Thrall Dies; Was Veteran Teacher," *Daily Dispatch* (Moline, Illinois), Wednesday 14 June 1950, p. 4, col. 5.
[529] Edith Thrall grave marker, image, College Hill Cemetery, Lebanon, St. Clair County, Illinois, memorial #12,068,898 for Edith L. Thrall by Alberta Daniels Withrow (findagrave.com).
[530] Leonidas W. Thrall in Freeburg to "Mother & Sister" in Bone Gap 7 July 1874; Flint–Thrall letter #17, in author's possession.

Years later Edith recalled her and younger brother Will's childhood:

> As a baby Will was not well and was fretful. My father [Leonidas] took a good deal of the care of him because mother was unable to do it. [At one point, suffering with asthma, she sat on the floor for four days and nights, because she could breathe more easily with her head leaning forward on a chair.] He would softly sing to him, 'Come Thou Fount of Every Blessing' to the tune of Greenville...
>
> During Will's first or second summer [1881 or 1882] I was ill and very puny. They sent me to Bone Gap for the country air and milk. While I was there they wrote that the baby [Will] was very ill. I was homesick enough any way but that was almost too much. But the worst was when Cousin Cretie [Lucretia Morgan, chapter 9] would play the organ and sing "Then scatter the seeds of kindness." I didn't have any feelings of a bad conscience but the verse that floored me went,
>
> "If we knew the baby fingers
> Pressed against the window pane
> Would be cold and stiff tomorrow
> Never trouble us again,
> Would the bright eyes of our darling
> Catch the frown upon our brow?
> Would the dainty baby fingers
> Vex us then as they do now?"[531]

---

[531] Edith Laura Thrall, "Will's Childhood," typescript of family memories written between his death (15 October 1941) and hers (14 June 1950).

Edith entered McKendree College in 1889 and graduated with the degree of A.B. in 1895. "She immediately entered upon a course of post-graduate study and was granted the degree of A.M. in 1896, and Ph.D. in 1898 by her Alma Mater. She was a member of the Clionian Literary Society."

An authority on Shakespeare and the Bible,[532] she rarely if ever left Illinois. She spent one year as assistant principal of Marissa (St. Clair County) high school; two years as teacher in the Lebanon (St. Clair County) public schools; one year as assistant principal of Morrison (Whiteside County) high school; and 25 years teaching at Jennings Seminary in Aurora (Kane County). A member of the Methodist Episcopal Church since early youth, she also engaged in deaconess work.[533] In 1906 she was at the Chicago Training School for City, Home, and Foreign Missions at 4949 Indiana Avenue.[534]

Later she was on the staff of the Methodist Old Peoples' Home on Foster Avenue in Chicago. "Her vacations were spent either in further study at the University of Chicago or visiting her family. At least one niece remembers her with special gratitude for her patient teaching clumsy little fingers skills like tatting, crocheting, and knitting. In all phases of her work, in addition to her knowledge and wisdom, she showed a remarkable integrity and empathy with people."[535]

In 1929 brother Will advised her on possible ways of getting her "reading report scheme" published.[536] In 1936 she was housemother at

---

[532] Rosalie (Thrall) Carmichael, "Thrall Genealogy" (17-page typescript on onion skin in red binder, by Rosalie Thrall Carmichael although no author is named), 8; in author's possession, tub 2, item 34.

[533] *Centennial McKendree College with St. Clair County History* (Lebanon, Illinois: McKendree College, 1928), 357. For Jennings Seminary, "Edith Thrall Dies; Was Veteran Teacher," Daily Dispatch (Moline, Illinois), Wednesday 14 June 1950, p. 4, col. 5.

[534] W. F. Thrall in Flora to Edith L. Thrall at 4949 Indiana Avenue, Chicago, letter, 1 November 1906; in author's possession, tub 13, binder 325.

[535] Rosalie (Thrall) Carmichael, "Thrall Genealogy" (17-page typescript on onion skin in red binder, by Rosalie Thrall Carmichael although no author is named), 8; in author's possession, tub 2, item 34.

[536] William F. Thrall in Chapel Hill, North Carolina, to Edith L. Thrall in Aurora, Illinois, letter, 28 August 1929; in author's possession, tub 13, binder 326. What the scheme was and what became of it is unknown.

the Methodist Hospital Nurses Home at 224 Crescent Avenue in Peoria, Peoria County, Illinois.[537] Her networking skills should not be overlooked. In the 1940s when her niece Elizabeth Henderson was considering what to do after medical school, Edith relayed information about the Pine Mountain Settlement School in remote southeastern Kentucky, where Elizabeth and her husband later spent several years. (Chapter 55)

In July 1944 Edith spoke on great deaconesses in the Methodist Church:

> Long remembered for a unique work in Rescue work among girls lost in the city of Chicago is Miss Lucy Hall. . . . One outstanding feature of her work was her almost instinctive knowledge as to where to look for the one she was to find. Also it was noteworthy that keepers of houses of ill fame were more afraid of her than of the police. She knew just what she had a legal right to do and they knew that she knew and that she was absolutely not to be bought off nor was she the least bit fearful. The girl was produced when Miss Hall appeared.

Edith was impressed in a different way when she helped Lucy Hall at a church service with the "girls" from the houses of ill repute. "They knew all the Sunday School songs we announced. The thought in my mind was that the S.S. had had a chance with them but had signally failed."[538]

---

[537] Edith L. Thrall entry, *Peoria (Peoria County, Illinois) City Directory 1936* (Peoria: R.L. Polk, 1936), p. 613, image 310 of 505 (ancestry.com).

[538] Edith L. Thrall, "Outstanding Women in the Deaconess Movement," 7–8, undated typescript of a talk late 1944 (it mentions the Normandy invasion) and probably given more than once, in author's possession.

Chapter 17

Ninth Generation

Victor Thrall– Carrie Jones Family
parents at chapter 5

"We will be besieged to go to war again. We will be told it is to save democracy."

17. VICTOR WORTHY^9 THRALL (*Leonidas^8, Worthy^7, Eliphas^6, Samuel^5, John$^{4-3}$, Timothy^2, William^1*)
Birth: 19 April 1877 in Hartford, Lyon County, Kansas
Death: 21 August 1963 in Knoxville, Knox County, Tennessee
Burial: College Hill Cemetery, Lebanon, St. Clair County[539]
Spouse: **CARRIE FRANCES JONES,** married 25 December 1903 [540]
Spouse's Birth: 3 April 1877 in St. Clair County[541]
Spouse's Death: 6 July 1952 in Knoxville, Knox County, Tennessee

---

[539] Rev. Victor W. Thrall grave marker, image, College Hill Cemetery, Lebanon, St. Clair County, Illinois, memorial #12,068,903 for Victor Worthy Thrall by Alberta Daniels Withrow (findagrave.com).

[540] "Weds Schoolmate," *Daily News Democrat* (Belleville, Illinois), Saturday 26 December 1903, p. 2, col. 5. For approximate wedding date, "Thrall–Bell Wedding Is Solemnized," *Enquirer and Evening News* (Battle Creek, Michigan), Sunday 27 August 1933, p. 6, col. 6. Granddaughter Evelyn Thrall married almost exactly 75 years after B. Caroline, her maternal grandmother.

[541] Alfred C. Jones household, 1880 US census, T2N R7W, St. Clair County, Illinois, ED 39, p. 162A, dwelling/family 9. Also, "Pastor to Wesley Church Named," *Chicago Tribune*, Saturday 13 December 1913, p. 16, col. 5.

Spouse's Burial: 9 July at College Hill Cemetery, Lebanon, St. Clair County[542]

Spouse's parents: Alfred C. and B. Cornelia (Hauser) Jones,[543] who were married in August 1858

Both Victor and Carrie excelled in oratory. He often recalled her being the only person who ever defeated him in an oratorical contest. This was at McKendree, a contest between the Plato, Philo, and Clio literary societies.[544]

The youngest of four children, Carrie was educated at McKendree and was valedictorian of the class of 1897, receiving the degree of A.B.[545] She taught school in O'Fallon, St. Clair County, for four years. She was "an accomplished musician and an elocutionist."[546] As of 8 June 1912, "Mrs. V. W. Thrall of Litchfield," Macoupin County, was visiting "her sister, Mrs. O. C. Pfennighausen"[547]— her oldest sister, Sara Evelyn.[548]

---

[542] "Obituaries . . . Thrall, Mrs. Carrie Jones," *Knoxville News-Sentinel* (Tennessee), Monday 7 July 1952, p. 13, col. 1. Also p. 12, col. 6. Also, Carrie Jones Thrall grave marker, image, College Hill Cemetery, Lebanon, St. Clair County, Illinois, memorial #12,068,896 for Carrie Frances Jones Thrall by Alberta Daniels Withrow (findagrave.com).

[543] Alfred C. Jones family grave marker, image, Shiloh Valley Cemetery, Shiloh, St. Clair County, Illinois, memorial #102,279,364 for Alfred Cowles Jones by Jimbo1937 (findagrave.com). Listed on the stone are father Alfred C. 1822–1913, mother B. Cornelia 1836–1915, and children: Mary L. 1859–1860, Charles F. 1861–1862, Gussie 1867–1872, Willie 1872–1872, and Cora Belle 1865–1875. Four others including Carrie, the youngest, lived at least until the 1880 census. Hauser surname from Rosalie Thrall Carmichael's typescript Thrall Genealogy, in author's possession, tub 2, folder 34.

[544] Rosalie (Thrall) Carmichael, "Thrall Genealogy" (17-page typescript on onion skin in red binder, by Rosalie Thrall Carmichael although no author is named), pp. 9–10; in author's possession, tub 2, item 34.

[545] *Centennial McKendree College with St. Clair County History* (Lebanon, Illinois: McKendree College, 1928), 369.

[546] "Weds Schoolmate," *Daily News Democrat* (Belleville, Illinois), Saturday 26 December 1903, p. 2, col. 5.

[547] "Personal Paragraphs," *News Democrat* (Belleville, Illinois), Saturday 8 June 1912, p. 2, col. 4.

[548] *Centennial McKendree College with St. Clair County History* (Lebanon, Illinois: McKendree College, 1928), 338–39.

Carrie was remembered by her children as beautiful, tall, willowy, dignified, poised, and affectionate—"a sprightly conversationalist but amazingly slow to show any anger whatever. . . . She had unusual success as an organizer and teacher of young adult Sunday School Classes. . . . They had the reputation of always leaving parsonage houses and grounds more attractive than they found them."[549]

Victor was salutatorian of McKendree's class of 1899. "After a year in the pastorate he entered Garrett Biblical Institute and received the degree of B.D. from that institution in 1903. He also received the degree of Ph.D. from McKendree." He was "much in demand as a speaker at Epworth League Institutes and other young peoples' assemblies."[550] Of his first 26 years in the ministry, nineteen years involved downtown city churches or churches attended by college and university students.[551]

Their charges included:
- Farina, Fayette County, Illinois, 1903–1906,[552] when they were married
- Altamont, Effingham County, Illinois, 1906[553]
- Lebanon, St. Clair County, Illinois, 1907–1910[554]

---

[549] Rosalie (Thrall) Carmichael, "Thrall Genealogy" (17-page typescript on onion skin in red binder, by Rosalie Thrall Carmichael although no author is named), pp 9-10; in author's possession, tub 2, item 34.

[550] *Centennial McKendree College with St. Clair County History* (Lebanon, Illinois: McKendree College, 1928), p. 369.

[551] "City's Religious Spirit Finds Expression," *Battle Creek Inquirer and Evening News* (Michigan), Tuesday 1 January 1929, section 3, p. 1, col. 5.

[552] "Conference Appointments 1905," *Minutes of the 54th Session of the Southern Illinois Conference of the Methodist Episcopal Church, East St. Louis, 27 September–2 October 1905*, p. 16, image 22 of 514 (babel.hathitrust.org). Also, "In Pulpit [*sic*] and Pew," *Republican* (Salem, Illinois), Thursday 4 May 1906, p. 8, col. 2, where Victor was said to be from Farina.

[553] "Conference Appointments 1906," *Minutes of the 55th Session of the Southern Illinois Conference of the Methodist Episcopal Church, Vandalia, 19–26 September 1906*, p. 19, image 151 of 514 (babel.hathitrust.org).

[554] "Conference Appointments 1907," first year, *Minutes of the 56th Session of the Southern Illinois Conference of the Methodist Episcopal Church, Mount Carmel, 18–23 September 1907*, p. 24, image 268 of 514 (babel.hathitrust.org). Similarly, 1908, second year, *57th Session, McLeansboro, 16–21 September 1908*, p. 27, image 403 of 514 (babel.hathitrust.org). Similarly, 1909, third year, *58th Session, Centralia, 22–27 September 1909*, p. 24, image 24 of 78 (archive.org). Similarly, 1910, fourth year, *59th Session, Olney, 28 September–3 October 1910*, p. 25, image 24 of 82 (archive.org).

- Litchfield, Macoupin County, 1911–12[555]
- Wesley Methodist, Belden and Halsted, Chicago, Cook County, approximately 1913–16[556]
- Evanston Covenant, Cook County, 1916–19[557]
- First Methodist, Clark and Washington, Chicago Loop, 1919–20, where he managed the Centenary program and raised $3.2 million[558]
- Dixon, Lee County, Illinois, 1920–21[559]
- Knoxville, Knox County, Tennessee 1921–25[560]
- Albion, Calhoun County, Michigan, 1925–28[561]

---

[555] "Conference Appointments 1911," first year, *Minutes of the 60th Session of the Southern Illinois Conference of the Methodist Episcopal Church, East St. Louis, 20–25 September 1911*, p. 22, image 22 of 25 (archive.org). Similarly, 1912, second year, *61st Session, Cairo, 25–30 September 1912*, p. 22, image 22 of 64.

[556] "Conference Appointments 1914," second year, *Minutes of the 75th Session of the Rock River Annual Conference of the Methodist Episcopal Church, Austin M.E. Church, 7–12 October 1914*, p. 48, image 210 of 912 (hathitrust.org). But Victor was not at Wesley in 1913: similarly, *76th Session*, "Conference Appointments 1913," p. 40, image 42 of 912, shows N. J. Harkness there, entering into his first year. Few relevant family letters survive to illuminate the years of this transition.

[557] Rev. W. B. Norton, "Warns Pastors They May Have Lower Salaries," *Chicago Tribune*, Tuesday 10 October 1916, p. 6, col. 1. Also, "Evanston Pastor To Take Up New Work," *Chicago Tribune*, Tuesday 9 September 1919, p. 18, col. 6.

[558] "News of the Religious World," *Chicago Tribune*, Sunday 7 December 1919, part 7, p. 8, cols. 3–4. Also, *Centennial McKendree College with St. Clair County History* (Lebanon, Illinois: McKendree College, 1928), 369. They were in Evanston in 1920: Victor W. Thrall household, 1920 US census, Evanston, Cook County, Illinois, Ward 6, ED 84, sheet 6B, dwelling 122, family 137.

[559] "Chicago Preacher Accepts Call from Dixon M.E. [Methodist Episcopal] Church," *Dixon Evening Telegraph* (Illinois), Friday 15 October 1920, p. 1, col. 8. "He is a young man, full of enthusiasm for his work, is a pulpit orator of ability and possesses a personality which it is felt sure will make him a host of friends in this community."

[560] "Big Reception for Dr. Thrall in New Charge," *Dixon Evening Telegraph* (Illinois), Monday 24 October 1921, p. 2, col. 6.

[561] "Rev. Thrall in Albion Pulpit," *Battle Creek Moon-Journal* (Michigan), Friday 2 October 1925, p. 9, col. 3.

- Battle Creek, Calhoun County, Michigan, 1928–33[562]
- District Superintendent, Big Rapids, Mecosta County, Michigan, 1933–38[563]
- Parchment, Kalamazoo County, Michigan, 1938–46[564]
- Lake Odessa, Ionia County, Michigan, 1946–48?[565]

In June 1950 they were living in Fountain City, Knoxville, Knox County, Tennessee.[566]

Victor was

> a very strong pulpit man with a warm outgoing personality . . . . That strong Thrall sense of humor was always there to keep life interesting. In the pulpit he excelled in attracting large night congregations to his outstanding dramatic religious book sermons. The books of Ian MacLaren and Robert Burns were particularly popular with the churches of his district. In appreciation of his generous use of his talent the churches of his district made him a present of a trip to Scotland enabling him to visit the settings of the books.[567]

---

[562] "New Ministers for Pulpits Here," *Enquirer and Evening News* (Battle Creek, Michigan), Sunday 9 September 1928, p. 8, cols. 4–5. Also, Victor W. Thrall household, 1930 US census, Battle Creek, Calhoun County, Michigan, ED 24, sheet 12B, dwelling 185, family 289.

[563] "Pastors Change at M.E. [Methodist Episcopal] Church," *Enquirer and Evening News* (Battle Creek, Michigan), Monday 1 January 1934, section 1A, p. 2, col. 6.

[564] "Bishop Changes One Pastor Here," *Enquirer and News* (Battle Creek, Michigan), Monday 10 June 1946, p. 2, col. 8.

[565] "Scholarship Created By Hastings Church," *Enquirer and News* (Battle Creek, Michigan), Friday 13 February 1948, p. 14, col. 3.

[566] "Edith Thrall Dies; Was Veteran Teacher," *Daily Dispatch* (Moline, Illinois), Wednesday 14 June 1950, p. 4, col. 5.

[567] Rosalie (Thrall) Carmichael, "Thrall Genealogy" (17-page typescript on onion skin in red binder, by Rosalie Thrall Carmichael although no author is named), pp 9–10; in author's possession, tub 2, item 34.

About 1917, in the shadow of war, Victor wrote his brothers from Evanston,

> Bishop Mitchell raised thunder at preacher's meeting Monday morning. He used some very indiscreet remarks in talking to the German brethren about how they 'have to keep your mouths shut now.' It was about the war [World War I]. Then he told how the German people here stood with respect to the kaiser. The German brethren spoke back, nothing in any way disloyal to the flag. Then he lost his balance and things flew hot for a while. It was a battle back and forth. There was no excuse in his doing what he did.[568]

No doubt this experience shaped Victor's attitude when the war drums were again being beaten in 1939: "We will be besieged to go to war again. We will be told it is to save democracy. We didn't save it the last time; we nearly lost it. . . . [The only way for Americans to save democracy] is to save it in America."[569]

In 1929, he wrote hopefully that the many Christian denominations would come together in the near future:

> One of the greatest movements in modern Christianity is that which looks toward organizing a union of the various Protestant churches. It is a movement with which I am heartily in accord. The Methodist church at its general conference in May, 1928, appointed a commission to receive overtures from and make overtures toward churches of like minds looking toward closer cooperation and organization of American churches. This is not limited to churches of similar creed, faith or

---

[568] Victor W. Thrall letter to "Dear Boys" (his brothers), dated "Wednesday afternoon" but on stationary for an August 1917 Epworth League Institute; in author's possession, tub 13, binder 326.

[569] "Dr. Thrall Warns 'Peace Trek' Of War's Danger to Democracy," *Enquirer and Evening News* (Battle Creek, Michigan), Sunday 12 November 1939, p. 6, cols. 2–3.

organization, but includes all those that have a mind to unite.

The Presbyterian church and the Methodist church are now considering such a merger. Both churches voted in favor of consolidation at their national conferences and all that remains to be done is an agreement as to organization. . . . These two systems [episcopal vs. congregational] will have to be compromised, probably with sacrifice on the part of both churches. However, I feel that both would be willing to forego some of their established customs to come to an agreement. . . . I look for a great deal of consolidation of this kind during the next ten years, and I shall use every influence in my power to help such a movement.[570]

Children of Victor Worthy[9] and Carrie Frances (Jones) Thrall:

50 i. EDITH FLINT[10] THRALL (*Victor W.[9], Leonidas[8], Worthy[7], Eliphas[6], Samuel[5], John[4-3], Timothy[2], William[1]*) was born 7 October 1904 in O'Fallon, St. Clair County, Illinois; and died 23 April 1989. She married 26 August 1926 in Albion, Calhoun County, Michigan, GEORGE ANSEL MOOERS.

51 ii. EVELYN GRACE[10] THRALL (*Victor W.[9], Leonidas[8], Worthy[7], Eliphas[6], Samuel[5], John[4-3], Timothy[2], William[1]*) was born 27 December 1907 in Illinois, died 15 June 1987 at the University of Tennessee hospital, and was buried at Ozone Cemetery, Cumberland County, Tennessee. She married in Battle Creek, Calhoun County, Michigan, 26 August 1933 JOSHUA "JESS" JENNINGS BIRD.

iii. FRANCES HELEN[10] THRALL (*Victor W.[9], Leonidas[8], Worthy[7], Eliphas[6], Samuel[5], John[4-3], Timothy[2], William[1]*) was born and died

---

[570] Victor W. Thrall letter to editor, *Enquirer and Evening News* (Battle Creek, Michigan), Sunday 9 June 1929, p. 8, col. 4.

1913,571 probably in Chicago (parents' residence), and died young.

    iv. UNNAMED DAUGHTER^{10} THRALL (*Victor W.^{9}, Leonidas^8, Worthy^7, Eliphas^6, Samuel^5, John$^{4-3}$, Timothy^2, William^1*) was reportedly born and died 15 March 1915.572

52   v. VICTOR WORTHY^{10} THRALL, JR. (*Victor W.^{9}, Leonidas^8, Worthy^7, Eliphas^6, Samuel^5, John$^{4-3}$, Timothy^2, William^1*) was born 10 February 1918 in Evanston, Cook County, and died 12 December 2000 in Pekin, Tazewell County. He married 10 May 1941 in Pekin DONNA M. BROWN.

---

571 Rosalie (Thrall) Carmichael in "Thrall Genealogy" (17-page typescript on onion skin in red binder, by Rosalie although no author is named), 9; in author's possession, tub 2, item 34.

572 Thrall daughter, #566, index entry, 15 March 1915; "Illinois, Cook County Deaths, 1878–1994," DGS 100,770,641, image 156 (familysearch.org). Also index entry for birth record, possibly at FHL 1,315,958, DGS 4,394,348, image 58, p. 428, line 21342 (familysearch.org).

Chapter 18

Ninth Generation

William Thrall–Enola Keisling Family
parents at chapter 5

"A man who could see around a corner"

18. **William Flint**^{9} **Thrall** (*Leonidas^8, Worthy^7, Eliphas^6, Samuel^5, John$^{4-3}$, Timothy^2, William^1*)
Birth: 15 December 1880 in Ashley, Washington County, Illinois
Death: 15 October 1941 of prostate cancer in Chapel Hill, North Carolina[573]
Burial: College Hill Cemetery, Lebanon, St. Clair County, Illinois[574]
Spouse: **Enola Loudicy Keisling,** married in Washington County, Illinois,[575] 6 January 1906
Spouse's parents: Willard and Charlotte Jane (Carter) Keisling[576]
Spouse's birth: 7 August 1878 in Brownstown, Fayette County, Illinois
Spouse's death: of cerebral thrombosis 17 August 1950 in East

---

[573] William Flint Thrall death certificate; "North Carolina, Death Certificates, 1909–1976" > Onslow > 1941 > October > image 13 of 17 (ancestry.com).

[574] William Flint Thrall grave marker, image, College Hill Cemetery, Lebanon, St. Clair County, Illinois, memorial #12,068,904 by Alberta Daniels Withrow (findagrave.com).

[575] Married in Irvington: "Items of Local Interest," *Salem Herald-Advocate* (Illinois), Friday 19 January 1906, p. 1, col. 1. Married in Richview: "William Flint Thrall," in Winfield Scott Downs, editor, *Encyclopedia of American Biography*, new series, 16:63–65 (New York: The American Historical Company, 1943). The Washington County towns are five miles apart.

[576] Enola Thrall death certificate #47666, 17 August 1950, East Cleveland, Cuyahoga County, Ohio; "Ohio Deaths, 1908–1953" > 1950 > 47201–50000 > image 509 of 3125 (familysearch.org). She had been living at 2588 Canterbury Road, Cleveland Heights. Informant was daughter Rosalie T. Carmichael. Also, for Charlotte's birth surname, undated email to author, early 2000s, from Kathryn Keisling Fanning.

Cleveland, Cuyahoga County, Ohio
Spouse's burial: with her husband[577]

Enola

In 1880 the Keisling family was farming in Sefton, Fayette County, Illinois.[578] Father Willard joined the Methodist "traveling ministry" in 1890.[579] In 1900 daughter "E.L." (Enola) was cashier in a department store and father Willard was preaching in Hutsonville, Crawford County, Illinois.[580]

Soon after 1910 Willard and Charlotte left Illinois for Florida. Granddaughter Rosalie recalled visiting them in the 1920s when "things were still a bit primitive. They did have a little hand pump at the kitchen sink but were still careful of water, which reminds me that water conservation is a real issue here in Florida because of our rapid growth

---

[577] Enola Keisling Thrall grave marker, image, College Hill Cemetery, Lebanon, St. Clair County, Illinois, memorial #12,068,900 for Enola L. Keisling Thrall by Alberta Daniels Withrow (findagrave.com).

[578] Willard Keisling household, 1880 US census, Sefton, Fayette County, Illinois, ED 97, p. 105A, dwelling 120, family 121.

[579] W. Kiesling [Keisling] 1890 entry, "Chronological Roll of the Southern Illinois Conference," *Minutes of the 58th Session of the Southern Illinois Conference of the Methodist Episcopal Church, Centralia, 22–27 September 1909*, p. 17, image 16 of 88 (archive.org). His name was in capital letters indicating that he was categorized as "non-effective" as of the 1909 conference.

[580] M. Kushing [Rev. W. Keisling] household, 1900 US census, Hutsonville, Crawford County, Illinois, ED 38, sheet 6A, dwelling/family 122. In 1910 he was a Methodist clergyman in Illinois: Willard Keisling household, 1910 US census, Lebanon, St. Clair, County, Illinois, ED 145, sheet 4B, dwelling 100, family 110. He was "supernumerary," evidently unable to minister at the time but not retired (1952 definition, umc.org/decisions/41059/P1200): *Minutes of the 59th Session of the Southern Illinois Conference of the Methodist Episcopal Church, Olney, 28 September–3 October 1910*, p. 34, image 34 of 82 (archive.org). As of 1928 he was a retired member of the Southern Illinois Conference of the Methodist Episcopal Church: *Centennial McKendree College with St. Clair County History* (Lebanon, Illinois: McKendree College, 1928), 375.

and the fact that most of us don't realize that there is *not* an unlimited supply."[581]

In 1920 Willard was a "grocery merchant" in southwestern Florida's DeSoto County.[582] Ten years later, in their 70s, he and Charlotte were in neighboring Highlands County (Lake Placid City) and reported no occupation.[583] Evidently they left for the northeast corner of the state prior to Willard's death in Jacksonville, Duval County, 17 October 1939. He was buried in Oaklawn Cemetery there.[584] In 1940 the widowed Charlotte was living in Jacksonville with her doctor son's large family.[585]

Enola sang in choirs, painted pictures and china, and wrote and illustrated children's books. "Her special hobby was writing sonnets—which she did the way some people do cross-word puzzles."[586] In 1902 she became part of a quartet at McKendree, which sang together for several years, in public programs, funerals, conventions, "and other occasions where good music was in demand." She graduated in 1905.[587]

Will

At an early age, Will took an interest in a United States map puzzle:

---

[581] Rosalie Carmichael to her Thrall first cousins, 3 April 1986; in author's possession (tub 6, folder 193).

[582] Willard Kesling [Keisling] household, 1920 US census, Precinct 21, Lake Childs, DeSoto County, Florida, ED 22, sheet 1B, dwelling/family 21.

[583] Willard Keisling household, 1930 US census, Lake Placid City, Highlands County, Florida, ED 9, sheet 1B, dwelling/family 23.

[584] Willard Keisling, no image of grave marker, Oaklawn Cemetery, Jacksonville, Duval County, Florida, memorial #97,264,964 by Pass It On and Vickye Blatherwick (findagrave.com). Dates are unsourced.

[585] Frederic Keisling household for mother Charalle [Charlotte] Keisling, 1940 US census, Jacksonville, Duval County, Florida, ED 68-36, Ward 4, sheet 2A, dwelling 211.

[586] Rosalie (Thrall) Carmichael, "Thrall Genealogy" (17-page typescript on onion skin in red binder, by Rosalie Thrall Carmichael although no author is named), 12; in author's possession, tub 2, item 34.

[587] *Centennial McKendree College with St. Clair County History* (Lebanon, Illinois: McKendree College, 1928), 314.

> We had one that had each state made into a separate piece. Will became so skillful with it that he could put it together blindfolded. It was there too that . . . he learned the population of most of the large cities and could give them so glibly that we were all amused. He was always high strung and had to go to the bottom or to the very end to finish anything. My father [Leonidas] was especially interested in that mental trait and often spoke of it.[588]

At age 13, Will wrote a lengthy letter 2–3 December 1894 to his siblings Edith and Victor and cousin Edith Gould. Among other events, he reported hearing "'Billy' Bryan of Nebraska speak here Thursday night at the court house on the subject of 'Money' advocating free silver bimetallism and nearly everything else."[589] "Billy" of course was William Jennings Bryan, "The Great Commoner" who later ran unsuccessfully for president in 1896, 1900, and 1908. Bryan's father Silas Lillard Bryan graduated from McKendree in 1849.[590]

Although Will's birth almost took his mother's life, they shared a close bond, as sister Edith L. Thrall later wrote:

> When Will was about fifteen [1895] mother was very ill and the doctor had told her she didn't have a half hour to live. He couldn't find any pulse. We were all in the room around the bed. It was in the middle of the night. Will was standing at the foot of the bed. She said afterwards that at the minute the doctor said she couldn't live much longer she glanced up and saw him looking at her and thought, "Yes, I will

---

[588] Edith Laura Thrall, "Will's Childhood," typescript of family memories written probably shortly after his death 15 October 1941 and certainly prior to hers 14 June 1950.

[589] W. F. Thrall in Salem to Victor and Edith Thrall and Edith Gould in Lebanon, letter, 2–3 December 1894; in author's possession.

[590] *Centennial McKendree College with St. Clair County History* (Lebanon, Illinois: McKendree College, 1928), 152.

live. I have to for him." She did live two years more.[591]

Will spent the summer of 1898 doing sales work, apparently door-to-door, in various towns, with at least some success. The specifics were not discussed (everybody knew them!) but in her letters, his mother reflected on the experience:

> You are climbing one of lifes hills this summer, Willie. There are still higher ones before you but you will never climb another with the inexperience with which you set out last June. You may have lost some faith in humanity but you are now better able to value the world's promises at their real price or worth.[592]

Will "apparently inherited his mother's 'asthmatic' weakness. After graduation from McKendree College where he was an active member of the Platonian Literary Society and also a member of the football team, Southern Illinois champions in 1900, and some time spent doing journalistic work at the St. Louis World's Fair, he spent two seasons teaching a one-room frontier school in Blue [now in Greenlee County], Arizona."[593] His letter home 4 November 1902 was published (probably in the *Albion Journal*):

> Our party of six left Luna, New Mexico, the morning of Aug. 11. . . . After a day and half of travel, mostly on horseback, we reached the White Mountains which lie in the extreme eastern edge of Arizona . . . The next morning we set out on a fishing expedition down the Black River. To me, who had never fished except for perch and cat fish in the muddy streams of Southern Illinois, this trip was a revelation. The waters ran perfectly clear and enabled us to see the sand and

---

591 Rosalie (Thrall) Carmichael, "Thrall Genealogy" (17-page typescript compiled by Rosalie although no author is named), 12; in author's possession, tub 2, item 34.

592 Edith (Flint) Thrall in Lebanon to son William F. Thrall in Flora, letter, 24 July 1898; Flint–Thrall letter #71, in author's possession. She added that Will had lately been "much like the little pig who ran about so fast that he could not be counted."

593 Rosalie (Thrall) Carmichael, "Thrall Genealogy" (17-page typescript on onion skin in red binder by Rosalie Thrall Carmichael although no author is named), 12; in author's possession, tub 2, item 34.

gravel at the river bottom through several feet of water. . . . We soon caught as many trout as we could use for two or three days...

In a recent letter to the Journal I spoke disparagingly of the Mormon religion. While I have little or no respect for the religion I must say that there are many fine people among the Mormons—simple, hospitable and industrious, but I am uncharitable enough to attribute these qualities not to their religion but rather that they are in spite of Mormonism.[594]

This sojourn may also have been made in hopes of Will's improving his health.[595] Later he spent five years (1904–1909) teaching Latin and English in Illinois high schools (including Flora and Decatur).

Then came what may have been a turning point for Will. "A chance meeting with Edwin Greenlaw" (a native of Flora visiting there and a professor himself) "changed a half discouraged student into a determined scholar and turned the course of a teacher from the classrooms of small high schools to the halls of college and university. How often Edwin Greenlaw did that; and how often Will Thrall did it for other students in turn."[596] William took master's and doctor's degrees at the University of Chicago in 1915 and 1920, and then went to the University of North Carolina,[597] where he rose from assistant to full professor in seven years.[598]

---

[594] W. F. Thrall, "The White Mountains," datelined Blue, Arizona, 4 November 1902, clipped from an issue of the *Journal* newspaper, date and place not known. Copy in author's possession.

[595] Colin Carmichael letter to Elizabeth (Thrall) Henderson, 19 February 1968; in author's possession, tub 4, item 131.

[596] Dr. Adams, "An Appreciation," memorial service for William F. Thrall October 1941, typescript, in author's possession, tub 7, folder 212.

[597] "Dr. William Thrall, English Teacher at Chapel Hill, Passes: Funeral Services on Friday for Beloved Carolina Professor," *Durham Morning Herald* (North Carolina), Thursday 16 October 1941, part 1, p. 10, col. 3.

[598] "William Flint Thrall," in Winfield Scott Downs, editor, *Encyclopedia of American Biography*, new series, 16:65 (New York: The American Historical Company, 1943).

In 1920 William, Enola, and Rosalie were living on College Street in Lebanon, St. Clair County, Illinois where he was teaching at McKendree College.[599] They soon moved to the University of North Carolina; his sister-in-law Elizabeth wrote, "We were sorry to hear that Will is going so far south, but I suppose he has a good offer & will like it."[600] In 1930 the family lived at 720 Gimghoul Road, Chapel Hill, North Carolina; their house was valued at $10,000; he was a university teacher and Rosalie a university librarian.[601] In 1940, after ten years of the Great Depression, the house's value had declined to $6750, still well above the statewide average of $1802.[602]

In those two decades, Will chaired Freshman English (1922–30); served as an advisory editor of the publication Studies in Philology; and collaborated with Dean Addison Hibbard of Northwestern University in creating the widely-used reference work, *Handbook to Literature*. He also wrote numerous articles and reviews in learned journals and served on various local boards and committees.[603]

The handbook explained words and phrases used in reading and studying literature, with entries longer and more thorough than a dictionary, but not too detailed. The authors undertook the task because, as teachers, they often had to interrupt the study of a piece of writing in order to explain various terms of art.

> **This handbook should minimize these interruptions.
> . . . In this handbook are included brief explanations
> of the various rhetorical terms; somewhat more**

---

[599] William F. Thrall household, 1920 US census, Lebanon, St. Clair County, Illinois, ED 194, sheet 5B, dwelling 109, family 113.

[600] Elizabeth Schriber Thrall in Cisco, Illinois, letter to "Mother, Edith & Mary V[irginia]" 21 April 1920; in author's possession.

[601] William F. Thrall household, 1930 US census, Chapel Hill, Orange County, North Carolina, ED 6, sheet 21A, dwelling 499, family 465.

[602] William F. Thrall household, 1940 US census, Chapel Hill, Orange County, North Carolina, Ward 3, ED 68-8, sheet 18B, dwelling 331. Statewide figures from US Census Bureau, Census of Housing, Historical Census of Housing Tables, Median Home Values Unadjusted 1940 (census.gov/hhes/www/housing/census/historic/values.html).

[603] "Dr. William Thrall, English Teacher at Chapel Hill, Passes: Funeral Services on Friday for Beloved Carolina Professor," *Durham Morning Herald* (North Carolina), Thursday 16 October 1941, part 1, p. 10, col. 3.

> complete discussions of historical periods, and the various literary types and the forms of poetry; and chronological material systematically arranged to make clear the progress of the literature of England and America throughout the centuries. The book is, then, a presentation of the skeleton of literature rather than of the flesh, blood, mind, and spirit of literature itself.

The terms discussed in the first edition ran alphabetically from "abstract words" and "academic drama" to "wit and humor" and "women as actors." The authors soon found why their effort was the first of its kind. "Once they were fairly launched on the book, they learned only too well why this thing had not been done before."[604]

In 1968 Will's son-in-law Colin Carmichael reflected, "Considering how well the book has done, it seems a shame that the authors had so much difficulty finding a publisher with as much vision as they had, and that they didn't live long enough to see how it really took hold."[605] A twelfth edition by William Harmon, also of the University of North Carolina, was published in 2011.

In 1943 Will was described as "an extraordinarily successful teacher" who "played his part in the Southern literary Renaissance. . . .

> His broad scholarship commanded the respect of his students, as of his colleagues, his informed and discriminating taste left its mark on all who sat under him and his infectious enthusiasm awakened a similar response. In academic councils he occupied an influential place and assumed many

---

[604] William Flint Thrall and Addison Hibbard, "Preface," *A Handbook to Literature With an Outline of Literary History English and American* (Garden City, New York: Doubleday, Doran, 1936), vii, viii. Copy in author's possession inscribed by W. F. Thrall "To Hal, Elizabeth, Elizabeth Rose, Miriam, and James with love . . . April 23, 1936." Carolina professors William Harmon and C. Hugh Holman published a 1972 version based on Thrall and Hibbard. The 12th edition was published in 2011.

[605] Colin Carmichael letter to Elizabeth (Thrall) Henderson, 19 February 1968; in author's possession, tub 4, item 131.

responsibilities, both in the field of scholarship and as an administrator. . . .

A man of imposing stature and presence, standing six feet tall and over two hundred pounds in weight, the force of his personality had as its ideal foil a fine intellect and his complete moral and scholarly integrity. For hundreds of students his keen sense of humor, his ready smile, his hearty laugh and his intense love for his work, clothed the dry bones of scholarship with life and spirit.

His colleagues looked to him "as a man who could see around a corner, who could give true counsel, who never debated for the sake of debate, who could listen before he talked. Thrall's special interests in the classroom and the library were the mediaeval romances, Edmund Spenser, and the non-dramatic literature of the English Renaissance. . . . Using the Socratic method, a friendly manner, a wholesome wit, he impressed undergraduate and graduate alike as the type of teacher who saw the forest and the trees, who never separated literary works from the life that made them, who was proud of his devotion to the art which builds with words."[606]

Child of William Flint^9 and Enola (Keisling) Thrall:

53 i. ENOLA ROSALIE^{10} THRALL (*William Flint^9, Leonidas^8, Worthy^7, Eliphas^6, Samuel^5, John$^{4\text{-}3}$, Timothy^2, William^1*) was born in Flora, Clay County, Illinois, 18 September 1907, and died 19 April 1999 at St. Petersburg Beach, Pinellas County, Florida. She married 11 March 1933 in Chapel Hill, Orange County, North Carolina, COLIN CARMICHAEL.

---

[606] "William Flint Thrall," in Winfield Scott Downs, editor, *Encyclopedia of American Biograpy*, new series, 16:63–65 (New York: The American Historical Company, 1943).

Story 3: Locating the high-school track meet

Will tried several careers. He taught Latin and English in Illinois high schools, but his heart was not in every aspect of high-school work.

In November 1906, when he was the high-school principal in Flora (Clay County), he wrote to sister Edith:

"Second month closes next Friday. We are today choosing a field to fit up for a track for the spring meet. I wish the meet was to be held in Hades. It would satisfy most of the patrons of a high school meet and give me a legitimate excuse for not attending or preparing for it."[607]

---

[607] W. F. Thrall in Flora to Edith L. Thrall at 4949 Indiana Avenue, Chicago, letter, 1 November 1906; in author's possession, tub 13, binder 325.

Chapter 19

Ninth Generation

Charles Thrall–Gertrude Gerking Family
parents at chapter 5

"A nationally known figure in the field of religious education"

19. CHARLES HAVEN^9 THRALL (*Leonidas^8, Worthy^7, Eliphas^6, Samuel^5, John$^{4-3}$, Timothy^2, William^1*)
Birth: 20 October 1883 in Grayville, Edwards County, Illinois
Death: 18 January 1968, Evenglow Lodge, Pontiac, Livingston County, Illinois
Burial: East Lawn Memorial Gardens Cemetery and Mausoleum, Bloomington, McLean County, Illinois
Spouse: **GERTRUDE GERKING,** married at Lebanon, St. Clair County, 27 August 1907[608]
Spouse's parents: George Washington and Kate (Jones) Gerking[609]
Spouse's birth: 22 July 1881 in Ingraham, Clay County, Illinois
Spouse's death: 20 January 1950 in Bloomington, McLean County
Spouse's burial: with her husband[610]

---

[608] "Charles H. Thrall," *Journal-Yearbook of the 145th Session, Central Illinois Conference of the United Methodist Church, Bloomington, 10–14 June 1968*, p. 264. Also, Charles Haven Thrall grave marker, East Lawn Memorial Gardens Cemetery and Mausoleum, Bloomington, Illinois, image, memorial #112,334,691 by obsessive journey (findagrave.com).

[609] For Kate's birth surname, see George W. Gerking–Kate Jones marriage license 13 October 1880, married 17 October, Clay County, Illinois, Register of Marriages (1878–1895) 1:41, license #529; "Illinois County Marriages, 1810–1940" > 004,539,325 > image 89 of 601; FHL 1,008,793, items 2–5, DGS 4,539,325 (familysearch.org). He was 26, she was 19; they were married in Ingraham, Clay County, Illinois, where they both lived; Nelson Stauffer, Minister of the Gospel, officiated.

[610] Gertrude Gerking Thrall grave marker, East Lawn Memorial Gardens Cemetery and Mausoleum, Bloomington, Illinois, memorial #112,334,663 by obsessive journey (findagrave.com).

Gertrude

In 1900 Gertrude was living at home and teaching music.[611] She studied at three Methodist institutions: McKendree College, where she was a member of the Clionian society and received a B. Mus. in 1901; the Chicago Training School for City, Home and Foreign Missions (4949 South Indiana) for one year; and Garrett Biblical Institute in Evanston for one year.[612] Gertrude's maternal aunt Emily Jones later married as his second wife Charles's father Leonidas (chapter 5). In 1880 the Jones family was in Pixley Township, Clay County.[613]

Charles

Charles "became a student in McKendree in 1896 and graduated in 1903, with the degree of A.B. He was a member of the Philosophian Literary Society. After teaching in the public schools two years, he entered Garrett Biblical Institute and graduated in 1908 with the degree of S.T.B. He was then for two years Professor of Greek and Hebrew in the Central Holiness University of Oskaloosa [Mahaska County], Iowa, and also possibly at John Fletcher College there. From 1910 to 1912 he was pastor of the Methodist Episcopal Church in St. Francisville [Lawrence County, Illinois]. He joined the Southern Illinois Conference in 1905 and in 1912 was transferred to the Illinois Conference." In 1928 he "led an important church building enterprise to a successful conclusion at Quincy [Adams County], Illinois."[614]

---

[611] George W. Gerking household for Gertrude age 18, 1900 US census, Pixley Township, Clay County, Illinois, ED 10, sheet 5A, dwelling 98, family 99. Also, "Mrs. Charles H. Thrall," *Journal and Year Book, 127th Session of the Illinois Conference of the Methodist Church, Bloomington 6–11 June 1950*, p. 655.

[612] During the Great Depression of the 1930s, CTS and Garrett merged and came under the wing of Northwestern University: "Our History," *Garrett-Evangelical Theological Seminary* (garrett.edu/about-us/our-history).

[613] Robert Jones household, 1880 US census, Pixley Township, Clay County, Illinois, ED 150, p. 32D, dwelling 5, no family number.

[614] *Centennial McKendree College with St. Clair County History* (Lebanon, Illinois: McKendree College, 1928), 381. Also, Paul and Chester Farthing, editors, *Philo History: Chronicles and Biographies of the Philosophian Literary Society of McKendree College* (Lebanon, Illinois: privately printed, 1911), 210.

He preached on trial in the Southern Illinois Conference in 1905. That spring, Vandalia District presiding elder John Wesley Flint (Charles's maternal uncle) called on him to fill an unfortunately and unexpectedly empty pulpit in Patoka, Marion County: "The pastors appointed last fall all went to their places [in the Vandalia district] and all have stayed through the year, except E. L. Voight, who left Patoka at the end of seven months and returned to Kansas. Charles H. Thrall has completed the work of the year in a satisfactory manner."[615]

Later he served Methodist churches in southern, western, and central Illinois:

- St. Francisville, Lawrence County (1910–12)
- Toledo, Cumberland County (1912)
- Westfield, Clark County (1913–15)
- McLean, McLean County (1916–21)
- Bowen, Hancock County (1922–23)
- Quincy Grace, Adams County (1924–27)
- Pittsfield, Pike County (1928–29)
- Jacksonville Centenary, Morgan County (1930–33)
- Peoria St. John's, Peoria County (1934–39).

From 1940 until his retirement in 1954 he served as executive secretary of the Conference Board of Education and became a nationally known figure in the field of religious education.[616] In 1950 he and Gertrude were living in Bloomington, McLean County, Illinois.[617]

---

[615] "Vandalia District" report, *Minutes of the 54th Session of the Southern Illinois Conference, Methodist Episcopal Church, East St. Louis, 22 September–2 October 1905*, p. 63, image 69 of 478 (babel.hathitrust.org).

[616] "Charles H. Thrall," *Journal-Yearbook of the 145th Session, Central Illinois Conference of the United Methodist Church* (1968), p. 264. Date 1911 for St. Francisville from Paul and Chester Farthing, editors, *Philo History: Chronicles and Biographies of the Philosophian Literary Society of McKendree College* (Lebanon, Illinois: privately printed, 1911), 210.

[617] "Edith Thrall Dies; Was Veteran Teacher," *Daily Dispatch* (Moline, Illinois), Wednesday 14 June 1950, p. 4, col. 5.

Child of Charles Haven⁹ and Gertrude (Gerking) Thrall:

54   i. ROBERT MCDOWELL¹⁰ THRALL (*Charles H.⁹, Leonidas⁸, Worthy⁷, Eliphas⁶, Samuel⁵, John⁴⁻³, Timothy², William¹*) was born 23 September 1914 in Toledo, Cumberland County, Illinois, and died 11 April 2006 in Philadelphia. He married 3 September 1936 NATALIE ELIZABETH HUNTER.

Chapter 20

Ninth Generation

Harold Thrall–Elizabeth Schriber Family
parents at chapter 5

"His patient analysis of problems made him a desired and valuable counselor."

20. **Harold Leonidas**[9] **Thrall** (*Leonidas*[8], *Worthy*[7], *Eliphas*[6], *Samuel*[5], *John*[4-3], *Timothy*[2], *William*[1])
Birth: 13 November 1885 in Metropolis, Massac County, Illinois
Death: 8 April 1966 in Galva, Henry County, Illinois[618]
Burial: Mount Hope Cemetery and Mausoleum, Urbana, Champaign County, Illinois[619]
Spouse: **Elizabeth Schriber,** married 9 May 1911 in Chicago[620]
Spouse's parents: Chas. [Matthew Carl] and Elizabeth (Joss) Schriber
Spouse's birth: 12 November 1884 in Franklin Grove, Lee County, Illinois[621]
Spouse's death: 9 July 1979 in Urbana, Champaign County, Illinois
Spouse's burial: with her husband[622]

---

[618] "Harold L. Thrall," *Journal-Yearbook, Central Illinois Conference of the Methodist Church, 143rd session, Jacksonville 12–16 June 1966*, pp. 941–42.

[619] Harold Leonidas Thrall grave marker, no digital image or source, Mount Hope Cemetery and Mausoleum, Urbana, Champaign County, Illinois, memorial #178,750,534 by Jeanette (findagrave.com).

[620] Rosalie Thrall Carmichael, "Thrall Genealogy," in author's possession, tub 2, folder 34.

[621] Female child born to Chas. and Elizabeth (Joss) Schriber, Franklin Grove, Lee County, Illinois, certified copy of birth report to Illinois State Board of Health. Also, Elizabeth Rose Thrall, Illinois birth certificate #4639, 15 September 1918. Both in author's possession.

[622] Elizabeth Schriber Thrall grave marker, no image or source, Mount Hope Cemetery and Mausoleum, Urbana, Champaign County, Illinois, memorial #178,750,767 by Jeanette (findagrave.com).

Elizabeth

The youngest child of Swiss emigrants, she grew up in semi-rural Lee County, Illinois, and later in Chicago. She graduated from the city's North-West Division High School 25 June 1903, in a class of 87, roughly two-thirds of whom were women. Also in her class was lifelong close friend Elsie M. Johnson, a skilled photographer and frequent visitor.[623]

Elizabeth attended college with the support of her mother and sisters. After graduating from Lewis Institute (now Illinois Institute of Technology) and Northwestern University in 1907, Elizabeth taught high school mathematics in Sycamore, DeKalb County, Illinois.[624] She met her future husband in their New Testament Greek class.[625]

In advance of the wedding Elizabeth became acquainted with various members of the Thrall family. Her soon-to-be sister-in-law Enola (Keisling) Thrall wrote about 1910:

> At last I met Elizabeth. She came out to 10554 S. Leavitt St. [far south side of Chicago] with Edith [Edith Laura Thrall?] to keep me company while Dearie [William F. Thrall] went to Decatur on business. She is very charming. I like her, who could help it. She is somewhere between Carrie and me in height and rather slender in figure; she has brown eyes and brown hair exactly the shade of Rosalie's. She puts it up and it strays down in little kinkles around her face; her cheeks are rosy and she has a pretty little dimple that peeps

---

[623] "Graduating Exercises," June 25, 1903, North-West Division High School, Chicago, including names of all graduates; in author's possession, tub 7, folder 229. Also, postcard from Elizabeth reporting death of Elsie's sister Etta, headed "Fri. 4 pm" and postmarked Altona, Illinois, 9 September, therefore almost certainly from 1960, and stating they had been friends for 60 years; tub 2, folder 60. Elsie was born about October 1884 in Wisconsin to Wesley and Julia [–?–] Johnson; siblings were Arthur (21 in 1900), Etta (17), and Leroy (12); Wesley Johnson household, 1900 US census, Chicago, Cook County, Illinois, Ward 15, ED 467, sheet 6B, dwelling 83, family 133.

[624] Rosalie Thrall Carmichael, "Thrall Genealogy," in author's possession, tub 2, folder 34.

[625] "Elizabeth (Schreiber) Thrall 1884–1979," *Official Journal-Yearbook of the Central Illinois Conference of the United Methodist Church, 1980*, pp. 2451–52.

out now and then when she smiles. Hal is making no mistake in his choice, the only mistake is the delay.[626]

A family story has it that Elizabeth was at first a bit shy of the bustling, chuckling, practical-joking Thrall brothers. One of her new sisters-in-law explained that while they might pick on one another in fun, they would never do anything that would embarrass one another in public.

Elizabeth was remembered as "a full partner with her husband in the ministry, joining in the pastoral calling, leading Sunday School classes, Bible School and women's church organizations. Her capacity for establishing warm, loving relationships with people, and for understanding and responding to their needs, made her much loved in each community they served."[627]

She surely loved justice and mercy," recalled Rev. Paul Unger at her memorial service.

> She saw these things as issues of simple fairness. . . . She lived through lots of social and cultural changes in her years and she stayed current with them all, always applying this measure of justice, 'Is it fair, or not?' Through questions of raising children and generational conflict, to questions of racial equality and international relations she applied the question of fairness. She hated harsh words but she could deal with the tough issues of justice and equality, and in the 60's, she, too, got around to reading the Autobiography of Malcolm X and understood the issues there, too.[628]

---

[626] Rosalie (Thrall) Carmichael postscript to Colin Carmichael letter to Elizabeth (Thrall) Henderson, 19 February 1968; in author's possession, tub 4, item 131.

[627] "Elizabeth (Schreiber) Thrall 1884-1979," *Official Journal-Yearbook of the Central Illinois Conference of the United Methodist Church*, *1980*, 2451–52.

[628] Rev. Paul Unger, "Meditation," at memorial service 12 July 1979; in author's possession.

She outlived all her siblings, most of her cousins, and her husband (by thirteen years). That experience may have prompted her to ask that William Cullen Bryant's poem "To A Waterfowl" be read at her funeral.[629] The poet watches a solitary migrating bird cross the sunset into the dark, "wandering, but not lost," and in the final stanza reflects:

> He, who, from zone to zone,
> Guides through the boundless sky thy certain flight,
> In the long way that I must trace alone,
> Will lead my steps aright.[630]

Harold

Harold "entered McKendree College in the fall of 1899 and graduated in 1905, receiving the degree of A.B. After teaching a year he entered Garrett Biblical Institute. There he completed his theological course and received the degree of S.T.B. in 1909. While he was in McKendree he was a member of the Philosophian Society."[631]

He helped initiate the first Epworth League Institute (later MYF Summer Camps) in the conference, and carried out the first Booth Festival (later "The Festival of Sharing"). "For many years he was chairman of the Conference Board of Qualifications, and later was Vice Chairman of the Board of Ministerial Training. As part of this work, he was responsible for giving counsel and guidance to local pastors . . . . His patient analysis of problems not only fitted him for this task, but also made him a desired and valuable counselor in his various charges."[632]

---

[629] Funeral program, memorial service for Elizabeth Schriber Thrall, 12 July 1979, Wesley United Methodist Church, Urbana, Illinois; in author's possession, tub 2, folder 59.
[630] *Poetry Foundation* (poetryfoundation.org/poems/51861/to-a-waterfowl).
[631] *Centennial McKendree College with St. Clair County History* (Lebanon, Illinois: McKendree College, 1928), 384.
[632] "Harold L. Thrall," *Journal-Yearbook, Central Illinois Conference of the Methodist Church, 143rd session*, 941–42.

"His keen sense of justice and his analytical mind prompted his father [Leonidas] to say, 'Harold would make a fine lawyer and judge.' However his choice was to dedicate himself to the gospel ministry."[633]

Harold became a "local preacher" in the Southern Illinois Conference 22 June 1905, and was admitted "on trial" a year later. During this time he was a "supply" (substitute) pastor in both northern and southern Illinois: at Vernon, Lake County (four months); West Salem, Edwards County (three months); South Elgin, Kane County (seven months); and Grayslake, Lake County (one year). After admission to full connection he and Elizabeth served at:

- Noble, Richland County (1909–11)
- Weedman, McLean/Dewitt County (1911–13), about 3½ hours south of Chicago on the Illinois Central Railroad. Elizabeth (four months married) wrote to her mother and sisters, "It must be a tiny place, but pays $800 a year, with a good parsonage of 6 rooms, garden & stables. It is a two point circuit so we are to keep our horse . . . . I enjoyed the morning service at conf[erence] which is all I have attended so far. Say it sounded good to hear the roll call: L. W. Thrall–V. W. Thrall–C. H. Thrall–H. L. Thrall & to hear 'Present' after each one."
- Gifford (Penfield), Champaign County (1913–15)
- Sadorus, Champaign County (1915–19), where Elizabeth was born
- Cisco, Piatt County (1919–23), where Miriam was born
- Mansfield, Piatt County (1923–27), where Jim was born
- Newman, Douglas County (1927–29)
- San Jose, Mason County (1929–34)
- Tolono, Champaign County (1934–38)
- Weldon, DeWitt County (1938–43)
- Lincoln Church, Danville, Vermilion County (1943–45)
  - Galva, Henry County (1945–58), an exceptionally long tenure, which for some years included both of the two Methodist churches in the town

---

[633] Rosalie (Thrall) Carmichael, "Thrall Genealogy" (17-page typescript on onion skin in red binder, by Rosalie although no author is named), 15; in author's possession, tub 2, item 34.

- Altona, Knox County (1958–61?)[634] after retirement

When they left Galva his parishioners took up a collection for a parting gift. The money kept coming in, and the congregation was able to present him with a new 1958 Chevrolet. After his official retirement he served in Altona at least three more years, then retired in Galva.

In the late 1920s he wrote in the same vein as brother Victor:

> Most of the changes now taking place in religion point . . . toward a higher standard of service by the church. . . . they are in harmony with the teachings of Jesus who so frequently likened the Kingdom of God to changing, growing things such as the mustard seed and the leaven. . . . Closely related to the growth of the spirit of tolerance is another change which may be realized in part in the not distant future. This is the unity of the church both spiritually and organically. . . . as church unites with church we may expect to see some needed simplification of doctrinal statements and some improvements in ecclesiastical organization. Unnecessary doctrinal requirements and cumbersome church machinery cannot easily pass over into the new unit created by the union of churches."[635]

His widow Elizabeth remembered him about 1975:

---

[634] Typed version of handwritten H. L. Thrall timeline, prepared at Fosters summer 1961. Also, local preacher's license for Harold L. Thrall 22 June 1905. Also, H. L. Thrall handwritten notes on a letter from General Board of Pensions. Also, Elizabeth Schriber Thrall letter to "Mother & Sisters," 20 September 1911, one page, both sides, incomplete. All in author's possession.

[635] "Changes in the Church are Vitally Necessary to Progress, Rev. Thrall of Newman Declares," newspaper clipping (typeface suggests *Chicago Tribune*?), definitely 1927–29 as he is identified as pastor at Newman, Illinois; in author's possession, tub 1, folder 17.

He was intellectual and informed, but never pedantic. He prepared his sermons carefully through the week; on Saturday nights he wrote the sermon and fixed the outline in his mind, but on Sunday he preached without notes. He had a fine voice and delivery, and his sermons were practical and personal, based on Biblical background. One lady complained that, "The new preacher just stood and talked to us, -- I wanted him to holler and pound the Bible," but she later said to a mutual friend, "I like those Thralls – they're just as common as we are."

He had the gift of having and expressing good will for people even while hating and fighting their sins. A saloon keeper in a town where Harold was, as usual, fighting the liquor interest, said, "That Mr. Thrall is the only minister in town who speaks to me!" He radiated kindness and happiness. A doctor once said to him, "I like you to call on my patients. They are always better after your visits!" A former pastor, after leaving Galva, wrote to a friend there saying, "You will like your new minister. If he should call on you on a dark gloomy day, you will feel that the sun has just burst out."

He was one of the kindest, most considerate men one could live with, and was possessed of a quiet sense of humor which we all enjoyed, as it never held any barbs.[636]

Children of Harold Leonidas[9] and Elizabeth (Schriber) Thrall:

i. CHARLES FRANKIE[10] THRALL (*Harold L.[9], Leonidas[8], Worthy[7], Eliphas[6], Samuel[5], John[+3], Timothy[2], William[1]*) was born 20 June 1916

---

[636] "Harold Leonidas Thrall," typescript by his widow, Elizabeth (Schriber) Thrall, about 1975, nine years after his passing. In author's possession, tub 1, item 8.

and died the next day.⁶³⁷ The family story has it that since the baby was a month early, Elizabeth suggested that it might make sense to create a warm dark environment for him; the doctor disagreed.

55   ii. ELIZABETH ROSE¹⁰ THRALL (*Harold L.⁹, Leonidas⁸, Worthy⁷, Eliphas⁶, Samuel⁵, John⁴⁻³, Timothy², William¹*) was born 15 September 1918 in Sadorus, Champaign County, Illinois; and died 18 May 2008 in St. Joseph County, Indiana. She married 6 March 1943 at Wesley Foundation, University of Illinois, Urbana, Champaign County, RONALD ATHOL HENDERSON.

56   iii. MIRIAM RUTH¹⁰ THRALL (*Harold L.⁹, Leonidas⁸, Worthy⁷, Eliphas⁶, Samuel⁵, John⁴⁻³, Timothy², William¹*) was born 20 March 1921 in Cisco, Piatt County, and died 7 April 2010 in Urbana, Champaign County. She married 29 May 1943 at Wesley Foundation, University of Illinois, Urbana, Champaign County, GEORGE NORTON FOSTER.

57   iv. HAROLD JAMES "JIM"¹⁰ THRALL (*Harold L.⁹, Leonidas⁸, Worthy⁷, Eliphas⁶, Samuel⁵, John⁴⁻³, Timothy², William¹*) was born 15 June 1925 in Mansfield, Piatt County, Illinois; died 20 October 2018 in Plymouth, Marshall County, Indiana; and was buried 27 October at Southlawn Cemetery, South Bend, St. Joseph County, Indiana. He married 29 January 1948 in Galva, Henry County, Illinois, JOAN E. WALKER.

---

⁶³⁷ "Mr. Thrall" entry, "Illinois, Deaths and Stillbirths Index, 1916–1947," FHL 1,530,532, image 1589, reference #2973. The index has him born 20 June 1916, died 22 June, buried 23 June in Sadorus Cemetery (Champaign County, Illinois). His memorial #112,338,738 (findagrave.com) does not give an image of his grave marker, and cites the index as its source. Sadorus Cemetery has an on-line list of burials (SW of town) on line, and the information there (https://peoplelegacy.com/cemetery/sadorus_cemetery-7A2q) refers to "Charles Frankie Thrall." So it may derive from the stone itself even though the site has none of the hallmarks of a local project, and many of the hallmarks of artificially "harvested" data. Note also an unnamed and so far unviewed Sadorus doctor's ledger 1892–1918, now held in the University of Illinois, "Illinois History and Lincoln Collections," 324 Main Library, 1408 West Gregory Drive, Urbana, 217/333-1777(https://www.library.illinois.edu/ihx/archon/?p=collections/controlcard&id=19 1).

Story 4: Horse and Buggy from Noble to Weedman, 1911

The 1978 drought in central Illinois put 93-year-old Elizabeth (Schriber) Thrall in mind of a drought sixty-seven years earlier. In 1911, she and her newly wedded husband were due to move 135 miles (a two-hour car trip in 2019) from Noble, Richmond County, Illinois, to his new charge in Weedman, on the DeWitt and McLean county line. She hesitated to write, but then recalled how she and her sisters begged for any crumb their aged mother might remember. She picked up her pen and wrote:

> Whatever rain had fallen that summer had missed Noble until the night before we were to drive northward. We heard sprinkles falling thru our tall pine on to our roof, then more & more until it was a regular deluge! All thru the night!
>
> The next day we were invited to eat supper & spend the night at a member's home about 10 mi. on our way north. It was a delightful spot, but the rain continued. Roads were flooded & everything else was *mud*! My shoes were heavy to walk in! The creek that we needed to cross was out of banks, & the farmer's big son rode his horse, swimming part way, out into it, to locate the best crossing & then had us follow with horse & buggy. If I were in that buggy now for that ride, I'd be scared. But *then* it was exhilarating!
>
> That eve as we ate supper in a little town (now forgotten) Harold asked a man how the road north would be. "Well," he said, "it might be pretty wet, but you can make it." So we did.
>
> It was a beautiful full moon shining down on what seemed almost a sea of water. The field posts were half covered in water from side to side of the wagon road, & the only sound we heard except our own breathing was the splash, splash of Dixie's hooves as he steadily walked thru the water. . . .

I held our suit case over the back of our seat, & put my feet up against the dash board as the water crept in over the floor. If Harold was worried that we might strike a hole or have any trouble elsewise, he never said anything about it, & *I*—well, *I* was with my strong & perfect husband, why would *I* be afraid of anything!

Friday night maybe 8 or 9 o'clock we figured we might be within 5 or 6 miles of Weedman, when Harold noticed a sign tucked up a tree. With the help of his lantern he read "bridge out"! "Well," he said with a sigh, "You hold Dixie & I'll walk back to that house we passed a bit ago & see what can be done."

The night was black, & everything still until a long mournful "Moooooo" almost lifted me from the buggy! It was only a cow! Harold came back. "Farmer said we better spend the night with them."

Such a quiet well cared for household I had never seen before & don't expect to again. At breakfast there were Daddy & Mother & 12 children. Dad & Mom each had one on lap, older children looked after younger, & after the meal each one on foot had a special job. One put the chairs back against the wall, one took out flatware, one cups, one plates etc. etc. As the Dad explained, "Every Little helps a little." The family name was Little. . . . When Harold wanted to pay for our lodging & breakfast they said, "No, indeed," they were members of his church & they were glad to have had the chance to help! . . .

Weedman housed the dear little white steeple church, parsonage, on a slight rise of land, 2 neighbor houses across the road, Post office . . . across the tracks, a house up the hill & other side of tracks (I.C. [Illinois Central Railroad]) & a house in a field nearby, back of parsonage (where we use to go for eggs & milk).[638]

---

[638] Elizabeth Schriber Thrall, "On our way from Noble to Weedman," 7 August 1978 manuscript; copy in author's possession.

Chapter 21

Ninth Generation

Mary Virginia Thrall–David Solomon Cover Family
parents at chapter 5

"A cultural influence through work in Illinois Woman's Club and local mission and reading circles"

21. MARY VIRGINIA^9 THRALL (*Leonidas^8, Worthy^7, Eliphas^6, Samuel^5, John$^{4-3}$, Timothy^2, William^1*)
Birth: 17 March 1902 in Lebanon, St. Clair County, Illinois
Death: March 1976, last residence Tunnel Hill, Johnson County, Illinois[639]
Burial: Not found
Spouse: **DAVID SOLOMON COVER,** married 31 July 1922[640]
Spouse's parents: William Henry and Pernecie "Necy" (Whittenberg) Cover[641]
Spouse's birth: 23 July 1899 in Illinois[642]

---

[639] Mary Cover entry, US Social Security Death Index.
[640] "Marriage Licenses," *Belleville News Democrat* (Illinois), Monday 31 July 1922, p. 1, col. 6.
[641] William Henry Cover–Necy Whittenberg marriage license #410, 3 October 1895, marriage 6 October, Johnson County, Illinois, marriage register 1 (1878–96):234; FHL 964,811 item 1, DGS 7,621,3090, image 246 of 589 (familysearch.org). William was a miller and farmer. They were married in Tunnel Hill, where they both lived; R. W. Laughlin, Minister of the Gospel, presided; witnesses were W. E. Gallener and S. Whitehead. Necy was 31, William 45; it was said to be the first marriage for both. Some indexes have the groom's surname as "Coner."
[642] David Solomon Cover WWI draft card, 12 September 1918, local board Vienna, Johnson County, Illinois, serial #983, order #A120; "US, World War I Draft Registration Cards, 1917–1918" > Illinois > Johnson County > Draft Card C > image 175 of 218 (ancestry.com). Also, William H. Hover [Cover] household for son David S., 1900 US census, Tunnel Hill Township, Johnson County, Illinois, ED 44, sheet 19A, dwelling/family 277.

Spouse's death: March 1970 in Illinois[643]
Spouse's burial: Not found

In 1918 David was farming; his nearest relative was Necy Cover (his mother); and he was tall and slender, with brown eyes and hair.[644] In June 1920 Mary Virginia, who had been at Jennings Seminary in Aurora, was staying at the G. W. Gerking home in Lebanon.[645]

When they were licensed to marry at the end of July 1922, David was 23, of Tunnel Hill, Johnson County, Illinois, and Virginia was 20, of Lebanon, St. Clair County, Illinois.[646] They both completed three years of college.[647] In 1930 David owned the farm in Tunnel Hill and they had a radio set; his mother-in-law Emily J. Thrall was with the family, age 65.[648]

In the summer of 1935 he was taking the "Keeley cure" at Dwight, Livingston County, Illinois.[649] On New Year's Eve 1935–36 he survived a collision with a Big Four freight train.[650] In 1940 the family was farming

---

[643] David Cover entry, US Social Security Death Index.

[644] David Solomon Cover WWI draft card, serial #983, order #A120, 12 September 1918, local board Vienna, Johnson County, Illinois; "US, World War I Draft Registration Cards, 1917–1918" > Illinois > Johnson County > Draft Card C > image 175 of 218 (ancestry.com).

[645] "Lebanon," *Belleville News Democrat* (Illinois), Thursday 17 June 1920, p. 5, col. 3.

[646] "Marriage Licenses," *Belleville News Democrat* (Illinois), Monday 31 July 1922, p. 1, col. 6.

[647] D. S. Cover household, 1940 US census, Tunnel Hill Township, Johnson County, Illinois, ED 44-14, sheet 11B, dwelling 210.

[648] David S. Cover household, 1930 US census, Tunnel Hill Township, Johnson County, Illinois, ED 14, sheet 7B, dwelling 147, family 148.

[649] Elizabeth (Schriber) Thrall letter to her sisters in Chicago, 19 July 1935; transcribed #30, p. 56, in privately printed booklet, "Schriber and Thrall Letters to Family: Windows on the Past," in author's possession.

[650] "Car Hits Train; 3 Hurt," *Rockford Morning Star* (Illinois), Thursday 2 January 1936, p. 7, col. 1. The family story is that he gave up drinking afterwards.

in Tunnel Hill and their house was valued at $1500,[651] well below the Illinois statewide average of $3277.[652]

> Virginia Thrall Cover attended college in Lebanon and in Naperville, Illinois. She married Dave Cover, an electrical engineer, who chose later to return to his inherited farm near Tunnel Hill in southern Illinois. There Virginia played the organ in the Methodist Church, taught in the church school, was active in Bible School work, and became a cultural influence through work in Illinois Woman's Club and local mission and reading circles.
>
> Dave Cover was a pioneer cattle man and a Conservation District director. He was an innovator. He started in the mid 30's during the Depression by improving 40 acres by liming and spreading rock phosphate on a 40-acre field. With the advent of fescue, he and his son rapidly expanded their operation by improving one field after another.[653]

Children of Mary Virginia^9 (Thrall) and David Cover:

58   i. WILLIAM HENRY^{10} COVER (*Mary Virginia Thrall^9, Leonidas^8, Worthy^7, Eliphas^6, Samuel^5, John$^{4-3}$, Timothy^2, William^1*) was born in Tunnel Hill, Johnson County, Illinois, 15 August 1923, died 6 February 1986 at Jewish Hospital, St. Louis; and was buried in New Salem Cemetery, north of Tunnel Hill, three days later. He married 22 November 1950 in Sandusky, Erie County, Ohio, RUTH ALICE PALMER.

---

[651] D. S. Cover household, 1940 US census, Tunnel Hill Township, Johnson County, Illinois, ED 44-14, sheet 11B, dwelling 210.

[652] Statewide figures from US Census Bureau, Census of Housing, Historical Census of Housing Tables, Median Home Values Unadjusted 1940 (census.gov/hhes/www/housingcensus /historic/values.html).

[653] Rosalie (Thrall) Carmichael, "Thrall Genealogy" (17-page typescript on onion skin in red binder, by Rosalie Thrall Carmichael although no author is named), 17; in author's possession, tub 2, item 23A.

59   ii. DAVID LEONIDAS ^{10} COVER (*Mary Virginia Thrall^9, Leonidas^8, Worthy^7, Eliphas^6, Samuel^5, John$^{4-3}$, Timothy^2, William^1*) was born in Lebanon, St. Clair County, Illinois, 17 May 1925; died 8 March 1990 in New Burnside, Johnson County, Illinois; and was buried with military rites on the 11th at New Salem Cemetery in Johnson County. He married first in 1951 BILLIE JEAN TAAKE, and second as her second husband 5 December 1973 in Vienna, Johnson County, Illinois, AVA MARIE (SIMMONS) GODDARD.

Chapter 22

Tenth Generation

Edgar Morgan–Addie Gould Family
parents at chapter 6

Twelve children

22. EDGAR ALSINIUS/ANSEL^{10} MORGAN (*Milton Worthy Morgan^9, Mary Elizabeth Thrall^8, Worthy^7, Eliphas^6, Samuel^5, John$^{4-3}$, Timothy^2, William^1*)
Birth: 2 August 1875 in Bone Gap, Edwards County, Illinois
Death: 17 April 1925 at 2213 East Virginia Street, Evansville, Vanderburgh County, Indiana, of myocarditis[654]
Burial: Bone Gap Cemetery[655]
Spouse: **ADELE "ADDIE" GOULD,** married 28 January 1897 at her father's place in Bone Gap[656]
Spouse's parents: Ansel and Serena A. (Marriott) Gould[657]
Spouse's birth: 4 October 1878 in Illinois

---

[654] Edgar A. Morgan obituary information from Evansville newspaper, *Browning Genealogy Evansville, Indiana Obituary Search* (browning.evcpl.lib.in.us).

[655] Edgar A. Morgan grave marker 1875–1925, image, Bone Gap Cemetery, Bone Gap, Illinois, memorial #140,868,926 by Janice (Teel) Crites (findagrave.com).

[656] Edgar A. Morgan–Addie Gould marriage #2604, license 23 January 1897, marriage 28 January, Edwards County Register of Marriages D:153; "Illinois County Marriages, 1810–1940" FHL 1,401,780, DGS 4,661,397, image 359 of 654 (familysearch.org). Addie's paternal line *may* have been Ansel, Philander, Ebenezer, Aaron, Jeremiah, and Samuel II (1701–1790); Solon's may have been Freeman, Nathan Jr., Nathan Sr., and Samuel II (1701–1790). Testing these conjectures is beyond the scope of this book.

[657] Addie Morgan death certificate, Indiana 63-012052, 6 March 1963; "Indiana, Death Certificates 1899–2011" > Certificate > 1963 > 05 > image 2061 of 2510 (ancestry.com). Unsourced family tree, "Ancestors of Addie Claudia Morgan," by Carol Ann Lyle, circa 1997, in author's possession.

Spouse's death: 6 March 1963 of hypertension and cardiovascular disease, at 616 Reis Avenue in Evansville[658]
Spouse's burial: with her husband[659]

In 1880 five-year-old Edgar was living in Albion with his grandmother Elizabeth and aunt "Lucretea."[660] In 1885 Edgar was not present in his father's Nebraska household.[661]

Addie and Edgar had at least twelve children.[662] Edgar had a variety of occupations both before and after the family moved to the city of Evansville about 1914:

> **1897:** teacher at the time of their marriage[663]
> **1900:** farmer[664]
> **1910:** bank cashier[665]

---

[658] Addie Morgan death certificate, Indiana 63-012052, 6 March 1963; "Indiana, Death Certificates 1899–2011" > Certificate > 1963 > 05 > image 2061 of 2510 (ancestry.com). Also, Ansel Gould household, 1880 US census, Albion Precinct, Edwards County, Illinois, ED 7, p. 68D, dwelling 601, family 612. The two-year-old daughter was called "Floy" that year.

[659] Addie Morgan obituary information from Evansville newspaper, *Browning Genealogy Evansville, Indiana Obituary Search* (browning.evcpl.lib.in.us). Also, Addie Morgan grave marker 1878–1963, image, Bone Gap Cemetery, Bone Gap, Illinois, memorial #140,869,006 by Janice (Teel) Crites (findagrave.com).

[660] Elizabeth Morgan household for "son" [grandson] Edgar age 4, 1880 US census, Albion, Edwards County, Illinois, ED 7, p. 424D, dwelling 565, family 574.

[661] M. W. Morgan household for Amanda age 21 and Myrtle age 1, 1885 Nebraska state census, Burnett Village, Jefferson Precinct, Madison County, Nebraska, p. 4, dwelling/family 33.

[662] Addie Morgan obituary information from Evansville newspaper, in *Browning Genealogy Evansville, Indiana Obituary Search* (browning.evcpl.lib.in.us).

[663] Edgar A. Morgan–Addie Gould marriage #2604, license 23, January 1897, marriage 28 January, Edwards County Register of Marriages D:153; "Illinois County Marriages, 1810–1940," FHL 1,401,780, DGS 4,661,397, image 359 of 654 (familysearch.org).

[664] Edgar A. Morgan household, 1900 US census, Bone Gap, Edwards County, Illinois, ED 16, sheet 5B, dwelling/family 97.

[665] Edgar Morgan household, 1910 US census, Bone Gap, Edwards County, Illinois, ED 16, sheet 2A, dwelling/family 33. Also, "Evansville Deaths…Mrs. Nina Rodgers," *Evansville Courier* (Indiana), Tuesday 21 September 1976, p. 4, col. 1. Also, "Age and Youth Not Spared by the Reaper," *Evansville Courier* (Indiana), Sunday 24 September 1916, p. 16, col. 7.

1915: living at 220 Goodell in Evansville, a warehouseman for wholesale grocers Seitz Smith and Company (Lewis Seitz, a partner, lived in Mount Carmel, Wabash County, Illinois, and might have been known to the Morgans before their move to the city)[666]

1916: living at 427 East Illinois: a "coffee roaster" for Neas-Sanderson Company[667]

1917–18: solicitor for Public Savings Insurance Company [PSIC], moving from East Illinois to 1812 Reis Avenue[668]

1919: living at 1302 Reed: clerk for PSIC[669]

1920: "special police" at the opera house[670]

1922: "agent" for PSIC[671]

1924: he and Emil and Curtis Rohner incorporated the Mechanics' Mutual Finance Corporation in Evansville; Edgar was manager.[672] The enterprise continued after Edgar's death.[673]

---

[666] Edgar A. Morgan, *Evansville City Directory 1915* (Evansville: Bennett Directory Company, 1915), p. 540, image 282 of 566; Seitz Smith & Company, p. 685, image 356 of 566 (ancestry.com). Edgar does not appear in earlier years.

[667] Edgar A. Morgan, *Evansville City Directory 1916* (Evansville: Bennett Directory Company, 1916), p. 524, image 276 of 560 (ancestry.com).

[668] Edgar A. Morgan, *Evansville City Directory 1917* (Evansville: Bennett Directory Company, 1917), p. 498, image 256 of 532; PSIC, p. 498, image 284 of 532. Similarly, 1918, p. 524, image 281 of 558 (ancestry.com).

[669] Edgar A. Morgan, *Evansville City Directory 1919* (Evansville: Bennett Directory Company, 1919), p. 306, image 166 of 359 (ancestry.com).

[670] Edgar H. [A.] Morgan household, 1920 US census, Evansville, Vanderburgh County, Indiana, Ward 6, ED 147, sheet 1A, dwelling 7, family 8. Also, Edgar A. Morgan, *Evansville City Directory 1920* (Evansville: Bennett Directory Company, 1920), p. 288, image 152 of 335 (ancestry.com).

[671] Edgar A. Morgan, *Evansville City Directory 1922* (Evansville: Bennett Directory Company, 1922), p. 345, image 177 of 385 (ancestry.com).

[672] "New Loan Company Incorporates Here," *Evansville Journal* (Indiana), Friday 2 May 1924, p. 13, col. 2. Also, Edgar A. Morgan, *Evansville City Directory 1924* (Evansville: Bennett Directory Company, 1924), pp. 398–99, image 207 of 443 (ancestry.com). Son Lawson, then about 17, was bookkeeper.

[673] *Evansville City Directory 1926* (Evansville: Bennett Directory Company, 1926), p. 339, image 174 of 380 (ancestry.com).

Children of Edgar[10] and Addie (Gould) Morgan: first ten born in Illinois (probably in Bone Gap, Edwards County), and the rest born in Indiana (probably Evansville, Vanderburgh County)

> i. NINA G.[11] MORGAN (*Edgar A.[10], Milton W. Morgan[9], Mary E. Thrall[8], Worthy[7], Eliphas[6], Samuel[5], John[4-3], Timothy[2], William[1]*) was born 1 April 1898;[674] died 20 September 1976 in Evansville;[675] and was buried as Nina Kloke in the Lutheran Cemetery there.[676] She married first 10 February 1920 in Vanderburgh County[677] JOHN FREDERICK KLOKE, son of Philip and Frances (Diefenbach) Kloke.[678] He was born 20 June 1893 in Vanderburgh County, Indiana; died 7 June 1942 in Evansville of "cardio vascular renal disease"; and was buried at the Lutheran Cemetery there.[679] John completed eight years of school, Nina two years of high school. She was a machine operator in a cigar factory; he worked in a refrigerator factory. They owned a house at 616 Reis Avenue valued at $2500, just about the statewide

---

[674] Edgar A. Morgan household for daughter Nina born April 1898, 1900 US census, Bone Gap, Edwards County, Illinois, ED 16, sheet 5B, dwelling/family 97. Similarly, 1910 for daughter Nina age 12; 1920 for daughter Nina age 21. For exact birth date, Nina G. Rodgers death certificate, Indiana #76–033983, 20 September 1976; "Indiana, Death Certificates, 1898–2011" > Certificate > 1976 > 12 > image 993 of 3034 (ancestry.com).

[675] "Evansville Deaths…Mrs. Nina Rodgers," *Evansville Courier* (Indiana), Tuesday 21 September 1976, p. 4, col. 1.

[676] Nina Kloke (1898–1976) grave marker, image, Lutheran Cemetery, Evansville, Vanderburgh County, Indiana, memorial #22,687,842 by Kathy G. Current (findagrave.com).

[677] John Kloke–Nina Morgan marriage index entry, 10 February 1920 Vanderburgh County, Indiana; "Indiana, Select Marriages Index, 1748–1993" (ancestry.com).

[678] Unnamed stillborn son, 2 November 1923, Indiana birth certificate #61334, Vanderburgh County; "Indiana Birth Certificates 1907–1940" > 1923 > 025 > image 1349 of 2518 (ancestry.com). "Evansville Deaths…Mrs. Nina Rodgers," *Evansville Courier* (Indiana), Tuesday 21 September 1976, p. 4, col. 1.

[679] John Frederick Kloke death certificate, Indiana #19319, 7 June 1942; "Indiana, Death Certificates, 1899–2011" > Certificate > 1942 > 07 > image 2799 of 2979 (ancestry.com).

average of $2406.$[680] Nina married second about June 1943 ONIE/ORIE RODGERS; he predeceased her.[681]

ii. CLEMMA[11] MORGAN (*Edgar A.[10], Milton W. Morgan[9], Mary E. Thrall[8], Worthy[7], Eliphas[6], Samuel[5], John[4-3], Timothy[2], William[1]*) was born April 1900[682] and died 5 December 1973 in Evansville. She married 9 March 1920 in Henderson, Henderson County, Kentucky, HENRY HAUSCHILD.[683] He was born about 1901; in 1940 they lived at 2803 Franklin, in a house valued at $2,000 (slightly below the statewide average of $2406). He worked as a cab driver and Clemma as a cigar roller. They both completed eight years of school.[684]

iii. GRACE CLARINE[11] MORGAN (*Edgar A.[10], Milton W. Morgan[9], Mary E. Thrall[8], Worthy[7], Eliphas[6], Samuel[5], John[4-3], Timothy[2], William[1]*) was born about 1902[685] and died 1 September 1987 in

---

[680] John F. Kloke household, 1940 US census, Evansville, Vanderburgh County, Indiana, ED 93-54, sheet 3B, dwelling 63. Statewide figures from US Census Bureau, Census of Housing, Historical Census of Housing Tables, Median Home Values Unadjusted 1940 (census.gov/hhes/www/housing/census/historic/values.html).

[681] "Marriage Licenses," *Evansville Courier* (Indiana), Tuesday 15 June 1943, p. 8, col. 6. Nina's death certificate, for which her sister Mrs. Grace Burgdorf was informant, called her a widow at her death: Nina G. Rodgers death certificate, Indiana #76–033983, 20 September 1976; "Indiana, Death Certificates, 1898–2011" > Certificate > 1976 > 12 > image 993 of 3034 (ancestry.com).

[682] Edgar A. Morgan household for daughter Clema/Glenna born April 1900, 1900 US census, Bone Gap, Edwards County, Illinois, ED 16, sheet 5B, dwelling/family 97. Similarly, 1910 for daughter Clema/Glenna age 10; 1920 for daughter Clema/Glenna age 19.

[683] "Golden Anniversaries of Area Interest…The Hauschilds," *Sunday Courier and Press* (Evansville, Indiana), p. 13B, cols 1–3. Also, "Evansville Deaths…Mrs. Clemma Hauschild," *Evansville Courier* (Indiana), Thursday 6 December 1973, p. 7, cols. 1–2.

[684] Henry Houshild [Hauschild] household, 1940 US census, Evansville, Vanderburgh County, Indiana, ED 93-85A, sheet 2A, dwelling 24. Statewide figures from *United States Census Bureau*, Census of Housing, Historical Census of Housing Tables, Median Home Values Unadjusted 1940 (census.gov/hhes/www/housing/census/historic/values.html).

[685] Edgar Morgan household for daughter Grace age 8, 1910 US census, Bone Gap, Edwards County, Illinois, ED 16, sheet 2A, dwelling/family 33. Similarly, 1920 for daughter Grace age 18.

Evansville.⁶⁸⁶ She married farmer FREDERICK LOUIS BURGDORF, son of Adam and Louisa (Kuno) Burgdorf, who was born 13 November 1897 in Vanderburgh County, Indiana, and died there 16 February 1985.⁶⁸⁷ He completed four years of school, Grace seven.⁶⁸⁸

iv. FRANCIS E.^{11} MORGAN (*Edgar A.^{10}, Milton W. Morgan^{9}, Mary E. Thrall^{8}, Worthy^{7}, Eliphas^{6}, Samuel^{5}, John$^{4\text{-}3}$, Timothy^{2}, William^{1}*) was born about 1903⁶⁸⁹; died 2 November 1963 in Redondo Beach, Los Angeles County, California;⁶⁹⁰ and probably was buried as Francis Egbert at Fort Rosecrans National Cemetery in San Diego.⁶⁹¹ He lived in Evansville and Brazil, Indiana; served in the Navy in World War II; and married NEVELYN EDITH PERKINS,

---

⁶⁸⁶ "Deaths…Grace Burgdorf," *Evansville Courier* (Indiana), Wednesday 2 September 1987, p. 13, col. 1. She was survived by brother Marion Morgan of Cincinnati, and sisters Addie Moore of Youngstown, Mahoning County, Ohio, and Mildred Sims of Nevada City, Nevada County, California.

⁶⁸⁷ Frederick L. Burgdorf, Indiana death certificate 85:007352, 16 February 1985; "Indiana, Death Certificates 1899–2011" > Certificate > 1985 > 03 > image 1384 of 3054 (ancestry.com).

⁶⁸⁸ For schooling, Fred L. Burgdorf household, 1940 US census, Union Township, Vanderburgh County, Indiana, ED 82-16, sheet 2A, dwelling 140.

⁶⁸⁹ Edgar Morgan household for son Francis age 7, 1910 US census, Bone Gap, Edwards County, Illinois, ED 16, sheet 2A, dwelling/family 33. Similarly, 1920 for son Francis age 17.

⁶⁹⁰ "Evansville Deaths…Francis E. Morgan," *Evansville Courier* (Indiana), Monday 4 November 1963, p. 17, col. 2. He was survived by brothers Reis Morgan of West Palm Beach, Palm Beach County, Florida, "Larson" Morgan of Montclair, Essex County, New Jersey, and Edgar Morgan of Birmingham, Jefferson County, Alabama.

⁶⁹¹ Francis Egbert Morgan, no grave marker image, Fort Rosecrans National Cemetery, San Diego, California, plot A-A 1904, memorial #3,419,944 by US Veterans Affairs (findagrave.com). This unsourced entry gives a middle name, dates his birth at 17 September 1901 (a tight fit chronologically among the siblings), and names his wife as Alice I. Morgan. This is probably a bureaucratic transposition of names, as Alice I. Morgan's memorial names her as the wife of Francis Bryan Morgan and her burial plot bears no relation to that of Francis Egbert Morgan: Alice I. Morgan (1903–1963), no grave marker image, Fort Rosecrans National Cemetery, San Diego, California, plot T, 237, memorial #3,419,915 by US Veterans Affairs (findagrave.com).

daughter of Alfred and Stella (Thumier) Perkins, born 16 September 1915 in Evansville.[692]

v. EDGAR ANSEL[11] MORGAN (*Edgar A.[10], Milton W. Morgan[9], Mary E. Thrall[8], Worthy[7], Eliphas[6], Samuel[5], John[4-3], Timothy[2], William[1]*) was born 11 April 1904 in Grayville, White County, Illinois;[693] died at age 68 in Birmingham, Jefferson County, Alabama, 8 March 1973; and was buried at Forest Hill Cemetery there. [694] He married first soon after 20 September 1930, probably in Jefferson County, CLARA SOPHIA HUCK,[695] born 3 March 1909 in Perry Township, Vanderburgh County, Indiana, the daughter of Frederick and Christina (Kurz) Huck.[696] She died reportedly 23 July 1964 in

---

[692] "Evansville Deaths...Francis E. Morgan," *Evansville Courier* (Indiana), Monday 4 November 1963, p. 17, col. 2. Also, Nevelyn Edith Perkins birth certificate #57025, Evansville, Indiana; "Indiana, Birth Certificates 1907–1940" > 1915 > 017 > image 1019 of 6051 (ancestry.com). Also, "Deaths . . . The Rev. Alfred Perkins," *Evansville Press* (Indiana), Tuesday 17 October 1950, p. 28, col. 4, naming his daughter Nevelyn as a resident of Brazil, Clay County, Indiana.

[693] Edgar Ansel Morgan WW2 draft card, Birmingham, Alabama, local board 9, serial #T274, order #10636, 14 February 1942; "Draft Registration Cards for Alabama, 10/16/1940–3/31/1947" (fold3.com/image/605201652–53). Also, Edgar A. Morgan [Jr.] grave marker, image, Forest Hill Cemetery, Birmingham, Alabama, memorial #179,965,143 by RR (findagrave.com). Also, Edgar Morgan household for son Edgar Jr. age 6, 1910 US census, Bone Gap, Edwards County, Illinois, ED 16, sheet 2A, dwelling/family 33. Similarly, 1920, son Edgar A. Jr. age 15.

[694] "Evansville Deaths...Edgar Morgan," *Evansville Courier* (Indiana), Friday 9 March 1973, p. 15, col. 1. He was reportedly survived by brother Marion of Cincinnati and six sisters: Mrs. Nina Rodgers, Mrs. Clemma Hauschild, and Mrs. Grace Bergdorf of Evansville; Mrs. Hallein Kelley of Hemet, Riverside County, California; Mrs. Addie Moore of Hinsdale, Cook County, Illinois; and Mrs. Mildred Sims of Nevada City, Nevada County, California. Also, Edgar A. Morgan [Jr.] grave marker, image, Forest Hill Cemetery, Birmingham, Jefferson County, Alabama, memorial #179,965,143 by RR (findagrave.com).

[695] Edgar Ansel Morgan—Clara S. Huck, marriage license, bond, affidavit, and examination for venereal disease, each dated 20 September 1930, p. 332; "Alabama, County Marriage Records, 1805–1967" > Jefferson > 1930–1931 > image 1351 of 1918 (familysearch.org).

[696] Clara Sophia Huck, Indiana birth certificate #47962, 3 March 1909, Perry Township, Vanderburgh County; "Indiana, Birth Certificates, 1907–1940" > 1909 > 020 (ancestry.com).

Birmingham.[697] Edgar and Clara Sophia both completed four years of high school. In 1930 she was a student nurse at Protestant Deaconess Hospital & Home in Evansville, Vanderburgh County, Indiana.[698] In the late 1930s they moved around, living in Cincinnati 1935, Alabama 1936, Kentucky 1937, and renting at 199 Rock Ridge in Birmingham 1940 for $18 a month (telephone 9-8861), when Edgar was a draftsman for a "bridge works."[699] As of 14 February 1942, Edgar stood 6 feet tall and weighed 200 pounds, with blue eyes, black hair, and a scar underneath his left ear; he resided at 425 80th Street in Birmingham and worked for structural engineer C. A. Wilmore.[700]

In 1945 and 1948 he was in Evansville.[701] He was back in Birmingham by 1953, working as draftsman for Menefee & Smith.[702] In 1960 Edgar was a draftsman at 7829 Seventh Avenue South in Birmingham, residing at 7801; his wife was Clara H.[703]

---

[697] Mrs. Clara H. Morgan entry, obituary index Birmingham newspapers, *Birmingham News* (Alabama), 24 July 1964, p. 20 (http://bpldb.bplonline.org/db/obituaries). Original not viewed.

[698] Clara Huck entry, 1930 US census, Evansville, Vanderburgh County, Indiana, 5th Precinct, ED 26, sheet 19A, line 15.

[699] Edgar A. Morgan household, 1940 US census, Birmingham, Jefferson County, Alabama, ED 37-59, sheet 20A, dwelling 393.

[700] Edgar Ansel Morgan WW2 draft card, Birmingham, Alabama, local board 9, serial #T274, order #10636, 14 February 1942; "Draft Registration Cards for Alabama, 10/16/1940–3/31/1947" (fold3.com/image/605201652–53).

[701] Evansville, Indiana, directories for Edgar A. Morgan, *1945*, p. 507, image 256 of 573; and *1948*, p. 585, images 295 of 658.

[702] Birmingham, Alabama, directory for Edgar A. Morgan, *1953*, p. 753, image 383 of 937.

[703] Edgar A. Morgan entry, *Polk's Birmingham (Jefferson County, Alabama), City Directory 1960* (Richmond, Virginia: R. L. Polk & Co., 1960), p. 899, image 636 of 1281 (ancestry.com).

He apparently married second after 1964, as at his death his wife was named as MERLE [–?–].[704]

vi. LAWSON ALLYN[11] MORGAN (*Edgar A.*[10], *Milton W. Morgan*[9], *Mary E. Thrall*[8], *Worthy*[7], *Eliphas*[6], *Samuel*[5], *John*[4-3], *Timothy*[2], *William*[1]) was born reportedly 15 February 1907 in Illinois;[705] died reportedly 18 November 1970; and was buried at Fort Rosecrans National Cemetery, San Diego, California.[706] He married EVELYN MAY KELLEY, who was born 22 May 1907 in Rhode Island, died 24 December 1990, and was buried with her husband. Lawson completed two years of high school, Evelyn three.[707] In 1936 he was training at Camp Ross, Great Lakes Naval Training

---

[704] There is a Merle M. Morgan in the SSDI, born 10 May 1908 and died April 1996 in Birmingham. She changed her name in Social Security to Merle M. Morgan 21 February 1973, shortly before Edgar's death, and made a claim 20 March 1973, shortly afterwards. She is therefore probably his second wife. Renamed again to Bailey (possibly third husband?) 10 November 1976, and perhaps back to Morgan on SSDI. If this is correct, she was the daughter of Earnest and Willie [–?–] Hayne, per 1920 census. In 1940 this Merle was divorced from a Penn, living with her aforementioned parents, and working as a telephone operator in a hotel. Birmingham Public Library doesn't have her obituary under any of these names, unless at 1935 "Noyes" counts. More information at FHL 2,242,016, DGS 4,200,742, image 1664, Ref. ID 7255 C (familysearch.org). These matters deserve further study, beyond the scope of this book.

[705] Edgar Morgan household for son Lawson age 3, 1910 US census, Bone Gap, Edwards County, Illinois, ED 16, sheet 2A, dwelling/family 33. Similarly, 1920, for son Lawson A. age 13. Also, Lawson Allyn Morgan grave marker, no image, Fort Rosecrans National Cemetery, San Diego, plot A-A, 0, 1904, memorial #1,011,500 by US Veterans Affairs (findagrave.com).

[706] The Lawson buried in San Diego is probably the family member: his given middle name "Allyn" is unusual and was his grand-uncle's, and his death date falls between those of two brothers: on 4 November 1963 he was listed as a survivor of brother Francis ("Evansville Deaths…Francis E. Morgan," *Evansville Courier* [Indiana], Monday 4 November 1963, p. 17, col. 2), and on 8 March 1973 he was not listed as a survivor of Edgar Jr. ("Evansville Deaths…Edgar Morgan," *Evansville Courier* [Indiana], Friday 9 March 1973, p. 15, col. 1).

[707] Evelyn May Morgan grave marker, no image, Fort Rosecrans National Cemetery, San Diego, plot A-A, 0, 1904, memorial #1,011,198 by U. S. Veterans Affairs (findagrave.com). For birth surname Kelley: Lawson Allyn Morgan [Jr.]–Marla Kipp marriage index, 2 August 1956, Indiana, p. 272; "Indiana, Marriages, 1810–2001" (ancestry.com). Original not viewed. For Rhode Island birthplace and years of schooling: Lawson Morgan household, 1940 US census, Vallejo Township, Solano County, California, ED 98, sheet 10B, dwelling 249.

Station, in North Chicago, Lake County, Illinois.[708] In 1959 they were living at 19 Berkeley Place, Montclair, Essex County, New Jersey.[709]

vii. LESTER "REIS"[11] MORGAN (*Edgar A.[10], Milton W. Morgan[9], Mary E. Thrall[8], Worthy[7], Eliphas[6], Samuel[5], John[4-3], Timothy[2], William[1]*) was born about February 1909 in Illinois[710] and died 27 June 1966 in Princeton, Gibson County, Indiana.[711] He married 28 August 1928[712] CATHERINE HAZEL CRABTREE, who was born 1910 (reportedly 28 August) in Evansville, Vanderburgh County, Indiana; died 24 January 1994; and was buried at Royal Palm Beach Memorial Gardens, West Palm Beach, Palm Beach County, Florida.[713] Her parents were said to be John and Minnie (Parrott) Crabtree.

In 1940 Reis was "Pro Manager" at the "O'boro [Owensboro, Daviess County, Kentucky] Country Club"; they had both completed four years of high school and were renting at 308 Veatch Road for $15 a month.[714]

viii. HALLEIN M.[11] MORGAN (*Edgar A.[10], Milton W. Morgan[9], Mary E. Thrall[8], Worthy[7], Eliphas[6], Samuel[5], John[4-3], Timothy[2], William[1]*) was

---

[708] "Personals," *Evansville Press* (Indiana), Sunday 23 August 1936, p. 10, col. 2.

[709] Lawson A. Morgan entry, *Montclair, Caldwell, Essex Fells, Verona, Cedar Grove, Glen Ridge Directory* (Newark: Price-Hall, 1959), p. 348, image 194 of 387 (ancestry.com).

[710] Edgar Morgan household for son Reis age 1 2/12, 1910 US census, Bone Gap, Edwards County, Illinois, ED 16, sheet 2A, dwelling/family 33. Similarly,1920 for son Lester R. age 10.

[711] "Evansville Deaths…Reis Morgan," *Evansville Courier* (Indiana), Monday 27 June 1966, p. 18, col. 5. His residence was West Palm Beach, Florida.

[712] Katherine Crabtree–L. Reis Morgan marriage index entry, 28 August 1928, Indiana, p. 258; "Indiana Marriages, 1810-2001" (ancestry.com). Original not viewed.

[713] Catherine Morgan grave marker, image and obituary for "Catherine H. (Katie) Morgan" from unknown newspaper, Royal Palm Memorial Gardens, West Palm Beach, Florida, memorial #177,097,876 by Camille Harden Glancy.

[714] Reis Morgan household, 1940 US census, Upper Town, Daviess County, Kentucky, ED 30-42, sheet 14A, dwelling 308.

born about 1911 (possibly 8 August 1910)[715] and died 24 April 1986 in Hemet, Riverside County, California. She married HARRY KELLEY,[716] perhaps born about 1908.[717]

ix. MARION WILSON[11] MORGAN (*Edgar A.[10], Milton W. Morgan[9], Mary E. Thrall[8], Worthy[7], Eliphas[6], Samuel[5], John[4-3], Timothy[2], William[1]*) was born 7 September 1912[718]; died 19 December 1998; and was buried at Mount Moriah Cemetery, Withamsville, Clermont County, Ohio.[719] He married after 1940 CATHERINE M. "PAT" MEISE, who was born 17 January 1917 and died 31 December 1997.[720]

x. ADDIE CLAUDIA[11] MORGAN (*Edgar A.[10], Milton W. Morgan[9], Mary E. Thrall[8], Worthy[7], Eliphas[6], Samuel[5], John[4-3], Timothy[2], William[1]*)

---

[715] Edgar H. [A.] Morgan household for daughter "Hellen" age 9, 1920 US census, Evansville, Vanderburgh County, Indiana, Ward 6, ED 147, sheet 1A, dwelling 7, family 8. Also, Addie Morgan household for daughter Hallein M. age 19 born in Illinois, 1930 US census, Evansville, Vanderburgh County, Indiana, Ward 6, ED 33, sheet 10A, dwelling 233, family 250. Exact birth date, unsourced, from Brehm/LaPella family tree (lapella.net/wordchartmead.doc).

[716] "Deaths…Hallein Kelley," *Evansville Courier* (Indiana), Friday 25 April 1986, p. 18, col. 2.

[717] Approximate birth date, unsourced, from Brehm/LaPella family tree (lapella.net/wordchartmead.doc).

[718] Marion Wilson Morgan grave marker, image, Section 5 S, Row 9 19, Mount Moriah Cemetery, Withamsville, Clermont County, Ohio, memorial #167,023,974 by Charlegirl (findagrave.com). Also, Edgar H. [A.] Morgan household for son Marion W. age 7, 1920 US census, Evansville, Vanderburgh County, Indiana, Ward 6, ED 147, sheet 1A, dwelling 7, family 8. Also, Addie Morgan household for son Marion W. age 17 born in Illinois, 1930 US census, Evansville, Vanderburgh County, Indiana, Ward 6, ED 33, sheet 10A, dwelling 233, family 250.

[719] Marion Wilson Morgan grave marker, image, Mount Moriah Cemetery, Withamsville, Clermont County, Ohio, memorial #167,023,974 by Charlegirl (findagrave.com).

[720] "Obituaries . . . Morgan," *Cincinnati Enquirer*, Friday 2 January 1988, p. 21 or B6, col. 6. Also, Catherine M. Morgan grave marker, image, Mount Moriah Cemetery, Withamsville, Clermont County, Ohio, memorial #151,693,739 by Dudley Petty (findagrave.com). Marion was single in 1940: Addie Morgan household for son Marion W. Morgan, 1940 US census, Evansville, Vanderburgh County, Indiana, Councilmanic Zone 4, ED 93-53, sheet 5A, dwelling 93.

was born reportedly 10 December 1913[721] and died 22 December 1994, last residence Youngstown, Mahoning County, Ohio.[722] She married before 1939 (first-known child) JOHN BUTLER MOORE,[723] who was born 26 March 1916 and died 1999. Addie and John were buried together at Block A, Forest Lawn Memorial Park Cemetery, Youngstown, Mahoning County, Ohio.[724]

They both completed four years of high school and in 1940 were living with John's parents Henry and Edith at 1921 Everett in Youngstown.[725] John worked as a die maker for Fitzsimmons Coal and Steel there from 1936 to November 1940; as a machinist for Republic Iron and Steel there from November 1940 to July 1946; and as a machinist for United Air Lines in Cheyenne, Wyoming, from July 1946 to October 1947, when he applied to Colorado Steelworks.[726]

xi. ELLIS G.^{11} MORGAN (*Edgar A.^{10}, Milton W. Morgan^9, Mary E. Thrall^8, Worthy^7, Eliphas^6, Samuel^5, John$^{4\text{-}3}$, Timothy^2, William^1*) was

---

[721] Addie C. Moore entry, U.S. Social Security Death Index. Edgar H. [A.] Morgan household for daughter Addie age 6, 1920 US census, Evansville, Vanderburgh County, Indiana, Ward 6, ED 147, sheet 1A, dwelling 7, family 8. Also, Addie Morgan household for daughter Addie C. age 16 born in Illinois, 1930 US census, Evansville, Vanderburgh County, Indiana, Ward 6, ED 33, sheet 10A, dwelling 233, family 250.

[722] Addie C. Moore entry, US Social Security Death Index. She was also in Youngstown in 1987: "Deaths…Grace Burgdorf," *Evansville Courier* (Indiana), Wednesday 2 September 1987, p. 13, col. 1.

[723] Addie Morgan 6 March 1963 retyped obituary abstract from Evansville newspaper, *Browning Genealogy Evansville, Indiana Obituary Search* (browning.evcpl.lib.in.us). Mrs. John Moore of Portland, Ohio, was one of the daughters named. Also, Henry Moore household for Moore granddaughter age 1, 1940 US census, Youngstown, Mahoning County, Ohio, Ward 7, ED 96-144, sheet 4A, dwelling 69.

[724] Addie C. Moore and John B. Moore, joint grave marker, Block A, Forest Lawn Memorial Park Cemetery, Youngstown, Ohio, image, memorials #178,984,544 and #178,984,513 respectively, by J. Rupert (findagrave.com). Exact birth date from John's 1947 application for employment at the Colorado Fuel and Iron Corporation; "Colorado Steelworks Employment Records, 1887–1979" > 1920–1960 > Monteal–Myrick > Moore–Moormann > image 25 of 163 (ancestry.com).

[725] Henry Moore household, 1940 US census, Youngstown, Mahoning County, Ohio, Ward 7, ED 96-144, sheet 4A, dwelling 69.

[726] John B. Moore application for employment at the Colorado Fuel and Iron Corporation; "Colorado Steelworks Employment Records, 1887–1979" > 1920–1960 > Monteal–Myrick > Moore–Moormann > image 25 of 163 (ancestry.com).

born April 1916; died 23 September 1916 in Evansville, Vanderburgh County, Indiana, age five months; and was buried in Bone Gap, Edwards County, Illinois.[727]

xii. MILDRED EILEEN[11] MORGAN (*Edgar A.[10], Milton W. Morgan[9], Mary E. Thrall[8], Worthy[7], Eliphas[6], Samuel[5], John[4-3], Timothy[2], William[1]*) was born 30 March 1921[728] and reportedly died 18 March 2008, last residence Yuba City, Sutter County, California.[729] She married 12 January 1945 in Evansville, Vanderburgh County, Indiana, DALE DWIGHT SIMS,[730] son of Jesse D. and Maud [–?–] Sims.[731] Dale was born 17 October 1915 in Memphis, Saunders County, Nebraska,[732] and died 13 August 1971[733]

---

[727] "Age and Youth Not Spared by the Reaper," *Evansville Courier* (Indiana), Sunday 24 September 1916, p. 16, col. 7.

[728] Mildred Eileen Sims entry, US Social Security Death Index. Original not viewed. Also, Addie Morgan household for daughter Mildred E. age 9 born in Indiana, 1930 US census, Evansville, Vanderburgh County, Indiana, Ward 6, ED 33, sheet 10A, dwelling 233, family 250.

[729] Mildred Eileen Sims entry, US Social Security Death Index.

[730] Sergeant Sims arrived 12 January from Camp Blanding, Florida, for his Sunday 14 January wedding in Evansville: "Personals," *Evansville Courier and Press*, Friday 12 January 1945, p. 22, col. 1. Also, Mildred E. Sims obituary abstract, "US, Obituary Collection, 1930–Current" (ancestry.com). Original not viewed.

[731] Jesse D. Sims household for wife Maud and son Dale (age 4), Memphis village, Clear Creek Precinct, Saunders County, Nebraska, ED 150, sheet 1B, dwelling/family 13. In 1944 the father was called J. B.: "His Cousin's Photo in British Magazine," *Nevada Herald* (Missouri), Thursday 23 March 1944, p. 4, col. 2.

[732] "Marriage Licenses" including Dale Sims age 29, *Evansville Courier and Press*, Saturday 13 January 1945, p. 5, col. 8. Also, Dale Dwight Sims WW2 draft card, Evansville local board #3, 16 July 1945, serial #4721, order #409A; "WW2 Draft Registration Cards for Indiana, 10/16/1940–3/31/1947" (fold3.com/image/651545187). The reverse of the card is not in numerical sequence so the information there may not pertain to Dale.

[733] Dale D. Sims entry, US Social Security Death Index.

in Nevada County, California.[734] In 1966 and 1987 Mildred was living in Nevada City there.[735]

Dale served in the US Army from 11 January 1940 (prior to US involvement in World War II) to 12 July 1945.[736] but was required to register for the draft when he got home. As of 16 July 1945 he was six feet tall, weighed 165 pounds, with gray eyes, brown hair, and a scar on his left knee.[737]

During the war he served with the Alaska Scouts intelligence unit; in 1944 he was a sergeant living in a tent, evidently stationed on the islands of Attu and Kiska. At his death he resided in Grass Valley, Nevada County, California, where he chaired the mathematics department at Nevada Union High School.[738]

---

[734] Dale D. Sims entry, "California Death Index, 1940-1997" (ancestry.com). Original not viewed.

[735] "Evansville Deaths...Reis Morgan," *Evansville Courier* (Indiana), Monday 27 June 1966, p. 18, col. 5. Mrs. Dale Sims of Nevada City, California, survived him. Also, "Deaths...Grace Burgdorf," *Evansville Courier* (Indiana), Wednesday 2 September 1987, p. 13, col. 1. Grace was survived by sister Mildred Sims of Nevada City, California.

[736] Dale D. Sims entry, "US, Department of Veterans Affairs, BIRLS Death File, 1850–2010" (ancestry.com). His obituary claimed that he served beginning in 1936: "Dale D. Sims," *Sacramento Bee* (California), Tuesday 17 August 1971, p. B2 or 20, col. 8.

[737] Dale Dwight Sims WW2 draft card, Evansville local board #3, 16 July 1945, serial #4721, order #409A; "WW2 Draft Registration Cards for Indiana, 10/16/1940–3/31/1947" (fold3.com/image/651545187). The reverse of the card is not in numerical sequence so the information there may not pertain to Dale.

[738] "His Cousin's Photo in British Magazine," *Nevada Herald* (Missouri), Thursday 23 March 1944, p. 4, col. 2. Also, "Dale D. Sims," *Sacramento Bee* (California), Tuesday 17 August 1971, p. B2 or 20, col. 8.

Chapter 23

Tenth Generation

Myrtle Morgan–Christopher Collins Family
parents at chapter 6

Ranching and farming in Arizona Territory and Los Angeles County

23. MYRTLE BELL[10] **MORGAN** (*Milton W. Morgan*[9], *Mary E. Thrall*[8], *Worthy*[7], *Eliphas*[6], *Samuel*[5], *John*[4-3], *Timothy*[2], *William*[1])
Birth: 29 January 1884 in Nebraska[739]
Death: 15 June 1965 in San Bernardino, California[740]
Burial: Not found
Spouse: **CHRISTOPHER COLUMBUS COLLINS,** married as his second wife 10 May 1910 in Phoenix, Maricopa County, Arizona Territory[741]
Spouse's parents: Isaac McClendon and Mary Eliza (Wright) Collins[742]

---

[739] For month, year, and state of birth: Amanda Morgan household for daughter Myrtle age 16, 1900 US census, Bone Gap, Edwards County, Illinois, ED 16, sheet 9A, dwelling 167, family 170.

[740] Myrtle B. Morgan entry, 15 June 1965, California Death Index.

[741] Myrtle B. Morgan–Christopher C. Collins marriage license and certificate, 10 January 1910, Phoenix, Maricopa County, Arizona Territory, Marriage Licenses 8:24; "Arizona, County Marriage Records, 1865–1972" > Maricopa > Marriage Licenses > image 38165 of 86651 (ancestry.com). Minister Robert S. Fisher officiated. Witnesses were Mrs. Amanda M. Morgan (Myrtle's mother) and Ray L. Morgan (Myrtle's brother).

[742] Named as parents of James Wright Collins (age 70), Arizona death certificate #5494, 25 October 1948; "Arizona Death Records, 1887–1960" > Maricopa > 1940–1949 > image 424 of 22540 (ancestry.com). Also, I. M. Collins household for apparent son James age 8, 1880 US census, Cucamonga, San Bernardino County, California, ED 63, p. 52 (penned), dwelling/family 432. Also, Isaac M. Collins household, 1910 US census, Cartwright Precinct, Maricopa County, Arizona Territory, ED 55, sheet 3B, dwelling/family 57. Isaac and Mary's ages are fairly consistent.

Spouse's birth: 14 September 1874 in California
Spouse's death: 24 May 1949 in Los Angeles[743]
Spouse's burial: Not found

Sixteen-year-old Myrtle was with her mother Amanda Teachout Morgan in Bone Gap, Edwards County, Illinois, in 1900,[744] and a student in Lincoln, Lancaster County, Nebraska, in 1903 and 1905.[745] She completed three years of high school; Christopher had eight years of schooling.[746]

"Columbus C. Collins" married first in Maricopa County, Arizona Territory, 17 February 1904 Della G. Harrer.[747] As of 15 April 1910 (just before his second marriage) Christopher was a widowed "stock man" on a cattle ranch, living with his brother Thomas and sister-in-law Inez in

---

[743] Christopher Columbus Collins WWI draft card, serial #592, order #A1709, Yavapai County Local Board; "US, World War I Draft Registration Cards" > Arizona > Yavapai > Draft Card C > image 460 of 806 (ancestry.com). Christopher Columbus Collins, death index entry, California Death Index 1940–1997. Also, I. M. Collins household for apparent son Columbus age 6, 1880 US census, Cucamonga, San Bernardino County, California, ED 63, p. 52 (penned), dwelling/family 432. An unsourced "Millennium File" (ancestry.com) has Christopher born 14 September 1872 in Pomona, Los Angeles County, and dying 24 May 1948. (Sometimes people remember days and months better than years.)

[744] Amanda Morgan household for daughter Myrtle B. age 16, 1900 US census, Bone Gap, Edwards County, Illinois, ED 16 sheet 9A, dwelling 167, family 170.

[745] Amanda Morgan "wid. M. W." lived on the north side of Miller, first east of Warren in 1901, on the northwest corner of College and Fowler in 1903, and at 302 E. Adams in *1905; Hoye's City Directory of Lincoln* (Lincoln: Hoye Directory, 1901), p. 384, image 191 of 351 (ancestry.com). Similarly, 1903, p. 438, image 225 of 445; and 1905, p. 143, image 73 of 485. The Morgans were not found in 1906 or 1907. In 1905 University Place was enumerated separately within the Lincoln directory. Student Myrtle (1903) and Myrtle B. (1905) was at the same address as Amanda.

[746] Christopher Collins household, 1940 US census, Pomona, San Jose Township, Los Angeles County, California, ED 19-722, sheet 2B, dwelling 65.

[747] Columbus C. Collins–Della G. Harrer marriage license, certificate, and return, 16–17 February 1904, marriage licenses 5:30; "Arizona, County Marriage Records, 1865–1972" > Maricopa > Marriage Licenses > image 36263 of 86651 (ancestry.com). Rev. F. B. Fisher officiated; C. Burrows and M.A. Fisher witnessed. The wedding took place at "D. B. Harrer's," presumably her father's place.

Kirkland Valley, Yavapai County, Arizona Territory.[748] In 1920 Chris and Myrtle and three children and were farming in Wilson Precinct, Maricopa County, Arizona.[749]

By 1928 Christopher was in Pomona, Los Angeles County, California, working at a gas station on Valley Boulevard and living on Spadra.[750] In 1930 they lived in a $25-a-month rental and he was a farm laborer in Pomona.[751] In 1931 the family was at 445 North Park there, where one or more family members remained for the next 20 years; Christopher was a "ranchworker."[752] In 1940 they owned the place and rented part of it for $15 a month to daughter Ruth and family.[753] Except for 1945, when he was again a "rancher," Christopher had no occupation thereafter.[754] In 1948 he and Myrtle registered to vote, he as a Democrat, she as a Republican.[755] In 1951 Myrtle was identified as his widow, and remained at the same address in 1959.[756]

---

[748] Thomas A. Collins household for brother Christopher C., 1910 US census, Zonia [Kirkland Valley], Yavapai County, Arizona Territory, ED 123, sheet 14B, dwelling 377, family 404.

[749] Chris Collins household, 1920 US census, Wilson Precinct, Maricopa County, Arizona, ED 19, sheet 14B, dwelling 347, family 348.

[750] Christopher C. Collins, *Pomona…Directory 1928* (Los Angeles: Los Angeles Directory, 1928), p. 72, image 39 of 398 (ancestry.com).

[751] Christopher C. Collins household, 1930 US census, Pomona, Los Angeles County, California, ED 1453, sheet 1A, dwelling/family 12.

[752] Christopher C. Collins, *Pomona (California) City Directory 1931* (Los Angeles: Los Angeles Directory, 1931), p. 73, image 40 of 535 (ancestry.com). Each family member was listed. In 1934 he was a laborer: p. 62, image 35 of 394 (ancestry.com).

[753] Christopher Collins and Jacob Hepner households, 1940 US census, Pomona, San Jose Township, Los Angeles County, California, ED 19-722, sheet 2B, dwellings 65–66.

[754] Christopher C. Collins in Pomona city directories, variously titled: *1937–8*, p. 83, image 44 of 514; *1940*, p. 77, image 39 of 153; *1945*, p. 67, image 35 of 209; *1948*, p. 84, image 41 of 238 (ancestry.com).

[755] Christopher C. Collins and Mrs. Myrtle B. Collins at 445 North Park Avenue, Index to Register of Voters, Pomona City Precinct 8, Los Angeles County, California, 1948; "California, Voter Registrations 1900–1968" > Los Angeles County > 1948 > Roll 71 > image 1115 of 1249 (ancestry.com).

[756] Myrtle B. Collins entry, *Pomona City Directory 1951*, p. 85, image 80 of 898, and 1959, p. 49, image 69 of 564 (ancestry.com).

Chapter 24

Tenth Generation

Raymond Morgan–Ada Vensel Family
parents at chapter 6

Farmer and rubber worker

24. RAYMOND LEE[10] **MORGAN SR.** (*Milton W. Morgan*[9], *Mary E. Thrall*[8], *Worthy*[7], *Eliphas*[6], *Samuel*[5], *John*[4-3], *Timothy*[2], *William*[1])
Birth: 14 May 1890 in Meadow Grove, Madison County, Nebraska[757]
Death: 27 March 1936 in Los Angeles[758]
Burial: with his mother at Rose Hills Memorial Park, Whittier, Los Angeles County, California[759]
Spouse: **ADA PEARL VENSEL,** married 16 February 1913 in Maricopa County, Arizona[760]
Spouse's parents: W. J. and Alice (Mosier) Vensel
Spouse's birth: 3 October 1892 in Arizona

---

[757] Ray Morgan WWI draft card, #3269 or 1072, Peoria Precinct, Maricopa County, Arizona, 5 June 1917; "US, World War I Draft Registration Cards, 1917–1918" > Arizona > Maricopa County > Draft Card M > image 1626 of 1890 (ancestry.com).

[758] Raymond L. Morgan death index entry, Los Angeles 1936; California Death Index, 1905–1939. Original not viewed.

[759] Amanda M. Morgan 1863–1946 and Raymond L. Morgan 1890–1936 grave markers, images, Rose Hills Memorial Park, Whittier, Los Angeles County, California, memorial #89,904,876 by David Kaspareit (findagrave.com).

[760] Raymond L. Morgan–Ada P. Vinsel marriage 16 February 1913, Maricopa County license, p. 246; "Arizona, County Marriage Records, 1865–1972" > Maricopa > Marriage Licenses > image 39662 of 86651 (ancestry.com).

Spouse's death: 7 February 1920 of bronchial pneumonia in Phoenix, six days after delivering her second child[761]
Spouse's burial: 10 February 1920, Greenwood Memory Lawn Cemetery, Phoenix[762]

Raymond was with his mother Amanda and family in Bone Gap, Edwards County, Illinois, in 1900, and soon thereafter a student in Lincoln, Lancaster County, Nebraska, in 1903 and 1905.[763] In January 1911 in Arizona, his mother Amanda transferred "lot 7 block 1 Athena Place" to him. Two years later, soon after his marriage, he transferred it to A. D. Crabb.[764]

In 1912 he was a clerk for Talbot & Hubbard, which sold "hardware, paints, oils, glass and blacksmiths' supplies." The following year he was a salesman for Shaw's Smoke House at 12 Central Avenue North.[765] In 1917, farming in Glendale, Maricopa County, Arizona, he was of medium height and build with grey eyes and brown hair. He named

---

[761] Ada Morgan death certificate Arizona #204, 7 February 1920; "Arizona, Death Records, 1887–1960" > Maricopa > 1920–1929 > image 13817 of 16104 (ancestry.com). W. J. was born in Pennsylvania, Alice in Missouri.

[762] Ada Vensel Morgan grave marker, image, Greenwood Memory Lawn Cemetery, Phoenix, Arizona, section 2, block 11, lot 3, space 7, memorial #33,494,863 by Gloria Simpson for Ada P. Vensel Morgan (findagrave.com).

[763] Amanda Morgan household for son Raymond, 1900 US census, Bone Gap, Edwards County, Illinois, ED 16 sheet 9A, dwelling 167, family 170. Also, Amanda Morgan "wid. M. W." lived on the north side of Miller, first east of Warren in 1901, on the northwest corner of College and Fowler in 1903, and at 302 East Adams in 1905; *Hoye's City Directory of Lincoln* (Lincoln: Hoye, 1901), p. 384, image 191 of 351 (ancestry.com). Similarly, 1903, p. 438, image 225 of 445; and 1905, p. 143, image 73 of 485. The Morgans were not found there in 1906 or 1907. In 1905 University Place was enumerated separately within the Lincoln directory. Student "Ray" (1903) or "Raymond" (1905) was at the same address as Amanda.

[764] "Real Estate Transfers," *Arizona Republican*, Tuesday 28 January 1911, p. 1, col. 2, and p. 2 col. 1, Saturday 25 January 1913.

[765] Raymond L. Morgan entries, *Phoenix 1912 City Directory*, pp. 172 and 229; similarly, *1913*, pp. 230 and 276.

mother and wife as dependents, but did not claim an exemption from the World War I draft.[766]

In 1920 they owned their home (with mortgage) at 720 East McKinley in Phoenix (having moved there from nearby Peoria, Arizona, five months earlier). Raymond was a salesman at a service station, and his mother Amanda, age 55, was a nurse.[767] In 1921 he was working for Nitrolene Sales Company.[768]

After Ada's death, the bereaved young family soon headed farther west. In 1925 Ray L. Morgan, "tirebldr" with no named wife, lived at 230 West Cedar in Compton, Los Angeles County, California. The following year he was a rubberworker at Samson Tire and Rubber Company, living at 805 Hickory in Compton.[769] In 1930 Raymond and his two children were at 812 Stewart Street in Los Angeles, renting for $30 a month.[770] In 1932 he was at 2435 East Anaheim in Long Beach, and in 1936 a rubber worker at 1115 Fraser Avenue in Los Angeles.[771]

---

[766] Ray Morgan WWI draft card, #3269 or 1072, Peoria Precinct, Maricopa County, Arizona, 5 June 1917; "US, World War I Draft Registration Cards, 1917–1918" > Arizona > Maricopa County > Draft Card M > image 1626 of 1890 (ancestry.com).

[767] Ray L. Morgan household, 1920 US census, Phoenix, Maricopa County, Arizona, ED 64, sheet 8B, dwelling 159, family 189. For the move, see Ada Morgan death certificate Arizona #204, 7 February 1920; "Arizona, Death Records, 1887–1960" > Maricopa > 1920–1929 > image 13817 of 16104 (ancestry.com).

[768] Morgan entries (Ray L. and Amanda widow of M. W.), *Phoenix and Salt River Valley Directory 1921* (Los Angeles: Arizona Directory, 1921), pp. 191–92, images 371–72 of 395 (ancestry.com).

[769] Ray L. Morgan, *Watts–Compton City Directory 1925* [mislabeled "Compton" by ancestry.com] (Los Angeles: Los Angeles Directory, 1925), p. 242, image 130 of 324 (ancestry.com). Ray was absent from the 1922–1923 directory. Similarly, 1927–1928, but copyright 1926, p. 221, image 223 of 524 (ancestry.com).

[770] Robert [Ray] L. Morgan household, 1930 US census, Los Angeles, Los Angeles County, California, ED 338, sheet 16A, dwelling/family blank. Next door a Stella L. Morgan, age 40 born in Kansas, was enumerated as a lodger; an arrow on the sheet may suggest that she belonged in Raymond's household. No other evidence has been found to support a second marriage.

[771] Morgan entries, *Polk's Long Beach California City Directory 1932* (Long Beach: R. L. Polk of California, 1932), 419, image 210 of 493 (ancestry.com). Similarly, *1936*, p. 1300, image 658 of 682 (ancestry.com).

Chapter 25

Tenth Generation

Ezra Leonidas Morgan–Mary Fletcher Flint Family
<u>parents at chapter 7</u>

"Conservation of the People and the Rural Community"

25. EZRA LEONIDAS "LON"[10] MORGAN (*Allyn T. Morgan[9], Mary E. Thrall[8], Worthy[7], Eliphas[6], Samuel[5], John[4-3], Timothy[2], William[1]*)
Birth: 22 August 1879 in Bone Gap
Death: 9 October 1937 in St. Louis City, "apparently of natural causes, while visiting Miss Jeanne Wiukerson [Wilkerson], a friend of his daughters, at 4953 Washington boulevard, . . . while thumbing through a book"[772]
Burial: 12 October 1937 in Columbia, Boone County, Missouri[773]
Spouse: **MARY FLETCHER FLINT,** married 26 June 1906 in Murphysboro, Jackson County, Illinois[774]
Spouse's parents: Rev. John W. and Minerva (Robertson) Flint

---

[772] "Prof. E. L. Morgan Funeral," *St. Louis Post-Dispatch*, Monday 11 October 1937, p. 3C, col. 2, stating that he died on Saturday. US Department of Agriculture, *Experiment Station Record 1938* (Washington, DC: Government Printing Office, 1939), 580, erroneously gives 12 October, likely the burial date (see following note).

[773] Ezra L. Morgan death certificate #35891, St. Louis City, 9 October 1937; *Missouri Digital Heritage* > Collections > Death Certificates > "Missouri Death Certificates, 1910–1967." He died of coronary occlusion and renal sclerosis en route to City Hospital #1; there was no attending physician; and an autopsy was performed. Ancestral information was scanty; the informant was Sam F. Hendricks of Jefferson City.

[774] "Morgan–Flint," *Paxton Record* (Illinois), Thursday 28 June 1906, p. 4, col. 1. The bride's father, Rev. John Wesley Flint, officiated. Her sisters and brother participated in the ceremony.

Spouse's birth: 9 June 1881 in Mount Vernon, Jefferson County, Illinois
Spouse's death: 29 December 1945 in Columbia, Boone County, Missouri, of coronary occlusion and influenza
Spouse's burial: 1 January 1946 at Columbia Cemetery there[775]

Mary F. Flint "entered McKendree in September 1899, and graduated in June 1903, with the degree of A.B. She was a member of the Clionian Literary Society. For two years after her graduation she was a teacher [and] assistant principal of the Trenton [Clinton County] high school." As of 1928 she and Ezra were both members of the Methodist Episcopal Church, residing in Columbia, Boone County, Missouri.[776]

Ezra grew up on a farm near Bone Gap, Edwards County, Illinois, and was educated in country schools. (For instance, he attended College Hill School for 20 days in April and May 1888.)[777] After attending the collegiate institute at Albion (Edwards County seat), he entered McKendree College in the spring term of 1901, and graduated in 1904 with an A.B. degree. He then worked six years for the YMCA—four in rural Ford County, Illinois, and two in Kansas.

He then studied economics and rural sociology at the University of Wisconsin 1910–12, receiving a Master of Arts there. During the summer of 1912 he was a lecturer for the National Lincoln Chautauqua System, speaking at 120 Chautauquas in seven states.[778] Chatauquas—affordable summer retreats that combined recreation and edifying lectures—were popular from the 1870s into the 1920s. The movement had some Methodist roots.[779] Among Ezra's most popular lectures were

---

[775] Mary Morgan, Missouri death certificate #40501, 29 December 1945. The informant was Mrs. F. J. Loomis of Columbia.

[776] *Centennial McKendree College with St. Clair County History* (Lebanon, Illinois: McKendree College, 1928), 379.

[777] "Miscellaneous School Records, Edwards County, Illinois, 1865, 1873–1875, 1878–1880, 1883 and 1888," College Hill month ending 4 May 1888, typescript evidently transcribed from a standard "Schedule of a Common School," 27–28; copy in author's possession, likely from Edwards County Historical Society, Albion, Illinois.

[778] "Prof. E. Lon Morgan," *Centennial McKendree College with St. Clair County History* (Lebanon, Illinois: McKendree College, 1928), 382.

[779] Cindy S. Aron, *Working at Play: A History of Vacations in the United States* (New York: Oxford University Press, 1999), 101–26.

"Conservation of the People and the Rural Community" and "Conservation of the Soil and Corn Culture."[780]

From 1913 to 1919 Ezra was "community field agent in the extension service" at the Massachusetts Agricultural College at Amherst,[781] and later "extension professor of rural organization." He then became national director of rural service in the American Red Cross. From 1921 to his death, he was professor and chairman of the department of rural sociology at the University of Missouri, Columbia,[782] and served as vice-chairman of the (Missouri) State Social Security Commission.[783]

---

[780] "Prof. E. Lon Morgan," *Centennial McKendree College with St. Clair County History* (Lebanon, Illinois: McKendree College, 1928), 382.

[781] *Fiftieth Annual Report of the Massachusetts Agricultural College*, Part 1 (Boston: Wright & Potter, February 1913), 10. Fifteen years later McKendree's centennial history glorified his position as "in charge of the department of Applied Sociology."

[782] US Department of Agriculture, *Experiment Station Record 1938* (Washington, DC: Government Printing Office, 1939), 580.

[783] "Prof E. L. Morgan of Missouri University Dead," undated clipping, likely from Albion newspaper, copy in author's possession.

Chapter 26

Tenth Generation

Earl Morgan–Effie Bankston Family
parents at chapter 7

Milk peddler to railroad switchman

26. **EARL AMOS**[10] **MORGAN** (*Allyn T. Morgan*[9], *Mary E. Thrall*[8], *Worthy*[7], *Eliphas*[6], *Samuel*[5], *John*[4-3], *Timothy*[2], *William*[1])
Birth: 10 June 1890 in Bone Gap, Edwards County, Illinois
Death: 17 March 1960 in Illinois Central Hospital, Cook County, Illinois[784]
Burial: Spencer Heights Memorial Cemetery, Mounds, Pulaski County, Illinois[785]
Spouse: **EFFIE GERTRUDE BANKSTON,** married 10 June 1920 in Mounds[786]

---

[784] Earl Amos Morgan, Application for Headstone or Marker, 13 June 1960; "US, Headstone Applications for Military Veterans, 1925–1963 > 1960–1961 > Moorehead–Nelson > image 291 of 4065 (ancestry.com). For place of birth, Earl Amos Morgan, WWI draft card #2212/581/196, Amherst, Massachusetts.; "US, World War I, Draft Registration Cards, 1917–1918" > Massachusetts > Amherst City > 8 > Draft Card M > image 390 of 482 (ancestry.com). Also, "Bone Gap Native Claimed by Death," *Republican-Register* (Mount Carmel, Illinois), Wednesday 23 March 1960, p. 7A, col. 4.

[785] Earl Amos Morgan grave marker, image, Spencer Heights Memorial Cemetery, Mounds, Pulaski County, Illinois, memorial #128,850,311 by Randy Watkins (findagrave.com).

[786] Earl Amos Morgan–Effie Gertrude Bankston marriage, 10 June 1920, Pulaski County, Illinois, Register of Marriages, 2:273; "Illinois, County Marriages, 1810–1940," FHL 960,486, DGS 5,202,971, image 567 of 618 (familysearch.org). The form had blanks for details and parents' names, but none were completed. Officiating was Earl's grandmother's brother, Rev. Charles W. Campbell (chapter 4).

Spouse's parents: Henry Judson and Elizabeth Frances (McCallum) Bankston[787]
Spouse's birth: 13 July 1891, Pulaski County, Illinois[788]
Spouse's death: 15 October 1987 in Springfield, Sangamon County, Illinois[789]
Spouse's burial: Spencer Heights Memorial Cemetery, Mounds, Pulaski County, Illinois[790]

Earl completed at least one year of college, Gertrude four years of high school.[791] He attended McKendree College.[792] Venturing farther from home, in 1917 he was a "milk peddler" working for H. G. Wentworth in Amherst, Massachusetts, where he also attended the Massachusetts Agricultural College (now University of Massachusetts Amherst) and was elected sergeant-at-arms of the class of 1919.[793] Earl served in World War I from 4 July 1917 to 16 August 1919 as 1st lieutenant

---

[787] Jepha [elsewhere Alpha] Bankston–Roy C. Connell marriage, 3 September 1911, Mounds, Pulaski County, Illinois, Register of Marriages 2:122; "Illinois, County Marriages, 1810–1940," image 410 of 618, naming her parents as Henry J. Bankston and Frances E. McCallum (ancestry.com). Also, Henry J. Bankston household for daughter Gertrude age 18, 1910 US census, Mounds, Pulaski County, Illinois, Ward 2, ED 89, sheet 11B, dwelling 180, family 186.

[788] Gertrude Bankston Morgan, grave marker, image, Spencer Heights Memorial Cemetery, Mounds, Illinois, memorial #128,850,312 by Randy Watkins (findagrave.com).

[789] Also, Henry J. Bankston household for daughter Gertrude age 18, 1910 US census, Mounds, Pulaski County, Illinois, Ward 2, ED 89, sheet 11B, dwelling 180, family 186.

[790] Gertrude Bankston Morgan, grave marker, image, Spencer Heights Memorial Cemetery, Mounds, Illinois, memorial #128,850,312 by Randy Watkins (findagrave.com).

[791] Earl Morgan Sr. household, 1940 US census, Harvey, Thornton Township, Cook County, Illinois, ED 16-90, sheet 10A, dwelling 249.

[792] "Bone Gap Native Claimed by Death," *Republican-Register* (Mount Carmel, Illinois), Wednesday 23 March 1960, p. 7A, col. 4.

[793] Earl Amos Morgan, WWI draft card #2212/581/196, Amherst, Massachusetts; "US, World War I, Draft Registration Cards, 1917–1918" > Massachusetts > Amherst City > 8 > Draft Card M > image 390 of 482 (ancestry.com). Also, "Hampshire County . . . Massachusetts Agricultural College," *Daily Republican* (Springfield, Massachusetts), Friday 1 October 1915, p. 15, cols. 3–4.

infantry, Company A, 15th Machine Gun Battalion, 5th Division, U. S. Army.[794]

Shortly before their 1920 marriage, Gertrude was living in her brother-in-law's household and teaching school in Mounds;[795] Earl was a "dairy laborer" in Bone Gap living with his parents,[796] and was also enumerated as a laborer at Edward and Alta Britton's place in Mounds.[797] (Earl was called "cousin" there—he and Ernest Britton were second cousins; Edward G. Britton was Earl's first cousin once removed by marriage.)

In 1930 and 1940 Earl was a switchman for the "steam railroad,"[798] in this case the Illinois Central. He seems to have shuttled between opposite ends of the state, but always near the railroad. In 1930 and 1931 Earl and Gertrude were far south in Mounds, Pulaski County, Illinois, where they owned their home (with a "radio set") on South McKinley Avenue, valued at $2000.[799] In 1940 they were back to renting ($35/month) far north, at 15219 Center Avenue, Harvey, Cook County, Illinois. After 35 years he retired to Mounds, where he was active in the

---

[794] Earl Amos Morgan, Application for Headstone or Marker, 13 June 1960; "US, Headstone Applications for Military Veterans, 1925–1963" > 1960–1961 > Moorehead–Nelson > image 291 of 4065 (ancestry.com).

[795] L. H. Corzine household for sister-in-law Gertrude Bankston, 1920 US census, Mounds, Pulaski County, Illinois, ED 98, sheet 1A, dwelling/family 14.

[796] Allyn T. Morgan household for son Earl A. Morgan, age 29, 1920 US census, Bone Gap, Edwards County, Illinois, ED 20, sheet 4B, dwelling 138, family 139.

[797] B. G. [E.G.] Britton household for Earl Morgan, "cousin," age 29, 1920 US census, Mounds, Pulaski County, Illinois, ED 987, sheet 1A, dwelling 645, family 696.

[798] Earl Morgan Sr. household, 1940 US census, Harvey, Thornton Township, Cook County, Illinois, ED 16-90, sheet 10A, dwelling 249.

[799] Earl A. Morgan household, 1930 US census, Mounds, Pulaski County, Illinois, Ward 1, ED 8, sheet 18B, dwelling 477, family 488. For 1931, "A.T. Morgan, One of County's Leading Residents, Is Dead," *Journal-Register* (Albion, Illinois), Thursday 3 December 1931, p. 1, col. 8. Also, "Shower for a Recent Bride," *Daily Republican-Register* (Mount Carmel, Illinois), Thursday 12 June 1930, p. 6, col. 2. Similarly, "Bone Gap News," Thursday 17 July, p. 5, col. 1.

Methodist church, as was Gertrude.[800] She was living in Mounds in 1981.[801]

---

[800] "Bone Gap Native Claimed by Death," *Republican-Register* (Mount Carmel, Illinois), Wednesday 23 March 1960, p. 7A, col. 4.

[801] "Lily M. Lackey," *Southern Illinoisan* (Carbondale), Tuesday 7 July 1981, p. 19, col. 2.

Chapter 27

Tenth Generation

Evart Morgan–Elsie Drury–Eva Brines Family
<u>parents at chapter 7</u>

From Pueblo to Bone Gap, "most of the 1,500 miles dirt road"

27. EVART WILLIAM[10] **MORGAN** (*Allyn Theodore Morgan*[9], *Mary Elizabeth Thrall*[8], *Worthy*[7], *Eliphas*[6], *Samuel*[5], *John*[4-3], *Timothy*[2], *William*[1])
Birth: 19 March 1892 in Bone Gap, Edwards County, Illinois[802]
Death: 2 March 1979 in Pueblo, Pueblo County, Colorado
Burial: 6 March 1979 at Imperial Memorial Gardens there[803]
Spouse #1: **ELSIE P. DRURY,** married 20 March 1912 in Bone Gap
Spouse #1's parents: John T. and Elizabeth (Thread) Drury
Spouse #1's birth: 2 February 1889 in Illinois
Spouse #1's death: 27 July 1914
Spouse#1's burial: Bone Gap Cemetery[804]
Spouse #2: **EVA BRINES,** married 25 October 1917 in West

---

[802] Everett [Evart] William Morgan WWI draft card #595/6, Bone Gap, Illinois; "US, World War I, Draft Registration Cards, 1917–1918" > Illinois > Edwards County > Draft Card M > image 187 of 210 (ancestry.com).

[803] Evart W. Morgan grave marker, Imperial Memorial Gardens, Pueblo, Colorado, image, memorial #64,542,116 for Evart William Morgan by Ralph & Donna Sullivan (findagrave.com).

[804] Evart W. Morgan–Elsie P. Drury marriage license #4086, 19 March 1912, marriage 20 March in Bone Gap, Illinois, marriage record 2:99; "Illinois, County Marriages, 1810–1940," image 477 of 654, FHL 1,401,780, DGS 4,661,397 (familysearch.org). For death, Elsie P. wife of E. W. Morgan grave marker, image, Bone Gap Cemetery, Bone Gap, Illinois, memorial #140,962,515 for Elsie P. Morgan by Janice (Teel) Crites (findagrave.com). Also, John T. Drury household for daughter Elsie born February 1888, 1900 US census, Bone Gap, Edwards County, Illinois, ED 16, sheet 4B, dwelling/family 76.

Salem, Edwards County, Illinois[805]
Spouse #2's parents: Morris and Jennie (Mull) Brines
Spouse #2's birth: 17 October 1889 Mount Carmel, Wabash County, Illinois
Spouse #2's death: September 1981
Spouse #2's burial: Imperial Memorial Gardens, Pueblo, Colorado[806]

Elsie was in her widowed father's household in 1900 and 1910.[807] In 1900 Eva lived with father Morris and apparent mother Jennie in Bellmont village, Wabash County, Illinois.[808] In 1910 she was a "sister-in-law" in the Fisher household there.[809]

Evart and Eva both completed eight years of schooling.[810] In 1917 he was described as tall and slender, with blue eyes and black hair. He claimed exemption from the draft due to "rheumatism in shoulder" and "throat trouble."[811]

They left the area in 1919 after a farewell dinner 24 August:

---

[805] Evart W. Morgan–Eav [Eva] B. Brines marriage 25 October 1917, Edwards County Register of Marriages p. 50, #4563; "Illinois, County Marriages, 1810–1940" > FHL 1,401,780, DGS 4,661,397 > image 560 of 654 (familysearch.org). Rev. P. M. Durham officiated; Norma Fisher and Harry Epler witnessed. Also, "Evart W. Morgan," *Pueblo Chieftain* (Colorado), Monday 5 March 1979, p. 8B, col. 3.

[806] For birth date and death month, Eva B. Morgan index entry, US Social Security Death Index. For years, Eva B. Morgan grave marker, Imperial Memorial Gardens, Pueblo, Colorado, image, memorial #64,542,133 for Eva Brines Morgan by Ralph & Donna Sullivan (findagrave.com). Place of birth and Eva's mother's maiden surname from marriage record above.

[807] John T. Drury household for daughter Elsie born February 1888, 1900 US census, Bone Gap, Edwards County, Illinois, ED 16, sheet 4B, dwelling/family 76. Similarly, John T. Druery [Drury], 1910, sheet 7B, dwelling/family 167.

[808] Morris Brines household for daughter Eva born October 1888, 1900 US census, Bellmont village, Wabash County, Illinois, ED 84, sheet 11B, dwelling 226, family 234.

[809] John Fisher household for sister-in-law Evah age 20, 1910 US census, Bellmont Precinct, Wabash County, Illinois, ED 170, sheet 12B, dwelling 246, family 249.

[810] Evart W. Morgan household, 1940 US census, Pueblo, Pueblo County, Colorado, ED 51-38, sheet 13A dwelling 273.

[811] Everett [Evart] William Morgan WWI draft card #595/6, Bone Gap, Illinois; "US, World War I, Draft Registration Cards, 1917–1918" > Illinois > Edwards County > Draft Card M > image 187 of 210 (ancestry.com).

> At the home of J. R. Fisher and family of Gards Point a farewell dinner was given Sunday for Evart Morgan and wife of Bone Gap, who leave this week for Pueblo, Colorado to make their future home. It was a very happy affair and all of Mrs. Morgan's brothers and sisters and their families were there. Those present were J. Schneck Brines and family, of Mount Carmel; J. R. Brines, Jr., and family, T. K. Wright and family, M. W. Brines and family, H. C. Bell and family, of Maud; Gilbert Brines and wife, of Groffs, Earl and Evart Morgan and wife, of Bone Gap; and J. R. Fisher and family.[812]

They didn't get to Pueblo right away, however. In 1920 Evart and Eva were living in Tulsa, Tulsa County, Oklahoma; he was a barber and they had five boarders in the house at 1236 Admiral.[813] One year later he was barbering in Pueblo and they lived at 832 East 4th Street.[814] They kept up family visits back to Illinois for more than fifty years. On their 1924 visit from Pueblo, "They drove through and found most of the 1,500 miles dirt road."[815]

In 1930 they owned a $1500 house at 731 Brown Avenue in Pueblo.[816] Evart reported that in eleven years of barbering, he had "never been late to work except four mornings." His trade was not their only support: "At their home they have one thousand chickens and get from 470 to 530 eggs per day. At five o'clock each morning the hen houses are lit up with electric lights."[817] By 1940 their house was said to be worth

---

[812] "Society: A Farewell Dinner," *Daily Republican-Register* (Mount Carmel, Illinois), Tuesday 26 August 1919, p. 3, col. 2.

[813] Edart [Evart] W. Morgan household, 1920 US census, Tulsa, Tulsa County, Oklahoma, Precinct 11, ED 225, sheet 8B, dwelling 147, family 151.

[814] Evart W. Morgan entry, *Pueblo City Directory 1921* (Colorado Springs: R. L. Polk, 1921), 232, image 121 of 277 (ancestry.com).

[815] "State Patrol Man on the Job," *Daily Republican-Register* (Mount Carmel, Illinois), Saturday 27 September 1924, p. 3, col. 5. Distance is about 1000 miles.

[816] Evart W. Morgan household, 1930 US census, Pueblo, Pueblo County, Colorado, ED 36, sheet 9B, dwelling 225, family 228.

[817] "Bone Gap News," *Daily Republican-Register* (Mount Carmel, Illinois), Thursday 5 February 1931, p. 5, col. 5.

$3000.[818] (Colorado's statewide average that year was $2091.)[819] They were still there in 1975.[820]

Evart was a member of Adriance Methodist Church, Pueblo AARP, and the local barbers' union, retiring in 1965.[821] Not only did they visit southeastern Illinois regularly, they also retained some farmland there. In August 1931 Evart's father Allyn, then 75 years old, spent a day in Wabash County looking after Eva's "farm interests" there.[822] Evart and Eva owned eighty acres in the west half of the southeast quarter of Section 17, Township 1 South, Range 13 West (in Wabash County), which rose in value from $7040 in 1966 to $11,880 in 1970.[823]

---

[818] Evart W. Morgan household, 1940 US census, Pueblo, Pueblo County, Colorado, ED 51-38, sheet 13A, dwelling 273.

[819] Statewide figures from US Census Bureau, Census of Housing, Historical Census of Housing Tables, Median Home Values Unadjusted 1940 (census.gov/hhes/www/housing/census/historic/values.html).

[820] Evart W. Morgan entry, *1975 Pueblo (Pueblo, Pueblo Co., Colo.) City Directory* (Kansas City, Missouri: R. L. Polk, 1975), 598, image 816 of 1688 (ancestry.com).

[821] "Evart W. Morgan," *Pueblo Chieftain* (Colorado), Monday 5 March 1979, p. 8B, col. 3.

[822] "Live Wires of Bone Gap Meet" (Bone Gap locals), *Daily Republican-Register* (Mount Carmel, Illinois), Friday 28 August 1931, p. 3, col. 4.

[823] "Official Publications of Assessment Roll for 1966," *Daily Republican-Register* (Mount Carmel, Illinois), Tuesday 26 July 1966, p. 10, col. 4; similarly, 1970, $11,880, Thursday 23 July 1970, p. 10, col. 3.

Chapter 28

Tenth Generation

Hale Morgan–Edna Wheeler Family
parents at chapter 8

Automobile mechanic for the motion picture industry

28. HALE EUGENE^{10} MORGAN (*Wilbur Amos Morgan^9, Mary Elizabeth Thrall^8, Worthy^7, Eliphas^6, Samuel^5, John$^{4-3}$, Timothy^2, William^1*)
Birth: 4 June 1886 in Bone Gap, Edwards County, Illinois[824]
Death: 28 December 1954 in Los Angeles County, California[825]
Burial: Mountain View Cemetery and Mausoleum in Altadena, Los Angeles County[826]
Spouse: **EDNA BLANCHE WHEELER,** married 25 January 1907 in Albion, Edwards County, Illinois[827]

---

[824] For birth date, Hale Eugene Morgan, WWI draft card, serial #5812, order #A54-29, Yakima County, Washington, 12 September 1918; "US, World War I, Draft Registration Cards, 1917–1918" > Washington > Yakima Co., H–Searle > image 3552 of 5763 (familysearch.org). For birth place, Hale Eugene Morgan, WW2 draft card, serial #484, order #189; "US, World War II, Draft Registration Cards, 1942" > California > Lother-Zwanzig > image 481 of 2392 (ancestry.com).

[825] Hale Eugene Morgan index entry, "California Death Index, 1940–1997." Original record not viewed.

[826] Hale E. Morgan (1886–1954) grave marker, grave 8, lot 1243, Radiant Meadow, Mountain View Cemetery and Mausoleum, Altadena, California, image, memorial #171,422,876 for Hale Eugene Morgan by RHare (findagrave.com).

[827] Hale E. Morgan–Edna B. Wheeler marriage license #3616, 25 January 1907, Edwards County, Illinois, marriage record 2:62; FHL 1,401,780, DGS 4,661,397, image 440 of 654 (familysearch.org). Hale was a merchant living in Bone Gap; Edna was living in Mount Vernon, Jefferson County, Illinois Rev. R. D. Woodley officiated.

Spouse's parents: John B. and Minnie (Henderson) Wheeler[828]
Spouse's birth: 5 May 1889
Spouse's death: November 1979[829]
Spouse's burial: with her husband[830]

In 1900 Hale was living with his family in Bone Gap and attending school with his next-door first cousins Myrtle and Raymond Morgan (children of Hale's late uncle Milton and aunt Amanda Morgan).[831] Hale completed two years of college, Edna four years of high school.[832] In 1910 they were married and he was running a general store.[833] Edna visited her grandparents, the John Hendersons, at Browns, Thursday 16 February 1911.[834]

At some point after 1912 (when a daughter was born in Illinois), the family broke away and went west. In 1920 they were in Sunnyside Precinct, Yakima County, Washington, with his mother "E. Jennie"; Hale

---

[828] John B. Wheeler household for mother Minnie J. and daughter Edna B. age 11, 1900 US census, Browns, Edwards County, Illinois, ED 17, sheet 7B, dwelling/family 144. Edna was the second oldest in a family of seven children. John was a "railroad boss." For Minnie's birth surname, Hale E. Morgan–Edna B. Wheeler marriage license #3616, 25 January 1907, Edwards County, Illinois, marriage record 2:62; FHL 1,401,780, DGS 4,661,397, image 440 of 654 (familysearch.org).

[829] Edna Wheeler index entry, born 5 May 1889, died November 1979, last residence Pasadena, US Social Security Death Index. Edna B. Morgan (1889–1979) grave marker, grave 8, lot 1243, Radiant Meadow, Mountain View Cemetery and Mausoleum, Altadena, California, image, memorial #171,422,785 for Edna Blanche Wheeler Morgan by Rhare (findagrave.com).

[830] Edna B. Morgan (1889–1979) grave marker, grave 8, lot 1243, Radiant Meadow, Mountain View Cemetery and Mausoleum, Altadena, California, image, memorial #171,422,785 for Edna Blanche Wheeler Morgan by Rhare (findagrave.com).

[831] William [Wilbur] Morgan household for Hale age 13, 1900 US census, Bone Gap, Edwards County, Illinois, ED 16, sheet 9A, dwelling 168, family 171.

[832] Hale E. Morgan household, 1940 US census, Pasadena Township, Los Angeles County, California, ED 19-539, sheet 11A, dwelling 265.

[833] Hale E. Morgan household, 1910 US census, Bone Gap, Edwards County, Illinois, ED 16, sheet 2B, dwelling/family 51.

[834] "County News . . . Browns," *Daily Republican-Register* (Mount Carmel, Illinois), Wednesday 22 February 1911, p. 3, col. 3. Mrs. Mary Speedy of Los Angeles also went.

was working as an automobile mechanic.[835] In 1930 he was foreman of a garage (likely auto repair); they owned a radio set and a $6500 house at 1851 Corson Street, Pasadena Township, Los Angeles County, California.[836] (Hale and Willard lived about 2½ miles apart.) After ten years of the Great Depression, their house value had dropped to $4000 (still above the statewide average of $3527); Hale remained an auto mechanic—for the "moving picture" industry.[837] In 1942 he was working for the same company as brother Willard: the Brown Valve and Manufacturing Company in Alhambra.[838]

As late as August 1945 Hale and Edna traveled together from California to visit relatives in Edwards County, Illinois,[839] and in 1946 they registered to vote as Republicans.[840] Evidently they divorced at some point after that; in 1951 they had separate listings at 1851 Corson. (Other couples were listed in the customary format as "John [Jane].")[841] As divorced people, on 25 October 1954 they married second for the second

---

[835] Hale E. Morgan household, 1920 US census, Sunnyside Precinct, Yakima County, Washington, ED 207, sheet 9A, dwelling/family 26.

[836] Hale E. Morgan household, 1930 US census, Pasadena Township, Los Angeles County, California, ED 1274, sheet 12A, dwelling 334, family 338. The site is now apparently an on-ramp to the 210.

[837] Hale E. Morgan household for wife Edna (the informant), 1940 US census, Pasadena Township, Los Angeles County, California, ED 19-539, sheet 11A, dwelling 265. (House value mistranscribed as $1,000.) Statewide figures from US Census Bureau, Census of Housing, Historical Census of Housing Tables, Median Home Values Unadjusted 1940 (census.gov/hhes/www/housing/census/historic/values.html).

[838] Hale Eugene Morgan, WW2 draft card, serial #484, order #189; "US, World War II, Draft Registration Cards, 1942" > California > Lother–Zwanzig > image 481 of 2392 (ancestry.com).

[839] "Bone Gap News," *Daily Republican-Register* (Mount Carmel, Illinois), Wednesday 29 August 1945, p. 3, cols 3–4.

[840] Hale E. Morgan and Mrs. Edna B. Morgan of 1851 Corson Street, Index to Register of Voters, Lamanda Precinct 2, Los Angeles County, California, 1946; "California, Voter Registrations, 1900–1968" > Los Angeles County > 1946 > Roll 65 > image 66 of 1048 (ancestry.com).

[841] Mrs. Edna Morgan and Hale Morgan, separate listings at 1851 Corson, *Thurston's Pasadena 1951 Directory* (Los Angeles: Los Angeles Directory, 1949?), p. 508, image 251 of 494 (ancestry.com). Edna but not Hale was listed in *1953*, p. 493, image 254 of 403, and in 1954, p. 423, image 254 of 717; neither appeared in *1955*, p. 521, image 624 of 746 (ancestry.com).

time in Pasadena.[842] Hale died two months and three days after their remarriage.[843] "Mrs. Edna B. Morgan" was still at 1851 Corson in 1962.[844]

---

[842] Hale Eugene Morgan–Edna B. Morgan marriage license #14124, 25 October 1954, Los Angeles County, California, marriage record 3777:47; "California, County Marriages, 1850–1952," FHL 1,343,396, DGS 5,686,345, image 1375 of 3153 (familysearch.org). Both reported having been divorced. (The 1948 Los Angeles Extended Area telephone directory includes too many Ednas to distinguish, and no Hales.)

[843] Hale Eugene Morgan index entry, "California Death Index, 1940–1997." Original record not viewed.

[844] Mrs. Edna B. Morgan entry, Pasadena Index to Register of Voters, Precinct 191 (alphabetical); "California, Voter Registrations, 1900–1968" > Los Angeles County > 1962 > Roll 164 > image 273 of 788 (ancestry.com).

Chapter 29

Tenth Generation

Glen Morgan–Elmina Sims– Ava B. [–?–] Family
<u>parents at chapter 8</u>

Oil-well equipment manufacture (three brothers)

29. GLEN WILBUR[10] **MORGAN** (*Wilbur Amos Morgan*[9], *Mary Elizabeth Thrall*[8], *Worthy*[7], *Eliphas*[6], *Samuel*[5], *John*[4-3], *Timothy*[2], *William*[1])
Birth: 25 June 1890 in Illinois[845]
Death: 27 November 1957 in Victorville, San Bernardino County, California, last residence Barstow[846]
Burial: Mountain View Cemetery and Mausoleum, Altadena, Los Angeles County, California[847]
Spouse #1: **ELMINA "MINA" LOIS SIMS,** married 1 September 1915 in Evansville, Vanderburgh County, Indiana
Spouse #1's parents: John H. and Lois M. (Leach) Sims

---

[845] Glen W. Morgan–Mina Sims marriage applications, license, and return, 1 September 1915, Vanderburgh County, Indiana, p. 219; FHL 1,479,611, DGS 7,579,770, image 253 of 712 (familysearch.org).

[846] "Obituary Notices . . . Morgan," *Pasadena Independent* (California), Friday 29 November 1957, p. 12, col. 4. Ava was his surviving wife.

[847] Glen W. Morgan (1890–1957) grave marker, grave 13, lot 469, Radiant Meadow, Mountain View Cemetery and Mausoleum, Altadena, California, image, memorial #171,429,886 for Glen Wilbur Morgan by Rhare (findagrave.com).

Spouse #1's birth: 10 October 1891 or 1892 in Illinois[848]
Spouse #1's death: 7 February 1979, last residence San Gabriel, Los Angeles County[849]
Spouse #1's burial: Rose Hills Memorial Park, Whittier, Los Angeles County[850]
Spouse #2: **AVA B. [–?–]**, married between 1950 and 1952[851]
Spouse #2's parents: Not known
Spouse #2's birth: Not known
Spouse #2's death: after 1964[852]
Spouse #2's burial: Not known

Mina's mother Lois was a daughter of Rev. Daniel Bassett Leach, likely a blacksmithing customer of Mina's husband's great-grandfather Worthy Thrall in the 1840s (chapter 1).[853]

---

[848] Born October 1892: Glen W. Morgan–Mina Sims marriage applications, license, and return, 1 September 1915, Vanderburgh County, Indiana, p. 219; FHL 1,479,611, DGS 7,579,770, image 253 of 712 (familysearch.org). W. B. Farmer officiated. Also, Mina Morgan entry, US Social Security Death Index. Born October 1891: John H. Sims household, 1900 US census for daughter Elmira [Elmina] Sims, Bone Gap, Edwards County, Illinois, ED 16, sheet 11A, dwelling 215, family 218. Also, Mina S. Morgan entry, "California Death Index 1940–1997." Original not viewed.

[849] Mina Morgan entry, US Social Security Death Index.

[850] Mina S. Morgan memorial #117,551,773, no image or sourcing, reportedly buried at Entrance Gate 1, Grave/Niche 1, Burial Lot 1009, Marigold Lawn Burial Section 3, Rose Hills Memorial Park, Whittier, California, by Stuart Strout Woodside Skolfield (ancestry.com).

[851] Index to Register of Voters, Alhambra City Precinct #10, Los Angeles County, California, 1950, Glen W. and Mrs. Mina S. Morgan; "California, Voter Registrations, 1900–1968" > Los Angeles County > 1950 > Roll 76 > image 28 of 792 (ancestry.com). Also, Index to Register of Voters, Alhambra City Precinct #6, Los Angeles County, California, 1952, Glen W. and Mrs. Ava B. Morgan; "California, Voter Registrations, 1900–1968" > Los Angeles County > 1952 > Roll 83 > image 40 of 1247 (ancestry.com).

[852] "Obituary Notices . . . Morgan," *Pasadena Independent* (California), Friday 29 November 1957, p. 12, col. 4. Ava was his surviving wife.

[853] Daniel Bassett Leach (10 August 1821–12 February 1909) grave marker, image, Bone Gap Cemetery, Bone Gap, Illinois, memorial #76,905,329 by Jeaniealogy (findagrave.com) with a newspaper clipping and family portrait.

Glen and Mina each completed two years of high school,[854] and soon thereafter left for the Golden West. In 1920 they were renting at the rear of 221 South Raymond Avenue in Alhambra, Los Angeles County, California; he was a machinist in a tractor factory, while she was a machine operator in a box factory.[855] Ten years later they owned a radio set and a $5000 house at 1819 Lemon Street. Glen was a "factory machinist."[856] In 1935 he was vice-president and manager of Brown Valve and Manufacturing Company.[857] In 1940 the family was living at 23 North El Molino, which they owned, valued at $4500 (above the statewide average of $3527), and Glen earned $2750 for 52 weeks' work as manager of an oil well equipment manufacturer, no doubt Brown Valve.[858]

In 1950 Glen and Mina registered to vote from 23 North El Molino in Alhambra. As usual she registered as a Democrat and he declined to say.[859] Two years later, Glen and apparent second wife Ava registered to vote from 24 North Third in a nearby precinct; both registered as Republicans, then and later.[860] Mina, living just a mile away, was reported as Glen's widow that year.[861]

---

[854] Glen Morgan household for wife Mina, 1940 US census, Alhambra, San Gabriel Township, Los Angeles County, California, ED 19-665, sheet 14B, dwelling 364.

[855] Glen W. Morgan household for wife Mina, 1920 US census, Alhambra, Los Angeles County, California, ED 16, sheet 2B, ED 574, sheet 11B, dwelling 267, family 280.

[856] Glen W. Morgan household for wife Nina [Mina] S., 1930 US census, Alhambra, Los Angeles County, California, ED 18, sheet 2A, dwelling 35, family 36.

[857] Glen W. Morgan entry, *Alhambra (California) City Directory 1935* (Los Angeles: Los Angeles Directory County, 1935), p. 108, image 107 of 463 (ancestry.com).

[858] Glen Morgan household, 1940 US census, Alhambra, San Gabriel Township, Los Angeles County, California, ED 19-665, sheet 14B, dwelling 364. Statewide figures from US Census Bureau, Census of Housing, Historical Census of Housing Tables, Median Home Values Unadjusted 1940 (census.gov/hhes/ www/housing/ census/historic/values.html).

[859] Glen W. and Mrs. Mina S. Morgan, Index to Register of Voters, Alhambra City Precinct #10, Los Angeles County, California, 1950; "California, Voter Registrations, 1900–1968" > Los Angeles County > 1950 > Roll 76 > image 28 of 792 (ancestry.com).

[860] Glen W. and Mrs. Ava B. Morgan, Index to Register of Voters, Alhambra City Precinct #6, Los Angeles County, California, 1952; "California, Voter Registrations, 1900–1968" > Los Angeles County > 1952 > Roll 83 > image 40 of 1247 (ancestry.com).

[861] Mina S. Morgan entry, *Alhambra City Directory 1952* (Los Angeles: Los Angeles Directory Company, 1952), p. 283, image 143 of 487 (ancestry.com).

Glen and Ava soon left Alhambra for Barstow, San Bernardino County, in the "Inland Empire" about 100 miles northeast. There they registered to vote in 1954 and 1956 at Rural Route 1, Box 222, Barstow; following Glen's death, she registered again in 1958 and 1962.[862] In 1964 she registered at 21483 West Highway 66 in Barstow (quite possibly the same location with a different label).[863]

---

[862] Glen W. and Mrs. Ava B. Morgan voter registration, p. 6; "California, Voter Registrations, 1900–1968" > San Bernardino County > 1954 > roll 18 (ancestry.com). Similarly, p. 8, 1956 > roll 20 > image 1201 of 1985. Similarly, Mrs. Ava B. Morgan, 1958, roll 22 > image 1326 of 1420. Similarly, 1962, roll 30 > image 174 of 1384.

[863] Mrs. Ava B. Morgan, 1964, Lenwood Precinct, San Bernardino County, p. 3; "California, Voter Registrations," 1900–1968 > San Bernardino County > 1964 > roll 34 > image 31 of 1678 (ancestry.com).

Genealogical puzzle #3: Who was Glen's second wife?

Conjectures and possibilities for further research:

(1) In 1979 an unidentified "Ava B. Morgan De Rousse" had property in San Bernardino County sold to the state, subject to redemption, for unpaid taxes of $24.95.[864]

(2) An Ava Bennington DeRousse, wife of Louis, reportedly born 23 September 1911 in Montana, died in Modesto, Stanislaus County, California, 9 December 1991, having lived in nearby Waterford since about 1973.[865] (Barstow and Modesto are more than 300 miles apart.)

(3) In 1964, a Louis E. DeRousse and Mrs. Carol R. DeRousse registered to vote as Republicans at 3696 Wall Avenue in San Bernardino.[866]

(4) Possibly a separate mystery: Glen's obituary names a daughter Dixie who did not appear in his 1940 household. Dixie is not found in 1930 or 1940, although in 1929 a sixteen-year-old woman appeared on a ship passenger list and among other things gave her place of birth as "Indian Point" in

---

[864] "Legal Notice . . . Delinquent tax notice," *Sun* (San Bernardino County, California), Saturday 8 September 1979, p. 34, col. 3; assessor's map book 434, p. 46, block 1, parcel 04.

[865] "Ava B. DeRousse," *Leader* (Oakdale, California), Wednesday 18 December 1991, p. A2, col. 1.

[866] Louis E. Derousse Jr., Index to Precinct Register, San Bernardino Precinct, p. 2, San Bernardino County, California; "California, Voter Registrations, 1900–1968" > San Bernardino County > 1964 > Roll 35 > image 443 of 965 (ancestry.com).

Illinois—very likely Indian Point Township, Knox County, Illinois.[867]

(5) Another candidate to be Glen's second wife is Ava Vivian Dale, supposedly the daughter of Martin and Ida (Keeler) Dale, who was born 11 April 1913 in Knox County, Illinois, and died 2 October 1989 in Sacramento. This tentative identification is weak, as her California Death Index entry has her mother's maiden name as Dalany, not Keeler.[868]

(6) In 1920 a six-year-old Illinois-born Ava lived in Mercer County, Illinois, with apparent parents Morton and Ida (Keeler) Dale, in Morton's brother's household (they were farm laborers).[869]

---

[867] Ava Vivian Dale ("known as Brown"), single, female, age 16, in List of United States Citizens, "Tourist Third Cabin," S.S. *Megantic*, from Liverpool 21 December 1929, arriving New York 31 December, born "Endian Point, Illinois" 11 April 1913, heading for aunt Mrs. E. Shrider at 2223 Seminary Avenue in Chicago; "New York, Passenger and Crew Lists (including Castle Garden and Ellis Island), 1820-1957" > Roll > T715, 1897–1957 > 4001–5000 > Roll 4652 > image 952 of 1059 (ancestry.com).

[868] Ava Vivian Morgan entry, California Death Index, 1940–1997 (ancestry.com).

[869] Thomas Dale household for niece Ava age 6, 1920 US census, ED 75, Mercer Township, Mercer County, Illinois, sheet 2A, no dwelling number, family 28. Ida Keeler and husband Martin Dale appeared on the marriage license for daughter Mildred Dale, who married Harry E. Riddell 17 January 1921 in Galesburg, Knox County, Illinois: "Illinois, County Marriage Records, 1800–1940," FHL 1,412,072, DGS 4,031,822, image 634 of 1709 (familysearch.org). Mildred appeared in the 1920 household, born in Missouri, age 17.

Chapter 30

Tenth Generation

Willard Morgan–Wilma Snider Family
parents at chapter 8

Accountant in manufacturing

30. **WILLARD AMOS**[10] **MORGAN** (*Wilbur Amos Morgan*[9], *Mary Elizabeth Thrall*[8], *Worthy*[7], *Eliphas*[6], *Samuel*[5], *John*[4-3], *Timothy*[2], *William*[1])
Birth: 20 November 1898, probably in Bone Gap[870]
Death: 13 September 1948 in Los Angeles[871]
Burial: Mountain View Cemetery and Mausoleum in Altadena, Los Angeles County, California[872]
Spouse: **WILMA ANN SNYDER,** married 23 October 1929 in Los Angeles, California[873]
Spouse's parents: William H. and Anna (Oertel) Snider
Spouse's birth: 19 September 1906 in Los Angeles

---

[870] William [Wilbur] Morgan household for Willerd [Willard] age 1, 1900 US census, Bone Gap, Edwards County, Illinois, ED 16, sheet 9A, dwelling 168, family 171. Also, Willard Amos Morgan entry, "California Death Index, 1940–1997" (ancestry.com). Original not viewed.

[871] Willard Amos Morgan entry, "California Death Index, 1940–1997" (ancestry.com). Original not viewed.

[872] Willard A. Morgan (1898–1948) grave marker, image, Mountain View Cemetery and Mausoleum, Altadena, Los Angeles County, California, memorial #188,610,903 for Willard Amos Morgan by Carolyn (Schmidt) Alves (findagrave.com).

[873] Willard A. Morgan–Wilma A. Snyder marriage license #17120, 23 October 1929, Los Angeles 904:61, certificate same date, "California, County Birth, Marriage, and Death Records, 1849–1980" > 5,698,489 > image 1637 of 2522. He was age 30 living in Pasadena; she was 23 in Los Angeles. Presbyterian minister S. H. Sutherland officiated. Witnesses were W. H. Snyder (probably her father) and W. A. Morgan. Also, "Announcement of Marriage Is Made by Bone Gap Folks," *Daily Republican-Register* (Mount Carmel, Illinois), Thursday 31 October 1929, p. 8, col. 1.

Spouse's death: 14 October 2001 in San Marino, Los Angeles County[874]
Spouse's burial: with her husband[875]

In 1910 Wilma's father William was a motorman on the L.A.R.R. (Los Angeles Rail Road) and the family owned their home.[876] Willard completed four years of college, Wilma five.[877] In 1930 they were renting a $47-a-month apartment at 325 West Magnolia in Compton, Los Angeles County. He was an accountant in manufacturing, she taught in a public school, and they owned a radio set.[878] In the fall of 1937 he visited his parents in Bone Gap for two weeks.[879]

In 1936 he was treasurer of the Brown Valve and Manufacturing Company in Alhambra.[880] The Depression decade appears to have been relatively good for the family: in 1940 they owned a $10,000 home at 1055 Winston Avenue in San Marino, well above the statewide average of $3527. (Hale and Willard lived about 2 ½ miles apart.) Willard earned

---

[874] Wilma Anna Morgan index entry including mother's birth surname, "US, Social Security Applications and Claims Index, 1936–2007" (ancestry.com). Last known residence from US Social Security Death Index. For additional parental information, Wm. H. Snider household for wife Anna (age 41) and daughter Wilma A. (age 3), 1910 US census, Los Angeles, Los Angeles County, California, ED 146, Precinct 101, sheet 4A–B, dwelling 95, family 98.

[875] Wilma A. Morgan (1906–2001) grave marker, Mausoleum, Mountain View Cemetery and Mausoleum, Altadena, Los Angeles County, California, image, memorial #188,610,917 for Wilma A. Snider Morgan by Carolyn (Schmidt) Alves.

[876] Wilma Anna Morgan index entry including mother's birth surname, "US, Social Security Applications and Claims Index, 1936–2007" (ancestry.com). Last known residence from US Social Security Death Index. For additional parental information, Wm. H. Snider household for wife Anna (age 41) and daughter Wilma A. (age 3), 1910 US census, Los Angeles, Los Angeles County, California, ED 146, Precinct 101, sheet 4A–B, dwelling 95, family 98.

[877] Willard A. Morgan household for wife Wilma (the informant), 1940 US census, San Marino City, San Gabriel Township, Los Angeles County, California, ED 19-701, sheet 20A, dwelling 384.

[878] Willard Morgan household, 1930 US census, Compton, Los Angeles County, California, ED 871, sheet 5A, dwelling 114, family 129.

[879] "Bone Gap News," *Daily Republican-Register* (Mount Carmel, Illinois), Wednesday 27 October 1937, p. 3, col. 5. These notices normally state "Mr. and Mrs." if both visited.

[880] Willard A. Morgan entry, *San Marino City Directory, Season 1936–1937* (South Pasadena, California: California Directory, 1936), p. 54, image 53 of 101 (ancestry.com).

$4000 for a full year's work in 1939.[881] In 1944 he and Wilma registered to vote as Republicans.[882] The Los Angeles Heart Association acknowledged gifts to its research fund in his and others' memory in 1950.[883]

---

[881] Willard A. Morgan household, 1940 US census, San Marino City, San Gabriel Township, Los Angeles County, California, ED 19-701, sheet 20A, dwelling 384. Statewide figures from US Census Bureau, Census of Housing, Historical Census of Housing Tables, Median Home Values Unadjusted 1940 (census.gov/hhes/www/housing/census/historic/values.html).

[882] Willard A. Morgan and Mrs. Wilma Morgan entries at 1055 Winston Avenue, Index to Register of Voters, San Marino City Precinct #15, Los Angeles County, California, 1944; "California, Voter Registrations, 1900–1968" > Los Angeles County > 1944 > Roll 60 > image 555 of 979 (ancestry.com).

[883] Los Angeles Heart Association advertisement, *Los Angeles Times*, Sunday 24 December 1950, p. 10, cols. 1–2.

Chapter 31

Tenth Generation

William Britton–Sarah Castile–Helen Ross Family
parents at chapter 9

*"Hornbook on the Law of Bills and Notes" and
two tons of geological specimens*

31. **WILLIAM EVERETT**[10] **BRITTON** (*Maria Lucretia "Cretie" Morgan*[9], *Mary Elizabeth Thrall*[8], *Worthy*[7], *Eliphas*[6], *Samuel*[5], *John*[4-3], *Timothy*[2], *William*[1])
Birth: 23 March 1887 in Bible Grove, Clay County, Illinois[884]
Death: reportedly 6 November 1965 in Los Angeles County, California[885]
Burial: Bone Gap Cemetery, Edwards County, Illinois[886]
Spouse #1: **SARAH MYRTLE CASTILE,** married 28 July 1916[887]
Spouse #1's parents: William and Mary E. (Watts) Casteel[888]

---

[884] James [Joseph] W. Britten [Britton] household for son William E. age 13, 1900 US census, Glenwood, Schuyler County, Missouri, ED 132, sheet 4B, dwelling/family 76. For exact date and place, William E. Britton WWI draft card, order #2040, serial #43, 5 June 1917, Urbana, Illinois; "US, World War I Draft Registration Cards, 1917–1918" > Illinois > Champaign County > 1 > Draft Card B > image 375 of 552 (ancestry.com).
[885] William E. Britton index entry; "California, Death Index, 1940–1997" (ancestry.com). Original not viewed.
[886] William E. Britton (1887–1965) grave marker, Bone Gap Cemetery, Bone Gap, Illinois, image, memorial #141,241314 by Janice (Teel) Crites (findagrave.com).
[887] William Everett Britton entry, *Who Was Who in America* (Wilmette, Illinois: Marquis Who's Who, 1989), vol. 9 (1985–1989):48. William and Sarah's names as given in Kent Gunnell Britton–Berdina Theresa Meck marriage, 18 July 1945, Hollywood, California, California marriage certificate #13086, Los Angeles County 2423:40; "California, County Marriages, 1850–1952" > 5698704 > image 2851 of 3191 (familysearch.org).
[888] William Casteel household for wife Mary E. and daughter Myrtle age 15, 1900 US census, Danville, Vermilion County, Illinois, Ward 6, ED 74, sheet 14B, dwelling 306, family 340. For mother's birth surname, Sarah C. Britton entry, "California, Death Index, 1940–1997" (ancestry.com). Original not viewed.

Spouse #1's birth: 6 March 1885 in Illinois[889]
Spouse #1's death: 19 June 1966 in Orange County, California[890]
Spouse #1's burial: not known
Spouse #2: **HELEN GLADYS ROSS,** married reportedly in Cook County, Illinois, 23 July 1949[891]
Spouse #2's parents: John G. and Nellie (McLennan) Ross[892]
Spouse #2's birth: 25 August 1901 in St. Louis County, Minnesota[893]
Spouse #2's death: San Francisco 24 July 1957
Spouse #2's burial: Duluth, St. Louis County, Minnesota[894]

In 1910 Helen's father John was clerk of the municipal court in Duluth, St. Louis County, Minnesota.[895] In later years in California, Helen was a member of the Bay Area Librarians and the American Association of Law Libraries.[896]

---

[889] For birthdate 1887, Sarah M. Britton entry, List of United States Citizens, S.S. *Delvangen* arriving New Orleans from Jamaica 25 September 1938; "New Orleans Passenger Lists, 1813–1963" > T905, New Orleans, 1903–1945 > 168 > image 331 of 505 (ancestry.com).

[890] Sarah C. Britton death index entry, "California, Death Index, 1940–1997" (ancestry.com). Original not viewed.

[891] William E. Britton–Helen G. Ross marriage index entry, 23 July 1949, "Cook County, Illinois, Marriage Index 1930–1960" (ancestry.com). For 30 July, William Everett Britton entry, *Who Was Who in America* (Wilmette, Illinois: Marquis Who's Who, 1989), vol. 9 (1985–1989):48.

[892] Helen Gladys Ross birth index entry, certificate #1901-38039, "Minnesota, Birth Index 1900–1934" (ancestry.com). Also, John G. Ross household for wife Nellie and daughter Helen age 8, 1910 US census, Duluth, St. Louis County, Minnesota, Ward 1, ED 146, sheet 1B, dwelling 16, family 17.

[893] William E. and Helen R. Britton, List of In-Bound Passengers, S.S. *Excambion*, arriving New York City 26 July 1950; "New York, Passenger Lists, 1820–1957" > Roll > T715, 1897–1957 > 7001–8000 > Roll 7684 > image 287 of 1278 (ancestry.com).

[894] "Helen Britton Funeral Rites Tomorrow," *San Francisco Chronicle*, Friday 26 July 1957, p. 18, col. 1.

[895] Helen Gladys Ross birth index entry, certificate #1901-38039, "Minnesota, Birth Index 1900-1934" (ancestry.com). Also, John G. Ross household for wife Nellie and daughter Helen age 8, 1910 US census, Duluth, St. Louis County, Minnesota, Ward 1, ED 146, sheet 1B, dwelling 16, family 17.

[896] "Helen Britton Funeral Rites Tomorrow," *San Francisco Chronicle*, Friday 26 July 1957, p. 18, col. 1.

William completed eight years of post-college education, Sarah four.[897] He came to McKendree College from Mounds and graduated with an A.B. in 1909.[898] In 1917 he was teaching in the College of Commerce at the University of Illinois and living at 605 Indiana Avenue, Urbana, Champaign County. Tall and slender, with gray eyes and light-colored hair, he claimed exemption from the draft on account of a "dependent wife."[899] In 1920 they had two children and he was teaching at the university; the family lived in apartment 2 at 1101 West Oregon in Urbana.[900]

In the early 1920s he taught briefly at Indiana University, soon returning to the University of Illinois 1925–1954. He also taught summer sessions at Northwestern, the University of North Carolina, and other schools.[901] From 1922 to 1925 he served on the National Conference Commissioners on Uniform State Laws. He wrote the *Hornbook on the Law of Bills and Notes*, published in 1943.[902] From 1945 to 1949, he was the university's legal counsel, dealing with projects including the gift of the Robert Allerton estate and the lease of Navy Pier in Chicago for new campus development. He also chaired the University's Committee on Accountancy from 1924 to 1954.[903]

---

[897] Kristian [William] Everett Britton household, 1940 US census, Urbana, Champaign County, Illinois, ED 10-39, sheet 62A, dwelling 25.

[898] Paul and Chester Farthing, editors, *Philo History: Chronicles and Biographies of the Philosophian Literary Society of McKendree College* (Lebanon, Illinois: privately printed, 1911), 177.

[899] William E. Britton WWI draft card, order #2040, serial #43, 5 June 1917, Urbana, Illinois; "US, World War I Draft Registration Cards, 1917–1918" > Illinois > Champaign County > 1 > Draft Card B > image 375 of 552 (ancestry.com).

[900] William E. Britton household, 1920 US census, Urbana, Champaign County, Illinois, Ward 4, ED 48, sheet 7A, dwelling 138, family 192.

[901] "Make Additions to U. of I. Faculty," *Decatur Herald* (Illinois), Sunday 15 June 1924, p. 1, col. 6. Also, "Judge Hemphill to Teach Law," *Alton Evening Telegraph* (Illinois), Wednesday 27 May 1936, p. 22, col. 3. Also, "Three Noted Jurists To Teach This Summer," *Durham Morning Herald* (North Carolina), Sunday 9 March 1941, part 2, p. 8, col. 1.

[902] William Everett Britton entry, *Who Was Who in America* (Wilmette, Illinois: Marquis Who's Who, 1989), 9:48.

[903] *Meeting of the Board of Trustees of the University of Illinois*, 21 June 1954, p. 1371, Record Series 1/1/802 (archives.library.illinois.edu/slc/egyptian-illinois-illini).

In 1930 the family lived at 307 Michigan in Urbana, in a house valued at $16,000.[904] In 1940 they lived at 305 Pennsylvania in a house valued at $20,000, about five times the statewide average that year.[905] On 26 July 1950 William and Helen, residents of 305 Pennsylvania, arrived at New York City from Marseilles on the S.S. *Excambion*.[906]

His dauntingly busy activities were not limited to legal affairs: he was president of the American Association of University Professors 1954–56. On retirement, he taught part-time at the University of California's Hunter College of Law in San Francisco until 1964.[907] When he left Illinois, he donated to the university's geology department two tons of geological specimens he had picked up as a hobby over many years.[908]

---

[904] William E. Britton household, 1930 US census, Urbana, Champaign County, Illinois, Ward 7, ED 76, sheet 9B, dwelling 214, family 236.

[905] Kristian [William] Everett Britton household, 1940 US census, Urbana, Champaign County, Illinois, ED 10-39, sheet 62A, dwelling 25. Statewide figures from US Census Bureau, Census of Housing, Historical Census of Housing Tables, Median Home Values Unadjusted 1940 (census.gov/hhes/www/housing/census/historic/values.html).

[906] William E. and Helen R. Britton, List of In-Bound Passengers, S.S. *Excambion*, arriving New York City 26 July 1950; "New York, Passenger Lists, 1820–1957" > Roll > T715, 1897–1957 > 7001–8000 > Roll 7684 > image 287 of 1278 (ancestry.com).

[907] William Everett Britton entry, *Who Was Who in America* (Wilmette, Illinois: Marquis Who's Who, 1989), 9:48.

[908] "Donates Specimens," *Rockford Morning Star* (Illinois), Sunday 22 August 1954, p. B7, col. 1. One hopes that they were labeled!

Chapter 32

Tenth Generation

Floyd Britton–Gladys Gaunt–Hazel Reck Family
parents at chapter 9

Making Illinois Gov. Len Small return $650,000 to the state treasury

32. FLOYD EVANSTON^{10} BRITTON (*Maria Lucretia "Cretie" Morgan^9, Mary Elizabeth Thrall^8, Worthy^7, Eliphas^6, Samuel^5, John$^{4-3}$, Timothy^2, William^1*)
Birth: 24 December 1890 in Marion, Williamson County, Illinois
Death: 3 June 1982 in Spread Eagle, Florence County, Wisconsin
Burial: Memorial Park Cemetery and Crematorium, Skokie, Cook County, Illinois[909]
Spouse #1: **GLADYS GAUNT,** married 25 December 1912 in Mound City, Pulaski County, Illinois[910]
Spouse #1's parents: Charles M. and Eleanor (Miller) Gaunt[911]
Spouse #1's birth: 16 February 1891

---

[909] "Floyd E. Britton," *Chicago Tribune*, 5 June 1982. For place of birth, Floyd E. Britton WWI draft card, order #814, serial #285, Springfield, Illinois, 29 May 1917; "US, World War I Draft Registration Cards, 1917–1918" > Illinois > Pulaski County > Draft Card B > image 251 of 338 (ancestry.com). Floyd E. Britton grave marker, Grave 3-W, Lot 632, Lakeside Section, Memorial Park Cemetery and Crematorium, Skokie, Cook County, Illinois, image, memorial #115,937,925 for Floyd Evanston Britton by Mick (findagrave.com).

[910] "Our Town," *Chicago Sunday Tribune*, Sunday 4 January 1953, part 3, p. 12, col. 5, recalling the siblings' joint wedding 40 years later. Also, Frank E. Britton–Gladys Gaunt marriage license 24 December 1912, marriage 25, Pulaski County Register of Marriages 2:142; "Illinois, County Marriages, 1810–1940 > 5292971 > image 430 of 618 (familysearch.org). Parental and other information was omitted.

[911] Charles Gaunt household for wife Ellanor [Eleanor] age 33 and daughter Gladys age 9, 1900 US census, Mound City, Pulaski County, Illinois, Ward 1, ED 70, sheet 2B, dwelling 31, family 34. Similarly, 1910, Mounds, ED 88, sheet 5A, dwelling 92, family 94. Also, Eleanor Miller–Charles M. Gaunt marriage index entry, Pulaski County, 13 October 1889; "Illinois, Marriage Index, 1860–1920" (ancestry.com).

Spouse #1's death: 8 March 1961 at 331 Kedzie, Evanston, Cook County, Illinois[912]

Spouse #1's burial: with her husband[913]

Spouse #2: **HAZEL (RECK) (CROCKER) THORSNESS,** married second as her third husband before 6 January 1963[914]

Spouse #2's parents: Peter and Grace (Watkins?) Reck

Spouse #2's birth: 17 July 1897 in Chicago[915]

Spouse #2's death: 7 May 1978 in Green Bay, Brown County, Wisconsin[916]

Spouse #2's burial: not known

Floyd was memorialized twice: 5 June at Iron Mountain, Dickinson County, Michigan, and 7 June in Skokie, Cook County, Illinois.[917]

---

[912] "Obituaries…Mrs. Floyd E. Britton," *Chicago Tribune*, Thursday 9 March 1961, part 4, p. 2, col. 3. Funeral at First Methodist Church in Evanston.

[913] Gladys Gaunt Britton grave marker, Grave 2-W, Lot 632, Lakeside Section, Memorial Park Cemetery and Crematorium, Skokie, Cook County, Illinois, image, memorial #115,938,103 for Gladys Gaunt Gaunt [*sic*] Britton by Mick (findagrave.com).

[914] "Evanston Couple Mark 50th Year of Marriage," *Chicago Tribune*, Sunday 6 January 1963, part 8, p. 4, col. 8, where she was identified as "the former Mrs. Charles Crocker."

[915] Peter Ruk [Reck] household for wife Grace age 26 and daughter Hazel age 2, 1900 US census, Chicago, Cook County, Illinois, Ward 25, ED 777, sheet 12B, dwelling 201, family 236. For birthdate and place, Hazel Thorsness born 15 July 1897 in Chicago, List of United States Citizens arriving Los Angeles on S.S. *President Garfield* 14 May 1940; "California, Passenger and Crew Lists, 1882–1959" > M1764, Los Angeles, Selected Suburbs, 1907–1948 > 102 > image 261 of 930 (ancestry.com). For Grace's probable birth surname, John Watkins household for daughter Gracie age 7, 1880 US census, Evanston, Cook County, Illinois, ED 218, p. 294C, dwelling 149, family 162. Also, Grace Elizabeth Reck death index entry 26 February 1921 naming father as Edward Wathins [Watkins]; "Illinois, Deaths and Stillbirths Index, 1916–1947," citing FHL 1,570,364, DGS 4,008,103 (familysearch.org).

[916] Hazel C. Britton death index entry, certificate #11460 "grba" (probably Green Bay); "Wisconsin, Death Index, 1959–1997" (ancestry.com). Also, "Kin of Local Woman Dies," *Journal Gazette* (Mattoon, Illinois), Monday 7 June 1982, p. 5, col. 4.

[917] "Floyd E. Britton," *Chicago Tribune*, 5 June 1982. For place of birth, Floyd E. Britton WWI draft card, order #814, serial #285, Springfield, Illinois, 29 May 1917; "US, World War I Draft Registration Cards, 1917–1918" > Illinois > Pulaski County > Draft Card B > image 251 of 338 (ancestry.com). Floyd E. Britton grave marker, Grave 3-W, Lot 632, Lakeside Section, Memorial Park Cemetery and Crematorium, Skokie, Cook County, Illinois, image, memorial #115,937,125 for Floyd Evanston Britton by Mick (findagrave.com).

Floyd's first wife Gladys grew up in Mounds, Pulaski County, Illinois, where her father Charles was at various times a merchant, sheriff, and later bank cashier.[918] She completed four years of high school.[919]

Floyd's second wife Hazel married first 17 April 1920 in Rogers Park, Chicago, Charles Henry Crocker, an insurance broker born there 3 October 1883, with whom she had two children.[920] She married second as his second wife between 1935 (when they were living in different places) and 1940 (when they were together in Kenilworth) Lionel G. Thorsness, a lawyer born 20 May 1895 in DeForest, Dane County, Wisconsin.[921]

Floyd completed four years of college.[922] He was one of seven graduates from Medora High School (Macoupin County, Illinois) 1 May

---

[918] Charles Gaunt household for wife Ellanor [Eleanor] Age 33 and daughter Gladys age 9, 1900 U. S. census, Mound City, Pulaski County, Illinois, Ward 1, ED 70, sheet 2B, dwelling 31, family 34. Similarly, 1910, Mounds, ED 88, sheet 5A, dwelling 92, family 94. Also, Eleanor Miller–Charles M. Gaunt marriage index entry, Pulaski County, 13 October 1889; "Illinois, Marriage Index, 1860–1920" (ancestry.com).

[919] Lionel Thorsness (age 44) household for wife Hazel (age 42), 1940 US census, ED 16-313, Kenilworth, New Trier Township, Cook County, Illinois, sheet 14A, dwelling 240 (?).

[920] Hazel C. Reck (age 22)–Charles H. Crocker (age 36) marriage, license #862,361, 12 April 1920, marriage 17 April, Cook County, Illinois; FHL 1,030,724, DGS 4,272,561, image 581 of 1444 (familysearch.org). Rev. Nichols of 6925 North Ashland officiated. For exact date and place and mother, Charles Henry Crocker, WWI draft card, serial #4065, order #1627, 4339 Hazel Avenue, Chicago; "US, World War I Draft Registration Cards, 1917–1918" > Illinois > Chicago City > 55 > Draft Card C > image 606 of 686 (ancestry.com). For occupation, Charles Crocker, 1930 US census, Kenilworth, Cook County, ED 3, sheet 8B, dwelling/family 81.

[921] Lionel Thorsness (age 44) household for wife Hazel (age 42), 1940 US census, ED 16-313, Kenilworth, New Trier Township, Cook County, Illinois, sheet 14A, dwelling 240 (?). Also, Leonel [Lionel] G. Thorsness, WWI draft card, #67, 53rd Ward, Chicago, 1 June 1917; "US, World War I Draft Registration Cards, 1917–1918" > Illinois > Chicago City > 79 > Draft Card T > image 173 of 387 (ancestry.com). Lionel married first about 1925 Alice M. Wagner: Lionel G. Thorsness (age 34) household for wife Alice (age 29), 1930 US census, Chicago, Cook County, Illinois, Ward 44, ED 1619, sheet 6A, family [blank], dwelling 243. He married third 4 August 1950 Dolores M. Molitor: Lionel G. Thorsness–Dolores M. Molitor marriage index entry, file 2144125, Cook County Clerk; "Cook County, Illinois, Marriage Index, 1930–1960" (ancestry.com).

[922] Floyd E. Britten [Britton] household, 1940 US census, Evanston, Cook County, Illinois, ED 16-206, sheet 13A, dwelling 381.

1908, where he presented an oration, "An Issue of Justice."[923] A University of Illinois Law School graduate, Evanston resident, and Chicago attorney, Floyd served as an Illinois state assistant attorney general in the 1920s, when the family lived in Springfield.[924] In 1917 he was living in Mounds when the state attorney general appointed him to "have charge of all the inheritance tax work outside of Cook county."[925] That fall he and others were delegated to help the St. Clair County state's attorney in prosecuting cases from the July race riots in East St. Louis.[926] In the mid-1920s he was involved in lawsuits against Governor Len Small, first as an assistant attorney general and later representing the Citizens Association of Chicago—at the end of which Small had to pay $650,000 into the state treasury.[927]

In 1938 Floyd himself was in the spotlight when vice-president Leslie Krumsick of the Fort Dearborn Securities Corporation killed himself. A subsequent raid by the state's attorney revealed a shortage of funds.

As president of the corporation, Floyd claimed he was an ignorant "figurehead." He stated, "This company was organized after the old Donoghue, Krumsick & Co. went into bankruptcy. Its function was to give Krumsick a chance to make good on the losses of the other company's customers. They took stock in the new one. Krumsick told me only a short while ago that Fort Dearborn Securities was in such shape it could be liquidated without loss to anyone. I was not familiar with the firm's affairs, and was seldom in the office. I believed him."[928]

---

[923] "Medora Commencement May 1st," *Daily Illinois State Register* (Springfield), Monday 20 April 1908, p. 1, col. 5. His father, Rev. J. W. Britton, gave the benediction.

[924] "Floyd E. Britton," *Chicago Tribune*, 5 June 1982.

[925] "J. W. Gullett to Assist Brundage," *Illinois State Register* (Springfield), Tuesday 27 March 1917, p. 8, col. 4.

[926] "Will Prosecute Riot Cases," *Daily Illinois State Register* (Springfield), Saturday 15 September 1917, p. 6, col. 1. Also, Elliott M. Rudwick, *Race Riot at East St. Louis July 2, 1917* (Carbondale: Southern Illinois University Press, 1964).

[927] "Chicagoans Seek Small Trial Entry," *Rockford Register-Gazette* (Illinois), Monday 1 June 1925, p. 2, col. 1. Also, Robert P. Howard, *Illinois: A History of the Prairie State* (Grand Rapids, Michigan: William B. Eerdmans, 1972), 465.

[928] "Broker Cheats Blue Sky Raid by Gas Suicide," *Chicago Tribune*, Wednesday 24 August 1938, p. 1, col. 4.

Assistant state's attorney John Philips agreed, finding that the secretary had altered the books and Floyd was in the clear: he had been named president at the suggestion of creditors of the earlier concern, "knew nothing of stocks and bonds," and "acted only in a supervisory capacity."[929]

In 1951 Floyd chaired the state bar association's section on commercial and bankruptcy law.[930] He was associated with the firm of Hubachek & Kelley until his retirement in 1964.[931] In 1930 the family rented for $150 a month in Chicago; in 1940 for $120 a month in suburban Evanston.[932] In 1952 they were living at 331 Kedzie there.[933]

---

[929] "Broker $25,000 Short, Ends Life in His Auto," *St. Louis Post-Dispatch*, Wednesday 24 August 1938, p. 2A, col. 8.

[930] "District Bar Meeting Set," *De Kalb Daily Chronicle* (Illinois), Wednesday 24 October 1951, p. 1, col. 3.

[931] "Floyd E. Britton," *Chicago Tribune*, 5 June 1982.

[932] Freidrich [Floyd] Britton household, 1930 US census, Chicago, Cook County, Illinois, Ward 41, ED 2871, sheet 4B, dwelling 5, family 99. Similarly, Floyd E. Britten [Britton], 1940, Evanston, ED 16-206, sheet 13A, dwelling 381.

[933] "Our Town," *Chicago Sunday Tribune*, Sunday 4 January 1953, part 3, p. 12, col. 5, recalling the siblings' joint wedding 40 years later.

Chapter 33

Tenth Generation

Lucile Britton–Timothy McKnight Family
parents at chapter 9

"The Minnesota Plan for Expert Testimony"

33. **LUCILE EVANGELINE**[10] **BRITTON** (*Maria Lucretia "Cretie" Morgan*[9], *Mary Elizabeth Thrall*[8], *Worthy*[7], *Eliphas*[6], *Samuel*[5], *John*[4-3], *Timothy*[2], *William*[1])
Birth: 22 September 1892 in Illinois, possibly Anna, Union County[934]
Death: 15 March 1975 at the Homestead Hotel in Evanston, Cook County, Illinois[935]
Burial: Memorial Park Cemetery and Crematorium, Skokie, Cook County, Illinois[936]
Spouse: **TIMOTHY IRLE MCKNIGHT,** married 25 December 1912 in Mound City, Pulaski County, Illinois[937]
Spouse's parents: William E. and Lucy Emily (Wilkin) McKnight
Spouse's birth: 10 June 1891 in Oblong, Crawford County, Illinois[938]

---

[934] For exact date and state, "Lucile" McKnight entry, US Social Security Death Index.

[935] Death Notice, "[Lucille Britton] McKnight," *Chicago Tribune*, 18 March 1975, no page or column given.

[936] Lucile Evangeline McKnight, no grave marker image, Memorial Park Cemetery and Crematorium, Skokie, Illinois, memorial #190,432,138 by Mick (findagrave.com).

[937] "Our Town," *Chicago Sunday Tribune*, Sunday 4 January 1953, part 3, p. 12, col. 5, recalling the siblings' joint wedding 40 years ago. Also, Lucile E. Britton–Timothy I. McKnight marriage license #24 December 1912, marriage 25, Pulaski County Register of Marriages 2:142; "Illinois, County Marriages, 1810–1940" > 5292971 > image 430 of 618 (familysearch.org). Parental and other information was left blank.

[938] Timothy Irle McKnight #7062, *Semi-Centennial Alumni Record of the University of Illinois* (Chicago: R. R. Donnelley & Sons, [1918?]), 587.

Spouse's death: 19 January 1973 at 1625 Hinman Avenue in Evanston, Cook County, Illinois[939]
Spouse's burial: with his wife[940]

Timothy graduated from McKendree College in 1912 (later serving as a trustee) and from the University of Illinois law school in 1915. Practicing law in Carrollton, Greene County, Illinois, he served as city attorney 1915–1920 and as state's attorney 1920–24 (elected twice).[941]

In 1927 the family moved to Evanston, Cook County, Illinois, where they rented for $135 per month; in 1940 they owned a $25,000 house at 2110 Central Park Avenue there. (Statewide average house value that year was $3,527.) Both he and Lucille completed four years of college.[942] In 1932 helped defend the case of Illinois Life Insurance Company director Ernest Stevens in which he argued that Stevens's transfer of funds from the insurance company to family-owned hotels was "an honest but ill-advised business transaction."[943] In 1946 he spoke at the annual conference of Sixth Circuit federal judges on "The Minnesota Plan for Expert Testimony," intended to provide closer scrutiny of dubious medical testimony.[944] In 1953–54 he was president of the Illinois Bar Association. He was associated with the firm of Peterson, Ross, Rall, Barber & Seidel of 135 S. La Salle Street in Chicago prior to his retirement in 1972.[945]

---

[939] Death Notice, "Timothy I. McKnight," *Chicago Tribune*, Sunday 21 January 1973.

[940] Timothy I. McKnight, no grave marker image, Memorial Park Cemetery and Crematorium, Skokie, Illinois, memorial #190,432,240 by Mick (findagrave.com).

[941] Timothy Irle McKnight entry, *Who Was Who in America* (Wilmette, Illinois: Marquis Who's Who, 1989), 9:243 (1985–1989).

[942] "Evanston Couple Mark 50th Year of Marriage," *Chicago Tribune*, Sunday 6 January 1963, part 8, p. 4, col. 8. Statewide figures from US Census Bureau, Census of Housing, Historical Census of Housing Tables, Median Home Values Unadjusted 1940 (census.gov/hhes/www/housing/census/historic/values.html).

[943] "Complete Jury to Try Stevens in Illinois Life Case," *Chicago Tribune*, Tuesday 26 September 1933, p. 5, col. 7, and p. 32.

[944] "Judges to Discuss Question of Need for Commissioners," *Cincinnati Enquirer*, Thursday 10 October 1946, p. 7, cols. 7–8.

[945] Death Notice, "Timothy I. McKnight," *Chicago Tribune*, Sunday 21 January 1973.

Chapter 34

Tenth Generation

Vivian Britton–Harry Hannah Family
parents at chapter 9

Mattoon Landmarks

34. **Vivian**[10] **Britton** (*Maria Lucretia "Cretie" Morgan*[9], *Mary Elizabeth Thrall*[8], *Worthy*[7], *Eliphas*[6], *Samuel*[5], *John*[4-3], *Timothy*[2], *William*[1])
Birth: 7 September 1894 in Novelty, Knox County, Missouri[946]
Death: 17 October 1991 in Mattoon, Coles County, Illinois
Burial: Dodge Grove Cemetery there[947]
Spouse: **Harry Ingalls Hannah,** married 29 June 1917 in Ashley, Washington County, Illinois[948]
Spouse's parents: John F. and Emma Jane (Donaldson) Hannah[949]
Spouse's birth: 12 June 1890 in Fithian, Vermilion County, Illinois
Spouse's death: 20 May 1973 in Mattoon, Coles County, Illinois
Spouse's burial: with his wife[950]

---

[946] "Vivian B. Hannah," *Journal Gazette* (Mattoon, Illinois), Friday 18 October 1991, p. B4, col. 4.

[947] "Vivian B. Britton Hannah," *Herald & Review* (Decatur, Illinois), Friday 18 October 1991, p. A6. Also, Vivian Britton Hannah grave marker, grave space 30, division C, section 6, Dodge Grove Cemetery, Mattoon, Illinois, image, memorial #70,239,913 by Tim Naab (findagrave.com).

[948] "Judge and Mrs. Hannah Have 50th Anniversary," *Journal Gazette* (Mattoon, Illinois), Wednesday 5 July 1967, p. 16, cols. 5–6. Also, death notice, "[Lucille Britton] McKnight," *Chicago Tribune*, 18 March 1975, naming sister Mrs. Harry I. Hannah.

[949] Harry Ingalls Hannah entry, *The Political Graveyard* (http://politicalgraveyard.com/geo/IL/masons.D-J.html).

[950] Harry Ingalls Hannah grave marker, grave space 30, division C, section 6, Dodge Grove Cemetery, Mattoon, Illinois, image, memorial #70,239,911 by Tim Naab (findagrave.com).

In May 1895, "Cretia came near losing her baby a short time ago [Vivian?] but it is better now."[951]

Harry began practicing law in Mattoon in 1915 and remained there. As of 5 June 1917, he was tall, of medium build, with light blue eyes and light hair. An attorney employed by Bryan H. Tivnen, he claimed exemption from the World War I draft on six different grounds:
- migraine,
- mastoiditis,
- bronchitis,
- tuberculosis,
- his occupation, and
- an application (apparently pending) with the US Department of Agriculture.[952]

More than a year later, having evidently recovered, he left Mattoon 25 September 1918 to enter "officers training camp" at Fort Taylor, Kentucky.[953] He was formally enlisted on 4 October and released six weeks later (14 November) following the armistice that ended the war.[954] Three years after his nominal military service, he chaired the local American Legion chapter's delegation to the Illinois state convention.[955]

In later years he was constantly active. Some years he was in the Mattoon newspaper as often as three times a week—visiting family, attending or guiding clubs, giving talks, running for office (without great success except eventually as judge), and frequently appearing in court as a working attorney. After presiding over the start of the local Lions Club, in September 1923, he "delivered a brief but stirring arraignment of those

---

[951] Edith Flint Thrall in Salem, Illinois, to Edith Laura and Victor Worthy Thrall in Lebanon, 23 May 1895; Flint–Thrall letter 63, in author's possession.

[952] Harry I. Hannah World War I draft card, Mattoon local board, 5 June 1917, order #1222, serial #88; "US, World War I Draft Registration Cards, 1917–1918" > Illinois > Coles County > Draft Card H > image 111 of 674 (ancestry.com).

[953] "Personals," *Journal Gazette* (Mattoon, Illinois) Friday 4 October 1918, p. 6, col. 7.

[954] Harry Hannah index entry, "US, Department of Veterans Affairs BIRLS Death File, 1850–2010" (ancestry.com).

[955] "Legion Delegates to State Convention," *Journal Gazette* (Mattoon, Illinois), Thursday 22 September 1921, p. 1, col. 3.

of the members who procrastinate in attendance," and suggested that they "should either attend or resign" to make room for others (although the newspaper account said it was an unusually well-attended meeting).

"He also laid considerable stress upon the formulation of a definite program of work for the fall and winter seasons, and called attention to the fact that girls' work, under the auspices of the club, could be made a most interesting undertaking, and that there was need for it. As evidence of this fact he called attention to the number of young boys and girls who were being haled into police court by the authorities, many of them being found out in country lanes on 'petting' parties as late as 1 and 2 o'clock in the morning."[956]

In the fall of 1931, in the heart of the Depression, he began campaigning for the Republican nomination for the Illinois State Senate, laying out a seven-point program that fell short in the primary:

- reduced government spending (while the other points would seem to require more);
- finding some way "whereby holders of fortunes built up of securities and other intangibles . . . pay their just portion";
- more public works for the unemployed;
- unspecified aid to farmers;
- "stricter regulation" and licensing of vehicles' length, breadth, and weight load on state highways;
- "early completion of our hard road system"; and
- "stricter state supervision of banking" to protect depositors.[957]

In 1935, he represented unionized shoe-factory workers in Mattoon and Charleston when they were accused of disturbing the peace of a non-union meeting.[958] That same year, he chaired a committee of the local American Legion that sent letters to every school board in Coles

---

[956] "Lions to Aid Community Exposition," *Journal Gazette* (Mattoon, Illinois), 20 September 1923, p. 10, col. 1.

[957] "Political Advertisement: Hannah for State Senator," *Journal Gazette* (Mattoon, Illinois) Tuesday 6 October 1931, p. 8, col. 5.

[958] "Coles Shoe Union 'Riot' Appeal Set for Jan. 30," *Daily Review* (Decatur), Friday 18 January 1935, p. 30, col. 3.

County, insisting that all teachers take a "loyalty oath" before being allowed to teach.[959]

In 1936, Harry ran for state Senate in the general election. In mid-October he received a telegram inviting him to ride on the special train carrying Republican Presidential nominee Alfred M. Landon, traveling from Danville to Decatur and possibly to St. Louis.[960] Neither man fared well at the polls that year, which produced a landslide for Franklin D. Roosevelt. Harry also served in the state attorney general's office from 1915 to 1933 and was elected circuit court judge in 1957.[961]

In the fall of 1948, the Hannahs took a "three months trip by plane around the world," with stops in Honolulu, Shanghai, Hong Kong, Bangkok, New Delhi, Istanbul, Rome, Geneva, Paris, and England. "Switzerland seemed more like the United States to the local couple than any other country."[962] (The year before, when first commercially available, such a trip cost about $4,000 per couple—roughly $46,000 in 2019 dollars.)[963]

Vivian was a musician, teacher of Latin, and active in the community as a member of the "old Treble Clef Club," the Literary Club, the Central Community Church, DAR, Library Board, and as first president of the Mattoon Hospital Auxiliary.[964]

---

[959] "Wants Teachers to Take Oath of Allegiance," *Journal Gazette* (Mattoon, Illinois), Thursday 31 January 1935, p. 4 col. 2.

[960] "Hannah Gets Invitation to Ride on Landon Train," *Journal Gazette* (Mattoon, Illinois), Wednesday 14 October 1936, p. 1, col. 7.

[961] "Judge Harry Hannah Dies," *Journal Gazette* (Mattoon, Illinois), Monday 21 May 1973, p. 1, cols. 1–2.

[962] "Hannahs Complete World Plane Trip," *Journal Gazette* (Mattoon, Illinois,), Wednesday 6 October 1948, p. 7, col. 1.

[963] Tony Long, "June 17, 1947: Pan Am Launches 'Round-the-World Service," *Wired*, 17 June 2009 (wired.com/2009/06/dayintech-0617). For comparison, *Measuring Worth* (measuringworth.com/index.php), using "real wage" equivalent; other comparisons are higher.

[964] "Vivian B. Hannah," *Journal Gazette* (Mattoon, Illinois), Friday 18 October 1991, p. B4, col. 4.

Chapter 35

Tenth Generation

Waldo Vincent Britton Family
parents at chapter 9

The music stopped too soon

35. WALDO VINCENT¹⁰ BRITTON (*Maria Lucretia "Cretie" Morgan⁹, Mary Elizabeth Thrall⁸, Worthy⁷, Eliphas⁶, Samuel⁵, John⁴⁻³, Timothy², William¹*)
Birth: 21 September 1897 in Greencastle, Sullivan County, Missouri
Death: 13 February 1926 in St. Louis, Missouri[965]
Burial: Bone Gap, Edwards County, Illinois, on the 16th

In 1917 Waldo registered for the World War I draft in Ashley, Washington County, Illinois, but gave his occupation as "materials checker" in Nitro, Kanawha County, West Virginia, some 400 miles to the east. He was of medium height and build, with blue eyes and sandy hair.[966]

He was a student at the University of Illinois (Champaign County) in 1919 when he visited sister Vivian Hannah in Mattoon.[967] In 1920 he was living with his family in Ashley, Washington County, Illinois, and working as a musician in an opera house.[968] In 1921 he was a sophomore in the Delta Phi fraternity at the university; in 1926 he was a senior

---

[965] Waldo Britton, Missouri death certificate #6306, St. Louis, 13 February 1926; *Missouri Digital Heritage* > Collections > Death Certificates > "Missouri Death Certificates, 1910–1967." Also, Waldo V. Britton grave marker, Bone Gap Cemetery, Bone Gap, Edwards County, Illinois, image, memorial #141,241,373 by Janice (Teel) Crites (findagrave.com).

[966] Waldo Vincent Britton, WWI draft card, serial #1340, order #A-1221, 6 September 1918; "US World War I Draft Registration Cards, 1917–1918" > Illinois > Washington County A–Z > image 414 of 3534 (familysearch.org).

[967] Untitled note, *Journal Gazette* (Mattoon, Illinois), p. 3, col. 7.

[968] Joseph W. Britton household for Waldo, 1920 US census, Ashley, Washington County, Illinois, ED 214, sheet 4A, dwelling 97, family 100.

there.[969] His last address was 1701 North 45th Street in East St. Louis, St. Clair County, Illinois (not near Champaign-Urbana).

His length of stay in St. Louis was "5 hours" on 13 February 1926—at Barnes Hospital. The signing doctor attended Waldo from 3:30 until 7:10 pm, when he died of "hemorrhagic nephritis, cause unknown" and acute dilation of the heart.[970]

---

[969] Waldo Vincent Britton entry, Delta Phi fraternity, *The 1921 Illio*, University of Illinois, p. 427, image 438 of 662; similarly, Waldo V. Britton, *1927*, p. 410, image 444 of 742 (ancestry.com).

[970] Waldo Britton, Missouri death certificate #6306, St. Louis, 13 February 1926; *Missouri Digital Heritage* > Collections > Death Certificates > "Missouri Death Certificates, 1910–1967." Also, Waldo V. Britton grave marker, Bone Gap Cemetery, Bone Gap, Edwards County, Illinois, image, memorial #141,241,373 by Janice (Teel) Crites (findagrave.com).

Chapter 36

Tenth Generation

Elsie Britton–Verla Crawley Family
parents at chapter 9

Road Builder

36. ELSIE MAE "PEG"^{10} **BRITTON** (*Maria Lucretia "Cretie" Morgan^9, Mary Elizabeth Thrall^8, Worthy^7, Eliphas^6, Samuel^5, John$^{4-3}$, Timothy^2, William^1*)
Birth: October 1899 in Missouri, probably Schuyler County, Missouri, based on parents' residence
Death: 1997
Burial: with her husband in Mount Hope Cemetery in Belleville, St. Clair County, Illinois ^{971}
Spouse: **VERLA C. CRAWLEY,** married 1930^{972}
Spouse's parents: William A. and Sarah M. (Hood) Crawley^{973}

---

^{971} For date of birth, William A. Crawley household for wife Sarah M. and son Verla (age 3), 1900 US census, Franklin Township, Hendricks County, Indiana, ED 31, sheet 1B, dwelling/family 27. For place of birth, Verla C. Brawley [Crawley] household for Elsie M., 1940 US census, Signal Hill, Centerville Township, St. Clair County, Illinois, ED 32-135, sheet 1B–2A, dwelling 20. For death date and burial, Elsie B. Crawley grave marker, Mount Hope Cemetery, Belleville, Illinois, image, memorial #144,032,374 by Robin (findagrave.com).

^{972} Death Notice, "[Lucille Britton] McKnight," *Chicago Tribune*, Tuesday 18 March 1975. For approximate date, Verla Crawley household, 1930 US census, East St. Louis, St. Clair County, Illinois, ED 55, sheet 23A, dwelling 734, family 521. Also, Verle Crowley–Elsie Mae Britton marriage index entry, file #338,047, "Illinois, County Marriage Records, 1800–1940" (ancestry.com).

^{973} William A. Crawley household for wife Sarah M. and son Verla (age 3), 1900 US census, Franklin Township, Hendricks County, Indiana, ED 31, sheet 1B, dwelling/family 27. For mother's birth surname, William A. Crawley–Sarah M. Hood license 29 January 1887, marriage 30 January; "Indiana, Marriages, 1810–2001" > Putnam > 1881–1887, vol. H7 > image 296 of 325 (ancestry.com).

Spouse's birth: 29 October 1896 in Fillmore, Putnam County, Indiana[974]
Spouse's death: 3 March 1964
Spouse's burial: Mount Hope Cemetery in Belleville, St. Clair County, Illinois[975]

Verla, the son of a blacksmith,[976] served in World War I in the 158th Depot Brigade.[977] He completed four years of college (with a Bachelor of Science in Civil Engineering from Purdue University in 1921), Elsie three.[978] In 1920 "Verlie" was with his parents (father, blacksmith for a carriage company), divorced sister Ada (a machine operator for a card company), and her children in a rented house at 608 Fourth Street, Lafayette, Tippecanoe County, Indiana.

In 1930 in East St. Louis, St. Clair County, Illinois, Verla and Peg were renting for $65 a month and owned a radio set; he was a civil engineer for state highways.[979] In 1938 he and the assistant district engineer met with local officials in Edwardsville, Madison County,

---

[974] Verla Crawley, WW2 draft card, serial #U3568; "US, World War II Draft Registration Cards, 1942" > Illinois > Crawford–Cress > Clyne–Diekemper > image 1002 of 2027 (ancestry.com). Mrs. Harvey Smith of Rural Route 2, Lafayette [Tippecanoe County], Indiana, would know his address.

[975] Verla Crawley grave marker, Mount Hope Cemetery, Belleville, Illinois, image, memorial #144,032,340 by Robin (findagrave.com).

[976] William A. Crawley household for wife Sarah M. and son Verla (age 3), 1900 US census, Franklin Township, Hendricks County, Indiana, ED 31, sheet 1B, dwelling/family 27. For mother's birth surname, William A. Crowley–Sarah M. Hood license 29 January 1887, marriage 30 January; "Indiana, Marriages, 1810–2001" > Putnam > 1881–1887, vol. H7 > image 296 of 325 (ancestry.com).

[977] Verla Crawley grave marker, Mount Hope Cemetery, Belleville, Illinois, image, memorial #144,032,340 by Robin (findagrave.com).

[978] Verla C. Brawley [Crawley] household, 1940 US census, Signal Hill, Centerville Township, St. Clair County, Illinois, ED 32-135, sheet 1B–2A, dwelling 20. Also, "Complete Official List of Members of Graduating Class at Purdue University," *Lafayette Journal and Courier* (Indiana), Tuesday 7 June 1921, p. 11, col. 2.

[979] Verla Crawley household, 1930 US census, East St. Louis, St. Clair County, Illinois, ED 55, sheet 23A, dwelling 734, family 521.

Illinois, to discuss widening Highway 159 through town, increasing parking, and adding a traffic light.[980]

In 1940 the family was renting in Signal Hill for $60 a month.[981] In 1943 they were living at 274 Julia Avenue in Belleville, St. Clair County, Illinois, and "V. C." was a civil engineer; fifteen years later they were at 35 Glenview and his job was the same.[982] In 1963 he worked for the David J. Johnston engineering firm and was interviewed for a consulting job on traffic issues—again in Edwardsville, twenty-five years later.[983]

---

[980] "Street Widening Job Is Discussed at Edwardsville," *Alton Evening Telegraph* (Illinois), Thursday 22 December 1938, p. 2, col. 6.

[981] Verla C. Brawley [Crawley] household, 1940 US census, Signal Hill, Centerville Township, St. Clair County, Illinois, ED 32-135, sheet 1B–2A, dwelling 20.

[982] V. C. Crawley entry, *Polk's Belleville (St. Clair County, Illinois) City Directory 1943* (St. Louis, Missouri: R. L. Polk, 1943), p. 73, image 33 of 215. Similarly, *1958*, p. 106, image 137 of 635 (ancestry.com).

[983] "Traffic Engineer Is Interviewed," *Edwardsville Intelligencer* (Illinois), Thursday 15 August 1963, p. 2, col. 6.

Chapter 37

Tenth Generation

Ethel Britton–Milton Hartman Family
parents at chapter 10

Sending Peaches to Georgia: Pulaski County Spark Plugs

37. **ETHEL LUCRETIA**^{10} **BRITTON** (*Alta Areta Gould^9, Laura Lucina Thrall^8, Worthy^7, Eliphas^6, Samuel^5, John$^{4-3}$, Timothy^2, William^1*)
Birth: January 1894 or 5 November 1893 in Mounds, Pulaski County, Illinois[984]
Death: 13 August 1984 in Sikeston, Scott County, Missouri
Burial: Cairo City Cemetery in Villa Ridge, Pulaski County, Illinois[985]
Spouse: **MILTON MILES HARTMAN,** married 23 December 1913 in Mounds[986]
Spouse's parents: Mahlon R. and Mary (Rumer) Hartman[987]

---

[984] Born January 1894: Edward Britton household for Ethel, 1900 US census, Burkville Precinct, Pulaski County, Illinois, ED 68, sheet 16B, dwelling 351, family 379. Born 5 November 1893: Ethel Lucretia Britton Hartman entry, *Who's Who of American Women 1977–1978* (Chicago: Marquis Who's Who, 1977), 374–75. Also, Ethel B. Hartman grave marker, image, Cairo City Cemetery, Villa Ridge, Pulaski County, Illinois, memorial #71,880,546 by Lisa Caponetto (findagrave.com).

[985] Death date and burial: Ethel B. Hartman grave marker, image, Cairo City Cemetery, Villa Ridge, Pulaski County, Illinois, memorial #71,880,546 by Lisa Caponetto (findagrave.com). Place of death: "Area Head Start Founder Ethel Hartman Dies," *Southern Illinoisan*, Tuesday 14 August 1984, p. 15, cols. 1–3.

[986] Ethel L. Brittan [Britton]–Milton M. Hartman marriage 23 December 1913, Pulaski County, Illinois, marriage register 2:162; "Illinois, County Marriages, 1810–1940" > FHL 960,486, DGS 5,202,971 > image 450 of 618 (familysearch.org).

[987] Mahlon Hartman–Mary Rumer marriage license 4 October 1881, married 6 October, Mascoutah, St. Clair County, Illinois, FHL 2,169,731, DGS 4,030,010, images 45–47 of 1605 (familysearch.org).

Spouse's birth: 9 December 1892[988]
Spouse's death: 18 October 1964
Spouse's burial: Cairo City Cemetery in Villa Ridge, Pulaski County, Illinois[989]

A Methodist, Ethel studied at McKendree College 1909–1913, attended the University of Illinois 1916–1917, and earned a Bachelor of Science in Education at Southern Illinois University in 1947.[990] Ethel's mother's first cousin Rev. Victor W. Thrall (chapter 17) came from Chicago to officiate at their southern Illinois wedding. It took place at what one newspaper called "the palatial country home of Mr. and Mrs. E. G. Britton, residing on Beechwood dairy farm, near Mounds."[991]

Ethel was a supervisor or administrator in various capacities in Pulaski County schools from 1919 to 1959.[992] Said to be the originator of the Head Start program in southern Illinois,[993] she was its director in Pulaski County from 1965 to 1973. A co-organizer of Mounds Public Library in 1935, she continued for more than four decades as a volunteer supervising librarian there. She also helped organize the Pulaski-Alexander County Cooperative Extension Service and the Pulaski County TB and Visiting Nurses Association. She was a member of the founding

---

[988] Mahlon Hartman household for son Milton M. age 7, 1900 US census, New Athens Township, St. Clair County, Illinois, ED 120, sheet 5A, dwelling 80, family 83.

[989] Milton M. Hartman grave marker, image, Cairo City Cemetery, Village Ridge, Pulaski County, Illinois, memorial #71,880,527 by Lisa Caponetto (findagrave.com).

[990] Ethel Lucretia Britton Hartman entry, *Who's Who of American Women 1977–1978* (Chicago: Marquis Who's Who, 1977), 374–75.

[991] "Freeburg Man Is a Benedict," *News Democrat* (Belleville, Illinois), Saturday 27 December 1913, p. 4, col. 3.

[992] Ethel Lucretia Britton Hartman entry, *Who's Who of American Women 1977–1978* (Chicago: Marquis Who's Who, 1977), 374–75.

[993] "Deaths: Ethel B. Hartman," *Pulaski Enterprise* (Illinois), Wednesday 22 August 1984, p. 2, cols. 3–6. Also, Ethel Lucretia Britton Hartman entry, *Who's Who of American Women 1977–1978* (Chicago: Marquis Who's Who, 1977), 374–75.

board of the Southern Illinois Electric Co-op,[994] and a charter member of the Pulaski-Alexander County Farm Bureau.[995]

Milton graduated in the class of 1914 at McKendree, and was a "dairyman" in 1928.[996] He reportedly came to Pulaski County in 1913 from Freeburg, St. Clair County, Illinois, to marry Ethel Britton, his college sweetheart.

> He remained a resident until his death 51 years later. . . . Milton furthered his education at the University of Illinois with an advanced degree in Agriculture. He soon became an active leader in the community and contributed significantly towards the advancement of agriculture in our area.
>
> He was an organizer, and member of the first board of Directors of the Pulaski Farm Bureau in 1922 (now Pulaski-Alexander Farm Bureau) . . . sharing his home with the first Extension Farm Advisor-Farm Bureau Manager until sufficient funds were available from the community to pay for these services. He served as charter board member of Fruit Belt Service Company in 1927; served on boards of the Ullin Mutual Insurance Company, Ullin Livestock Shipping Association, and Villa Ridge Shippers Association, as well as leading the first 4-H Club in Pulaski County.
>
> Milton was an orchardist and horticulturist. His delicious peaches attracted not only area people but large trucks would come up empty from Georgia to fill up and haul Hartman peaches to their southern distributors. His fresh vegetables and other fruits were shipped to Chicago and St. Louis markets.

---

[994] Ethel Lucretia Britton Hartman entry, *Who's Who of American Women 1977–1978* (Chicago: Marquis Who's Who, 1977), 374–75.

[995] "Deaths: Ethel B. Hartman," *Pulaski Enterprise* (Illinois), Wednesday 22 August 1984, p. 2, cols. 3–6.

[996] *Centennial McKendree College with St. Clair County History* (Lebanon, Illinois: McKendree College, 1928), 401.

Milton and Ethel enjoyed camping, in fact, they honeymooned by covered wagon touring the hills of Southern Illinois.[997]

---

[997] "Milton Miles Hartman, Sr.," Pulaski County History Book Committee, *Pulaski County, Illinois, 1987* (Paducah, Kentucky: Turner, 1987), 179.

Chapter 38

Tenth Generation

Ernest Britton–Martha Hughes Family
parents at chapter 10

School superintendent in Effingham and Midland

38. ERNEST RAYMOND[10] BRITTON (*Alta Areta Gould⁹, Laura Lucina Thrall⁸, Worthy⁷, Eliphas⁶, Samuel⁵, John⁴⁻³, Timothy², William¹*)
Birth: 23 March 1903 in Illinois
Death: 31 October 1983, last residence in Midland, Midland County, Michigan[998]
Burial: Midland City Cemetery, Midland County, Michigan[999]
Spouse: **MARTHA E. HUGHES,** married about 1925[1000]
Spouse's parents: William L. and Maggie L. (Folck) Hughes[1001]
Spouse's birth: 30 November 1902 in Illinois

---

[998] Ernest Britton index entry; "Michigan Death Index, 1971–1996" (ancestry.com). Social Security Death Index gives November 1983. For birth date and middle name, Ernest Raymond Britton WWII draft card, serial #949, order #10537; "World War II Draft Registration Cards" > Illinois > B > Br > Britton, Ernest Raymond, 1903 > p. 1 (fold3.com/image/1/654589104).

[999] Ernest R. Britton (1903–1983) grave marker, image, Section Y, Midland City Cemetery, Midland, Michigan, memorial #177,039,622 by Rosemarie (findagrave.com).

[1000] Ernest Britton household, 1930 US census, Mound City, Pulaski County, Illinois, ED 6, sheet 18B, dwelling 407, family 413. Both reported being five years younger when first married. Also, Martha E. Britton index entry, US Social Security Death Index.

[1001] For mother's birth surname, William L. Hughes–Lulu M. Folck marriage license #80 on 3 April 1895, Crawford County, Illinois, marriage record C (1874–1911):86 on 4 April; FHL 1,310,116, image 216 of 627 (familysearch.org). Rev. Andrew Dewhirst officiated. Also, William L. Hughes household for daughter Martha E. age 3, 1910 US census, Martin Township, Crawford County, Illinois, sheet 19A, dwelling 254, family 257. William was born in Kentucky, as was Martha Britton's father in 1930.

Spouse's death: 3 July 1993 in Midland, Midland County, Michigan[1002]
Spouse's burial: Midland City Cemetery, Midland County, Michigan[1003]

Ernest and Martha both had at least four years of college.[1004] They graduated from McKendree College in 1924, and he was teaching in Mound City in 1928.[1005]

1930: they were renting at $25 per month at 420 Main Street in Mound City, Pulaski County, Illinois. They owned a radio set and both were teaching high school.[1006]

1934: he was high-school principal in Athens, Menard County, Illinois, when he moved on to be superintendent of schools in Effingham, Effingham County, Illinois, where he served for about twelve years.[1007]

1940: they owned a $5200 house (the statewide average was $3277) at 619 Fourth Street in Effingham.[1008]

1942: he stood 5 feet 10½ inches, weighed 165 pounds, and had gray eyes, brown hair, and a dark complexion.[1009]

[1002] Martha E. Britton index entry, US Social Security Death Index.

[1003] Martha E. Britton (1902–1993) grave marker, image, Section Y, Midland City Cemetery, Midland, Michigan, memorial #177,039,577 by Rosemarie (findagrave.com).

[1004] Earnest [Ernest] Britton household, 1940 US census, Effingham, Effingham County, Illinois, ED 25-8, sheet 14A, dwelling 306.

[1005] *Centennial McKendree College with St. Clair County History* (Lebanon, Illinois: McKendree College, 1928), 430.

[1006] Ernest Britton household, 1930 US census, Mound City, Pulaski County, Illinois, ED 6, sheet 18B, dwelling 407, family 413.

[1007] "School Head Will Resign," *Herald* (Decatur, Illinois), Thursday 13 December 1945, p. 8, col. 2.

[1008] Earnest [Ernest] Britton household, 1940 US census, Effingham, Effingham County, Illinois, ED 25-8, sheet 14A, dwelling 306. Statewide figures from US Census Bureau, Census of Housing, Historical Census of Housing Tables, Median Home Values Unadjusted 1940 (census.gov/hhes/www/housing/census/historic/values.html).

[1009] Ernest Raymond Britton WWII draft card, serial #949, order #10537; "World War II Draft Registration Cards" > Illinois > B > Br > Britton, Ernest Raymond, 1903 > p. 2 (fold3.com/image/1/654589106).

1945: they moved to Midland, Midland County, Michigan, where he was superintendent through at least 1960.[1010]

1955: he was also president of the Michigan Association of School Administrators.[1011]

He held a doctorate from Columbia University Teachers College in New York City, and taught at the University of Michigan, Michigan State University, Northern Michigan University, and Central Michigan University.[1012]

[1010] "Whirlpool Executive Heads State Group," *Herald-Palladium* (Benton Harbor–St. Joseph, Michigan), Thursday 4 December 1975, p. 3, cols. 4–5. Dr. Ernest R. Britton, "a Midland school administrator," was treasurer of an organization called the Michigan Association of the Professionals.

[1011] "Schoolmen Discuss Taxes and Financing," *Times Herald* (Port Huron, Michigan), Wednesday 16 February 1955, p. 7, col. 6.

[1012] "Midland's School Chief Will Speak," *Herald-Palladium* (Benton Harbor–St. Joseph, Michigan), Tuesday 19 November 1963, section 2, p. 4, cols. 4–5.

Chapter 39

Tenth Generation

Kathleen Pifer–Hugh McNelly Family
parents at chapters 10, 11

"A new life for the rebellious little redhead"

39. KATHLEEN VIRGINIA^{10} PIFER (*Alta Areta Gould^9, Laura Lucina Thrall^8, Worthy^7, Eliphas^6, Samuel^5, John^{+3}, Timothy^2, William^1*), foster child ("niece") of Ed and Alta^{1013}
Birth: about 1914 (possibly 11 February, age 66 at death) in Covington, Alleghany County, Virginia^{1014} (for biological relatives, see Chapter 11)
Death: 13 October 1980 of diabetes and heart disease, last residence Lake Hopatcong, Morris County, New Jersey^{1015}
Burial: not known
Spouse: **REV. HUGH JOHN MCNELLY,** married 20 August 1935 near Mounds, Pulaski County, Illinois
Spouse's parents: John O. and Nannie Belle (Samson) McNelly^{1016}

---

^{1013} "Golden Wedding Day Observed," *Daily Republican-Register* (Mount Carmel, Illinois), Monday 29 April 1940, p. 5, cols. 4–5. Similarly, "Bone Gap News," Wednesday 4 September 1935, p. 6, col. 6, calling her their niece.

^{1014} Edward G. Britton household for Cathleen Pifer, 1930 US census, Mounds Precinct, Pulaski County, Illinois, ED 9, sheet 5B, dwelling/family 134.

^{1015} "Kathleen Virginia McNelly," *Journal and Yearbook of the Northern New Jersey Annual Conference, The United Methodist Church, 124tht Session, Madison, New Jersey, 31 May–3 June 1981,* pp. 333–34.

^{1016} "Bone Gap News," *Republican-Register* (Mount Carmel, Illinois), Wednesday 4 September 1935, p. 6, col. 5. Kathleen was described as the niece of Edward and Alta. Kathleen's adoptive uncle, Rev. Virgil Gould, officiated. For parents, John O. McNalley [McNelly] household for wife Nannie age 37 and son Hugh J. age 9, 1920 US census, Chester, Randolph County, Illinois, Ward 3, ED 112, sheet 7B, dwelling 159, family 166. Also, John McNelly household for wife Belle age 21, married 2 years, no children, 1910 US census, East St. Louis, St. Clair County, Illinois, Ward 6, ED 127, sheet 13B, dwelling 283, family 290. For Nannie Belle's birth name, J.O. McNelly–Nannie Belle Samson marriage, license #3346, 2 May 1908, marriage Renault, Monroe County, Illinois, 6 May, marriage register 2:19; FHL 1,006,360, DGS 5,204,661 (familysearch.org). John was evidently married three times.

Spouse's birth: about 1911 in Illinois[1017]
Spouse's death: 27 July 1997 in Milford, Hunterdon County, New Jersey[1018]
Spouse's burial: not known

In 1981, more than half a century after the events, Rev. Hugh John McNelly wrote a brief sketch of this family connection (also quoted in Chapter 11):

> Kathleen Virginia Pifer was born in Covington [Alleghany County], Virginia, on February 11, 1914. Her family was broken up when she was 2 years old, and her mother had to place her in a series of foster homes. Her 'deliverance' came this way—Rev. Virgil Gould, a Methodist Minister in Illinois, had married Kathleen's aunt [Dora Sophia Leighton]. Kathleen was sent north to them, but Rev. Gould could not afford to keep her, so his sister 'Aunt Alta' Britton, took Kathleen into her home at Mounds, Illinois. At the age of 7, a new life began from the rebellious little redhead. She was a part of a loving Christian family! There she found Christ as her personal Savior. Piano lessons were provided for her. After High School the Brittons sent her to the same college their son and daughter had attended—McKendree. She graduated with a major in piano and a minor in pipe organ, plus the State Public School Music Certificate.[1019]

[1017] Rev. Hugh McNelly household, 1940 US census, Fishkill village, Dutchess County, New York, ED 14-26, sheet 4B, no dwelling number. Parents' birth states were asked of only a small fraction of those enumerated, of which Hugh was one. Unfortunately, this census taker marked every single person on the page as NY-born; in 1920 and 1930 Hugh was shown as Illinois-born of Illinois-born parents.

[1018] "Hugh John McNelly," *Journal and Yearbook of the Northern New Jersey Annual Conference, The United Methodist Church, 141st Session,* Madison, New Jersey, 4–6 June 1998, p. 220.

[1019] "Kathleen Virginia McNelly," *Journal and Yearbook of the Northern New Jersey Annual Conference, The United Methodist Church, 124th Session,* Madison, New Jersey, 31 May–3 June *1981,* pp. 333–34.

Kathleen graduated from McKendree College in June 1935; brother Melvin attended the ceremony.[1020] The story was later told that they became acquainted on campus when he was taking voice lessons and she became his accompanist.[1021]

Hugh and Kathleen both graduated from McKendree College and Drew Theological Seminary. In 1939, in Fishkill, Dutchess County, New York, he earned $1375 as a Methodist minister, Kathleen $100 as a musician and teacher.[1022] Serving the Methodist Church for 45 years, "she was a member of the National Association of Methodist Musicians and she had been an official music director in the Northern New Jersey Conference of the United Methodist Church," and played the organ at her husband's charge in Hurdtown.[1023]

"She usually used her music to supplement what was already being done—often organizing and directing children's choirs, boy's choirs, youth choirs. When necessary she would serve as organist and/or choir director. Private piano lessons provided extras and sometimes necessities for the parsonage budget. She only bought one thing for herself with the lesson money—her grand piano."[1024] She did more than music, in 1956 leading a Methodist study group on "the Indian problem."[1025]

Hugh was ordained in Vandalia 30 September 1934. He came east in part to study at Drew Theological Seminary, where he graduated in

---

[1020] "Bone Gap News," *Republican-Register* (Mount Carmel, Illinois), Thursday 13 June 1935, p. 6, col. 1.
[1021] Louis J. Clark, "Tenafly Methodists Mark Anniversary," *Record* (Hackensack, New Jersey), Saturday 21 March 1959, p. 32, with photo.
[1022] Rev. Hugh McNelly household, 1940 US census, Fishkill village, Dutchess County, New York, ED 14-26, sheet 4B, no dwelling number.
[1023] "Obituaries . . . Kathleen McNelly," *Daily Record* (Morristown, New Jersey), Tuesday 14 October 1980, p. 2, col. 4.
[1024] "Kathleen Virginia McNelly," *Journal and Yearbook of the Northern New Jersey Annual Conference, The United Methodist Church, 124th Session, Madison, New Jersey, 31 May–3 June 1981*, pp. 333–34.
[1025] "Church Group Studies Indian," *Record* (Hackensack, New Jersey), Saturday 4 February 1956, p. 10, col. 5.

1939.[1026] He and Kathleen served churches in three states over 45 years:

- Hartford and South Roxana, Madison County, Illinois (1929–33)[1027]

- Granite City, Madison County, Illinois, in 1935 (?) and 1936[1028]

- Port Murray, Warren County, New Jersey

- Rockaway Valley, Morris County, New Jersey, 1938[1029]

- Fishkill, Dutchess County, New York (1939–43)[1030]

- Beacon, Poughkeepsie, Dutchess County, New York (1941?)[1031]

- Ellenville, Ulster County, New York (1943)[1032]

[1026] Louis J. Clark, "Tenafly Methodists Mark Anniversary," *Record* (Hackensack, New Jersey), Saturday 21 March 1959, p. 32, with photo.

[1027] "Rev. Souers Assigned to Mount Carmel," *Evening Telegraph* (Alton, Illinois), Monday 30 September 1929, p. 1, col. 2. Hartford and South Roxana are two miles apart, just east of the Mississippi River, between Alton and Edwardsville. Similarly, 29 September 1930, p. 1, col. 5; 5 October 1931, p. 1, col. 4. Similarly, Monday 2 October 1933, p. 1, col. 4, stating that McNelly had been replaced at Hartford.

[1028] "District M. E. Conference To Be Held Here," *News-Democrat* (Belleville, Illinois), Tuesday 21 April 1936, p. 7, col. 5. Hugh was secretary of the East St. Louis district.

[1029] "Edmund Stickle Dies of Illness," *Morning Call* (Paterson, New Jersey), Saturday 8 January 1938, p. 12, col. 4.

[1030] "Pastor Accepts Call," *Daily Freeman* (Kingston, New York), Monday 13 December 1943, p. 4, col. 5.

[1031] "Personal Mention," *Journal* (Poughkeepsie, New York), Thursday 4 September 1941, p. 14, col. 3. Later Hugh was described as the former pastor of Beacon: "Mrs. Margaret Lane, Fishkill, Dies at 87," *Journal* (Poughkeepsie, New York), Saturday 26 July 1947, p. 10, col. 3.

[1032] "Pastor Accepts Call," *Daily Freeman* (Kingston, New York), Monday 13 December 1943, p. 4, col. 5.

- Marlborough, Ulster County, New York (1946)[1033]

- Middle Hope (Newburgh), Orange County, New York

- Milton, Marlboro, and Middle Hope, Ulster County, New York (1948)[1034]

- Morsemere, Yonkers, Westchester County, New York (1949–54)[1035]

- Tenafly, Bergen County, New Jersey (1954-59)[1036]

- Grace Church, Paterson, Passaic County, New Jersey (1959)[1037]

- Wesley Church, Roselle, Union County, New Jersey (1964)[1038]

- Bloomingdale, Passaic County, New Jersey (1965–75)[1039]

[1033] "Thomas Troncilito Weds Miss Joan Cosman, Both of Marlborough," *Daily Freeman* (Kingston, New York), Tuesday 13 August 1946, p. 8, col. 7.

[1034] "Summer Church Planned at Milton," *Journal* (Poughkeepsie, New York), Saturday 15 May 1948, p. 5, col. 5.

[1035] "Methodist Conference Appointments," *Daily Freeman* (Kingston, New York), Monday 14 May 1951, p. 11, col. 3. He was at Morsemere from 1949: "Rev. McNelly Named To Tenafly Church," *News* (Paterson, New Jersey), Tuesday 27 April 1954, p. 30, col. 8.

[1036] "Church to Get New Minister," *Evening Record* (Bergen, New Jersey), Wednesday 7 April 1954, p. 27, col. 5.

[1037] "New Pastors for 8 Methodist Churches," *Evening News* (Paterson, New Jersey), Monday 15 June 1959, p. 6, col. 1. During Hugh's five-year tenure at Tenafly the church's membership increased 41 percent.

[1038] "Methodist Church Changes Affect Pastorates in Area," *Herald-News* (Passaic, New Jersey), Monday 21 June 1965, p. 2, cols. 7–8.

[1039] "Methodist Church Changes Affect Pastorates in Area," *Herald-News* (Passaic, New Jersey), Monday 21 June 1965, p. 2, cols. 7–8. Similarly, "Alfred J. Koones," Wednesday 29 September 1965, p 13, col. 3. Similarly, "His Congregation's Farewell," Friday 16 May 1975, p. 22, cols. 1–3.

- Hurdtown, Morris County, New Jersey (1975–80)[1040]

[1040] "Kathleen Virginia McNelly," *Journal and Yearbook of the Northern New Jersey Annual Conference, The United Methodist Church, 124tht Session, Madison, New Jersey, 31 May–3 June 1981*, pp. 333–34. Her husband Hugh wrote this memoir, giving a more detailed account of their charges than the memoir written after his demise. "Hugh John McNelly," *Journal and Yearbook of the Northern New Jersey Annual Conference, The United Methodist Church, 141st Session, Madison, New Jersey, 4–6 June 1998*, p. 220. Fishkill was their location in the 1940 census: Rev. Hugh McNelly household, 1940 US census, Fishkill village, Dutchess County, New York, ED 14-26, sheet 4B, no dwelling number.

Chapter 40

Tenth Generation

Edwin Malcolm Gould–Rhodean Alice Perdue Family
parents at chapter 12

Music as "physical control to the nth degree"

40. EDWIN "EDWY" MALCOLM¹⁰ GOULD (*Virgil Nathan Gould⁹, Laura Lucina Thrall⁸, Worthy⁷, Eliphas⁶, Samuel⁵, John⁴⁻³, Timothy², William¹*)
Birth: 11 September 1894 in Bone Gap, Edwards County, Illinois¹⁰⁴¹
Death: 15 February 1993 in Palm Beach County, Florida¹⁰⁴²
Burial: Not known
Spouse: **RHODEAN ALICE PERDUE,** married 26 December 1921 in Marissa, St. Clair County, Illinois¹⁰⁴³
Spouse's parents: Samuel and Sophronia "Fronia" Jane (Thompson) Perdue¹⁰⁴⁴

---

¹⁰⁴¹ Born 1894: Edwin Malcolm Gould WWI draft card, serial #2326, order #106, 5 June 1917, Elkville, Illinois; "US, World War I Draft Registration Cards, 1917–1918" > Illinois > Jackson County > Draft Card G > image 185 of 369. Also, *Centennial McKendree College with St. Clair County History* (Lebanon, Illinois: McKendree College, 1928), 628. Born 1895: Florida Death Index entry and "US, World War II Draft Registration Cards, 1942" > Missouri > Gordon–Govero > images 1821–22 of 2065 (ancestry.com). Either way, he is not to be confused with the Edwin Goulds who were son and grandson of Gilded Age financier Jay Gould (https://en.wikipedia.org/wiki/Edwin_Gould_Sr.).

¹⁰⁴² Edwin Malcolm Gould death index entry, Palm Beach County, Florida, 15 February 1993; "Florida Death Index 1877–1998" (ancestry.com).

¹⁰⁴³ "Society," *News-Democrat* (Belleville, Illinois), Monday 26 December 1921, p. 2, col. 4. Edwin's father officiated.

¹⁰⁴⁴ Samuel Perdue household, 1910 US census, Marissa, St. Clair County, Illinois, ED 148, sheet 15A, dwelling 321, family 359. For Sophronia's birth surname, Everett James Perdue death index entry, 25 January 1941, "Illinois Deaths and Stillbirths, 1916–1947" (ancestry.com). More information is likely available through Family History Center, Marissa, St. Clair County, Illinois, FHL 1,832,443, DGS 4,008,570, image 358, cn 3820. Samuel's parents were born in France and Ireland, Sophronia's in Georgia and Illinois.

Spouse's birth: probably 21 February 1903,[1045] probably in Marissa (parents' residence)[1046]
Spouse's death: North Palm Beach, Palm Beach County, Florida, 21 February 1992[1047]
Spouse's burial: Not known

Rhodean and Edwin both completed five years of college.[1048] They were married for more than 70 years.[1049]

In 1917 Edwin was a farmer and a student working for E. M. Casleton in Elkville, Jackson County, Illinois. He served eight months as a musician in Company L of the 4th Illinois National Guard, and was described as tall and slender, with blue eyes and light-colored hair.[1050] After graduating from McKendree College with a B.S. in 1921,[1051] he was hired as bandmaster for the Bloomington, McLean County, Illinois, high

---

[1045] For 1900: Rhodean Alice Gould, Florida Death Index, 1877–1998 (ancestry.com); and death notice (transcribed), Rhodean A. Gould age 92, *Miami Herald* (Florida), no page or col. number (genealogybank.com). For 1901: Samuel Perdue household for daughter Rhodean age 9, 1910 US census, Marissa, St. Clair County, Illinois, ED 148, sheet 15A, dwelling 321, family 359. For 1903: Edwin M. Gould household for wife "Dean," 1930 US census, Logansport, Cass County, Indiana, 5th Ward, ED 20, sheet 6B, dwelling 160, family 169; and "Saphona" Perdue household for daughter "Rodine," 1920 US census, Marissa, St. Clair County, Illinois, ED 197, sheet 19B, dwelling 474, family 476. For 21 February 1903: Dean A. Gould death index entry, US Social Security Death Index.

[1046] Samuel Perdue household, 1900 US census, Marissa Township, St. Clair County, Illinois, ED 115, sheet 11B, dwelling 233, family 241. Similarly, 1910, ED 148, sheet 15A, dwelling 321, family 359. Samuel was a coal miner born in Kentucky to father born France and mother in Ireland.

[1047] "Rhodean A. Gould," *Post* (Palm Beach, Florida), Saturday 22 February 1992, p. 7B, col. 1. Her Florida Death Index entry has her dying on her 92nd birthday in Broward County.

[1048] Edwin M. Gould household, 1940 U.S census, St. Louis City, Missouri, ED 96-596, sheet 4A, dwelling 78.

[1049] "Rhodean A. Gould," *Post* (Palm Beach, Florida), Saturday 22 February 1992, p. 7B, col. 1.

[1050] Edwin Malcolm Gould WWI draft card, serial #2326, order #106, 5 June 1917, Elkville, Illinois; "US, World War I Draft Registration Cards, 1917–1918" > Illinois > Jackson County > Draft Card G > image 185 of 369.

[1051] *Centennial McKendree College with St. Clair County History* (Lebanon, Illinois: McKendree College, 1928), 424.

school, where he was to "devote his entire time to the teaching of individuals." (A newspaper account said that this upgrading of the band program was "in the face of a great crying out against jazz"; Edwin's opinions were not quoted.)[1052] In 1924 they lived at 506 East Jefferson there.[1053]

In 1926 he taught at the summer session of Teachers College in Emporia, Lyon County, Kansas.[1054] In 1927 they were in Asheville, Buncombe County, North Carolina, where he commented on the difficult demands of instrumental music:

> Considered from a physical standpoint, the reading and playing of one note on a wind instrument requires the correct tension, control, and synchronization of somewhere from 50 to a 100 different muscles of the eye, face, tongue, arms, fingers, and breathing apparatus; furthermore, this muscular adjustment must be changed, always under perfect control, at a rate of speed anywhere from four to 12 times per second. Obviously, this is physical control to the nth degree.[1055]

Edwin was a musician as well as a teacher, playing first French horn in the St. Louis Philharmonic Orchestra and later with the Tampa (Florida) symphony.[1056]

[1052] "Notes and Comments of Music World: Schools Reach More Children," *Daily Pantagraph* (Bloomington, Illinois), Saturday 16 September 1922, p. 9, col. 2.

[1053] Edwin M. Gould and wife "Rhodian" entry, *Polk's Bloomington and Normal City Directory, 1924–25* (Chicago: R.L. Polk, 1924), p. 204, image 102 of 349 (ancestry.com).

[1054] "Strengthen Faculty for Summer School," *Daily Gazette* (Emporia, Kansas), Tuesday 8 Jun 1926, p. 6, col. 3.

[1055] "One Teacher Resolves to Put Emphasis on Quality," *News and Observer* (Raleigh, North Carolina), Friday 26 August 1927, p. 15, cols. 6–7. The original article appeared in the September 1927 issue of *North Carolina Teacher*.

[1056] "Edwin Malcolm Gould," *Post* (Palm Beach, Florida), Wednesday 17 February 1993, p. 14, col. 4.

1930: he was teaching instrumental music in Logansport, Cass County, Indiana, and they were renting at 2214 Broadway for $40 a month;[1057] they were still there in 1935.

1940: he was teaching music in the St. Louis public schools part-time (19 weeks in 1939), while Rhodean, the census informant, was working 52 weeks as a doctor's receptionist. Each brought in $720 for the year. They rented at 6320 Arsenal in the city for $28 a month.[1058]

1948: In the spring he was conducting the 65-member Normandy High School band there.[1059]

1957: he was music supervisor in the public schools at Nokomis, Montgomery County, Illinois.[1060]

1960: they moved to Bradenton, Manatee County, Florida.[1061]

1967: North Palm Beach, Palm Beach County, Florida.[1062]

[1057] Edwin M. Gould household, 1930 US census, Logansport, Cass County, Indiana, 5th Ward, ED 20, sheet 6B, dwelling 160, family 169.

[1058] Edwin M. Gould household, 1940 U.S census, St. Louis City, Missouri, ED 96-596, sheet 4A, dwelling 78. Rhodean's given age of 28 seems to be a mistake.

[1059] "Lincoln Tomb Notes," *Illinois State Journal* (Springfield), Thursday 20 May 1948, p. 22, col. 2.

[1060] "Dora S. Gould, Mother of CV Doctor, Dies," *Star-News* (Chula Vista, California), Thursday 5 December 1957, p. 8A, col. 3.

[1061] "Rhodean A. Gould," *Post* (Palm Beach, Florida), Saturday 22 February 1992, p. 7B, col. 1.

[1062] "Edwin Malcolm Gould," *Post* (Palm Beach, Florida), Wednesday 17 February 1993, p. 14, col. 4.

Chapter 41

Tenth Generation

Victor Leighton Gould–Ella Lippert–Geraldine Hacke Family
parents at chapter 12

St. Louis to Chula Vista

41. Victor Leighton[10] Gould (*Virgil Nathan Gould^9, Laura Lucina Thrall^8, Worthy^7, Eliphas^6, Samuel^5, John$^{4-3}$, Timothy^2, William^1*)
Birth: 23 November 1898[1063] in Bone Gap, Edwards County, Illinois
Death: about 11 July 1983 in Los Banos, Merced County, California
Burial: Los Banos Cemetery, Merced County, California[1064]
Spouse #1: **Ella Lippert,** married 11 December 1919 (as stated in her 1933 divorce petition) or soon after the 1920 census (when Victor was enumerated as single and living with his parents)[1065]
Spouse #1's parents: William F. and Leona (Walter) Lippert[1066]

[1063] For November 1898, Virgil N. Gould household, 1900 US census, Bone Gap, Edwards County, Illinois, ED 16, sheet 4B, dwelling/family 73. Also, *Centennial McKendree College with St. Clair County History* (Lebanon, Illinois: McKendree College, 1928), 617.

[1064] Victor Leighton Gould, no grave marker image, Los Banos Cemetery, Merced County, California, memorial #81,604,491 by seacowz (findagrave.com). His obituary stated that he died "last week": "Dr. Victor Gould, delivered 3,500 babies," *Star-News* (Chula Vista, California), Thursday 21 July 1983, p. 22, col. 1.

[1065] Virgil N. Gould household for Victor L. Gould, 1920 US census, Trenton, Ward 1, Sugar Creek, Clinton County, ED 21, sheet 3A, dwelling/family 75. Also, "Wife of Dr. V. L. Gould Files Suit for Divorce," *St. Louis Globe-Democrat* (Missouri), Wednesday 28 June 1933, p. 17, col. 3.

[1066] For Leona's birth surname, Leona Lippert death certificate #214, 29 June 1931 in Belleville, St. Clair County, Illinois; "Illinois, Deaths and Stillbirths Index, 1916–1947" > FHL 1,653,850, DGS 4,008,288, item 2 > image 252 of 2439 (familysearch.org). Leona's parents were reported as Steve and Mary (Fuss) Walter, both born in Germany.

Spouse #1's birth: September 1895 or 1896 in Missouri[1067]
Spouse #1's death: 8 April 1988 likely in St. Louis[1068]
Spouse #1's burial: Mount Hope Cemetery, Belleville, St. Clair County, Illinois[1069]
Spouse #2: **GERALDINE ERNESTINE HACKE,** married 12 September 1933 De Soto, Jefferson County, Missouri[1070]
Spouse #2's parents: Max G. and Laura Henrietta (Smith) Hacke[1071]
Spouse #2's birth: 31 December 1912 in Missouri
Spouse #2's death: 2 January 2000 in Los Banos, Merced County, California[1072]
Spouse #2's burial: Los Banos Cemetery, Merced County[1073]

In 1900 and 1910 Ella was the youngest child, living with her family in a rented house at 2408 West Main in Belleville, St. Clair County,

---

[1067] William E. Lippert household for daughter Ella age 4, born September 1895, 1900 US census, Belleville, St. Clair County, Illinois, Ward 4, ED 84, sheet 12B, dwelling 232, family 257. Also, Victor Gould household for wife Ella age 33, 1930 US census, St. Louis City, Missouri, Ward 24, ED 148, sheet 40A, dwelling 724, family 836.

[1068] Ella L. Gould index entry, US Social Security Death Index. This index gives her birth as 27 September 1896.

[1069] Ella L. Gould grave marker, Mount Hope Cemetery, Belleville, Illinois, image, memorial #140,443,593 by Chief Easton (findagrave.com).

[1070] Dr. Victor L. Gould–Geraldine Ernestine Hacke marriage license #249, 10 September 1933, marriage 12 September, De Soto, Jefferson County, Missouri, p. 555; "Missouri, Marriage Records, 1805–2002" > Jefferson > Record images for Jefferson > 1930–1936 > image 282 of 621 (ancestry.com).

[1071] Max G. Hacke household for daughter Geraldine age 7, 1920 US census, De Soto, Jefferson County, Missouri, Ward 1, ED 45, sheet 14B, dwelling 335, family 340. Also, Laura Hacke 1888–1964 grave marker, City Cemetery, De Soto, Missouri, image, memorial #20,492,979 for Laura Smith Hacke by TLH (findagrave.com). For birth surname and parents, Laura Henrietta Hacke death 25 June 1964, Missouri certificate #23610; Missouri Secretary of State, *Missouri Digital Heritage* (sos.mo.gov/mdh) > Collections > Quick Links > Death Certificates > "Missouri Death Certificates, 1910–1967").

[1072] "Geraldine Gould, worked in doctor-husband's office," *Star-News* (Chula Vista, California), Saturday 8 January 2000, p. 4, cols. 2–5. Also, Victor L. Gould household for wife Geraldine E. age 27, born Missouri, 1940 US census, St. Louis City, Missouri, Ward 24, ED 96-777, sheet 13A, dwelling 394. Also, Geraldine E. Gould index entry, US Social Security Death Index.

[1073] Geraldine Earnestine Gould, no grave marker image, Los Banos Cemetery, Merced County, California, memorial #81,604,490 by seacowz (findagrave.com).

Illinois, and ten years later at 2207, which they owned.[1074] Ella completed four years of college,[1075] being a 1919 McKendree College graduate from Belleville. Victor "attended McKendree two years, graduated from Illinois University in 1922, and from Washington University Medical School in 1926." In 1928 he was an intern at the new Maternity Hospital of Washington University.[1076]

In 1920 Victor was single and living with his parents in Sugar Creek, Clinton County.[1077] He was a veteran of World War I.[1078] In 1930 Victor was a physician; he and Ella had two daughters, and they were renting for $50 a month at 2759 Sulphur, St. Louis City.[1079] In 1933 they lived at 2807A Watson Road before separating 18 March 1933. On 27 June 1933 she filed for divorce on the grounds that he was "cold and indifferent and criticised her without cause."[1080]

In 1940 Ella and her daughters were in Ella's St. Louis household; she was a YWCA dietitian who earned $700 for 52 weeks of work in 1939. She paid $65 a month rent but had space for five female lodgers.[1081]

[1074] William F. Lippert household for 4-year-old daughter Ella, 1900 US census, Belleville, St. Clair County, Illinois, Ward 4, ED 84, sheet 12B, dwelling 232, family 257. Similarly for 14-year-old daughter Ella, 1910, Ward 3, ED 88, sheet 8B, dwelling 176, family 203. William was foreman/supervisor in a "glass works." Ella's 1900 siblings were Florence 14, Leona 12, Walter 10, and Charles 8.

[1075] Ella L. Gould household, 1940 US census, St. Louis City, Missouri, ED 96-634A, sheet 3B, dwelling 92.

[1076] *Centennial McKendree College with St. Clair County History* (Lebanon, Illinois: McKendree College, 1928), 406, 617.

[1077] Virgil N. Gould household for son Victor L. (age 21 and single), 1920 US census, Trenton, Sugar Creek Township, Clinton County, Illinois, Ward 1, ED 21, sheet 3A, dwelling/family 75.

[1078] "Dr. Victor L. Gould Delivers Own Grandson—And In Total Darkness," *Star-News* (Chula Vista, California), Thursday 31 January 1957, p. 1, cols. 4–5. Also, 1930 census below.

[1079] Victor Gould household, 1930 US census, St. Louis City, Missouri, Ward 24, ED 148, sheet 40A, dwelling 724, family 836.

[1080] "Wife of Dr. V. L. Gould Files Suit for Divorce," *Globe-Democrat* (St. Louis, Missouri), Wednesday 28 June 1933, p. 17, col. 3.

[1081] Ella L. Gould household, 1940 US census, St. Louis City, Missouri, ED 96-634A, sheet 3B, dwelling 92.

In 1936 Victor owned the Alton Automobile Company, dealer of Auburn and Cord automobiles in the St. Louis area.[1082] In 1940 he and second wife Ernestine were in a $14,000 house at 6352 Devonshire in St. Louis (six times the statewide average of $2392).[1083] Probably early in 1946 Victor sold the house[1084] and they went west.

In April 1947 their son was attending "school camp" in Chula Vista, San Diego County, California, and Victor was taking the examination to be licensed as a physician in California.[1085] In 1957 he delivered his own grandson during a power failure at the Chula Vista hospital.[1086] In 1969 he was practicing medicine at 721 Third Avenue and residing at 344 Hilltop Drive in Chula Vista.[1087] Trained at Deaconess Hospital in St. Louis in 1932, Geraldine worked as his nurse from 1946 to 1980.[1088] Victor retired in 1982 due to illness.[1089]

[1082] "Alton Firm Appointed as Auburn-Cord Dealer," *Star-Times* (St. Louis, Missouri), Wednesday 29 January 1936, p. 24, col. 5.

[1083] Victor L. Gould household, 1940 US census, St. Louis City, Missouri, Ward 24, ED 96-777, sheet 13A, dwelling 394. Statewide figures from US Census Bureau, Census of Housing, Historical Census of Housing Tables, Median Home Values Unadjusted 1940 (census.gov/hhes/www/housing/census/historic/values.html).

[1084] Real estate advertisement and photograph, *Star-Times* (St. Louis, Missouri), Friday 7 June 1946, p. 26, col. 5, showing "Six-room residence in St. Louis Hills at 6352 Devonshire av., bought by Oliver F. Johnson from Dr. Victor L. Gould through the Cyrus Crane Willmore Organization, Inc."

[1085] "Sixth Grade Students Attend School Camp," *Star*, (Chula Vista, California), Friday 11 April 1947, p. 4A, col. 4. Similarly, "Dr. Victor Gould Takes State Exam for Medical License," Friday 25 July 1947, p. 1, col. 2.

[1086] "Dr. Victor L. Gould Delivers Own Grandson—And In Total Darkness," *Star-News* (Chula Vista, California), Thursday 31 January 1957, p. 1, cols. 4–5.

[1087] Victor L. Gould and Geraldine entries, *Polk's San Diego Suburban (San Diego, California) Directory 1969* (Monterey Park, California: R. L. Polk, [1969]), p. 320, image 456 of 1680 (ancestry.com).

[1088] "Geraldine Gould, worked in doctor-husband's office," *Star-News* (Chula Vista, California), Saturday 8 January 2000, p. 4, cols. 2–5. There are some slight variances on dates between his and her obituaries.

[1089] "Dr. Victor Gould, delivered 3,500 babies," *Star-News* (Chula Vista, California), Thursday 21 July 1983, p. 22, col. 1.

Chapter 42

Tenth Generation

Paul Glenwood Gould–Ada L. Shaffer–Rosa Germanini Family
parents at chapter 12

School principal in mid-Illinois towns

42. **PAUL GLENWOOD**[10] **GOULD** (*Virgil Nathan Gould*[9]*, Laura Lucina Thrall*[8]*, Worthy*[7]*, Eliphas*[6]*, Samuel*[5]*, John*[4-3]*, Timothy*[2]*, William*[1])
Birth: 21 February 1901, possibly Bone Gap, Edwards County, Illinois, where parents lived in 1900[1090]
Death: 2 December 1998 in Lake Worth, Palm Beach County, Florida
Burial: Lake Worth Memory Gardens Cemetery[1091]
Spouse #1: **ADA L. SHAFFER,** married in the early 1930s
Spouse #1's parents: William E. and Viola (Bumpus) Shaffer[1092]
Spouse #1's birth: 26 April 1905 in Illinois

[1090] Born 1901: Virgil N. Gould household for son Paul age 9, 1910 US census, Sumner, Lawrence County, Illinois, ED 123, sheet 8B, dwelling 193, family 212. Born 21 February 1900: *Centennial McKendree College with St. Clair County History* (Lebanon, Illinois: McKendree College, 1928), 617. The year is likely a mistake for 1901, as Paul was absent from the family household in the 1900 census, when the date of record was 1 June and the household was enumerated 7 June. Other evidence also leans toward 1901. He was said to be age 97 at death 2 December 1998: "Paul G. Gould," *Post* (West Palm Beach, Florida), Sunday 6 December 1998, p. 8C, col. 2. Also, Florida Death Index entry has birth 21 February 1901. Also, Virgil N. Gould household for son Paul, age 18, 1920 US census, Trenton, Sugar Creek Township, Clinton County, Illinois, Ward 1, ED 21, sheet 3A, dwelling/family 75. Also, Paul G. Gould, lodger, age 28, 1930 US census, Centralia, Marion County, Illinois, ED 61, sheet 24B, dwelling [blank], family 573. Also, Paul Gould age 39, 1940 US census, Shelbyville, Shelby County, Illinois, Ward 2, ED 87-28, sheet 3B, dwelling 65.

[1091] "Paul G. Gould," *Post* (West Palm Beach, Florida), Sunday 6 December 1998, p. 8C, col. 2.

[1092] William E. Shafer [Shaffer] for daughter Ada L. born Illinois, 1910 US census, Elk Prairie Township, Jefferson County, Illinois, ED 96, sheet 6A, dwelling 116, family 117.

Spouse #1's death: 4 December 1985 in Palm Beach County, Florida[1093]
Spouse #1's burial: Lake Worth Memory Gardens there[1094]
Spouse #2: as her second husband **ROSA LEE (BURDETTE) GERMANINI,** married between 20 April 1986 and 30 March 1987[1095]
Spouse #2's parents: Wiley H. and Carrie (Miller) Burdette
Spouse #2's birth: 26 May 1909 in Atlanta, Fulton County, Georgia[1096]
Spouse #2's death: 19 July 1993 in Palm Beach County, Florida
Spouse #2's burial: Lake Worth Memory Gardens there[1097]

Paul was a graduate of McKendree College (1928) and Northwestern University.[1098] His career path took him from southern Illinois into mid-Illinois,[1099] where he served as:

[1093] "Ada S. Gould," *Pantagraph* (Bloomington, Illinois), Saturday 14 December 1985, p. C6, col. 4. Ada Gould index entry, US Social Security Death Index. For state of birth, 1910 US census above.

[1094] Ada S. Gould grave marker, Lake Worth Memory Gardens, Palm Beach County, Florida, image, memorial #59,169,810 for Ada Shaffer Gould by DebStarrett (findagrave.com).

[1095] Presumably after she was called "Rosa Germanini" 20 April 1986: Sallie James, "Lighthouse Helps Blind Handle Life," *Post* (West Palm Beach, Florida), Sunday 20 April 1986, p. C11, col. 3. Social Security changed Rosa Lee's surname to Gould 30 March 1987: Rosalee Gould index entry, "US, Social Security Applications and Claims Index, 1936–2007" (ancestry.com).

[1096] Rosalee Gould index entry, "US, Social Security Applications and Claims Index, 1936–2007" (ancestry.com). Also, Hillis [Willis] Burdett household for wife Carrie and daughter Rosa L. age 11 months, 1910 US census, Black Hall District, Fulton County, Georgia, ED 122, sheet 5B, dwelling 119, family 122.

[1097] "Rosa Lee Gould," *Post* (West Palm Beach, Florida), Thursday 22 July 1993, p. 4B, col. 2.

[1098] *Centennial McKendree College with St. Clair County History* (Lebanon, Illinois: McKendree College, 1928), 33 and 431 (for his middle name).

[1099] "Mid-Illinois" is the coinage of James Krohe, Jr., in *Corn Kings & One-Horse Thieves: A Plain-Spoken History of Mid-Illinois* (Carbondale: Southern Illinois University Press, 2017), 1–2. It refers to that part of Illinois between interstates 70 and 80, "where Southerners' tolerance for treelessness, flatness, and cold overlapped most Northerners' tolerance for Southerners."

- seventh-grade teacher in Freeburg, St. Clair County, 1926–27[1100]
- principal of Irving School in Centralia, Marion County, 1928–30[1101] (Ada, his future wife, was also there)[1102]
- principal of the elementary school in Freeburg, St. Clair County, 1931–36
- principal of the Main Street grade school in Shelbyville, Shelby County, starting in 1936;[1103] they owned a $2000 house at 2514 North Long Street there in 1940 (the statewide average was $3277)[1104]
- principal at Mossville, Peoria County, in 1951[1105]
- teacher in Bloomington-Normal, McLean County, from 1952 on; in 1952 he was to teach 5th and 6th grades in outlying Towanda[1106]

In 1952 they settled in and bought a house at 210 North University in Normal, McLean County, Illinois, from Alice E. Ward.[1107] Ada earned a bachelor's degree from Southern Illinois University in

---

[1100] "Freeburg," *News Dispatch* (Belleville, Illinois), Friday 23 April 1926, p. 7, col. 6, and Friday 6 May 1927, p. 12, col. 3.

[1101] "Freeburg," Friday 8 February 1929, *News-Democrat* (Belleville, Illinois), p. 16, col. 3. Also, Paul G. Gould, lodger, age 18, 1930 US census, Centralia, Marion County, Illinois, ED 61, sheet 24B, dwelling [blank], family 573. The written census page is catastrophically disorganized.

[1102] George B. Gorham household for roomer Ada Shaffer, 1930 US census, Centralia, Marion County, Illinois, Ward 4, ED 8, sheet 3A, dwelling/family 65.

[1103] "Shelbyville Board Hires School Head," *Review* (Decatur, Illinois), Saturday 5 September 1936, p. 8, col. 2.

[1104] Paul Gould household, 1940 US census, Shelbyville, Shelby County, Illinois, Ward 2, ED 87-28, sheet 3B, dwelling 65. Statewide average from *United States Census Bureau*, Census of Housing, Historical Census of Housing Tables, Median Home Values Unadjusted 1940 (census.gov/hhes/www/housing/census/historic/values.html).

[1105] "Mossville School Registration Slated," *Journal* (Peoria, Illinois), Thursday 23 August 1951, p. 13A, col. 6.

[1106] "Unit District 5 Employs Ten New Teachers," *Pantagraph* (Bloomington, Illinois), Friday 29 August 1952, p. 10, cols. 1–5, including a picture of Paul and an indication (unlikely) that Mossville was his "home town."

[1107] "Spencer Ewing Home Sold to James Owen: Deed Transfers In 14 Sales Total $225,100," *Pantagraph* (Bloomington, Illinois), Sunday 31 August 1952, p. 2, cols. 1–2.

1956;[1108] the following year they were both teaching in Bloomington-Normal.[1109] She taught at Central School and later Chiddix Junior High School in Normal.[1110] In 1972 Paul sold their house in Normal for $28,500.[1111] They moved to Florida soon thereafter, where they were involved at Good Shepherd United Methodist Church in West Palm Beach.[1112]

Paul's second wife Rosa Lee lived most of her life in Florida. A member of Good Shepherd United Methodist Church, she was a joint steward of the Biscayne Bay Yacht Club in Miami, Florida, for over 30 years, an active participant in the Lighthouse for the Blind (where she learned to get around with only peripheral vision), and "a very avid shopper."[1113]

[1108] Ada Shaffer Gould entry, press release from Southern Illinois University Information Service, 2 August 1956, p. 6 (archive.org/details/southernillinois1956sout).

[1109] Paul and Ada Gould entries, *Polk's Bloomington (McLean County, Illinois) City Directory 1957* (St. Louis: R.L. Polk, 1957), 315, image 171 of 444 (ancestry.com). Also, "Dora S. Gould, Mother of CV Doctor, Dies," *Chula Vista Star-News* (California), Thursday 5 December 1957, p. 8A, col. 3.

[1110] "Ada S. Gould," *Pantagraph* (Bloomington, Illinois), Saturday 14 December 1985, p. C6, cols. 4–5.

[1111] "McLean County Real Estate Transfers," *Pantagraph* (Bloomington-Normal, Illinois), Sunday 22 October 1972, p. B10, col. 4.

[1112] "Paul G. Gould," *Post* (West Palm Beach, Florida), Sunday 6 December 1998, p. 8C, col. 2.

[1113] "Rosa Lee Gould," *Post* (West Palm Beach, Florida), Thursday 22 July 1993, p. 4B, col. 2. Also, Sallie James, "Lighthouse Helps Blind Handle Life," *Post* (West Palm Beach, Florida), Sunday 20 April 1986, p. C11, col. 3.

Chapter 43

Tenth Generation

Areta Hope Gould–Emery Martin Family
parents at chapter 12

Teacher-Coach at Ziegler, DuQuoin, and Gillespie

43. **Areta Hope**^{10} **Gould** (*Virgil Nathan Gould^9, Laura Lucina Thrall^8, Worthy^7, Eliphas^6, Samuel^5, John$^{4-3}$, Timothy^2, William^1*)
Birth: 18 October 1907 in Geff (Jeffersonville), Wayne County, Illinois
Death: 15 December 1998 in Urbana, Champaign County, Illinois
Burial: the 19th in Woodlawn Cemetery there[1114]
Spouse: **Emery H. Martin,** married 23 December 1928 in Freeburg, St. Clair County, Illinois[1115]
Spouse's parents: Marion and Melissa (Moore) Martin
Spouse's birth: 8 January 1906 in Sumner, Lawrence County, Illinois
Spouse's death: 5 July 1987 in Savoy, Champaign County, Illinois
Spouse's burial: Woodlawn Cemetery, Urbana, Champaign County, Illinois[1116]

[1114] "Areta H. Martin," *State Journal-Register* (Springfield, Illinois, 17 December 1998, p. 38, col. 4.

[1115] "Freeburg," *Belleville Daily News-Democrat* (Illinois), Saturday 29 December 1928, p. 14, cols. 3–4. Her father officiated. No parents or guests were named for the groom. Listed guests included attendants Miss Lillian Hell ("an intimate friend of the bride") and Mr. Paul Gould ("a brother of the bride"), Rev. and Mrs. Virgil Gould, Mr. and Mrs. Britton, Mr. and Mrs. Milton Hartman, Lucille and Kathryn Pfeiffer of Mounds, Mr. and Mrs. Edward Gould of Ashville, North Carolina, Dr. and Mrs. Victor Gould of Belleville, and Mrs. Emily Hell," along with "a few friends and teachers of Granite City" where Areta had taught.

[1116] "Emery Martin," *Champaign-Urbana News-Gazette* (Illinois), Monday 6 July 1987, p. B6, cols. 2–3.

In 1910 both two-year-old Areta and five-year-old Emery were living in Christy Township, Lawrence County, Illinois.[1117] Areta "studied one year at Illinois Wesleyan, Bloomington, [McLean County], and one year at McKendree"; she completed two years of college, Emery five.[1118] In 1927 she was hired to teach music and penmanship at Granite City High School in Madison County, Illinois.[1119]

In 1930 Emery and Areta and their baby daughter lived next door to her parents in the coal-mining town of Zeigler in Franklin County; both households had radio sets.[1120] In 1940 the Martins were renting a house in DuQuoin, Perry County, for $25 a month; Emery was coach and athletic director at the township high school and was paid $1800.[1121]

She and Emery visited her brother Victor in Chula Vista, San Diego County, California, in June 1951.[1122] In 1954 she taught music at Gillespie, Macoupin County, Illinois.[1123] A widow in 1993, she was living in Champaign, Champaign County, Illinois.[1124]

[1117] Virgil H. Gould household for Areta H., 1910 US census, Sumner, Christy Township, Lawrence County, Illinois, ED 123, Ward 3, sheet 8B, dwelling 193, family 212. Similarly, Marion Martin for Emory [Emery], 1910, Christy Township, ED 122, sheet 10A, dwelling/family 208. Virgil was a preacher, Marion a railroad section laborer.

[1118] *Centennial McKendree College with St. Clair County History* (Lebanon, Illinois: McKendree College, 1928), 617. For college years, Emery Martin household, 1940 US census, DuQuoin, Perry County, Illinois, ED 73-10, sheet 3A, dwelling 48.

[1119] "Freeburg," *Belleville News-Democrat* (Illinois), Friday 10 June 1927, p. 9, col. 3.

[1120] Augie Fowld [Virgil Gould] household, 1930 US census, Zeigler, Franklin County, Illinois, ED 37, sheet 8A, dwelling/family 187. Similarly, Emery Martin household, sheets 8A–B, dwelling/family 188.

[1121] Emery Martin household, 1940 US census, DuQuoin, Perry County, Illinois, ED 73-10, sheet 3A, dwelling 48.

[1122] "Illinoian Visitors at Victor Gould's Home," *Chula Vista Star* (California), Thursday 21 June 1951, p. 10, col. 3.

[1123] "List Faculty for Unit 7: Gillespie Schools Reopen August 31," *Illinois State Journal* (Springfield), Thursday 19 August 1954, p. 18, col. 3.

[1124] "Edwin Malcolm Gould," *The Palm Beach Post* (West Palm Beach, Florida), Wednesday 17 February 1993, p. 14, col. 4.

Emery graduated from McKendree in 1928 (when he was described as "invincible on the field of college sports")[1125] and received a master's degree from the University of Illinois in 1940. "He began teaching and coaching at Zeigler in 1928 and continued his career at DuQuoin and Gillespie." [1126]

He rose through the ranks from coach to Gillespie High School principal in 1949 and superintendent of schools in 1956. He ran unsuccessfully as a Republican for Macoupin County Superintendent of Schools in 1962.[1127] He retired in 1965.[1128]

[1125] "Emery H. Martin," senior class, *Centennial McKendree College with St. Clair County History* (Lebanon, Illinois: McKendree College, 1928), 30.

[1126] "Emery Martin," *Champaign-Urbana News-Gazette* (Illinois), Monday 6 July 1987, p. B6, cols. 2–3.

[1127] "Jacksonville and Gillespie Preps Get New Coaches," *Daily Illinois State Journal* (Springfield), Monday 15 August 1949, p. 10 col. 2. Also, "Litchfield, Hillsboro Want Federal Aid," Saturday 25 February 1956, p. 1, cols 4-6, and p. 2, col. 3. Also, "Midstate Election Returns...Macoupin County," Wednesday 7 November 1962, p. 8, col. 1.

[1128] "Emery Martin," *Champaign-Urbana News-Gazette* (Illinois), Monday 6 July 1987, p. B6, cols. 2–3.

Chapter 44

Tenth Generation

Margaret Louise/Lucille Pifer–George Young King Family
parents at chapters 11, 13

"To introduce Music in the Pulaski county schools" (3800 children)

44. MARGARET LOUISE/LUCILLE^{10} PIFER (*Edith Evelyn & Alice Flo Gould^9, Laura Lucina Thrall^8, Worthy^7, Eliphas^6, Samuel^5, John$^{4-3}$, Timothy^2, William^1*)
Birth: 3 April 1911 in Covington, Alleghany County, Virginia[1129] (for biological relatives, Chapter 11)
Death: 12 March 1983 in Sun City, Maricopa County, Arizona
Burial: Sunland Memorial Park there[1130]
Spouse: **GEORGE YOUNG KING,** married 18 March 1934 at home of her "aunt and uncle" Mr. and Mrs. E. G. Britton near Mounds[1131]
Spouse's parents: Jefferson F. and Martha V. (Young) King[1132]

[1129] Margaret Lucille Pifer delayed birth certificate (1941), Virginia #9732, 3 April 1911; "Virginia, Birth Records, 1912–2016, Delayed Birth Records 1854–1911" > Delayed > 1868–1912 > 09424–09757 > image 323 of 350 (ancestry.com). Aunt Eula B. Baker, age 62, attested to the information 11 September 1941. Also, Edith E. Gould household for sister "Alice F." and "adopted child" Lucille Pifer, 1920 US census, Bone Gap, Edwards County, Illinois, ED 20, sheet 1A, dwelling/family 11.

[1130] Beulah Ridens, "Bone Gap News...Personals," *Daily Republican-Register* (Mount Carmel, Illinois), Wednesday 13 April 1983, p. 14, col. 7. Also, "Obituaries...Margaret King," *Arizona Republic* (Phoenix), Friday 18 March 1983, p. D3 or 39, col. 3.

[1131] "Pifer–King," *Daily Republican-Register* (Mount Carmel, Illinois), Thursday 29 March 1934, p. 3, cols. 5–6. Sister Kathleen played the wedding march. Uncle Virgil N. Gould of Zeigler officiated. Also, Beulah Ridens, "Bone Gap News...Personals," *Daily Republican-Register* (Mount Carmel, Illinois), Wednesday 13 April 1983, p. 14, col. 7.

[1132] J. F. King–Martha V. Young marriage license #29 January 1889, marriage 31 January, Williamson County, Illinois; "Illinois, County Marriages, 1810–1940," FHL 965,417, DGS 5,204,407, image 44 of 587 (familysearch.org). Also, Jefferson King household for son George, 1920 US census, McLeansboro, Hamilton County, Il., ED 54, sheet 7A, dwelling 142, family 143.

Spouse's birth: 29 January 1904 in Illinois,[1133] reportedly in "Marrion"[1134]
Spouse's death: 13 November 2003 in Peoria, Maricopa County, Arizona[1135]
Spouse's burial: Not known

In 1920 George was with his parents and family in McLeansboro, Hamilton County, Illinois; Lucille was living with Edith and Alice Gould in Bone Gap, Edwards County, Illinois.[1136] In 1928 Lucille and adoptive aunt Mrs. Virgil Gould (that is, Dora Sophia [Leighton] Gould) visited relatives "in Asheville, North Carolina, and Covington, Virginia."[1137]

Lucille graduated from Bone Gap Community High School in 1929,[1138] and entered the Louisville Conservatory of Music that fall,[1139] where she took the "public school music course" and majored in violin.[1140] In June 1930 she returned from conservatory to offer violin and piano lessons.[1141] In the summer of 1931 she was taking a course in Carbondale, Jackson County, Illinois.[1142] From 1931 to 1933 she was the

---

[1133] George Y. King index entry, US Social Security Death Index.

[1134] "Obituaries . . . George King," *Arizona Republic* (Phoenix), Wednesday 19 November 2003, p. B7, col. 1.

[1135] George King household, 1940 US census, East Peoria, Tazewell County, Illinois, ED 90-12, sheet 7A, dwelling 143. For exact birth and death dates, George Y. King index entry, US Social Security Death Index.

[1136] Jefferson King household for son George, 1920 US census, McLeansboro, Hamilton County, Illinois, ED 54, sheet 7A, dwelling 142, family 143. Similarly, Edith E. Gould household for sister Alice F. and "adopted child" Lucille Pifer, Bone Gap, Edwards County, Illinois, ED 20, sheet 1A, dwelling/family 11.

[1137] "Interesting News Items from Bone Gap," *Daily Republican-Register* (Mount Carmel, Illinois), Thursday 26 July 1928, p. 5, col. 3.

[1138] Beulah Ridens, "Bone Gap News…Personals," *Daily Republican-Register* (Mount Carmel, Illinois), Wednesday 13 April 1983, p. 14, col. 7.

[1139] "Country Club Holds Meeting at Bone Gap," *Daily Republican-Register* (Mount Carmel, Illinois), Wednesday 11 September 1929, p. 6, col. 2.

[1140] "Bone Gap News," *Daily Republican-Register* (Mount Carmel, Illinois), Monday 30 December 1929, p. 4, col. 5.

[1141] "Instruction," classified advertisement by Edith Gould, *Daily Republican-Register* (Mount Carmel, Illinois), Monday 9 June 1930, p. 7, col. 1.

[1142] "Bone Gap News," *Daily Republican-Register* (Mount Carmel, Illinois), Tuesday 21 July 1931, p. 6, cols. 6–7.

director and music teacher at Keensburg, Wabash County, Illinois.[1143]

Lucille performed and taught music locally.[1144] In the fall of 1933 she undertook a three-month contract "to introduce music in the Pulaski county schools"; she had "entire supervision of 3800 children in the fifty-six high and graded schools in that county."[1145] This may well be where they met.

George completed five years of college, Lucille three.[1146] He taught in McLeansboro, Hamilton County, Illinois, from 1930 to 1933, when he moved to Mounds Township High School in Pulaski County as coach. In a trifecta that says much about rural Illinois, their engagement was announced at a banquet at the local Methodist Church 22 February 1934, held to honor the basketball team's victory in the county tournament.[1147]

In 1940 Lucille and George owned a $3800 house (a bit above the statewide average of $3277) at 111 Pierson Avenue in East Peoria, Tazewell County, Illinois; he was a high-school teacher[1148] in East Peoria.

[1143] "Bone Gap Personals," *Daily Republican-Register* (Mount Carmel, Illinois), Friday 6 November 1931, p. 5, col. 5. Similarly, "Plan Concert at Keensburg," Friday 17 March 1933, p. 2, col. 4.

[1144] "Special Coach Carries Band Over Southern," *Daily Republican-Register* (Mount Carmel, Illinois), Monday 20 June 1927, p. 6, cols. 4–5. Also, "Lick Prairie," *Daily Republican-Register* (Mount Carmel, Illinois), Thursday 16 July 1929, p. 4, col. 5.

[1145] "Takes Position in Music Work in Pulaski County," *Daily Republican-Register* (Mount Carmel, Illinois), Tuesday 19 September 1933, p. 2, col. 1.

[1146] George King household, 1940 US census, East Peoria, Tazewell County, Illinois, ED 90-12, sheet 7A, dwelling 143.

[1147] "Bone Gap News," *Daily Republican-Register* (Mount Carmel, Illinois), Saturday 6 January 1934, p. 2, col. 2, when he was a guest at Edith's. Also, "Announce Engagement," *Daily Republican-Register* (Mount Carmel, Illinois), Tuesday 27 February 1934, p. 3, col. 3, reprinted from the *Independent* (Mounds, Illinois).

[1148] George King household, 1940 US census, East Peoria, Tazewell County, Illinois, ED 90-12, sheet 7A, dwelling 143. For statewide house value average, *United States Census Bureau*, Census of Housing, Historical Census of Housing Tables, Median Home Values Unadjusted 1940 (census.gov/hhes/www/housing/census/historic/values.html).

As of 16 February 1942, he was six feet tall and weighed 205 pounds, with brown eyes and brown hair.[1149] In 1960 they were still in East Peoria.[1150]

Reportedly they first retired to "Galedia" (likely an error for Goleta, Santa Barbara County) in California, and then in 1977 or 1978 to Sun City, Maricopa County, Arizona. George married second after 1983 Helen [–?–].[1151] In 1997 only George was listed at 10104 West Royal Oak Road in Sun City.[1152]

[1149] George Young King, WW2 draft card, Tazewell County Local Board #2, serial #T620, order #T10687; "US WWII Draft Cards Young Men, 1940–1947" > Illinois > Kanel–Kurka > Kindt–King > images 1913–14 of 2131 (ancestry.com).

[1150] "Edith Evelyn Gould Graveside Services Held Sunday," clipping from unknown newspaper (quite possibly the *Albion Journal*) dated 16 November 1960, in author's possession.

[1151] "Obituaries . . . George King," *Arizona Republic* (Phoenix), Wednesday 19 November 2003, p. B7, col. 1. Also, Margaret Louise/Lucille's obituary says they moved five years before her 1983 death, implying 1978: "Obituaries…Margaret King," *Arizona Republic* (Phoenix), Friday 18 March 1983, p. D3 or 39, col. 3.

[1152] George Y. King entry, *Polk Cross-Reference Directory for Phoenix Suburban Arizona*, p. 316.

Chapter 45

Tenth Generation

Cecil Melvin Pifer–Rosalie Galeener–Kathryn Williams Family
parents at chapters 11, 13

Schoolteacher to USAF Lieutenant Colonel

45. CECIL MELVIN^{10} PIFER (*Edith Evelyn & Alice Flo Gould^9, Laura Lucina Thrall^8, Worthy^7, Eliphas^6, Samuel^5, John$^{4-3}$, Timothy^2, William^1*)
Birth: 14 July 1915 in Covington, Alleghany County, Virginia[1153] (for biological relatives, Chapter 11)
Death: 15 June 1995, last residence Phoenix, Maricopa County, Arizona[1154]
Burial: Not known
Spouse #1: **ROSALIE F. GALEENER,** married 17 June 1938
Spouse #1's parents: William Kenneth and Adela Pauline (Carrier) Galeener[1155]
Spouse #1's birth: 23 December 1919 in Illinois[1156]

[1153] Cecil Melvin Pifer–Kathryn Sande marriage license 25794 (21 March 1950), Cascade County, Montana; "Montana, Marriage Records, 1943–1986" > 1943–1956 > Cascade > Cas 2706–Cas 6250 > image 2426 of 3548 (ancestry.com).

[1154] Cecil Pifer index entry; "US, Department of Veterans Affairs BIRLS Death File, 1850–2010" (ancestry.com). For last residence, US Social Security Death Index entry.

[1155] "Announce Engagement," *Daily Republican-Register* (Mount Carmel, Illinois), Tuesday 31 May 1938, p. 4, col. 2. Melvin's parents were described as "the late Mr. and Mrs. William Pifer of Covington, Va.," although the father was probably not deceased. For Rosalie's parents: William Kenneth Galeener–Adela Pauline Carrier marriage 17 June 1914, license #4199, Urbana, Champaign County, Illinois, marriage register 5:237; "Illinois, County Marriages, 1810–1940," FHL 1,032,314, DGS 4,539,342, image 468–69 of 672 (familysearch.org).

[1156] "Rosalie F. Aukland," *Baraboo News-Republic* (Wisconsin), Thursday 6 March 2008, no p. or col. number, transcription at genealogybank.com. Also, William K. Glienders [Galeener] household for daughter Boasil [Rosalie] age 1/12, 1920 US census, Jasper Township, Wayne County, Illinois, ED 157, sheet 7A, dwelling 140, family 144. Also, Melvin Pifer household for wife Rosalie, 1940 US census, La Rose, Marshall County, Illinois, ED 62-1, sheet 1B, dwelling 25.

Spouse #1's death: 2 March 2008 in Baraboo, Sauk County, Wisconsin[1157]
Spouse #1's burial: Not known
Spouse #2: **KATHRYN INEZ (WILLIAMS) SANDE,** married second 23 July 1950 as her second husband in Great Falls, Cascade County, Montana
Spouse #2's parents: John G. and Ann (Fraser) Williams
Spouse #2's birth: 28 March 1917 in Manlius, Bureau County, Illinois[1158]
Spouse #2's death: June 1984 in Phoenix, Maricopa County, Arizona[1159]
Spouse #2's burial: Not known

Most likely Melvin came to Bone Gap, Edwards County, Illinois, in the early 1920s.[1160] He was in a group that "motored" to Flora for an Epworth League (Methodist youth) gathering in 1929.[1161] In 1930 he was "foster son" of Edith Gould in Bone Gap.[1162] He visited sister Lucille in Carbondale in the summer of 1931, as well as friends in Zeigler and Mounds.[1163] Graduating from Bone Gap High School second in his class,[1164] he entered the University of Illinois in 1934.[1165] He "gained a 4 years scholarship at the University & has a F.E.R.A. job that nets in 15 a

---

[1157] "Rosalie F. Aukland," *News-Republic* (Baraboo, Wisconsin), Thursday 6 March 2008, no p. or col. number, transcription at genealogybank.com.

[1158] Cecil Melvin Pifer–Kathryn Sande marriage license 25794 (21 March 1950), Cascade County, Montana; "Montana, Marriage Records, 1943–1986" > 1943–1956 > Cascade > Cas 2706–Cas 6250 > image 2426 of 3548 (ancestry.com). She was called Catherine Inez Williams in Ruth S. Widdison, compiler, *Wixom Family History Supplement* (Salt Lake City: privately printed, 1988), unpaginated, under listing #14370.

[1159] Kathryn Pifer index entry, June 1984, US Social Security Death Index.

[1160] He was in Virginia at the time of the 1920 census: Virginia S. Leighton household for grandson Melvin Pifer age 4 9/12 and "widowed" daughter Willie Pifer age 33, 1920 US census, Covington, Alleghany County, Virginia, ED 5, sheet 4B, dwelling 70, family 72.

[1161] "Goes to Take Training Course in Health Work," *Daily Republican-Register* (Mount Carmel, Illinois), Thursday 20 June 1929, p. 4, col. 4.

[1162] Edith Gould household for Melvin Pifer, 1930 US census, Bone Gap, Edwards County, Illinois, ED 3, sheet 2B, dwelling/family 65.

[1163] "Bone Gap News," *Daily Republican-Register* (Mount Carmel, Illinois), Tuesday 21 July 1931, p. 6, cols. 6–7.

[1164] "Announce Engagement," *Daily Republican-Register* (Mount Carmel, Illinois), Tuesday 31 May 1938, p. 4, col. 2.

[1165] "Bone Gap News," *Daily Republican-Register* (Mount Carmel, Illinois), Wednesday 5 December 1934, p. 4, col. 6.

mo. Edith Gould sends him food from her little farm twice a week, & he & a room mate do light house keeping."[1166]

In 1935 he was living in Champaign, Champaign County, Illinois.[1167] In the summer of 1937 he visited with Mortimer Piper of Rantoul, and had six weeks' military training at Camp Custer in Michigan.[1168]

Melvin's first wife Rosalie Galeener graduated from University High School in Champaign.[1169] Likely divorced between the 1940 census and 23 July 1950, she married second Owen Maller, who was born in 1930 and died 2005.[1170] In the late 1950s they were living at 607 West White in Champaign, Champaign County, Illinois, when Owen was a university student[1171]—most likely a graduate student, as he received a bachelor of science degree there in 1952.[1172]

After they parted ways, Rosalie married third Raymond Aukland, and Owen married second about 1974 Alma Sollod. Owen's career included a University of Illinois doctorate in psychology in 1964, research at North Carolina State University and the Veterans Administration, co-authorship of the book *Chemical Senses and Nutrition* in 1977, and later (on

---

[1166] Letter from Elizabeth Schriber Thrall in Tolono to her Schriber sisters in Chicago, 29 November 1934; in author's possession. Her husband was first cousin of Edith Gould. "F.E.R.A." = "Federal Emergency Relief Administration," one of President Roosevelt's Depression-era jobs programs

[1167] Melvin Pifer household, 1940 US census, La Rose, Marshall County, Illinois, ED 62-1, sheet 1B, dwelling 25.

[1168] "Neighbors Meet at Gillette Home," *Daily Republican-Register* (Mount Carmel, Illinois), Thursday 17 June 1937, p. 3, col. 4.

[1169] "Announce Engagement," *Daily Republican-Register* (Mount Carmel, Illinois), Tuesday 31 May 1938, p. 4, col. 2.

[1170] "Obituaries . . . Dr. Owen Maller, 75," *Philadelphia Enquirer*, Friday 26 August 2005, p. B7, col. 4.

[1171] Owen Maller and Rosalie F. entries, *Polk's Champaign-Urbana (Champaign County) City Directory 1960* [Illinois] (St. Louis, Missouri: R. L. Polk, 1960), p. 311 (image 220 of 431) (ancestry.com). Similarly, 1957, p. 379, image 201 of 476; 1958, p. 316, image 223 of 429; 1959, p. 320, image 218 of 427.

[1172] Owen Maller degree, Board of Trustees, University of Illinois, 19 June 1952, p. 1558 (https://archives.library.illinois.edu/ erec/University%20Archives/ 0101802/02_volume_sections/1950-1952/23_meeting_1952-06-19.pdf).

a volunteer stint at Lankenau Hospital, Wynnewood Township, Pennsylvania) entertaining patients as "Dr. Hugh Moore."[1173]

Melvin's second wife Kathryn completed two years of college and taught school.[1174] She had married first 10 March 1943 in Phoenix, Maricopa County, Arizona, Charles Bernard Sande.[1175] Charles was born 24 October 1915 in Laurel, Yellowstone County, Montana, and died 23 May 1992 in Billings, Yellowstone County, Montana,[1176] the son of Charles B. and Mary (Parchet/Sarchet) Sande.[1177] In 1944 Kathryn and Charles were living at 33 Burlington Avenue in Billings; he was in the army and she was "cash[ier]" for Consolidated Freightways.[1178] She divorced him 16 December 1946 in Roundup, Musselshell County, Montana, on grounds of "extreme cruelty."[1179]

In 1938 Melvin completed the ROTC (Reserve Officers' Training Corps) course at the University of Illinois which led to the rank of second

---

[1173] "Obituaries . . . Dr. Owen Maller, 75," *Philadelphia Enquirer*, Friday 26 August 2005, p. B7, col. 4.

[1174] J. G. Williams household for daughter Kathryn, 1940 US census, Great Falls, Cascade County, Montana, ED 7-4, sheet 9A, dwelling 293.

[1175] Charles Bernard Sande–Kathryn Williams marriage license and certificate 10 March 1943, Phoenix, Maricopa County, Arizona, p. 211; "Arizona, County Marriage Records, 1865–1972" > Maricopa > Marriage Licenses > image 13675 of 86651 (ancestry.com).

[1176] Charles B. Sande index entry, died 23 May 1992, US Social Security Death Index.

[1177] Charles B. Sande–Mary Parchet/Sarchet marriage 24 July 1907, Anaconda, Deer Lodge County, Montana, #3055, Marriage Record p. 1121; "Montana, County Marriages, 1865–1987" > Deer Lodge > Marriage Records, v. 2–4, 1897–1907 > image 902 of 919 (ancestry.com). In different places on the same form, the first letter of her surname is clearly S and clearly P. Also, Charles B. Sande, 24 October 1915, Montana birth certificate #72 or 66-199; "Montana, Birth Records, 1897–1919" > 1915 > 66 > image 395 of 1994 (ancestry.com).

[1178] Chas. B. and Kathryn I. Sande entries, *Polk's Billings (Yellowstone County, Montana) City Directory 1944* (Salt Lake City: R. L. Polk, 1944), p. 328, image 163 of 358 (ancestry.com).

[1179] Kathryn Sande, plaintiff, vs. Charles B. Sande, defendant, case #5233, Montana Divorce or Annulment Certificate, 16 December 1946; "Montana, Divorce Records, 1943–1986" > 1943–1956 > Musselshell > Musl1–Musl175 > image 71 of 177 (ancestry.com).

lieutenant.[1180] In 1940 he and Rosalie were living in a $9-a-month apartment in La Rose, Marshall County, Illinois, where he earned $1700 for 44 weeks' work teaching school in 1939.[1181] His three Air Force enlistments totaled almost twenty years: 2 to 15 July 1939, 20 August 1941 to 30 November 1957, and 6 January 1958 to 31 December 1961,[1182] retiring as a lieutenant colonel.[1183]

In later years he and Kathryn lived in Cedar Rapids, Linn County, Iowa (1953); Peoria, Peoria County, Illinois (1956–59);[1184] and Phoenix, Maricopa County, Arizona (1960).[1185]

[1180] "188 Illini Complete ROTC Course," *Daily Illini* (University of Illinois), 28 May 1938, p. 1, col. 7.

[1181] Melvin Pifer household, 1940 US census, La Rose, Marshall County, Illinois, ED 62-1, sheet 1B, dwelling 25.

[1182] Cecil Pifer index entry; "US, Department of Veterans Affairs BIRLS Death File, 1850–2010" (ancestry.com).

[1183] "Cecil Melvin Pifer," newspaper clippings (newspaper not identified) 21 June 1995, col.3; "Arizona, Payson Obituaries, 1948–2008," DGS 100,743,143, image 2480 of 8664 (familysearch.org). Biological parents from Cecil Melvin Pifer index entry, "US, Social Security Application and Claims Index, 1936–2007" (ancestry.com).

[1184] Cecil M. and Kathryn Parker entries: *Polk's Cedar Rapids (Linn County, Iowa), City Directory 1953* (Omaha, Nebraska: R. L. Polk, 1953), p. 499, image 266 of 594. *Polk's Peoria (Peoria County, Illinois), City Directory 1956* (St. Louis, Missouri: R. L. Polk, 1956), p. 603, image 513 of 836. Similarly, *1957*, p. 581, image 389 of 709; *1958*, p. 598, image 410 of 725; and *1959*, p. 606, image 419 of 740 (ancestry.com).

[1185] "Edith Evelyn Gould Graveside Services Held Sunday," clipping from unknown newspaper (likely the *Albion Journal*) dated 16 November 1960, in author's possession.

Chapter 46

Tenth Generation

Carrie Eleanor Marshall–Howard Lee Daughenbaugh Family
parents at chapter 14

Forty-six years on the Southern Pacific Railroad (including the 1937 Rose Bowl)

46. CARRIE ELEANOR^{10} MARSHALL (*Etta Jane Campbell^9, Hannah Caroline Thrall^8, Worthy^7, Eliphas^6, Samuel^5, John$^{4-3}$, Timothy^2, William^1*)
Birth: 1 November 1900 in Louisiana
Death: 31 January 1977
Burial: Greenwood Cemetery, Jennings, Jefferson Davis Parish, Louisiana[1186]
Spouse: **HOWARD LEE DAUGHENBAUGH,** married 17 December 1919 in Lake Charles, Calcasieu Parish, Louisiana[1187]
Spouse's parents: Henry and Philomene (Miller) Daughenbaugh[1188]

[1186] "Carrie E. Marshall wife of Howard L. Daughenbaugh Sr." grave marker, Greenwood Cemetery, Jennings, Louisiana, memorial #140,858,188 by Bobby (findagrave.com). Also, Harvey Marshall household for daughter Carrie, 1910 US census, Calcasieu Parish, Police Jury Ward 10, ED 51, sheet 23B, dwelling 450, family 402.

[1187] Carrie Elenor Marshall–Howard Lee Daughenbaugh marriage 17 December 1919, Calcasieu Parish, 11:498; FHL 1,405,694, DGS 4,705,923, image 118 of 1118 (familysearch.org). Carrie's adoptive grandfather Charles W. Campbell officiated. Also, witnesses were Mr. Lynn L. Daughenbaugh and Ruth Marshall: "Daughenbaugh–Marshall," *Jennings Daily Times-Record* (Louisiana), Thursday 18 December 1919, p. 1, col. 3.

[1188] Henry Doughenbough [Daughenbaugh] household for son Henry L. age 1 born June 1898, 1900 US census, Acadia Parish, Louisiana, Ward 4, ED 6, sheet 15B, dwelling 262, family 264. For Philomene's birth surname, Ivan Henry Daughenbaugh–Eula Mae Langley marriage 1 May 1924, record D:257; "Louisiana, Parish Marriages, 1837–1957" > Jefferson Davis Parish > FHL 1,378,075, DGS 4,705,663 > image 570 (familysearch.org).

Spouse's birth: 6 June 1898 in Louisiana
Spouse's death: 27 August 1964 in Calcasieu Parish
Spouse's burial: Greenwood Cemetery[1189]

Howard reportedly began his railroad career about 1917 as "station agent on the Lafayette division."[1190] After their 1919 wedding, the young couple planned to live with Howard's parents "until located at a home of their own in Jennings."[1191] In 1930 Carrie and Howard were renting at $30 a month and owned a radio.[1192] In 1937, "widely known in south Louisiana," he was promoted to general agent at Birmingham, Jefferson County, Alabama.[1193] In 1940 they lived at 427 Helen in Lake Charles in a house valued at $8,000 (statewide average was $1414); he earned $3600 for 52 weeks of work.[1194] In 1930 and 1940 Carrie's parents Harvey and Etta Marshall were with them.[1195] In 1955 the family was living in New Orleans.[1196]

Howard worked various jobs for the Southern Pacific Railroad for 46 years, retiring in 1963: a clerk at Jennings and Opelousas; traveling

---

[1189] Howard L. Daughenbaugh grave marker, Greenwood Cemetery, Jennings, Louisiana, memorial #121,297,158 by Marie (findagrave.com). Also, "H.L. Daughenbaugh," *American Press* (Lake Charles, Louisiana), Friday 28 August 1964, p. 2, col. 1.

[1190] "Railroad Man Here Is Given Promotion," *Meridional* (Abbeville, Louisiana), Saturday 6 March 1937, p. 8, col. 5.

[1191] "Daughenbaugh–Marshall," *Daily Times-Record* (Jennings, Louisiana), Thursday 18 December 1919, p. 1, col. 3.

[1192] Howard L. Daughenbaugh household, 1930 US census, New Iberia City, Iberia Parish, Louisiana, Ward 6, ED 8, sheet 2A, dwelling 27, family 32.

[1193] "Railroad Man Here Is Given Promotion," *Meridional* (Abbeville, Louisiana), Saturday 6 March 1937, p. 8, col. 5.

[1194] Howard L. Daughenbaugh household, 1940 US census, Lake Charles, Calcasieu Parish, Louisiana, ED 10-15, sheet 23 B, dwelling 555. Statewide figures from US Census Bureau, Census of Housing, Historical Census of Housing Tables, Median Home Values Unadjusted 1940 (census.gov/hhes/www/housing/census/historic/values.html).

[1195] Howard L. Daughenbaugh household for in-laws Harvey and Etta Marshall, 1930 US census, New Iberia City, Iberia Parish, Louisiana. Ward 6, ED 8, sheet 2A, dwelling 27, family 32. Also, Howard L. Daughenbaugh household, 1940 US census, Lake Charles, Calcasieu Parish, ED 10-15, sheet 23B, dwelling 555.

[1196] "Society," *Times-Picayune* (New Orleans), Friday 23 December 1955, p. 29, col. 2.

agent at Lake Charles, New Iberia, and Birmingham; district freight and passenger agent at Lake Charles from 1938 to 1952; and assistant general freight and passenger agent in New Orleans from 1952 to 1963.

He was also a member of the New Orleans, Lake Charles, and Mobile Traffic Clubs, and an active lay leader in the Louisiana Conference of the Methodist Church.[1197] In 1947 he spoke to a PTA meeting on raising school standards and teachers' salaries.[1198]

On Christmas night 1937, a special train, "California and Rose Bowl bound," was to depart Montgomery, Alabama, at 10:33 p.m. According to agents Daughenbaugh (Southern Pacific) and W. M. Hays (Louisville & Nashville), the 75 passengers with reservations were the largest group "ever to follow the Alabama football team to California for a Rose Bowl battle." The special train was to be made up in Montgomery, join a special from Birmingham, and add five sleepers and two dining cars at New Orleans along the way.

"Mr. Daughenbaugh plans to make the trip as a loyal rooter of the Crimsons during the big contest. In addition to those making the trip by train, a number of other local fans will be leaving today and tomorrow by automobile. Maj. Aubrey Hornsby, ace pilot of Maxwell Field, plans to fly to the Pacific Coast next week for the game."

After four days in Los Angeles, the return train was to head home 2 January.[1199] The return trip may have seemed longer, as the Tide was at ebb that year, losing to California 13-0 before a crowd of 90,000.[1200]

[1197] "Daughenbaugh Funeral Today," *Times-Picayune* (New Orleans), Friday 28 August 1964, p. 20, col. 3. For his stint at Lake Charles, "SP Railroad District Agent Here Promoted," American Press (Lake, Charles, Louisiana), Saturday 22 June 1963, p. 1, col. 5.

[1198] "Teachers Should Be Paid Higher Salaries, States Speaker at Gueydan Meet," *Meridional* (Abbeville, Louisiana), Saturday 7 June 1947, p. 4, col. 1.

[1199] "Largest Crowd Follows Alabama to Pasadena Game," *Advertiser* (Montgomery, Alabama), Saturday 25 December 1937, p. 5, col. 2.

[1200] "1938 Rose Bowl," *Wikipedia* (https://en.wikipedia.org/wiki/1938_Rose_Bowl).

Chapter 47

Tenth Generation

Beulah Marshall Family
parents at chapter 14

Nursing in Louisiana and Texas

47. BEULAH F.^{10} MARSHALL (*Etta Jane Campbell^9, Hannah Caroline Thrall^8, Worthy^7, Eliphas^6, Samuel^5, John$^{4-3}$, Timothy^2, William^1*)
Birth: 11 August 1904 in Louisiana
Death: 29 December 1983 in Louisiana, last residence New Iberia, Iberia Parish[1201]
Burial: Not known

In 1910 five-year-old Beulah lived with her parents and siblings in Ward 10 of Calcasieu Parish, where her father was a rice farmer.[1202] In 1920 the family was in Lake Charles, Calcasieu Parish, at 1002 Second Boulevard, and owned the duplex they lived in.[1203] Beulah attended a family gathering for her Marshall grandmother 30 December 1920.[1204]

[1201] Harvey Marshall household for daughter Beulah, 1910 US census, Calcasieu Parish, Police Jury Ward 10, ED 51, sheet 23B, dwelling 450, family 402. For month and year of death, and last known residence, Beulah Marshall index entry, US Social Security Death Index. For exact date, Beulah Marshall index entry, "US, Department of Veterans Affairs BIRLS Death File, 1850–2010" (ancestry.com).
[1202] Harvey Marshall household, 1910 US census, Calcasieu Parish, Police Jury Ward 10, ED 51, sheet 23B, dwelling 450, family 402.
[1203] Harvey Marshall household, 1920 US census, Lake Charles, Calcasieu Parish, Louisiana, Ward 3, ED 42, sheet 8A, dwelling 144, family 149.
[1204] "Family Reunion Held in Honor of Mother, Mrs. Ellen Marshall," *Daily Times-Record* (Jennings, Louisiana), Saturday 31 December 1921, p. 5, col. 4.

1930: Beulah was a student nurse living at the St. Patrick's Sanitarium Nurses Home on South Ryan Street in Lake Charles.[1205]

1934: supervisor of nurses at the Eye, Ear, Nose, and Throat Hospital in New Orleans.[1206]

1935–1940: she and Marie Keaton, both trained nurses, shared a New Orleans apartment at 3122 Cleveland that rented for $22 a month. Beulah earned $1500 in 1939.[1207] (This Beulah Marshall should not be confused with the Louisiana-born Beulah [usually Beulah F.] who was a couple of years older and lived with husband John G. Marshall and daughter in Pasadena, California, in 1940.[1208])

1945: in the army near the end of World War II, 24 May to 23 December 1945.[1209]

1952 and 1955: in Wichita Falls, Wichita County, Texas.[1210] She was still there in 1955, when the 1930 class of student nurses observed its 25th anniversary,[1211] but soon returned to her native state.

[1205] Beulah Marshall, lodger, 1930 US census, St. Patrick's Sanitarium Student Nurses Home, Lake Charles City, Calcasieu Parish, Louisiana, Ward 4, ED 12, sheet 17A, dwelling 333, family 355.

[1206] "Boy Veteran of 35 Operations Dictates Letter to Santa," *Times-Picayune* (New Orleans), Wednesday 12 December 1934, p. 1, col. 6. Includes a photo of the boy and nursing supervisor Beulah Marshall.

[1207] Beulah Marshall, partner in Marie Keaton household, 1940 US census, New Orleans, Orleans Parish, Louisiana, Ward 3, ED 36-56, sheet 62B (dwelling numbers are random).

[1208] John G. Marshall household for Beulah F. age 37, 1940 US census, Pasadena, Los Angeles County, California, Ward 47, ED 19-497, sheet 17B, dwelling 431.

[1209] Beulah Marshall index entry, "US, Department of Veterans Affairs BIRLS Death File, 1850–2010" (ancestry.com). Also, Social Security Death Index.

[1210] Elta [Etta] Campbell, Texas death certificate #53703, 7 December 1952, Wichita Falls; "Texas, Death Certificates, 1903–1982" > Wichita > 1952 > Oct–Dec > image 170 of 240 (ancestry.com).

[1211] "Nurses Class of 1930 to Hold Reunion," *American-Press* (Lake Charles, Louisiana), Sunday 8 May 1955, p. 6, col. 1.

1957, 1960, and 1963: she owned her home at 607 Kirk in New Iberia, Iberia Parish, and worked as nursing supervisor at Dauterive Hospital.[1212]

1966 and 1969: at 207 Dodson with the same job.[1213]

1977: in New Iberia.[1214]

[1212] Beulah Marshall entry, *New Iberia Louisiana ConSurvey City Directory 1957–58* (New Iberia: Mullin-Kille and Chamber of Commerce, 1958), p. 576, image 561 of 612 (ancestry.com). Similarly, *1960*, p. 684, image 535 of 665 (ancestry.com); *1963*, p. 582 (not on line).

[1213] Beulah Marshall entry, *New Iberia Louisiana ConSurvey City Directory 1966*, p. 595; *1969*, p. 598.

[1214] "Daughenbaugh," *Times-Picayune* (New Orleans), Wednesday 2 February 1977, p. 16, col. 7.

Chapter 48

Tenth Generation

Leona Mae Campbell–Chester E. "Jackie" Pearson Family
parents at chapter 15

Cobden to St. Louis

48. LEONA "LENA" MAE^{10} CAMPBELL (*Leo Frank Campbell^9, Hannah Caroline Thrall^8, Worthy^7, Eliphas^6, Samuel^5, John$^{4-3}$, Timothy^2, William^1*)
Birth: 1920 (possibly 13 September) in or near Cobden (parents' residence), Union County, Illinois[1215]
Death: 1999 (possibly 31 July)
Burial: Block 10, lot 2D, grave 5 in Cobden Cemetery, Cobden, Union County, Illinois[1216]
Spouse: **CHESTER EDWARD "JACKIE" PEARSON,** married at Jackson, Cape Girardeau County, Missouri, 19 August 1938[1217]
Spouse's parents: Roscoe and Millie (Peterman) Pearson[1218]

[1215] Leo F. Campbell household, 1920 US census, Cobden, Union County, Illinois, ED 138, sheet 9A, dwelling 64, family 65.

[1216] Leo F. Campbell household for daughter Leona Mae age 10, 1930 US census, Cobden, Union County, Illinois, ED 9, sheet 13B, dwelling/family 95. Also, Leona Mae Pearson grave marker, Cobden Cemetery, Cobden, Illinois, image, memorial #43,921,566 for Leona Mae Campbell Pearson by Alethea England (findagrave.com).

[1217] C. E. Jackie Pearson–Lena Mae Campbell marriage license and return #3372, Cape Girardeau County, Missouri, 19 August 1938; "Missouri, Marriage Records 1805–2002" > Cape Girardeau > Record images for Cape Girardeau > 1936–1939 > image 249 of 779 (ancestry.com). Baptist minister S. H. Hardy officiated.

[1218] Roscoe Pearson household for son Chester age 4, 1920 US census, Cobden, Union County, Illinois, ED 137, sheet 7A, dwelling 130, family 144. For Millie's birth surname, Roscoe Pearson and spouse Millie Peterman entries, "US, Social Security Applications and Claims Index, 1936–2007" (ancestry.com). Also, Millie Peterman age 8 in Wm. J. Peterman household, 1900 US census, Goreville, Johnson County, Illinois, ED 41, sheet 6A, dwelling 104, family 108. Roscoe was a railroad laborer.

Spouse's birth: 11 January 1915, probably in Cobden (parents' residence 1910 and 1920)[1219]
Spouse's death: 31 August 1995, last residence Cobden[1220]
Spouse's burial: with his wife[1221]

At the time of their marriage, Jackie was living in West Paducah, McCracken County, Kentucky, and Leona was in Cobden, Union County, Illinois, some 60 miles northwest.[1222] They both completed four years of high school.

1940: they were renting an $8-a-month apartment in Cobden; he was a draftsman for the federal government's Works Progress Administration (WPA).[1223] Chester served in the US Navy during World War II.

1945: aboard the U.S.S. *Farenholt* (DD491) he was disbursing storekeeper, 2nd class (SKD 2c).[1224]

[1219] Raeve [Roscoe] Pearson household, 1910 US census, Cobden, Union County, Illinois, ED 131, sheet 9B, dwelling/family 198. Similarly, Roscoe Pearson household for son Chester age 4, 1920, ED 137, sheet 7A, dwelling 130, family 144.

[1220] Chester E. Pearson entry, US Social Security Death Index.

[1221] Chester E. Pearson grave marker, Cobden Cemetery, Cobden, Union County, Illinois, image, memorial #44,165,557 for Chester Edward "Jack" Pearson by Alethea England (findagrave.com).

[1222] C. E. Jackie Pearson–Lena Mae Campbell marriage license and return #3372, Cape Girardeau County, Missouri, 19 August 1938; "Missouri, Marriage Records 1805–2002" > Cape Girardeau > Record images for Cape Girardeau > 1936–1939 > image 249 of 779 (ancestry.com).

[1223] C. E. Pearson household, 1940 US census, Cobden, Union County, Illinois, ED 91-9, sheet 3A, dwelling 57.

[1224] Chester E. Pearson grave marker, Cobden Cemetery, Cobden, Illinois, image, memorial #44,165,557 for Chester Edward "Jack" Pearson by Alethea England (findagrave.com). Also, Chester E. Pearson entry, Navy Cruise Books, 1918–2009 > F > 1945 > pp. 46 and 52 (https://www.fold3.com/image/1/301648353 and https://www.fold3.com/image/1/301648365). Also, *The Bluejackets' Manual, U.S. Navy, 1944*, 12th edition (Annapolis, Maryland: United States Naval Institute, 1944), pp. xx, 73, 82.

1962–63: in St. Louis as "C. Jack" and "Mae." Jack's father died near Cobden in the spring of 1963.[1225]

1964-69: at 5951 Marwinette Avenue in St. Louis; he was office manager for Loomis Brothers Equipment at 2823 Locust.[1226] (The brothers were Burton P. and Charles H., residing in St. Louis County.)[1227]

About 1969: moved out to 11331 Five Oaks Parkway, Concord Village in St. Louis County, where Jack was in charge of the Claymont Laundry at 901 Clayton Road.[1228]

About 1972: moved to 10558 Kamping Lane and Jack was working at Penney's (probably the department store).[1229]

[1225] "Roscoe Pearson, 73, Dies Near Cobden," *Southern Illinoisan* (Carbondale), Sunday 10 March 1963, p. 24, col. 2. Also, "Leo F. Campbell, Father of Paducah Resident, Dies," Sun-Democrat (Paducah, Kentucky), 23 February 1962, p. 16A, col. 1.

[1226] C. Jack Pearson (Mae) entries, *Polk's St. Louis (Missouri) City Directory* (Detroit: R. L. Polk), p. 1109; *1966*, p. 1279; 1967–8, p. 1208; *1969*, p. 887.

[1227] Loomis Brothers Equipment, *Polk's St. Louis (Missouri) City Directory 1964* (Detroit: R. L. Polk), p. 873.

[1228] Jack Pearson (Mae) entries, *Polk's St. Louis Suburban Directory 1969* (Detroit: R. L. Polk), p. 1145; *1970*, pp. 260, 1132; *1971*, p. 1132.

[1229] Jack Pearson (Mae) entry, *Polk's St. Louis Suburban Directory (Detroit: R. L. Polk), 1972–73*, p. 881.

Chapter 49

Tenth Generation

Mary Anna Campbell–Edward August Kohler Family
parents at chapter 15

Materials Engineering and Music

49. MARY ANNA^{10} **CAMPBELL** (*Leo Frank Campbell*^{9}, *Hannah Caroline Thrall*^{8}, *Worthy*^{7}, *Eliphas*^{6}, *Samuel*^{5}, *John*$^{4-3}$, *Timothy*^{2}, *William*^{1})
Birth: about 1932 (possibly 17 August 1931) in Illinois[1230]
Death: 30 October 2013 in Paducah, McCracken County, Kentucky
Burial: 2 November 2013 at Mount Kenton Cemetery there
Spouse: **EDWARD AUGUST KOHLER JR.**, married about 1951[1231]
Spouse's parents: Edward August (Sr.) and Grace (Rendleman) Kohler
Spouse's birth: 9 March 1928 in Alto Pass, Union County, Illinois
Spouse's death: 1 December 2016 in Paducah, McCracken County, Kentucky
Spouse's burial: 5 December 2016 with his wife[1232]

Edward served in the US Navy, attended Southern Illinois University, and worked 44 years for Martin Marietta Systems.[1233] In 1956

[1230] Leo Campbell household for daughter Mary A. age 8, 1940 US census, Cobden, Union County, Illinois, ED 91-9, sheet 6A, dwelling 122. Exact date is unsourced at Mary Anna Campbell Kohler memorial (no image) #119,591,439 by AZLITE (findagrave.com).

[1231] "Funeral Notice . . . Mary Anna Kohler," *Sun* (Paducah, Kentucky), Wednesday 30 October 2013, p. A10, cols. 1–2.

[1232] "Edward A. Kohler," *Sun* (Paducah, Kentucky), Sunday 4 December 2016, p. A11, cols. 3–4.

[1233] "Edward A. Kohler," Sun (Paducah, Kentucky), Sunday 4 December 2016, p. A11, cols. 3–4.

he and Mary lived at 1527 North 13th in Paducah, Kentucky; he was a materials engineer for Union Carbide. In 1957 they moved to 3227 Pines Road where they remained for at least 41 years. In 1959 he was a "junior account engineer."[1234] In 1968 and 1976 he was an "engineer aide" at Union Carbide.[1235] In 1990 he was a supervisor at Martin Marietta.[1236] By 1996 he had retired.

They were members of Broadway United Methodist Church, where Mary Anna "was an excellent musician and used her musical talents as a soloist, piano teacher, choir director, and church organist and pianist."[1237]

[1234] Edward Kohler entries, *Caron's Paducah City Directory 1956* (St. Louis, Missouri: Caron Directory Company, 1956), p. 215, image 119 of 451. Similarly, *1957*, p. 342, image 186 of 454; and *1959*, p. 244, image 183 of 444 (ancestry.com). No Kohlers were recorded in 1954. For retirement in place, *1996*.

[1235] Edward Kohler entries, *Caron's Paducah City Directory 1968*, p. 368, and 1976, p. 177.

[1236] Edward Kohler entry, *Caron's Paducah City Directory 1990*, p. 201.

[1237] "Funeral Notice . . . Mary Anna Kohler," *Sun* (Paducah, Kentucky), Wednesday 30 October 2013, p. A10, cols. 1–2.

Chapter 50

Edith Flint Thrall–George Ansel Mooers Family
parents at chapter 17

Artist and minister in Michigan and Pennsylvania

50. EDITH FLINT[10] **THRALL** (*Victor Worthy*[9], *Leonidas*[8], *Worthy*[7], *Eliphas*[6], *Samuel*[5], *John*[4-3], *Timothy*[2], *William*[1])
Birth: 7 October 1904 in O'Fallon, St. Clair County[1238]
Death: 23 April 1989, last residence Columbus, Franklin County, Ohio[1239]
Burial: Not known
Spouse: **GEORGE ANSEL MOOERS,** married 26 August 1926 in Albion, Calhoun County, Michigan[1240]
Spouse's parents: Charles Ansel and Gertrude (Broome) Mooers
Spouse's birth: 20 July 1899 in Knoxville, Knox County, Tennessee
Spouse's death: 10 September 1987 in Columbus, Franklin County, Ohio
Spouse's burial: Muskegon, Muskegon County, Michigan[1241]

[1238] For exact date, Edith T. Mooers entry, Social Security Death Index. For location, D. Stephen Thrall and Grant Leslie Thrall, compilers, *Thrall Genealogy 1630–1965: Descendants of William Thrall* (N.p.: privately printed, circa 1965), p. 155, family 965.

[1239] Edith T. Mooers entry, Social Security Death Index.

[1240] George A. Mooers–Edith F. Thrall marriage license #492, 12 August 1926, marriage 26 August, Calhoun County, Michigan; "Michigan, Marriage Records, 1867–1952" > Calhoun–Emmett > Calhoun (1926–1930) > image 539 of 3061 (ancestry.com). Edith's father Rev. Victor Thrall officiated. Witnesses were Carrie J. Thrall (Edith's mother) and Charles A. Mooers (George's father). Also, "Society," *News* (Knoxville, Tennessee), Thursday 26 August 1926, p. 6, col. 2.

[1241] "George Ansel Mooers," *1988 Official Journal and Year Book Western Pennsylvania Annual Conference, The United Methodist Church, Grove City, Pennsylvania, 14–17 June 1988*, p. 371.

In 1920 Edith was living with her parents and siblings in Evanston, Cook County, Illinois.[1242] She studied at the University of Tennessee, Northwestern University, and Albion College. "She led and participated in dramatic productions in different communities. She organized and directed children's choirs in various churches. She did extensive entertaining of the entire church membership at the parsonages in which she lived."[1243]

In 1900, baby George was with his parents (father born in Maine, mother in England), who were renting half of a duplex in South Knoxville, Knox County, Tennessee.[1244] In 1910 they rented at 1016 Coleman in Knoxville, and Charles was a university teacher. George was evidently an only child.[1245] In 1918 they were at 815 East Maine; George was 19, a tall slender student with brown eyes and brown hair.[1246] After serving in the military during World War I, he was discharged 3 October 1918.[1247] In 1920 the family had a mortgaged house at 2826 East Fifth Avenue in Knoxville, and Charles was a "university chemist"—a bit of an

---

[1242] Victor W. Thrall household for daughter Edith age 15, 1920 US census, Evanston, Cook County, Illinois, Ward 6, ED 84, sheet 6B, dwelling 122, family 137.

[1243] "Edith Flint Thralls [Thrall] Mooers," *1990 Official Journal and Year Book Western Pennsylvania Annual Conference, The United Methodist Church, Grove City, Pennsylvania, 14–17 June 1990, p. 313.*

[1244] Charles A. Mooers household for son Georg [George] A. age 10/12 (not 14 as stated by ancestry.com), 1900 US census, South Knoxville, Knox County, Tennessee, Civil District 14, sheet 3A, dwelling 49, family 51.

[1245] Charles A. Moores [Mooers] household, 1910 US census, Knoxville, Knox County, Tennessee, Ward 1, ED 79, dwelling 23, family 26. Both 1900 and 1910 censuses reported that his mother had one child, one living.

[1246] George Ansel Mooers WWI draft card, serial 2892, order 2555, first division local board, Knoxville, Tennessee, 12 September 1918; "US, World War I Draft Registration Cards, 1917–1918" > Tennessee > Knoxville City > 1 > Draft Card M > image 125 of 993 (ancestry.com).

[1247] George Ansel Mooers delayed birth record TN D-558282, sworn to by Charles 11 July 1961 and filed 22 June 1964, Tennessee Department of Public Health. The record included a brief abstract of Enlistment-Discharge US Army by Harry B. Johnson, Captain Infantry USA, 10-3-18.

understatement as he was a pioneer in agronomy and soil surveys in the South.[1248]

Son George earned degrees from the University of Tennessee, Garrett Biblical Institute, and Adrian College, with additional study at the University of Chicago and Northwestern University. In 1927 he and his father-in-law Rev. Victor Thrall preached the morning and evening services at Knoxville First Methodist.[1249]

In addition to serving as a Methodist minister, he was an artist who painted regularly until the age of 84. In more than 40 years in three states beginning in 1925 he served the following charges:

- Coal City, Grundy County, Illinois
- Reading, Hillsdale County, Michigan, 1927–28[1250]
- Belding, Ionia County, Michigan
- Charlotte, Eaton County, Michigan
- St. Joseph, Berrien County, Michigan, 1938
- Holland, Ottawa County, Michigan
- Muskegon, Muskegon County, Michigan, 1952[1251]
- Bellevue, Allegheny County, Pennsylvania, 1954–62

[1248] "The death of Charles Mooers, Emeritus Director of the Tennessee Agricultural Experiment station on August 2, 1970, marked the end of a long and distinguished career in agricultural research and administration. When Mooers was appointed Assistant Chemist in 1893, there were only 7 other professional members on the staff of the fledgling institution. Mooers was associated with the Station almost from its beginning and continued for the next 53 years. He served not only as chemist, but also as Agronomist in 1905 and, from 1923 until his retirement in 1946, as Director." (https://ag.tennessee.edu/plantsciences/Documents/RetireeBiographies/CharlesMooersBio.pdf)

[1249] "Visitors at First M.E.," *News-Sentinel* (Knoxville, Tennessee), Sunday 2 January 1927, p. 5D, col. 5.

[1250] "Entertainment at Huffine Home for Visitors," *News-Sentinel* (Knoxville, Tennessee), Tuesday 4 January 1927, p. 21, col. 5, identifying Mr. and Mrs. George Mooers of Reading, Michigan.

[1251] "Thrall, Mrs. Carrie Jones," *News-Sentinel* (Knoxville, Tennessee), Monday 7 July 1952, p. 13, col. 1.

- Connellsville District Superintendent, Pennsylvania, 1962–68
- Mount Washington, Pittsburgh, Allegheny County, Pennsylvania, 1969–70

"He was a romantic at heart.... His gentle spirit, his wry sense of humor, his appreciation of art forms... conveyed the beauty and glory of the gospel."[1252] In 1984 they lived at 341 South Columbia in Columbus, Franklin County, Ohio.[1253]

[1252] "George Ansel Mooers," *1988 Official Journal and Year Book Western Pennsylvania Annual Conference, The United Methodist Church, Grove City, Pennsylvania, 14–17 June 1988*, p. 371. For 1928 in Reading, see *Centennial McKendree College with St. Clair County History* (Lebanon, Illinois: McKendree College, 1928), 369.

[1253] Polly Mooers letter to Elizabeth and Ronald Henderson, 27 June 1984; in author's possession, tub 8, folder 243.

Chapter 51

Tenth Generation

Evelyn Grace Thrall–Joshua "Jess" Jennings Bird Family
parents at chapter 17

Subsistence homesteading and the "strawberry walk"

51. EVELYN GRACE[10] **THRALL** (*Victor Worthy*[9], *Leonidas*[8], *Worthy*[7], *Eliphas*[6], *Samuel*[5], *John*[4-3], *Timothy*[2], *William*[1])
Birth: 27 December 1907 in Illinois,[1254] probably Lebanon, St. Clair County, based on parents' residence (Chapter 17)
Death: 15 June 1987 at the University of Tennessee hospital[1255]
Burial: Ozone Cemetery, Cumberland County, Tennessee[1256]
Spouse: **JOSHUA "JESS" JENNINGS BIRD,** married Battle Creek, Calhoun County, Michigan, 26 August 1933
Spouse's parents: Samuel and Harriett (Jennings) Bird[1257]

[1254] Victor W. Thrall household for daughter Evelyn age 2 born Illinois, 1910 US census, Lebanon, St. Clair County, Illinois, Ward 1, ED 145, sheet 3B, dwelling 69, family 65.

[1255] "Obituaries . . . Bird, Mrs. Evelyn Thrall," *News-Sentinel* (Knoxville, Tennessee), Tuesday 16 June 1987, p. 7, col. 2.

[1256] Evelyn T. Bird grave marker, image, Ozone Cemetery, Cumberland County, Tennessee, memorial #58,954,643 for Evelyn Thrall Bird by Larry Moore (findagrave.com).

[1257] "Evelyn Thrall to Be Married To Belding Man," *Enquirer and Evening News* (Battle Creek, Michigan), Tuesday 2 May 1933, p. 10, col. 7. Also, "Thrall–Bell Wedding Is Solemnized," *Enquirer and Evening News* (Battle Creek, Michigan), Sunday 27 August 1933, p. 6, col. 6. For Harriet's birth surname, Jess Jennings Bird–Evelyn Grace Thrall marriage license #131,308, 27 July 1933, certificate 26 August 1933, Ingham County, Michigan; "Michigan, Marriage Records, 1867–1952" > Certificates, 1926–1942 > Ingham > Ingham (1932–1935) > image 516 of 7729 (ancestry.com). Evelyn's father presided; witnesses were Delmer H. LaVoi of East Lansing and the bride's sister Edith T. Mooers of Belding, Ionia County, Michigan.

Spouse's birth: reportedly 19 May 1903 in Bandon, Ireland[1258]
Spouse's death: 3 January 1982 in Crossville, Cumberland County, Tennessee[1259]
Spouse's burial: with his wife[1260]

In 1928–29 Evelyn was teaching school in Holland, Ottawa County, Michigan.[1261] Jess, from nearby Belding, Ionia County, Michigan, earned an agriculture degree from Michigan State University 23 June 1930.[1262]

Their 1933 Battle Creek marriage ceremony was described as "one of the most elaborate and beautiful weddings of the year," after which the couple "motored" to Tennessee, where they were to spend a week at a friend's estate in the Smoky Mountains. Evelyn carried "a lace handkerchief which belonged to her maternal grandmother, Mrs. Alfred Jones, who was married 75 years ago yesterday." After marriage they lived at 531 Ann in East Lansing, Ingham County, Michigan, where Jess was "connected with Michigan State college [now Michigan State University] in the crops improvement division."[1263]

[1258] Joshua Jennings Bird birth index entry, April–June 1903, Bandon, Ireland, vol. 5, p. 3; "Ireland, Civil Registration Indexes, 1845–1958," FHL 101,069, DGS 4,193,983, image 386 (familysearch.org). For Ireland about 1904 as birth, Samuel Bird Sr. household, 1920 US census, ED 142, Winfield, Montcalm County, Michigan, sheet 6B, dwelling 146, family 145. According to this record the family immigrated in 1910 and Samuel had taken out "first papers" for citizenship.
[1259] "Bird, Ex-UT Horticulture Prof, Dies," *News-Sentinel* (Knoxville, Tennessee), Tuesday 5 January 1982, p. B5, col. 1.
[1260] Jess J. Bird grave marker, image, Ozone Cemetery, Cumberland County, Tennessee, memorial #58,954,584 by Larry Moore (findagrave.com).
[1261] "First Methodist Church Members Are to Greet New Minister Today," *Enquirer and Evening News* (Battle Creek, Michigan), Saturday 29 September 1928, p. 2, col. 6.
[1262] "M.S.C. to Give 471 Degrees at Commencement Rites June 23," *State Journal* (Lansing, Michigan), Saturday 7 June 1930, p. 9, col. 1.
[1263] "Thrall–Bell Wedding Is Solemnized," *Enquirer and Evening News* (Battle Creek, Michigan), Sunday 27 August 1933, p. 6, col. 6.

In 1940 the family lived in rural Cumberland County, Tennessee, in a $1000 house, somewhat below the statewide average that year of $1826. Jess completed five years of college, Evelyn four.[1264]

> When he came to UT [the University of Tennessee], Bird headed an agricultural experiment station on the Cumberland Plateau and conducted an experiment in subsistence homesteading after the Depression, teaching persons to make their living on small farms. He returned to the Knoxville campus in 1947 and served on the UT Agricultural Extension Service as a horticulturist until he retired [in 1969].
>
> Bird helped strawberry production statewide when he started a pick-your-own farm and demonstrated the 'strawberry walk,' a three-step method for planting strawberries. He established the Bird Peach Farm in Lenoir City, another pick-your-own farm which is still in operation. He also helped in the initial planning of Cumberland State Park near Crossville. . . . He was an archer, woodworker, and a member of the Southern Handicraft Guild.[1265]

[1264] Jess J. Bird (informant) household, 1940 US census, 3rd District, Cumberland County, Tennessee, ED 18-7, sheet 5B, dwelling 80. Statewide figures from US Census Bureau, Census of Housing, Historical Census of Housing Tables, Median Home Values Unadjusted 1940 (census.gov/hhes/www/housing/census/historic/values.html).

[1265] "Bird, Ex-UT Horticulture Prof, Dies," *News-Sentinel* (Knoxville, Tennessee), Tuesday 5 January 1982, p. B5, col. 1. For retirement date and an interstate highway story, Elmer Hinton, "Down to Earth: Certain Price for Progress," *Tennessean* (Nashville), Thursday 10 April 1969, p. 16, col. 3.

Chapter 52

Tenth Generation

Victor Worthy Thrall Jr.–Donna M. Brown Family
parents at chapter 17

Salesman and bank director

52. **Victor Worthy**^{10} **Thrall, Jr.** (*Victor Worthy*^{9}, *Leonidas*^{8}, *Worthy*^{7}, *Eliphas*^{6}, *Samuel*^{5}, *John*$^{4-3}$, *Timothy*^{2}, *William*^{1})
Birth: 10 February 1918 in Evanston, Cook County, Illinois
Death: 12 December 2000 in Pekin, Tazewell County, Illinois[1266]
Burial: Meadow Lawn Cemetery, Manito, Mason County, Illinois[1267]
Spouse: **Donna M. Brown,** married 10 May 1941 in Pekin
Spouse's parents: Harry T. and Mary Alice (Kear) Brown[1268]
Spouse's birth: 22 November 1917 in Peoria, Peoria County, Illinois
Spouse's death: 25 February 2013 in Pekin
Spouse's burial: Meadow Lawn Cemetery, Manito[1269]

[1266] "Victor Thrall Jr." obituary, clipping from *Times* (Pekin, Illinois), no page or exact date given but likely 13 December 2000; in author's possession, tub 13, binder 325.

[1267] Victor Worthy Thrall, Jr., no grave marker image, Meadow Lawn Cemetery, Manito, Mason County, Illinois, memorial #131,722,393 by Jeannette (findagrave.com).

[1268] Harry T. Brown household for wife Mary A. and daughter Dona [Donna], 1920 US census, Manito, Mason County, Illinois, ED 85, sheet 4B, dwelling 104, family 111. Also named in what appears to be a transcription of Donna's Pekin newspaper obituary: Donna M. Brown grave marker, no image, Meadow Lawn Cemetery, Manito, Mason County, Illinois, memorial #105,827,481 by Meadow Lawn Cemetery (findagrave.com).

[1269] "Victor Thrall Jr." obituary, clipping from *Pekin Times* (Illinois), no page or exact date given but likely 13 December 2000; in author's possession, tub 13, binder 325.

Victor Jr. graduated from Illinois Wesleyan University in 1939 in business administration.[1270] In 1940 he was a salesman for a paper mill in Kalamazoo County, Michigan, and lived with his parents there. In 1935 they had all been in Big Rapids, Mecosta County, Michigan.[1271]

Donna and Victor both completed four years of college; in 1940 Donna was a schoolteacher, earning $480 a year and living with her parents at 603 South 6th Street in Pekin, Tazewell County, Illinois. Her father Harry was co-owner of a confectionery there. The house was valued at $6000, almost double the statewide average of $3277.[1272]

Victor Jr. served in the Army Air Forces during World War II. After the war, he worked for Oakford Company, a grocery wholesaler in Pekin; for Peoria-based Brown & Bigelow in advertising specialties; and for Illini Welding (later Praxair) in Pekin, managing medical and safety sales.[1273]

In 1972 Victor and Donna executed the will of Mary Brown.[1274] In September 1977 he was elected to the board of directors of the Pekin State Bank.[1275] At various times he also served on the boards of Grace United Methodist Church, the Pekin Public Library, the Heart Fund, and the Creve Coeur Council of the Boy Scouts of America. He served as president of the Central Illinois Chapter of the Cystic Fibrosis Foundation

---

[1270] "Victor Thrall Jr." obituary, clipping from *Pekin Times* (Illinois), no page or exact date given but likely 13 December 2000; in author's possession, tub 13, binder 325.

[1271] Victor Thrall household for Victor Jr., 1940 US census, Parchment, Kalamazoo County, Michigan, ED 39-49, sheet 3B, dwelling 57.

[1272] Harry Brown household for daughter Danna [Donna], 1940 US census, Pekin, Tazewell County, Illinois, ED 90-44, Ward 6, sheet 10B, dwelling 240. Statewide figures from US Census Bureau, Census of Housing, Historical Census of Housing Tables, Median Home Values Unadjusted 1940 (census.gov/hhes/www/housing/census/historic/values.html).

[1273] "Victor Thrall Jr." obituary, clipping from *Pekin Times* (Illinois), no page or exact date given but likely 13 December 2000; in author's possession, tub 13, binder 325.

[1274] "Court Notes, Tazewell County," *Pantagraph* (Bloomington, Illinois), Wednesday 12 January 1972, p. C5, col. 4.

[1275] "Pekin Bank Names Officers," *Pantagraph* (Bloomington-Normal, Illinois), Sunday 18 September 1977, p. B14, col. 1.

and the Peoria Society of Safety Engineers. He was a member of the Rotary Club and the Pekin Country Club.[1276]

[1276] "Obituaries... Victor Thrall," *Journal Star* (Peoria, Illinois), Thursday 14 December 2000, p. B4. Also, Victor Worthy Thrall, Jr., no grave marker image, Meadow Lawn Cemetery, Manito, Mason County, Illinois, memorial #131,722,393 by Jeannette (findagrave.com).

Chapter 53

Tenth Generation

Enola Rosalie Thrall–Colin Carmichael Family
parents at chapter 18

Machine Design Award and Genealogy

53. Enola Rosalie[10] **Thrall** (*William Flint*[9], *Leonidas*[8], *Worthy*[7], *Eliphas*[6], *Samuel*[5], *John*[4-3], *Timothy*[2], *William*[1])
Birth: 18 September 1907 in Flora, Clay County, Illinois[1277]
Death: 19 April 1999 at St. Petersburg Beach, Pinellas County, Florida[1278]
Burial: Chapel Hill Memorial Park, Largo, Pinellas County[1279]
Spouse: **Colin Carmichael,** married 11 March 1933, Chapel Hill, Orange County, North Carolina[1280]
Spouse's parents: John and May [–?–] Carmichael

[1277] Rosalie Thrall Carmichael, membership application to the Daughters of the American Revolution, 24 August 1974; copy in author's possession.

[1278] "Carmichael, Rosalie T.," *Times* (St. Petersburg, Florida), 21 April 1999, p. 9B.

[1279] Colin Carmichael, no image of grave marker, Chapel Hill Memorial Park, Largo, Pinellas County, Florida, memorial #89,131,647 by RobMinteer57 (findagrave.com).

[1280] Colin Carmichael–Rosaline [Rosalie] Thrall marriage license #623, 8 March 1933, marriage 11 March; "North Carolina, Marriage Registers, 1741–2011" > Orange > Marriage Register (1851–1962) > image 679 of 1799 (ancestry.com). Rev. Ronald J. Tamblyn officiated; witnesses were Christine Carmichael, W. F. Thrall, and Georgia H. Faison. It was a sunrise wedding; Christine was Colin's sister, residing in Canada: "Miss Thrall and Mr. Carmichael Wed," *Daily News* (Greensboro, North Carolina), Sunday 19 March 1933, p. B5, col. 3. For Colin's parents: Colin Carmichael–Rosalie Thrall marriage license #623 and return, 11 March 1933; "North Carolina, Marriage Records, 1741–2011" > Orange > Marriage Licenses (1809–1962) > image 10866 of 24454 (ancestry.com).

Spouse's birth: 22 February 1905[1281] in Glasgow, Lanarkshire, Scotland[1282]
Spouse's death: 16 October 1978 in St. Petersburg[1283]
Spouse's burial: Chapel Hill Memorial Park, Largo, Pinellas County[1284]

Rosalie was a librarian who moved from Cleveland to Florida in 1970.[1285] She and Colin both completed five years of college.[1286] He was one of five new faculty members in engineering at the University of North Carolina in the fall of 1931,[1287] and received his master's in mechanical engineering there in 1934.[1288] In the summer of 1935 they traveled to Scotland and back. Colin was described as 5 feet 11 inches tall, with a fair complexion, light brown hair, blue eyes, and a small wart on the left side of his nose.[1289]

1935: in North Carolina[1290]

[1281] Rosalie Thrall Carmichael, membership application to the Daughters of the American Revolution, 24 August 1974; copy in author's possession.

[1282] Colin Carmichael household, 1940 US census, Highland Park, Middlesex County, New Jersey, ED 12-26, sheet 4B, dwelling 89.

[1283] Colin Carmichael death index entry; "Florida Death Index, 1877–1998" (ancestry.com). Original not viewed. For city, US Social Security Death Index entry. The 1976 death year on findagrave.com appears to be erroneous.

[1284] Rosalie T. Carmichael, no image of grave marker, Chapel Hill Memorial Park, Largo, Pinellas County, Florida, memorial #89,131,264 by RobMinteer57 (findagrave.com).

[1285] "Carmichael, Rosalie T.," *Times* (St. Petersburg, Florida), 21 April 1999, p. 9B.

[1286] Colin Carmichael household, 1940 US census, Highland Park, Middlesex County, New Jersey, ED 12-26, sheet 4B, dwelling 89. Also, "Clothier Warns Maintenance of Research Integrity Vital," *Daily Home News* (New Brunswick, New Jersey), Saturday 9 October 1937, p. 1, cols. 6–7, and p. 2, col. 2.

[1287] "Many New Men on North Carolina Faculty," *News and Observer* (Raleigh, North Carolina), Sunday 20 September 1931, p. 3, col. 8.

[1288] "Represents UNC," *Sun* (Durham, North Carolina), Thursday 27 May 1948, p. 11A, col. 2.

[1289] Colin Carmichael, "List or Manifest of Alien Passengers for the United States Immigration Officer at Port of Arrival," *SS Caledonia* leaving Glasgow 28 August 1935 and arriving New York 6 September 1935, line 21, pp. 146–47; "New York, Passenger and Crew Lists" (including Castle Garden and Ellis Island), 1820–1957 > Roll > T715, 1897–1957 > 5001–6000 > Roll 5699 > images 613–14 of 728 (ancestry.com).

[1290] Colin Carmichael household, 1940 US census, Highland Park, Middlesex County, New Jersey, ED 12-26, sheet 4B, dwelling 89.

1937: Ithaca, Tompkins County, New York, where he was an assistant professor at Cornell University and they lived at 128 Blair.[1291] They were in New Jersey no later than 1939.[1292]

1940: at 48 Lawrence Avenue in Highland Park, Middlesex County, New Jersey, where they rented for $55 a month and he was a professor at Rutgers University.[1293] Also in 1942.[1294]

1950: he chaired the machine design division of the American Society of Mechanical Engineers (ASME)[1295] and edited a 1660-page reference for mechanical engineers on design and production, as part of the 12th edition of Kent's *Mechanical Engineers Handbook*.[1296]

1952: as editor of *Machine Design* magazine, he warned of a shortage of design engineers due to increasingly complex design problems and a lack of interest from young engineers. "Now, there is nothing you or I can do to halt this trend toward increased complexity in design. But we can perhaps do something about the other factor, this seeming lack of interest in design work."[1297]

[1291] Colin Carmichael, *Manning's Ithaca (New York) Directory for the year beginning January, 1937* (Schenectady, New York: H.A. Manning Co., 1937), p. 138, image 65 of 248 (ancestry.com).

[1292] Colin Carmichael household, 1940 US census, Highland Park, Middlesex County, New Jersey, ED 12-26, sheet 4B, dwelling 89. Their one-year-old son was born in New Jersey.

[1293] Colin Carmichael household, 1940 US census, Highland Park, Middlesex County, New Jersey, ED 12-26, sheet 4B, dwelling 89. Also, "Clothier Warns Maintenance of Research Integrity Vital," *Daily Home News* (New Brunswick, New Jersey), Saturday 9 October 1937, p. 1, cols. 6–7, and p. 2, col. 2.

[1294] Colin Carmichael, *Polk's New Brunswick (Middlesex County, New Jersey) City Directory 1942* (Pittsburgh: R.L. Polk & Company), 1942), p. 102, image 98 of 932 (ancestry.com).

[1295] "Double Panel at Conference: Machine Design," *Journal-Sentinel* (Milwaukee, Wisconsin), Sunday 29 January 1950, business section, p. 9, col. 2.

[1296] Burrows store advertisement for technical and business books, item T33, *Plain Dealer* (Cleveland, Ohio), Sunday 29 October 1950, p. 7B, cols. 4–8.

[1297] "Design Engineers in Short Supply," *News and Observer* (Raleigh, North Carolina), Tuesday 1 April 1952, p. 5, col. 3.

1963: he received the $1000 "Machine Design Award" from the ASME's Machine Design Division (now Design Engineering Division).[1298]

He was responsible for proposing and researching the enshrinement of the USS *Olympia* as a National Historic Mechanical Engineering Landmark: in 1892 it had been one of the first ships with a vertical reciprocating steam engine; it was also involved in the US conquest of the Philippines in 1898.[1299]

In the late 1960s Colin and Rosalie traveled around the world by boat, taking 4½ months. Soon thereafter Colin had a major health issue requiring seven hours of surgery and 21 units of whole blood; they spent time in Key West for recuperation.[1300] Colin bought a condominium apartment in Pinellas County, Florida, 23 February 1970, for $23,800.[1301] In retirement he frequently wrote letters to local newspapers.[1302]

In retirement in St. Petersburg, Rosalie was a member of Pass-a-Grille Beach Community Church, the DAR Boca Ciega chapter, the St. Petersburg Garden Club, and Pi Beta Phi Sorority.[1303]

As a genealogist, Rosalie kept in touch with relatives. She authored and updated a Thrall family history in typescript with photographs

---

[1298] ASME, "Machine Design Award" (https://www.asme.org/about-asme/participate/honors-awards/achievement-awards/machine-design-award).
[1299] "National Historic Mechanical Engineering Landmark, Vertical Reciprocating Steam Engines, USS *Olympia*, Penn's Landing, Philadelphia, Pennsylvania, March 30, 1977, The American Society of Mechanical Engineers" (https://www.asme.org/wwwasmeorg/media/ResourceFiles/AboutASME/Who%20We%20Are/Engineering%20History/Landmarks/22-USS-Olympia-Vertical-Reciprocating-Steam-Engi.pdf).
[1300] Colin Carmichael letter to Elizabeth (Thrall) Henderson, 19 February 1968; in author's possession, tub 4, item 131.
[1301] "Pinellas County Deeds," *Times* (St. Petersburg, Florida), Thursday 19 March 1970, p. 10C, col. 6. The condo might be Rosalie's later address, 5555 Gulf Boulevard, Apartment 309, St. Pete Beach, Florida (Elizabeth Henderson's comb-bound address book, in author's possession, tub 10, folder 282).
[1302] Rosalie (Thrall) Carmichael letter to Elizabeth (Thrall) Henderson, 26 June 1990; in author's possession, tub 4, item 131.
[1303] "Carmichael, Rosalie T.," *Times* (St. Petersburg, Florida), 21 April 1999, p. 9B.

attached that carried Worthy and several descendants in generations 7 through 11 up into the middle 1970s, and introduced at least one budding genealogist to the quest. Her correspondence and conversations with cousins and older relatives preserved priceless memories and stories in the Thrall and James families.[1304]

It is said that she had a chocolate cup that came from Wales. She also told the story of a Sunday in Wales in the late 1700s involving her great-grandfather Simon James (whose youngest daughter married Worthy Thrall). Simon was in church with galleries all around; when the minister said, "Lift up your eyes to behold wondrous things," he did so and saw his future wife.

[1304] "Thrall Genealogy," 17-page typescript on onion skin in red binder, by Rosalie Thrall Carmichael although no author is named; in author's possession, tub 2, item 34.

Chapter 54

Robert McDowell Thrall–Natalie Elizabeth Hunter Family
parents at chapter 19

Mathematics, open housing, and Planned Parenthood

54. **ROBERT MCDOWELL^{10} THRALL** (*Charles Haven^9, Leonidas^8, Worthy^7, Eliphas^6, Samuel^5, John$^{4\text{-}3}$, Timothy^2, William^1*)
Birth: 23 September 1914 in Toledo, Cumberland County, Illinois
Death: 11 April 2006 in Philadelphia
Burial: cremation
Spouse: **NATALIE ELIZABETH HUNTER,** married 3 September 1936
Spouse's parents: Alexander and Mary (Kiser) Hunter
Spouse's birth: 18 October 1913 in Pittsfield, Pike County, Illinois
Spouse's death: 5 December 2004 in Philadelphia[1305]
Spouse's burial: cremation

Natalie grew up on a non-electrified farm and earned spending money by running a trapline for muskrats and beavers. She rode her horse into town to attend high school in Pittsfield, Pike County, Illinois; graduated summa cum laude from MacMurray College in Jacksonville, Morgan County, Illinois; and earned a master's degree in classics from the University of Illinois. She and Robert helped sponsor an Open Housing Covenant through the First Methodist Church in the 1950s in Ann Arbor, Michigan; the library at Planned Parenthood in Houston, Texas, was named after her.

[1305] "Robert McDowell Thrall 1914–2006, In Memoriam," four-page typescript biography, in author's possession. Also, "Natalie Hunter Thrall 1913–2004," 4-page typescript from her children, in author's possession.

Robert graduated from Illinois College in Jacksonville, Morgan County, in 1935. As a 22-year-old newly minted Ph.D. from the University of Illinois, he joined the Department of Mathematics at the University of Michigan in Ann Arbor.[1306] In the early 1940s he spent two years at Princeton University's Institute for Advanced Study. From 1944 to 1946 he reportedly worked in MIT's secret Radiation Lab. He consulted extensively for the RAND Corporation (1951–74), the US Army (1958–78), and Holt, Rinehart, and Winston (1961–76). He co-authored *College Algebra* (1950), *Vector Spaces and Matrices* (1957), and *Linear Optimization* (1970), and was editor-in-chief of *Management Science* and related journals.[1307]

Mathematician and historian Walter Meyer described Robert's role in the post-WWII efflorescence of math and social science:

> Starting in the fall of 1950, in cooperation with the departments of economics, philosophy, sociology, and psychology, mathematician Robert M. Thrall organized a seminar at the University of Michigan on newer applications of mathematics, focusing especially on the social sciences. This seminar attracted the participation of such notable social scientists as the psychologist Clyde Coombs and the economists Paul Samuelson and Lawrence Klein. . . In 1952, Thrall and some of his colleagues at Michigan obtained funding from the Ford Foundation, the RAND Corporation, and the Office of Naval Research to hold an 8-week seminar in Santa Monica, at which researchers from various disciplines and various universities met to discuss mathematical approaches to the behavioral sciences.

[1306] "Robert McDowell Thrall 1914–2006, In Memoriam," four-page typescript biography, in author's possession. Also, "Natalie Hunter Thrall 1913–2004," 4-page typescript from her children, in author's possession.

[1307] Robert McDowell Thrall entry, *Who Was Who in America* 2006–2007 (New Providence, New Jersey: Marquis Who's Who, 2007), 18:241. Rad Lab from family knowledge.

One of the results of this seminar was the book *Decision Processes*.[1308]

In 1969 he became chairman of the Department of Mathematical Sciences at Rice University in Houston, Texas. He took particular interest in teaching, interdisciplinary work, and mathematical modeling.[1309]

In 1986 Robert co-authored an article on evaluating sites for a high-energy physics laboratory in Texas.[1310] In 1996, at the age of 82, he published "Duality, classification, and slacks in DEA [Data Envelopment Analysis]" in *Annals of Operations Research*.[1311] According to the Mathematics Genealogy Project, as of 15 August 2020 he had 307 mathematician "descendants" in the profession.[1312]

[1308] Walter Meyer, "The Origins of Finite Mathematics: The Social Science Connection," *College Mathematics Journal* 38 (March 2007):106–18, at 111.

[1309] "Robert McDowell Thrall 1914–2006, In Memoriam," four-page typescript biography, in author's possession.

[1310] R.G. Thompson, F.D. Singleton Jr., R.M. Thrall, and B.A. Smith, 1986, "Comparative site evaluation for locating a high-energy physics lab in Texas," *Interfaces* 16:35–49.

[1311] Robert M. Thrall, "Duality, classification and slacks in DEA," *Annals of Operations Research* 66(1996):109–38 (https://link.springer.com/article/ 10.1007/ BF02187297).

[1312] *Mathematics Genealogy Project* (genealogy.math.ndsu.nodak.edu/mission.php), whose stated goal is to track all mathematics doctorate holders.

Chapter 55

Tenth Generation

Elizabeth Rose Thrall–Ronald A. Henderson Family
parents at chapter 20

"Time will pass, but will you?"

55. ELIZABETH ROSE^{10} THRALL (*Harold Leonidas^9, Leonidas^8, Worthy^7, Eliphas^6, Samuel^5, John$^{4-3}$, Timothy^2, William^1*)
Birth: 15 September 1918 in Sadorus, Champaign County, Illinois
Death: 18 May 2008 in St. Joseph County, Indiana[1313]
Burial: cremation
Spouse: **RONALD ATHOL HENDERSON,** married 6 March 1943 at Wesley Foundation, University of Illinois, Urbana, Champaign County, Illinois[1314]
Spouse's parents: Alexander and Elin Ida (Boring) Henderson[1315]
Spouse's birth: 4 October 1914 at Swedish Covenant Hospital in Chicago, Cook County, Illinois
Spouse's death: 12 July 2002 in Farmington, Fulton County, Illinois[1316]
Spouse's burial: cremation

[1313] Elizabeth T. Henderson, 18 May 2008, South Bend, Indiana Certificate of Death; in author's possession (tub 23, folder 483).

[1314] Ronald A. Henderson-Elizabeth Rose Thrall marriage license #21046, 6 March 1943. The bride's father, Rev. Harold L. Thrall, officiated. The bride's siblings, Miriam and H. James, witnessed.

[1315] Ronald A. Henderson, 12 July 2002, Illinois death certificate, in author's possession (tub 2, folder 52). Parents named Alexander Henderson and Ellen Boring; on the 1943 marriage license his mother's name was given as Ida Ellen.

[1316] Ronald A. Henderson obituary, *Journal Star* (Peoria, Illinois), 15 July 2002.

"I know I haven't told you before," Elizabeth Schriber Thrall wrote to her mother and sisters 29 April 1918 from DuQuoin, Illinois, where Leonidas Thrall's life was drawing to a close. "We have hopes for a little one in Sept., and I'm not taking any chances on trouble that I can avoid."[1317]

Elizabeth and Ronald met at Wesley Foundation at the University of Illinois in the early 1940s. Either she needed help with physics or he needed help with chemistry (the stories differ); in any event they were the third generation in this Thrall line to meet at college.[1318]

Elizabeth earned an M.D. at the University of Illinois in Chicago in December 1943, at a time when women doctors were a curiosity (the class contained 157 men and eight women).[1319] Her downstate origins also made her an outsider in Chicago. She recalled puzzling fellow med students when she told them she planned to practice medicine in downstate Illinois: "Why, you won't have any patients!"

Active in the Fellowship of Reconciliation, she and her husband opposed US entry into World War II. From 1944 to 1950 they worked in remote Harlan County, Kentucky, at Pine Mountain Settlement School (now an environmental center), then accessible only by a rough switchback road over the mountain from Harlan.

She wrote home 11 November 1945:

[1317] Elizabeth (Schriber) Thrall in DuQuoin, Illinois, to her mother and sisters in Chicago 29 April 1918; transcribed copy in author's possession.

[1318] This and later items in this chapter not footnoted are personal knowledge of the author.

[1319] University of Illinois College of Medicine, Class of December 1943, Medical Alumni Day May 21, 1968, booklet containing names, addresses or death dates, and some very brief comments; in author's possession, tub 2, folder 64. Totals by counting; one male was included for whom there was "no official record" as a student.

> About 3:45 a.m. Thursday morning we were wakened by a strange man knocking on the door. He said, "I came to take the doctor out to my house." I asked, "Who is sick?" "A baby is about to be born." So I dressed and packed my bag and climbed into the truck he had brought and we started out. There had been a light snow. We arrived about one half hour before the baby did at 5 a.m. and all went well.
>
> Worked by the combined light of my puny flashlight and wood fire in fireplace, and two kerosene lamps. Shortly before starting back to P. Mt. I held the baby by the lamp in order to look in its mouth to see if there was a tongue tie to clip. I smelled something, heard a sizzle, and saw a wisp of smoke as I looked up. Someone said, "The doctor has burned her hair." And sure enough, I had sizzled my top knot. Lucky I did not all go up in smoke. Sure felt silly.

A few days later a 12-year-old boy broke his leg when he was thrown from a mule at home. The family lived in Cutshin, miles from the nearest road.

> The next morning the boy's father made a stretcher from 2 saplings and nailed a couple of blankets onto it and he and his wife set out to carry the boy the 6 miles up a trail . . . to the road at Big Laurel where they could catch the mail truck and bring him to us [the hospital at the settlement school]. They picked up neighbors on the way so that they got some rests in the carrying, but it seemed quite a feat to me just the same.

> We have the boy put up in an improvised traction setup in the hospital living room and are trying to get him to Louisville under the Ky. Crippled Childrens Commission as I fear he will need a bone graft to make the leg heal properly.[1320]

After their second child was born in 1950, the family moved back to Illinois and Ronald tried various jobs. They stayed with her parents in Galva, and then moved to Galesburg. He worked in an "Autolite" parts store, and auditioned for a radio job, where his voice was considered too deep. He and Elizabeth had at least one conversation about whether he could take the job in good conscience if it was offered, given that he might have to read commercials he didn't believe in.

In the summer of 1951, Russell Troxel, the high-school principal in Farmington, Fulton County, Illinois, needed a math teacher to fill a last-minute vacancy. He consulted Harold Thrall, who was both a fellow singer in a regional men's chorus (Mannerchor), and Ronald's father-in-law. The last-minute hire stayed for decades.

Elizabeth's taste for adventure and making do was not slaked by the Pine Mountain experience. When the children were small she did not practice medicine; later she connected with various doctors in West Virginia (not far from Pine Mountain in distance or culture) and for several years in the late 1950s and early 1960s took the children along every summer to the small towns where she filled in for vacationing local doctors, while Ronald stayed in Illinois to work on his master's degree at Illinois State University in Normal, McLean County, Illinois. In later years she traveled to the Dakotas and Nicaragua to provide medical care, and in January 1991 (age 72) she and her sister traveled to Baja California to camp on the beach with a tour group and view a total solar eclipse.[1321]

[1320] Elizabeth T. Henderson at Pine Mountain Settlement School to her parents Harold L. and Elizabeth S. Thrall in Illinois, letters 11 and 21 November 1945, #43 and #44, as transcribed in privately printed family booklet, "Schriber and Thrall Letters to Family: Windows on the Past."

[1321] Elizabeth T. Henderson notebook, in author's possession, tub 2, folder 57.

As a boy growing up in Chicago, Ronald learned the fascinations of astronomy at the then-new Adler Planetarium in 1931. "I had a lot of free time and went to 10 out of 12 monthly lectures in a row. . . . I was actually interested before that. But growing up in Chicago I didn't get to see much of the sky." When he and Elizabeth went to Kentucky in the late 1940s he bought his first telescope.[1322] In Farmington his portable reflecting telescope was frequently set up for "star parties" in the driveway, with a clear western horizon for watching and measuring eclipses, nebulas, meteors, variable stars, occultations, artificial satellites, the moon, and other planets and their moons.

Some astronomical events could be viewed during the day as well, with the sun's image projected onto a sheet of white paper so as to show the current crop of dark "sun spots" on its surface. A memorable trip took the family to northern Maine in the summer of 1963 to view a total solar eclipse.

Ronald enjoyed teaching, and his approach often involved puns and humor. Every classroom in the high school had a prominently placed clock, but only his had this sign underneath: "Time will pass. But will you?"

He retired after 29 years of teaching math and physics in Farmington. After retirement he volunteered tutoring students in math at the community college in nearby Canton. A member of the Peoria Astronomical Society and the National Council of Teachers of Mathematics, he organized the high school's Scholastic Bowl team for 20 years.[1323] He and Elizabeth lived happily for more than 50 years in Farmington, but none of their children chose to stay.

[1322] Carla Fisher, "Astronomer waits for Kohoutek," *Daily Ledger* (Canton, Illinois), Saturday 5 January 1974, p. 1. In author's possession.

[1323] Ronald A. Henderson obituary, *Journal Star* (Peoria, Illinois), 15 July 2002.

Chapter 56

Tenth Generation

Miriam Ruth Thrall–George Norton Foster Family
parents at chapter 20

Art, music, and runner-up to the St. Louis Arch

56. **MIRIAM RUTH**[10] **THRALL** (*Harold Leonidas*[9], *Leonidas*[8], *Worthy*[7], *Eliphas*[6], *Samuel*[5], *John*[4-3], *Timothy*[2], *William*[1])
Birth: 20 March 1921 in Cisco, Piatt County, Illinois
Death: 7 April 2010 in Urbana, Champaign County, Illinois[1324]
Burial: Clements Cemetery, Champaign County[1325]
Spouse: **GEORGE NORTON FOSTER,** married 29 May 1943 at Wesley Foundation, University of Illinois, Urbana, Champaign County
Spouse's parents: Lane and Mamie (Barnett) Foster[1326]
Spouse's birth: 4 January 1918 in Ridgway, Gallatin County, Illinois[1327]
Spouse's death: 31 May 1999 in Urbana[1328]
Spouse's burial: Clements Cemetery, Champaign County[1329]

[1324] Miriam T. Foster index entry, US Social Security Death Index.

[1325] Miriam T. Foster grave marker, image, Clements Cemetery, Urbana, Champaign County, Illinois, memorial #50,859,420 for Miriam Thrall Foster by Bob & Nancy Cannon (findagrave.com).

[1326] For Mamie's birth surname, death index entry for unnamed female Foster infant 18 April 1919, Ridgway Township, Gallatin County, Illinois; "Illinois Deaths and Stillbirths, 1916–1947," citing FHL 1,544,466, DGS 4,008,037, image 2302 (familysearch.org). Original not viewed.

[1327] For birth date, George N. Foster funeral program, 5 June 1999; in author's possession.

[1328] "George Foster" obituary, transcribed from *News-Gazette* (Champaign-Urbana, Illinois), 2 June 1999 (genealogybank.com).

[1329] George N. Foster grave marker, image, Clements Cemetery, Urbana, Champaign County, Illinois, memorial #11,503,817 for George Norton Foster by Cheryl Behrend (findagrave.com).

As of 16 October 1940, George was studying at the University of Illinois; he was 5 feet 4 inches tall, weighed 123 pounds, and had blue eyes and brown hair.[1330] At the time of their wedding George was in the US Navy, assigned to a merchant marine ship as a radio operator.[1331] As of 30 June 1943, he was rated RM3/c (Radioman Third Class) aboard the US MSTS (United States Maritime Service Training Ship, soon shortened to TS) *American Mariner*.[1332]

After the war, in 1947, the Jefferson National Expansion Memorial Association announced a contest for a monumental new design for the St. Louis waterfront. George collaborated with two other University of Illinois graduate students, William Eng of Urbana and Gordon A. Phillips of Aurora, to create an entry. Out of 172 entries, their design was among the five finalists, and in the end finished second (prize $20,000) to Eero Saarinen's now-famous Gateway Arch.[1333] George's share of the prize helped build a house on what was then the western edge of Champaign at 208 South Mattis, across from a cornfield.

[1330] George Norton Foster WW2 draft card, serial #653, order #298, Local Board, Gallatin County, Illinois; "US WWII Draft Cards Young Men, 1940–1947" > Illinois > Erzinger–Geiger > Foster–Foster > images 551–52 of 2143 (ancestry.com).

[1331] "Plans Wedding Weldon Girl," *Pantagraph* (Bloomington, Illinois), Friday 28 May 1943, p. 8, col. 4.

[1332] George Norton Foster, Report of Changes, US MTSS American Mariner, month ending 30 June 1943, p. 2 (https://www.fold3.com/image/ 303089632?rec= 271578283); National Archives and Records Administration, Record Group 24, "Muster rolls of US Navy ships, stations, and other naval activities, 1939–1949," roll 32662_239244. Also, Bill Lee, "American Mariner: Sturdy Ship of Several Services Still Survives," April 2018; Newport News Shipbuilding Apprentice Association (http://www.nnapprentice.com/alumni/letter/AMERICAN_MARINER.pdf). Also, Bill Lee, "Apprentice School and Other NNS Memories" (http://www.nnapprentice.com /alumni/letter/log.htm).

[1333] "St. Louis Waterfront Plan Features Steel Arch," *Chicago Daily Tribune*, Friday 20 February 1948, p. 12, col. 3. Also, "Michigan Architect Awarded Jefferson Memorial Prize," *Jacksonville Daily Journal* (Illinois), Thursday 19 February 1948, p. 1, col. 7. Also, Christopher Klein, "The Monumental Designs Rejected for the Gateway Arch," 28 October 2015 (history.com/news/the-monumental-designs-rejected-for-the-gateway-arch), including an image of each.

In the 1960s George rode the river towboat "Jayne Houghland" down the Mississippi and the IntraCoastal Canal to Houston—a trip arranged by the Paducah (Kentucky) Art Guild—making sketches later used in larger drawings and paintings exhibited in July 1968.[1334]

He taught art and design at the University of Illinois for 38 years, receiving a bachelor of fine arts degree there in 1940 and a master's degree in 1950. He attended the Pennsylvania Academy of Fine Arts in 1942 and studied sculpture at the University of Denver in 1958. His oil paintings, litho paintings, drawings, and metal collages were exhibited nationally, regionally, and locally, receiving numerous awards. His contributions in teaching included field drawing courses taught in the southwestern United States and in Europe.[1335]

Miriam received a degree in music education in 1943 from the University of Illinois. In 1974 she returned to school, earned a master's degree in education, and taught adult learners for ten years in Urbana. A devoted pianist and piano teacher, she saw to it that all of her sons studied musical instruments, so there was always music in the home. A humanitarian by nature, she was active in civil rights and peace activities in the 1960s and 1970s. Later she was a hospice volunteer for ten years. Animals were always a significant part of the household, not only dogs and cats, but often rescued birds and squirrels. She and George were both good, thoughtful listeners and active members of Wesley United Methodist Church in Urbana.[1336]

[1334] "Foster Exhibits River Scenes," *Evansville Courier* (Indiana), Monday 8 June 1968, p. 13, col. 2.

[1335] "George Foster" obituary, transcribed from *News-Gazette* (Champaign-Urbana, Illinois), Wednesday 2 June 1999, no p. or col. number (genealogybank.com).

[1336] "Miriam Foster" obituary, transcribed from *News-Gazette* (Champaign-Urbana, Illinois), Friday 9 April 2010, no p. or col. number (genealogybank.com).

Chapter 57

Harold James "Jim" Thrall–Joan E. Walker Family
<u>parents at chapter 20</u>

From D-Day to Libby's and Nestlé

57. HAROLD JAMES "JIM"[10] **THRALL** (*Harold Leonidas*[9], *Leonidas*[8], *Worthy*[7], *Eliphas*[6], *Samuel*[5], *John*[4-3], *Timothy*[2], *William*[1])
Birth: 15 June 1925 in Mansfield, Piatt County, Illinois
Death: 20 October 2018 in Plymouth, Marshall County, Indiana
Burial: 27 October at Southlawn Cemetery, South Bend, St. Joseph County, Indiana[1337]
Spouse: **JOAN E. WALKER,** married 29 January 1948 in Galva, Henry County, Illinois
Spouse's parents: Melvin and Lottie (Brown) Walker
Spouse's birth: 11 January 1924 in Galva, Henry County, Illinois[1338]
Spouse's death: 17 May 2006 in South Bend, St. Joseph County, Indiana[1339]
Spouse's burial: Southlawn Cemetery, St. Joseph County

Joan grew up and attended school in Galva, Henry County, Illinois, where her future father-in-law would minister in the 1940s and 1950s.

[1337] "Harold James Thrall" obituary (http://johnson-danielson.com/Obit.php?ID=3091).

[1338] Joan E. Thrall death 17 May 2006, South Bend, St. Joseph County, Indiana, state certificate #018093, local 1078; "Indiana, Death Certificates, 1899–2011" > Certificate > 2006 > 15 > image 612 of 1029 (ancestry.com). Also, Melvin Walker household, 1940 US census, Galva, Henry County, Illinois, Ward 1, ED 37-19, sheet 4A, dwelling 69.

[1339] Joan E. Thrall death 17 May 2006, South Bend, St. Joseph County, Indiana, certificate #018093, local 1078; "Indiana, Death Certificates, 1899–2011" > Certificate > 2006 > 15 > image 612 of 1029 (ancestry.com).

The Walker family's house at 603 Southeast 2ⁿᵈ Street was worth $3500 in 1930—and $1500 in 1940 after a decade of the Great Depression (statewide average that year was $3277).[1340] Joan's older sister Marie lived there for many years.[1341]

As a boy Jim traveled in the early 1930s with his parents and maternal grandmother (Elizabeth Schriber) to visit the rock-strewn farm where the grandmother had grown up outside Winesburg, Holmes County, Ohio. (Perhaps the experience sparked his ongoing interest in family history.)

As of 15 June 1943, Jim was living in Weldon, De Witt County, Illinois, and attending high school. He was 5 feet 8 inches tall and weighed 140 pounds, with brown eyes and red hair.[1342] At summer's end he enlisted in the US Navy 1 September 1943 in Chicago, service number 854 28 57. "Pvt. Harold James Thrall, son of the Rev. and Mrs. H. L. Thrall of Danville, Illinois, formerly of San Jose, was inducted September 7 as a navy seabee and is now stationed at Camp Farragut, Idaho."[1343]

Less than eight months later, he was received on board USS *LST-504*[1344] on 21 April 1944.[1345] This particular LST ("Landing Ship, Tank") had been "laid down" 21 July 1943 in Jeffersonville, Clark County,

---

[1340] Melvin Walker household, 1930 US census, Galva, Henry County, Illinois, ED 52, sheet 7B, dwelling 201, family 212. Similarly, 1940, Ward 1, ED 37-19, sheet 4A, dwelling 69.

[1341] Elizabeth T. Henderson address book, in author's possession, tub 10, folder 282.

[1342] Harold James Thrall WW2 draft card, serial #W128, order #11378, Local Board 1, DeWitt County, Illinois; "US WWII Draft Cards Young Men, 1940–1947" > Illinois > Terry–Walton > Thorsen–Thundall > images 778–79 of 2092 (ancestry.com).

[1343] "San Jose Service News," *Pantagraph* (Bloomington, Illinois), Friday 24 September 1943, p. 14, col. 3. Enlistment evidently preceded induction.

[1344] "Landing Ship, Tank," *Wikipedia* (https://en.wikipedia.org/wiki/Landing_Ship,_Tank).

[1345] Harold James Thrall entry, Muster Roll of the Crew, p. 4, quarter ending 30 June 1944 (https://www.fold3.com/image/305811827?rec=281761277); National Archives and Records Administration, Record Group 24, "Muster rolls of U.S. Navy ships, stations, and other naval activities, 1939–1949," roll 32861_250195. "Branch of Service" was USN-I.

Indiana, and commissioned 18 December.[1346] These vessels were built to carry "tanks, vehicles, cargo, and landing troops directly onto shore with no docks or piers," thus expediting amphibious assaults on almost any beach. "The bow of the LST had a large door that would open with a ramp for unloading the vehicles" and "a special flat keel that allowed the ship to be beached and stay upright."[1347]

It is reported but not confirmed that "As part of Operation Overlord, LST-504 departed Weymouth, England, on June 4th 1944. However, she turned back due to bad weather and would later re-embark on the night of June 5th. LST-504 reached Omaha beach the next morning, and dropped anchor about a half mile off shore to avoid floating mines. In subsequent round trips made over the course of 30 days, the ship did land directly on the beach."[1348] Recently promoted to HA1c (Hospital Apprentice 1st Class),[1349] Jim attended to the troops during the D-Day Invasion as they stormed Omaha and Utah beaches in Normandy, France—a pivotal moment in history, but a troubling memory.

As of 31 July 1944 he was still on USS LST-504.[1350] According to one unconfirmed account, "Following her service in Operation Overlord, LST-504 was directed towards Sicily to prepare for the invasion of Southern France. En route, the convoy that LST-504 now led spotted a German ship. Orders were given for the convoy to turn, however one ship misinterpreted the order and turned the wrong way. A collision with

---

[1346] "USS LST-504," *Wikipedia* (https://en.wikipedia.org/wiki/USS_LST-504)

[1347] "Landing Ship, Tank," *Wikipedia* (https://en.wikipedia.org/wiki/Landing_Ship,_Tank).

[1348] "USS *LST-504*," *Wikipedia* (https://en.wikipedia.org/wiki/USS_LST-504), citing "Charles Heller's Autobiography" (1993), which has not been viewed. It does not appear on WorldCat and may not have been published.

[1349] Harold James Thrall entry, Report of Changes, p. 3 (https://www.fold3.com/image/305811814?rec=281761136). Also, "US Navy: World War II Enlisted Rates: Special Branch After January 1, 1944" (http://uniform-reference.net/insignia/usn/usn_ww2_enl_special.html).

[1350] Harold James Thrall entry, Report of Changes, p. 5, month ending 31 July 1944 (https://www.fold3.com/image/305811836?rec=281761365).

that ship damaged the bow door of LST-504. The 504 was diverted to Bizerte, Tunisia, for repairs."[1351]

On 7 September 1944 Jim was a passenger on USS *Hubbard* (DE-211).[1352] A destroyer escort, it shepherded two convoy crossings of the Atlantic following July 1944.[1353] Later he was on the crew of the USS *Marblehead* (CL12) in the quarter ending 31 March 1945,[1354] and on the crew of the USS *Mercer* (APB-39) in the quarter ending 1 January 1946. His rating at that point was PhM3c(T) Pharmacist's Mate Third Class.[1355] *Mercer* was reportedly a barracks ship built on an LST hull in 1944, and commenced its career of berthing and messing large numbers of naval personnel at New York on 7 November 1945. Transferred to the Inactive Fleet in January 1946, it had many later assignments.[1356]

Jim was honorably discharged 8 April 1946 and married Joan in Galva 29 January 1948. "He also attended Illinois Wesleyan University in Bloomington, Illinois, and obtained his Bachelor's Degree in 1950." In

---

[1351] "USS LST-504," *Wikipedia* (https://en.wikipedia.org/wiki/USS_LST-504), citing "Charles Heller's Autobiography" (1993), which has not been viewed. It does not appear on WorldCat and may not have been published.

[1352] Harold James Thrall entry, Report of Changes (https://www.fold3.com/image/308329643?rec=290316709).

[1353] "USS *Hubbard* (DE-211), *Wikipedia* (https://en.wikipedia.org/wiki/USS_Hubbard_[DE-211]). See also James L. Mooney, *Dictionary of American Naval Fighting Ships* (Washington, DC: Navy Department, Office of the Chief of Naval Operations, Naval History Division, 1959), also available as an ebook.

[1354] Harold James Thrall entry, Muster Roll of the Crew, p. 19, quarter ending 30 June 1944 (https://www.fold3.com/image/309724336?rec=294595048).

[1355] Harold James Thrall entry, Muster Roll of the Crew, p. 5, quarter ending 1 June 1946 (https://www.fold3.com/image/303761785?rec=275347114). Also, "US Navy: World War II Enlisted Rates: Special Branch After January 1, 1944" (http://uniform-reference.net/insignia/usn/usn_ww2_enl_special.html).

[1356] "USS *Mercer* (APL-39)," *Wikipedia* (https://en.wikipedia.org/wiki/USS_Mercer_[APL-39]).

1959, he completed post-graduate studies at IMEDE in Lausanne, Switzerland.[1357]

Jim's work for Libby's Foods, later Nestlé, for 35 years sent him all over the world, and he ended his career as a group vice president.

Eventually retiring to Granger, St. Joseph County, Indiana, in 1994, he was an active member of Grace United Methodist Church for 20 years. In 2013, he moved to Plymouth, Marshall County, Indiana, and joined Trinity United Methodist Church. He enjoyed reading about American history, politics, and business. "He loved the Old English Sheep dogs that his family had throughout the years. But mostly, he loved being with his family."[1358]

[1357] "Harold James Thrall" obituary (http://johnson-danielson.com/ Obit.php?ID=3091). IMEDE (Institut pour l'Etude des Méthodes de Direction de l'Entreprise) was established in 1956 in Lausanne by Nestlé in coordination with Harvard Business School. The institute operated under this name until 1989, when it merged with another entity to become the International Institute for Management Development (imd.org/why-imd/Origins-History). For additional information and references, see en.wikipedia.org/wiki/International_Institute_for_Management_Development.

[1358] "Harold James Thrall" obituary (http://johnson-danielson.com/ Obit.php?ID=3091).

Chapter 58

Tenth Generation

William Henry Cover–Ruth Alice Palmer Family
parents at chapter 21

Fertilizer and teaching children to read

58. **WILLIAM HENRY**[10] **COVER** (*Mary Virginia Thrall*[9], *Leonidas*[8], *Worthy*[7], *Eliphas*[6], *Samuel*[5], *John*[4-3], *Timothy*[2], *William*[1])
Birth: 15 August 1923, Tunnel Hill, Johnson County, Illinois
Death: 6 February 1986 at Jewish Hospital, St. Louis
Burial: New Salem Cemetery, north of Tunnel Hill[1359]
Spouse: **RUTH ALICE PALMER,** married 22 November 1950 in Sandusky, Erie County, Ohio
Spouse's parents: Bernard Michael and Ada (Lutes) Palmer[1360]
Spouse's birth: 21 February 1927 in Ohio
Spouse's death: 29 January 2013 in Sandusky, Erie County, Ohio[1361]
Spouse's burial: Oakland Cemetery, Sandusky[1362]

[1359] "Deaths... William H. Cover," *Southern Illinoisan* (Carbondale), Saturday 8 February 1986, p. 6, col. 2.

[1360] "Engagement of Ruth Palmer to Willi[a]m H. Cover Is Announced," *Register-Star-News* (Sandusky, Ohio), Thursday 21 September 1950, p. 8, cols. 4–5. For announced wedding date, "Shower Honors Miss Ruth Palmer," *Register-Star-News* (Sandusky, Ohio), Thursday 16 November 1950, p. 8, col. 3.

[1361] "Ruth P. Hunker," obituary from *Register* (Sandusky, Ohio), Tuesday 29 January 2013, transcribed at genealogybank.com. For birth place, Bernard Palmer household for daughter Ruth age 3, 1930 US census, Sandusky, Erie County, Ohio, Ward 3, ED 20, sheet 14A, dwelling 359, family 360.

[1362] Ruth Palmer Cover-Hunker, no image of grave marker, Oakland Cemetery, Sandusky, Erie County, Ohio, memorial #111,733,701 by D'Anna Rotsinger Nemitz (findagrave.com). Also, "Ruth P. Hunker," obituary from *Register* (Sandusky, Ohio), Tuesday 29 January 2013, transcribed at genealogybank.com (see note below).

Graduating from Mary Manse College in Toledo, Ruth taught in Ohio and Missouri schools for 30 years, specializing in reading in the primary grades. She and William divorced in 1974;[1363] she married second Francis "Sam" Hunker, who died in 2011.[1364]

William Henry graduated from the University of Illinois 10 February 1946 with a Bachelor of Science degree in agriculture.[1365] As of 26 June 1942 he was 6 feet 3 inches tall, weighed 165 pounds, and had blue eyes and brown hair. He was living in Tunnel Hill, Johnson County, where his phone number was 177F11.[1366] He served as an ensign in the US Naval Air Corps during World War II (1 September 1943 to 22 December 1945).[1367] As of 3 December 1943, he was in the crew of the USS NAPTC (Naval Air Primary Training Command).[1368] In 1950 he was a salesman at Armour Fertilizer Works.[1369] Later he worked as executive sales trainer for the agriculture department of Monsanto Chemical Company.

[1363] Rosalie (Thrall) Carmichael, "Thrall Genealogy" (17-page typescript on onion skin in red binder, by Rosalie Thrall Carmichael although no author is named), 17; in author's possession, tub 2, item 34.

[1364] "Ruth P. Hunker," obituary from *Register* (Sandusky, Ohio), Tuesday 29 January 2013, transcribed at genealogybank.com.

[1365] University of Illinois commencement program 15 September 1946, about p. 13 (archive.org).

[1366] William Henry Cover WW2 draft card, serial #N130, order #10682, Local Board 1, Johnson County, Illinois; "US WWII Draft Cards Young Men, 1940–1947" > Illinois > Clapper–DeGrazia > Courtney–Cowan > images 1168–69 of 2132 (ancestry.com).

[1367] "Engagement of Ruth Palmer to Willi[a]m H. Cover Is Announced," *Register-Star-News* (Sandusky, Ohio), Thursday 21 September 1950, p. 8, cols. 4–5. For service dates, William Cover index entry, "US, Department of Veterans Affairs BIRLS Death File, 1850–2010" (ancestry.com).

[1368] "Muster Roll of the Crew of the USS NAPTC," quarter ending 31 December 1943. He was said to have enlisted 3 November 1942 (seemingly contrary to his BIRLS Death File, above) and first received on board 3 December 1943; WWII Navy Muster Rolls > N > Naval Air Primary Training Command (fold3.com/image/313351185?rec=311261070). His service number was 7257956.

[1369] "Engagement of Ruth Palmer to Willi[a]m H. Cover Is Announced," *Register-Star-News* (Sandusky, Ohio), Thursday 21 September 1950, p. 8, cols. 4–5.

He had two funerals: one in Bopp Chapel, Kirkwood, St. Louis County, Missouri;[1370] the other in Lee County, Florida, where a memorial service was held for him 20 February 1986 at the First Church of Religious Science in Cape Coral.[1371] His estate was administered in Lee County Circuit Court there.[1372]

[1370] "Deaths... William H. Cover," *Southern Illinoisan* (Carbondale), Saturday 8 February 1986, p. 6, col. 2.

[1371] "Deaths, Funerals... Lee County, William Henry Cover," *News-Press* (Fort Myers, Florida), Wednesday 19 February 1986, p. 4B, col. 1.

[1372] "Notice of Administration... Estate of William H. Cover," *News-Press* (Fort Myers, Florida), Saturday 25 October 1986, p. 7B, col. 9.

Chapter 59

Tenth Generation

David Leonidas Cover–Billie Jean Taake– Ava Marie Goddard Family
parents at chapter 21

Conservation Farmer of the Year 1974 and a St. Louis inner-city settler

59. David Leonidas[10] **Cover** (*Mary Virginia Thrall*[9]*, Leonidas*[8]*, Worthy*[7]*, Eliphas*[6]*, Samuel*[5]*, John*[4-3]*, Timothy*[2]*, William*[1])
Birth: 17 May 1925, Lebanon, St. Clair County, Illinois
Death: 8 March 1990 in New Burnside, Johnson County, Illinois
Burial: 11 March 1990 at New Salem Cemetery in Johnson County, Illinois
Spouse #1: **Billie Jean Taake,** married first in 1951 (before 7 June, when she completed her student teaching as Billie Cover),[1373] divorced 1956[1374]
Spouse #1's parents: Howard and Clara (Will) Taake[1375]
Spouse #1's birth: 28 July 1929 in Christopher, Franklin County, Illinois
Spouse #1's death: 8 November 2014 in St. Louis

[1373] "Deaths: David Cover," *Southern Illinoisan* (Carbondale), Saturday 10 March 1990, p. 24, col. 1. Similarly, "81 at S.I.U. Finish Student Teaching Chores," Thursday 7 June 1951, p. 8, col. 5.

[1374] Rosalie (Thrall) Carmichael, "Thrall Genealogy" (17-page typescript on onion skin in red binder, by Rosalie Thrall Carmichael although no author is named), 17; in author's possession, tub 2, item 34.

[1375] "Deaths . . . Howard Taake," *Southern Illinoisan* (Carbondale-Herrin-Murphysboro-Marion), Thursday 19 June 1980, p. 21, col. 1. Also, "Services Pending for Christopher Woman," *Southern Illinoisan* (Carbondale), Sunday 7 June 1970, p. 33, col. 1, where Billie was called Clara's daughter.

Spouse #1's burial: bequeathed body to the Washington University School of Medicine for research[1376]
Spouse #2: **AVA MARIE (SIMMONS) GODDARD,** married second as her second husband 5 December 1973 in Vienna, Johnson County, Illinois
Spouse #2's parents: Earl and Mary "Dodie" (Johnson) Simmons[1377]
Spouse #2's birth: 28 September 1926 in Tunnel Hill, Johnson County, Illinois
Spouse #2's death: 7 May 2010 in Vienna, Johnson County, Illinois
Spouse #2's burial: 10 May 2010 New Salem Cemetery[1378]

As of 17 May 1943, David was just over six feet tall, weighed 145 pounds, and had brown eyes and brown hair. He had a "white jagged scar" on his right leg and a scar from upper lip to nose.[1379] A veteran of World War II, he graduated from Southern Illinois University-Carbondale in 1951 and was named Conservation Farmer of the Year in 1974 by the Johnson County Soil and Water Conservation District.

A cattleman and hog producer, he was a member of the Egyptian Livestock Marketing Association, Illinois Feeder Calf Association, Interstate Producers Livestock Association, the Advisory Council for the University of Illinois, the Johnson County Farm Bureau, and the Beggs-Gurley VFW Post 522 in Vienna.[1380]

[1376] "Billie Chamblin," *Southern Illinoisan* on line, 3 December 2014, no page or column number (https://thesouthern.com/news/local/obituaries/ billie-chamblin/article_449e682d-ed74-541b-b618-208a644aa8f7.html).

[1377] "Deaths: Mary Simmons," *Southern Illinoisan* (Carbondale), Monday 26 January 1987, p. 4, col. 2.

[1378] "Ava Cover," *Sun* (Paducah, Kentucky), Saturday 8 May 2010, p. 14A, col. 1. Also, Ava Marie Simmons Goddard, lengthy transcribed obituary from unnamed newspaper, likely 8 or 9 May 2010; no grave marker and no sourcing, memorial #74,001,910 by Tim Hawkins (findagrave.com).

[1379] David Leonidas Cover WW2 draft card, serial #W85, order #10852, Local Board 1, Johnson County, Illinois; "US WWII Draft Cards Young Men, 1940–1947" > Illinois > Clapper–DeGrazia > Courtney–Cowan > images 1113–14 of 2132 (ancestry.com).

[1380] "Deaths: David Cover," *Southern Illinoisan* (Carbondale), Saturday 10 March 1990, p. 24, col. 1.

In 1930 Billie Jean was in her Will grandparents' household in Christopher, Franklin County, Illinois; in 1940 she was with her parents in West Virginia.[1381] She married second between 1956 and 1966 Robert J. Chamblin;[1382] in 1966 she was a technician at City Hospital in St. Louis.[1383] In 1979 they were living at 10007B Sakura Drive in Sappington, St. Louis County, Missouri.[1384] On 22 May 1984 she quit-claimed Franklin County land to family members.[1385]

In the early 1990s she retired, bought property in St. Louis's McRee Town neighborhood, and moved in. "The property is cheap and I'm willing to put in the time and money," she told a newspaper reporter in 1995.

"These are good, sturdy buildings, and I love the old St. Louis architecture." She moved into a shooting war between two gang factions that killed eight people. She often couldn't watch television or use the telephone because of the noise.

"Some of the drug dealers could give faster, better service than Burger King. I often went to work on four hours' sleep. Things have improved"—in part due to increased police presence, a neighborhood organization, and property owners' drawing up a standard lease agreement to screen potential tenants.[1386]

[1381] Amos Will household for granddaughter Billie J. Taake, 1930 US census, Christopher, Franklin County, Illinois, ED 51, sheet 4B, dwelling 103, family 104. Also, Howard Taake household for daughter Billy Jean, 1940 US census, Big Creek, McDowell County, West Virginia, ED 24-17, dwelling 413.

[1382] "Billie Chamblin," *Southern Illinoisan* on line, 3 December 2014, no page or column number (https://thesouthern.com/news/local/obituaries/billie-chamblin/article_449e682d-ed74-541b-b618-208a644aa8f7.html).

[1383] Mrs. Bille [Billie] J. Chamblin entry, *Polk's St. Louis (Missouri) City Directory 1966* (Detroit: R. L. Polk, 1967), p. 273.

[1384] Robt. J. and Billy C. Chamblin entry, *St. Louis Suburban City Directory 1979* (no title page), p. 178.

[1385] "Franklin County Land Transfers," *Southern Illinoisan*, Wednesday 6 June 1984, p. F2, col. 1.

[1386] Bill Bryan, "Killing Fields Drying Up; Neighborhood Rebounding," *Post-Dispatch* (St. Louis, Missouri), Monday 30 January 1995, p. B1.

David's second wife Ava Marie Simmons lived with her parents in 1930 (as Ava, age 3) and 1940 (as Marie, age 13). Her parents each completed six years of school; her father was a farm laborer. In 1930 they were renting and had no radio set; in 1940 they owned a $250 house in Tunnel Hill (well below the statewide average of $3277).[1387]

Ava married first in Piggott, Clay County, Arkansas, 17 July 1945 Everett Samuel Goddard; he died 14 December 1954. She worked as a cook at the Tunnel Hill Grade School and later at the Hillview Health Care Center in Vienna. A member of the New Salem Baptist Church, she also enjoyed reading, sewing, quilting, yard sales, and spending time with her grandchildren.[1388]

[1387] Earl Simmons household for daughter Ava age 3, 1930 US census, Tunnel Hill, Johnson County, Illinois, ED 14, sheet 7B, dwelling 153, family 154. Similarly, daughter Marie age 13, 1940, sheet 5B, dwelling 97. Mother-in-law Mary Johnson was living with the family in 1940. For average Illinois house cost in 1940, *United States Census Bureau*, Census of Housing, Historical Census of Housing Tables, Median Home Values Unadjusted 1940 (census.gov/hhes/www/housing/census/historic/values.html).

[1388] "Ava Cover," *Sun* (Paducah, Kentucky), Saturday 8 May 2010, p. 14A, col. 1. Also, Ava Marie Simmons Goddard, lengthy transcribed obituary from unnamed newspaper, likely 8 or 9 May 2010; no grave marker and no sourcing, memorial #74,001,910 by Tim Hawkins (findagrave.com). The obituaries do not contradict one another, but the first seems more precise and the second more colorful.

Index

NOTE: Footnotes are not indexed. Names are indexed under their surnames. Places (towns, counties, etc.) are indexed under state or nation. Titles such as "Dr." or "President" or "Rev." are not used in alphabetizing.

[-?-]

Ann E. (Bailey) [-?-], 119
Ava B. [-?-], 115, 238-240
Eliza [-?-], 110
Helen [-?-], 301
Inez [-?-], 214
Maud [-?-], 211
May [-?-], 335
Merle [-?-], 207

A

AARP, 232
Account book, 19-21
Activities, 3
Adams, William Henry Harrison, 4
Adler Planetarium, Chicago, 349
Adoption/fostering, 1, 3, 56, 96, 131, 137, 138
Adrian, Eunice B. (Schofield), 99
Air Force, 307
Alabama, 3, 206
        Birmingham, Jefferson County, 205, 206, 310, 311
        Montgomery, Montgomery County, 311
Alaska, Attu and Kiska islands, 212
Allerton, Robert, estate, 249
Allied Families
        Gould-Thrall, 45 (Tree 1)
        Jones-Thrall, 74 (Tree 2)
        Flint-Morgan, 93, 104 (Tree 4)
        Schofield-Thrall-Morgan, 99, 103 (Tree 3)
        Thrall-Morgan, 95
        Thrall-Morgan-Gould-Britton, 125, 129 (Tree 5)
American Association of University Professors, 250
American Legion, 260-262
American Red Cross, 223
American Society of Mechanical Engineers, Machine Design Division, 337

Anderson, Fred, on success in rural economies, 21
Anthony, Susan B., 61
Arbitration, 71
Arizona, 217
    Black River, 175
    Blue (now Greenlee County), 175
    Glendale, Maricopa County, 218
    Kirkland Valley, Yavapai County, 215
    Maricopa County, 83, 85, 138, 148, 214, 217
    Peoria, Maricopa County, 219, 300
    Phoenix, Maricopa County, 83-85, 148, 213, 218, 219, 303, 304, 307
    Sun City, Maricopa County, 137, 299, 301
    University Addition, 83
    White Mountains, 175
    Wilson Precinct, Maricopa County, 215
Arkansas
    Methodist Conference, 49, 55
    Piggott, Clay County, 368
Armstrong, Rebecca, 111
Astronomy, 348, 349
Aukland
    Raymond, 305
    Rosalie (Galeener) (Pifer) (Maller), 305, 307
Austin Methodist Conference, 49, 53
Autobiography of Malcolm X, 187
Autolite parts store, 348

B

Bailey
    Ann E. [-?-], 119
    James H. Bailey, 119
    Mary (Britton), 119
Baja California, 348
Bankston
    Effie Gertrude (Morgan), 102, 225
    Elizabeth Frances (McCallum), 226
    Henry Judson, 226
Baptists, 4
Barnett, Mamie (Foster), 351
Beechwood Dairy, 129
Beeney, Harriet (Britton), 117, 127
Beggs, Mary (Meeks), 97
Bell, H. C., 231
Bernays, Thecla, 63
Bircket, John W., 112

Bird
    Evelyn Grace (Thrall), 169, 327
    Harriet (Jennings), 327
    Joshua "Jess" Jennings, 169, 327
    Peach Farm, 329
    Samuel, 327
Bisbee
    Lawson, 82
    Ruth Ann (Marr) (Teachout), 78, 80, 82
Biscayne Bay Yacht Club, 294
Bittman, E. S., 84
Blackard, Mrs. Abigail C. "Abbie" (Schofield), 98, 99
Bobbitt
    Hannah Maria (Doty), 89
    William, 89
Books (inheritance), 43
Booth Festival (later "Festival of Sharing"), 188
Boring, Elin Ida (Henderson), 345
Bride, Mr., 24
Brines
    Eva (Morgan), 102, 229
    Gilbert, 231
    Jennie (Mull), 230
    J. R. Jr., 231
    J. Schneck, 231
    Morris, 230
    M. W., 231
Britton, 299
    Alta Areta (Gould), 43, 50, 118, 127-130, 133, 278
    Elsie Mae "Peg" (Crawley), 122, 124, 265
    Ethel Lucretia (Hartman), 12, 130, 269
    Edward George, 43, 118, 127, 129, 130, 227, 270
    Ernest Raymond, 131, 227, 273
    Floyd E., 123, 251, 253, 254
    Gladys (Gaunt), 123, 251, 253
    Harriet (Beeney), 117, 127
    Hazel (Reck) (Crocker) (Thorsness), 123, 252, 253
    Helen Gladys (Ross), 123
    Henry E., 130
    John Edward, 117, 127
    Rev. Joseph Walter, 11, 31, 32, 117, 119, 129
    Lucile Evangeline, 121, 123
    Lucretia "Crete" (Morgan), 24, 31, 32, 50, 91, 111, 117-119, 121, 122, 128, 129, 200
    Martha E. (Hughes), 131, 273
    Mary (Bailey), 119, 123
    Ralph, 130
    Sarah Myrtle (Castile), 123, 247

       Virgil C., 131
       Vivian (Hannah), 121, 124, 259, 260, 263
       Waldo Vincent, 122, 124, 263, 264
       William Everett, 12, 121, 123, 247, 249-250

Broome, Gertrude (Mooers), 323

Brown
       Donna M. (Thrall), 170, 331
       Harry T., 331
       John, 18
       Lottie, 355
       Lydia, 18
       Mary, 134
       Mary Alice (Kear), 331, 332
       Mary Louise (Stuple) (Haynes) (Clausen?), 138
       M. D., 134
       Orilla (Thrall), 14
       Virginia Susan (Leighton), 134, 139

Brown Valve and Manufacturing Company, 3, 114, 235, 239, 244

Bryan
       Silas Lillard, 174
       William Jennings, 174

Bryant, William Cullen 187

Bumpus, Viola (Shaffer), 291

Burdette
       Carrie (Miller), 292
       Rosa Lee (Germanini), 291, 292
       Wiley H., 292

Burdocks, 70

Burgdorf
       Adam, 204
       Clarine (Morgan), 203
       Frederick Louis, 204
       Louisa, 204

Burkey, Nels and Bertha, 83

Burns, Robert, 167

Businesses
       Alton Automobile Company, 290
       Armour Fertilizer Works, 362
       Brown & Bigelow (advertising specialties), 332
       Colorado Steelworks, 210
       Consolidated Freightways, 306
       David J. Johnston (engineering), 267
       Fitzsimmons Coal and Steel, Youngstown, Ohio, 210
       Holt, Rinehart, and Winston, 342
       Illinois Welding (later Praxair), 332
       Libby's Foods (later Nestlé), 359
       Loomis Brothers Equipment, 319
       Martin Marietta Systems, 321, 322

        Monsanto Chemical Company, 362
        Nitrolene Sales, 84, 219
        Oakford Company, 332
        Oil well equipment manufacture, 237
        Rand Corporation, 342
        Republic Iron and Steel, Youngstown, Ohio, 210
        Samson Tire and Rubber Company, Compton, California, 219
        Shaw's Smoke House, 218
        Talbot & Hubbard, 83, 218
        Union Carbide, 322
        United Air Lines, 210
Bust, Mand Watts, 64

C

California, 4, 84, 113, 214
        Alhambra, Los Angeles County, 114, 239, 240
        Barstow, San Bernardino County, 240, 241
        Chula Vista, San Diego County, 143, 290, 296
        Compton, Los Angeles County, 84, 219, 244
        Goleta (miscalled "Galedia"), Santa Barbara County, 301
        Grass Valley, Nevada County, 212
        Hemet, Riverside County, 209
        Long Beach, 219
        Los Angeles, 78, 85, 115, 243, 311
        Los Angeles County, 78, 114, 123, 214, 215, 219, 233, 247
        Los Angeles Heart Association, 245
        Los Baños, Merced County, 144, 287, 288
        Modesto, Stanislaus County, 241
        Montebello Township, East Los Angeles, 84
        Nevada City, Nevada County, 212
        Orange County, 248
        Pasadena, Los Angeles County, 109, 235, 236
        Pomona, Los Angeles County, 215
        Redondo Beach, Los Angeles County, 204
        Sacramento, 242
        San Bernardino, 85, 213, 241
        San Francisco, 248
        San Gabriel, Los Angeles County, 238
        San Marino, Los Angeles County, 244
        Santa Monica, 342
        Victorville, San Bernardino County, 114-115, 237
        Waterford, 241
        Whittier, Los Angeles County, 78, 85
        Yuba City, Sutter County, 211
Campbell
        Rev. Charles Wesley, 11, 26, 47, 49, 50-56, 151, 154, 155

Etta Jane "Ettie," 50-52, 56, 149, 150, 155
Fleeta M. (Cantwell), 57, 153, 155-157
Hannah Caroline "Carrie" (Thrall), 12, 17, 19, 22, 26, 47, 49, 50-52, 118, 128, 151, 154, 159
Helen Marie, 157
Leo Frank, 57, 151, 153, 155-157
Leona "Lena" Mae (Pearson), 157, 317
Mary Anna (Kohler), 157, 321
Phoebe (Young), 48
Silas C., 48

Canada
Toronto, 63

Cantwell
Annie (Payne), 153
Fleeta M. (Campbell), 57, 153, 155-157
John, 153

Carmichael
Colin, 178, 335
Enola Rosalie (Thrall), 179, 335
John, 335
May [-?-], 335

Carrier, Adela Pauline (Galeener), 303
Carter, Charlotte Jane (Keisling), 171
Casleton, E. M., 284

Castile/Casteel
Mary E. (Watts), 247
Sarah Myrtle (Britton), 123, 247
William, 247

Causes of Death
Acute dilation of heart, **264**
Bronchial pneumonia, 218
Cancer of pancreas, 149
Cardio vascular renal disease, 202
Cerebral thrombosis, 172
Consumption, 94
Diabetes, 131, 137, 277
Gangrene, 134
Heart Disease, 131, 137, 277
Hemorrhagic nephritis, 264
Hypertension and cardiovascular disease, 200
Myocarditis, 199
Pelvic Inflammatory Disease, 136
Pneumonia, 157
Prostate cancer, 171
Stroke, 87

Cemeteries
Bone Gap, Illinois, 13, 14, 27, 28, 33, 76, 85, 87-89, 109, 117, 118, 123, 136, 139, 145, 146, 199, 229, 247, 263

Cairo City Cemetery, Villa Ridge, Pulaski County, Illinois, 127, 128, 130, 269, 270
Chapel Hill Memorial Park, Largo, Pinellas County, Florida, 335, 336
Clements Cemetery, Champaign County, Illinois, 351
Cobden Cemetery, Union County, Illinois, 153, 157, 317
College Hill, Lebanon, St. Clair County, Illinois, 59, 60, 159, 163, 164, 171, 172
Columbia Cemetery, Boone County, Missouri, 222
Dodge Grove, Mattoon, Coles County, Illinois, 124, 259
East Lawn Memorial Gardens, Bloomington, McLean County, Illinois, 181
Ebenezer Cemetery, Wayne County, Illinois, 101
Forest Hill Cemetery, Birmingham, Alabama, 205
Forest Lawn Memorial Park, Youngstown, Ohio, 210
Fort Rosecrans National Cemetery, San Diego, California, 204, 207
Fredonia City Cemetery, Wilson County, Kansas, 119
Greenwood Cemetery, Jennings, Jefferson Davis Parish, Louisiana, 152, 309, 310
Greenwood Memory Lawn Cemetery, Phoenix, Arizona, 217
Imperial Memorial Gardens, Pueblo, Colorado, 102, 229, 230
Jennings, Jefferson Davis Parish, Louisiana, 149
Lake Worth Memory Gardens Cemetery, Palm Beach County, Florida, 144, 291, 292
Los Banos Cemetery, Merced County, California, 287, 288
Louisville Conservatory of Music, Kentucky, 300
Lutheran Cemetery, Evansville, Vanderburgh County, Indiana, 202
Meadow Lawn Cemetery, Manito, Mason County, Illinois, 331
Memorial Park Cemetery and Crematorium, Skokie, Illinois, 123, 251, 252, 257, 258
Midland City Cemetery, Midland, Michigan, 273, 274
Mountain View Cemetery and Mausoleum, Altadena, California, 233, 237, 243, 244
Mount Hope Cemetery and Mausoleum, Urbana, Champaign County, Illinois, 185
Mount Hope Cemetery, Belleville, St. Clair County, Illinois, 265, 266, 288
Mount Kenton Cemetery, Paducah, Kentucky, 157, 321
Mount Moriah Cemetery, Withamsville, Ohio, 209
Mount Pleasant Cemetery, Alleghany County, Virginia, 134, 136, 137
Muskegon, Muskegon County, Michigan, 323
New Salem Cemetery, Johnson County, 198, 199, 361, 365, 366
Oakland Cemetery, Sandusky, Ohio, 361
Oak Lawn, Jacksonville, Duval County, Florida, 173
Old Albion, Illinois, 100
Orange Grove Cemetery, Lake Charles, Calcasieu Parish, Louisiana, 48
Ozone Cemetery, Cumberland County, Tennessee, 327, 328
Rose Hills Memorial Park, Whittier, Los Angeles County, California, 217, 238
Royal Palm Beach Memorial Gardens, West Palm Beach, Florida, 208
Southlawn Cemetery, South Bend, St. Joseph County, Indiana, 192, 355
Spencer Heights Memorial Cemetery, Mounds, Pulaski County, Illinois, 102, 225, 226

Sunland Memorial Park, Maricopa County, Arizona, 148, 299
Woodlawn Cemetery, Champaign County, Illinois, 144, 295
Chamberlain, President, 64
Chamblin
    Billie Jean (Taake) (Cover), 199, 364, 365, 367
    Robert J., 367
Chattel mortgage, 91
Chautauquas, 222
Chemical Senses and Nutrition, 306
Church union, 168-169, 190
Citizens Association of Chicago, 254
Civil rights and peace activities, 353
Civil War, 4, 35, 36, 80, 83
    "Detachment to Recruit Negroes," 37
    Pension applications, 38-40, 83, 92, 93, 147
    Shiloh, 36
Clark
    John H., 79
    Martha Clementine (Morgan), 31, 76, 79, 85
    Mary (?), 76
    Robert, 76
Clausen (?), Mary Louise (Stuple) (Haynes) (Brown), 138
Clionian Literary Society, 49, 61, 63, 161, 182, 222
College Algebra, 342
Colleges, Universities, Preparatory Schools
    Adrian College, 325
    Albion College, 324
    Central Holiness University, Oskaloosa, Mahaska County, Iowa, 182
    Central Michigan University, 275
    Chicago North-West Division High School, 186
    Chicago Training School for City, Home, and Foreign Missions, 161, 182
    Columbia University Teachers College, 275
    Cornell University, Ithaca, Tompkins County, New York, 337
    Drew Theological Seminary, 279
    Garrett Seminary/Biblical Institute, Evanston, Cook County, Illinois, 119, 165, 182, 188, 325
    Hunter College of Law, San Francisco, California, 250
    Illinois College, Jacksonville, Morgan County, Illinois, 342
    Illinois State University, Normal, McLean County, Illinois, 348
    Illinois Wesleyan University, Bloomington, McLean County, Illinois, 49, 112, 296, 331, 358
    IMEDE (now International Institute for Management Development), 359
    Indiana University, Bloomington, Monroe County, Indiana
    John Fletcher College, Oskaloosa, Mahaska County, Iowa, 182
    Knox College, Galesburg, Knox County, Illinois, 119
    Lewis Institute (now Illinois Institute of Technology), Chicago, Cook County, Illinois, 186
    MacMurray College, Jacksonville, Morgan County, Illinois, 341

Mary Manse College, Toledo, Ohio, 362
Massachusetts Agricultural College (now UMass Amherst), 226
McKendree College (now University), Lebanon, St. Clair, Illinois, 8, 22, 23, 34, 49, 50, 61, 64, 65, 67, 68, 71, 72, 133, 146, 161, 164, 165, 173-175, 177, 182, 188, 222, 226, 249, 258, 270, 271, 274, 278, 279, 284, 289, 292, 296, 297
Methodist Deaconess Training School, Northwestern University, Evanston, Illinois, 146
Michigan State University, 275, 328
MIT Radiation Lab, 342
North Carolina State University, 305
Northern Michigan University, 275
Northwestern University, 186, 249, 292, 324, 325
Oberlin College, 9
Ohio State Normal, Lebanon, Ohio, 119
Pennsylvania Academy of Fine Arts, 353
Princeton University, Institute for Advanced Study, 342
Protestant Deaconess Hospital & Home, Evansville, Indiana, 206
Purdue University, West Lafayette, Indiana, 266
Rice University, Houston, Texas, 342
Rutgers University, New Jersey, 337
Southern Illinois University, 270, 293, 321, 366
Teachers College, Emporia, Kansas, 285
University of Chicago, 161, 176, 325
University of Denver, 353
University of Illinois, 249, 254, 258, 263, 270, 271, 289, 297, 304-306, 341, 342, 346, 352, 353, 362
University of Michigan, 275, 342
University of Missouri, Columbia, 223
University of North Carolina, 176-178, 249, 336
University of Tennessee, 324, 325
University of Wisconsin, 222
Washington University Medical School, St. Louis, 289

Collins
Christopher Columbus, 85, 215
Della G. (Harrer), 214
Inez [-?-], 214
Isaac McClendon, 213
Mary Eliza (Wright), 213
Myrtle Bell (Morgan), 85, 215
Ruth, 215
Thomas, 214

Colorado
Pueblo, Pueblo County, 102, 229, 231

Connecticut, 2, 6

Conservation Farmer of the Year (1974), 366

Coombs, Clyde, 342

Cooper
Caroline (Thrall), 14-16

Samuel, 16
Cover
 Ava Marie (Simmons) (Goddard), 199, 364
 Billie Jean (Taake) (Chamblin), 199, 364, 365, 367
 David Leonidas, 2, 73, 195, 198, 364, 365
 David Solomon, 195-197
 Leon, 72
 Mary Virginia (Thrall), 72, 73, 195, 196, 198
 Pernecie "Necy" (Whittenberg), 195, 196
 Ruth Alice (Palmer) (Humker), 198, 361, 362
 William H. "Billie," 2, 72
 William Henry, 195, 197, 361, 362
Crabb, A. D., 218
Crabtree
 Catherine Hazel (Morgan), 208
 John, 208
 Minnie (Parrott), 208
Crawley, Elsie Mae "Peg" Britton, 122, 124, 265
 Sarah M. (Hood), 265
 Verla C., 4, 124, 265
 William A., 265
Crocker
 Charles Henry Crocker, 253
 Hazel (Reck) (Thorsness) (Britton), 123, 252, 253
Crooks, Guy, 20
Crowder, S./H., 20

D

Dairying, 129
Dakotas, 348
Dale
 Ava Vivian, 242
 Ida (Dalany? Keeler?), 242
 Martin? Morton?, 242
Daughenbaugh
 Carrie Eleanor (Marshall), 152, 309
 Henry, 309
 Howard Lee, 152, 309, 311
 Philomene (Miller), 309
Davis
 Capt., 37
 Dr. Henry W., 37
D-Day, 357, *see also* World War II
Deaconess Home (Chicago), 63
Death places by generation, 4
Decision Processes, 343

De Rousse
    Ava B. Morgan, 241
    Ava Bennington, 241
    Carol R., 241
    Louis E., 241
Divorce, 97, 136, 235, 266, 287, 289, 305, 306, 362, 365
Dodd, Leo W., 54, 154
Dodds
    Samuel F., 111
    William, 111
Donaldson, Emma Jane (Hannah), 259
Donoghue, Krumsick & Co., 254
Doty
    Hannah Maria (Schofield), 89, 96, 99
    William B., 96
Drury
    Elizabeth (Thread), 229
    Elsie P. (Morgan), 102, 229
    John T., 113, 229
DuBois, H. A., 156

E

Eng, William, 352
Epworth League (Methodist youth), 62, 165
Epworth League Institute (later MYF Summer Camps), 188
Exhorters, 18, 120

F

Family Trees, *see "Allied Families"*
Farm Bureau, 129
Farming close-ups, 3
    Britton 1930, 128-29
    Cover 1930s, 198
    Gould 1880, 42
    Gould 1893-1907, 140
    Morgan 1860, 28-29
    Morgan 1880, 91
    Thrall 1850, 17-18
    Thrall 1860, 22
Fellowship of Reconciliation, 346
Fisher, John R., 230, 231
Fishing, 175-176
Flint

Edith Marie (Thrall), 8, 26, 49, 59, 61, 64, 65, 69, 72, 93, 146
Rev. John Wesley, 183, 221
Mary Fletcher (Morgan), 93, 101
Mary (Gedney), 59, 93
Minerva (Robertson), 221
William, 59, 93
Florida, 4, 122, 294, 336
- Bradenton, Manatee County, 286
- Cape Coral, Lee County, First Church of Religious Science, 363
- DeSoto County, 173
- Jacksonville, Duval County, 173
- Key West, 338
- Lake Placid City, Highlands County, 173
- Lake Worth, Palm Beach County, 144, 291
- Miami, 294
- North Palm Beach, Palm Beach County, 284, 286
- Palm Beach County, 143, 283, 292
- Pinellas County, 338
- St. Petersburg Beach, Pinellas County, 179, 335, 336
- West Palm Beach, Palm Beach County, 294

Folck, Maggie L. (Hughes), 273
Ford Foundation, 342
Fort Dearborn Securities Corporation, 254
Fort Donelson, 36
Fort Pickering (Memphis), 38
Foster
- George N., 4, 351
- Lane, 351
- Mamie (Barnett), 351
- Miriam Ruth (Thrall), 72, 189, 192, 351

Fostered children, *see* Adoption/Fostering
Fox River, Virginia (later West Virginia), 8
Fraser, Ann (Williams), 304
Frauli, Clarinda (McKrell), 92, 147
Frazier, 94
Freedman's Aid School for colored boys & girls in Houston, Texas, 51-52
French Creek, Virginia (later West Virginia), 8
Fruit Belt Service Company, 271

G

Galleener
- Adela Pauline (Carrier), 303
- Rosalie F. (Pifer) (Maller) (Aukland), 138, 148, 303, 305, 307
- William Kenneth, 303

Gash
    Andrew Langston, 94
    Homer
    Louisa A. (Thrall) (Morgan), 31, 87, 88, 94, 101
Gateway Arch (St. Louis), 352
Gaunt
    Charles M., 251
    Eleanor (Miller), 251
    Gladys, 251, 253
Gedney, Mary (Flint), 59, 93
Genealogical puzzles, 86, 105, 241
Genealogy standards, 1
Generation Nine, 4
Generation Ten, 4
Geoffroy
    Frank, 105
    Lulu Irene (Thrall? Lankston?), 105
Georgia
    Atlanta, Fulton County, 292
    recipient of Illinois peaches, 271
Gerking
    George Washington, 181, 196
    Gertrude (Thrall), 66, 67, 72, 73, 181, 182, 184
    Kate (Jones), 66, 181
Germanini, Rosa (Gould), 291
Germans, 168
Goddard, Ava Marie (Simmons) (Cover), 199, 364, 366
Gould
    Ada L. (Shaffer), 291, 293
    Adele "Addie" (Morgan) 85, 199, 202
    Alice Flora, 41, 43, 44, 137, 140, 145-148, 300
    Alta Areta (Britton), 43, 50, 118, 127-130, 138, 146, 148
    Ansel, Sr., 18, 199
    Areta Hope (Martin), 144, 295
    Calvin C., 8, 43
    Charles F., 8, 43
    Dora Sophia (Leighton), 44, 133, 139, 140, 144, 147, 278, 300
    Dorcas (Ward), 7, 33, 42
    Edith Evelyn, 41, 43, 44, 137, 140, 145-148, 173, 300, 304, 305
    Edward, 138
    Edwin "Edwy" Malcolm, 143, 283-285
    Ella (Lippert), 144, 287, 289
    Freeman, 7, 33, 42
    Geraldine Ernestine (Hacke), 144, 290
    Laura Lucina (Thrall), 8, 17, 23, 25, 34, 42
    Paul Glenwood, 144, 291
    Rhodean Alice (Perdue), 283
    Rosa (Germanini), 291

Serena A. (Marriott) Gould, 199
Solon Harper, 4, 8, 17, 23, 25, 33, 35-36, 40-43, 46, 140, 147
Stephen B., 43
Unknown, 143
Unknown, 144
Victor Leighton, 4, 143, 144, 148, 287, 289, 290
Rev. Virgil Nathan, 11, 43, 44, 133, 135, 136, 139-143, 278

Grand Army of the Republic, Bone Gap Post, 41
Great Depression (1930s), 177, 197, 235, 244, 261, 329, 356
Greenlaw, Edwin, 176
Gulf Mission Methodist Conference, 49, 54

H

Hacke
    Geraldine Ernestine (Gould), 144, 288, 290
    Laura Henrietta (Smith) Hacke, 288
    Max G., 288
Hades, 180
Hall, Lucy, 159, 162
Hamline, Leonidas Lent, 67
Hammer, Emily E. (Jones), 60
Handbook to Literature, 12, 177-178
Haney, Rev. Richard, 18
Hannah
    Emma Jane (Donaldson), 259
    Harry Ingalls, 4, 124, 259
    John F., 259
    Vivian (Britton), 259, 260, 263
Harmon
    Dr. J. F., 55
    William, 178
Harms, Jacob, 17
Harrer, Della G. (Collins), 214
Harrison, President Benjamin, 80
Hartman
    Ethel Lucretia (Britton), 12, 130, 269
    Mahlon R., 269
    Mary (Rumer), 269
    Milton Miles, 130, 269
Hauschild,
    Clemma (Morgan), 203
    Henry, 203
Hauser
    B. Cornelia (Jones), 164
Haynes
    Edgar L., 138

　　　　Mary Louise (Stuple) (Brown?) (Clausen?), 138
　　　　Maud (Thompson), 138
　　　　Richard Edgar, 138
Henderson
　　　　Alexander, 346
　　　　Elin Ida (Boring), 346
　　　　Elizabeth Rose (Thrall), 72, 162, 189, 192
　　　　John B., 234
　　　　Minnie (Wheeler), 234
　　　　Ronald Athol, 192, 346, 348, 349
Hendricks, C. T.(?), 20
Henshaw
　　　　Ada, 91
　　　　Anderson, 91
　　　　Julia (Whittaker) (Smith), 90, 92
Hibbard, Addison, 177
Hill
　　　　Pinkney, 111
　　　　Thomas C., 111
Hinde, Thomas S., 5
Hoard's Dairyman, 129
Hocking
　　　　James, 18
　　　　John, 18
　　　　Lucinda, 18
　　　　Susanna, 18
Holding, Elizabeth, 63
Holton family, 5
Honchin/Houchin
　　　　Deanna (Saunders) (Smith), 109, 110
　　　　William Anderson, 110
Hood, Sarah M. (Crawley), 265
Hooper
　　　　Florence (Thrall), 105
　　　　Lulu Irene, 105, 106, *see also* Geoffroy
　　　　Mary Cynthia (Kirby), 105, 106
Hornbook on the Law of Bills and Notes, 249
Hornsby, Maj. Aubrey, 311
Horton, Agnes A. "Mrs. Albert," (Schofield), 98, 99
Houses of ill fame, 162
　　　　House values, 143, 177, 197, 202-203, 231-232, 235, 239, 244, 250, 258, 274, 290, 293, 301, 310, 329, 332, 356, 368
Houston Heights, 54
Hubachek & Kelley, 255
Huck
　　　　Christina (Kurz), 205
　　　　Clara Sophia (Morgan), 205
　　　　Frederick, 205

Hughes
    Maggie L. (Folck), 273
    Martha E. (Britton), 131, 273
    William L., 273
Hughey, Dr. G. W., 49
Hunker, Francis "Sam," 362
Hunter
    Alexander, 341
    Mary (Kiser), 341
    Natalie Elizabeth (Thrall), 184, 341
Hypes, Mrs., 62

I

Idaho, Camp Farragut, 356
Illinois, 79, 80, 119, 120, 131, 133, 149, 157, 169, 195, 196, 199, 207, 208, 229, 237, 238, 248, 273, 278, 291, 303, 321, 348
    Adams County, 60, 66, 67, 72
    Albion, Edwards County, 39, 89, 98, 99, 112, 120, 150, 175, 200, 222, 233
    Alexander County, 56
    Altamont, Effingham County, 165
    Altona, Knox County, 190
    Alto Pass, Union County, 321
    Anna, Union County, 57, 120, 123, 153, 257
    Ashley, Washington County, 69, 70, 73, 122, 171, 259, 263
    Athens, Menard County, 274
    Aurora, Kane County, 66, 72, 352
    Barnhill Township, Wayne County, 88
    Beaver Creek, Bond County, 121
    Belleville, St. Clair County, 265-267, 288, 289
    Bellmont, Wabash County, 230
    Benton, Franklin County, 120, 153
    Bible Grove, Clay County, 120, 123, 247
    Bloomington, McLean County, 49, 67, 112, 181, 183, 284, 285
    Bloomington-Normal, McLean County, 293, 294
    Bond County, 70
    Bone Gap, Edwards County, 8-10, 14, 17-19, 21-23, 25-28, 31, 33, 41, 43, 44, 47, 48, 59, 79, 81-83, 85, 87, 93, 96, 97, 99, 101, 102, 110, 112-115, 117, 118-119 (Morgan's Addition), 124, 127, 133, 134, 138-140, 143-146, 148, 160, 199, 200, 202, 211, 214, 218, 221, 222, 225, 227, 229, 231, 233, 234, 243, 244, 283, 287, 291, 300, 304
    Bowen, Hancock County, 183
    Brighton, Macoupin County, 122
    Browns, 9, 234
    Brownstown, Fayette County, 171
    Cairo, 55, 129

Calhoun, 9
Camp Ross, Great Lakes Naval Training Center, North Chicago, Lake County, 207-208
Canton, Fulton County, 349
Carbondale, Jackson County, 300, 304
Carrollton, Greene County, 258
Centralia, Marion County, 293
Champaign, Champaign County, 296, 305, 352
Chicago, 99, 166, 169, 186, 189, 252, 254, 255, 258, 271, 345, 346, 349
Christopher, Franklin County, 55, 365, 367
Christy Township, Lawrence County, 296
Cisco, Piatt County, 189, 192, 351
Cisne, Wayne County, 142
Clay County, 60, 65, 70
Coal City, Grundy County, 325
Cobden, Union County, 156, 317-319
Coles County, 48, 118
College Hill, Edwards County, 140, 146
Cook County, 123, 225, 248
Dalton City, Moultrie County, 98, 99
Danville, Vermilion County, 189, 262, 356
Decatur, Macon County, 176, 186, 262
Dixon, Lee County, 166
Douglas County, 72
DuQuoin, Perry County, 26, 59, 70, 296, 297, 346
Dwight, Livingston County, 196
East Peoria, Tazewell County, 301, 302
East St. Louis, St. Clair County, 53, 254, 264, 266
East St. Louis Settlement House, 142
Edwards County, 4, 6, 8-10, 13, 17-19, 21-23, 25-29, 31-33, 39, 41, 43, 44, 47, 48, 50, 59, 76, 81, 87, 91, 109, 111, 117, 235
Edwardsville, Madison County, 266, 267
Effingham County, 128, 274
Elkville, Jackson County, 141, 284
Evanston, Cook County, 119, 124, 166, 170, 252, 254, 255, 257, 258, 324, 331
Fairfield, Wayne County, 105, 107
Farina, Fayette County, 122, 165
Farmington, Fulton County, 345, 349
Fithian, Vermilion County, 259
Flora, Clay County, 70, 176, 179, 180, 304, 335
Ford County, 222
Franklin County, 367
Franklin Grove, Lee County, 185
Freeburg, St. Clair County, 69, 72, 142, 144, 159, 293, 295
Galesburg, Knox County, 348
Gallatin County, 38
Galva, Henry County, 72, 73, 185, 190-192, 348, 355, 357
Gards Point, Wabash County, 231

Gifford (Penfield), Champaign County, 189
Gillespie, Macoupin County, 143, 296, 297
Granite City, Madison County, 142, 280, 296
Grayslake, Lake County, 189
Grayville, White County, 9, 70, 73, 181, 205
Greenville, Bond County, 70
Harrisburg, Saline County, 70, 71
Hartford, Madison County, 280
Harvey, Cook County, 227
Henry County, 72, 73
Huey, Clinton County, 121
Hutsonville, Crawford County, 172
Indian Point/Indian Point Township, Knox County, 241, 242
Ingraham, 60, 181
Jacksonville, Morgan County, 183
Jasper County, 60
Jeffersonville ("Geff"), Wayne County, 141, 144, 295
Jennings Seminary (Aurora, Kane County), 66, 161, 196
Johnson County, 56, 72
Johnston City, 56
Jonesboro, Union County, 141
Kane County, 66, 72
Keensburg, Wabash County, Illinois, 301
Kewanee, Henry County, 159
Knox County, 242
La Rose, Marshall County, 307
Lawrenceville Circuit (Methodist), 19
Lawrenceville, Lawrence County, 139, 143
Lebanon, St. Clair County, 23, 53, 59, 60, 66, 70, 73, 161, 165, 177, 181, 195, 196, 199, 327, 365
Lee County, 186
Liberty, 69
Litchfield, Macoupin County, 166
Livingston County, 73
Macoupin County, 297
Madison Township, Richland County, 111
Manlius, Bureau County, 304
Mansfield, Piatt County, 66, 189, 192, 355
Marion County, 70
Marion, Williamson County, 120, 123, 251, 300
Marissa, St. Clair County, 143, 161, 283, 284
Massac County, 70, 73
Mattoon, Coles County, 118, 124, 156, 259, 260
Maud, Wabash County, 231
McLean County, 49, 67
McLean, McLean County, 183
McLeansboro, Hamilton County, 300, 301
Medora, Macoupin County, 121, 253

Merriam, Wayne County, 105
Metropolis, 70, 73, 185
Mid-Illinois, 292
Morrison, Whiteside County, 161
Mossville, Peoria County, 293
Mound City, Pulaski County, 123, 124, 257, 274
Mounds, Pulaski County, 55, 102, 128-131, 146, 148, 225, 227, 228, 249, 253, 269, 270, 277, 278, 299, 301, 304
Mount Carmel, Wabash County, 5, 10, 39, 140, 147, 201, 230, 231
Mount Olive, Macoupin County, 121
Mount Vernon, Jefferson County, 18, 122, 222
Murphysboro, Jackson County, 101, 221
Naperville, DuPage and Will counties, 198
Navy Pier, Chicago, 249
New Athens, St. Clair County, 142
New Burnside, Johnson County, 199, 365
Newman, Douglas County, 72, 189
Noble, Richland County, 141, 189, 193
Nokomis, Montgomery County, 286
Normal, McLean County, 293, 294
Oblong, Crawford County, 120, 257
O'Fallon, St. Clair County, 50, 56, 164, 169, 323
Olive Branch, 56
Olney, 9, 24, 50, 81, 89, 98, 109
Orient, Franklin County, 142
Paradise Township, 48
Parkersburg, Richland County, 9, 109
Patoka, Marion County, 183
Pekin, Tazewell County, 170, 331, 332
Peoria, 66, 148, 183, 307, 331
Peoria County, 66
Perry County, 26, 59, 69, 70
Piatt County, 66
Pinckneyville, 69
Pittsfield, Pike County 183, 341
Pixley, Clay County, 65, 182
Pontiac, Livingston County, 73, 181
Pulaski County, 55, 56, 127, 128, 226, 270, 301
Quincy, 60, 66, 67, 72, 182, 183
Reevesville, Johnson County, 56
Richland County, 9, 10, 24, 50, 110
Ridgway, Gallatin County, 351
Rochester Mills, Wabash County, 35
Rock Island, Rock Island County, 38
Rock Island County, 38
Rose Hill, Jasper County, 60
Sadorus, Champaign County, 192, 345

St. Clair County, 8, 23, 50, 53, 56-60, 66, 69, 70, 72, 73, 142-144, 159, 161, 163-165, 169, 171, 177, 195, 196, 198, 254, 264-267, 271, 283, 288, 293, 295, 323, 327, 365
St. Francisville, Lawrence County, 182, 183
St. John, Perry County, 153
St. John's Methodist, Peoria, 66
Salem, Monroe County, 146
Salem Precinct, Edwards County, 91, 113
Saline County, 70, 71
San Jose, Mason County, 189, 356
Savoy, Champaign County, 295
Sefton, Fayette County, 172
Seigert, Edwards County, 9
Shawneetown, Gallatin County, 38
Shelby Precinct, Edwards County, 96, 97
Shelbyville, Shelby County, 293
Signal Hill, St. Clair County, 267
Skokie, Cook County, 252
South Elgin, Kane County, 189
South Roxana, Madison County, 280
Springfield, Sangamon County, 226, 254
Steeleville, Randolph County, 141
Sugar Creek, Clinton County, 289
Sumner Circuit, Lawrence County, 141
Sumner, Lawrence County, 295
Sycamore, DeKalb County, 186
Tilden, Randolph County, 122
Toledo, Cumberland County, 183, 184, 341
Tolono, Champaign County, 189
Towanda, McLean County, 293
Trenton, Sugar Creek Township, Clinton County, 142, 222
Troy, Madison County, 121
Tunnel Hill, Johnson County, 72, 195, 196, 198, 361, 362
Union County, 57
Urbana, Champaign County, 144, 185, 192, 249, 250, 295, 345, 351, 352
Vandalia, Fayette County, 280
Vandalia District (Methodist), 70, 183
Vergennes, Jackson County, 122
Vernon, Lake County, 189
Vienna, Johnson County, 199, 366
Villa Ridge, Pulaski County, 55, 56
Wabash County, 4-6, 10, 14, 16, 28, 35, 39, 232
Waltonville, Jefferson County, 142
Washington County, 69, 70, 73, 171
Wayne County, 94, 105, 106
Weedman, McLean/Dewitt counties, 189, 193
Weldon, DeWitt County, 189, 356
Westfield, Clark County, 183

       West Salem, Edwards County, 9, 189, 229-230
       West Union, Clark County, Illinois, 119
       Wheeler, Jasper County, 141
       White County, Illinois, 9, 69, 70, 73
       Williamson County, 56
       Yankeetown School, Edwards County, 50, 111, 118, 128
       Zeigler, Franklin County, 142, 296, 297, 304

Illinois Bar Association, 258
Illinois Central Railroad, 55, 129, 189, 194, 227
Illinois Life Insurance Company, 258
Illinois Methodist Conference, 182
Illinois Woman's Club, 198
Illnesses
       Asthma, 160
       Cancer, 147
       Diabetes, 70
       Rheumatism, 230
       "Throat trouble," 230

Indiana, 9, 78, 98
       Brazil, Clay County, 204
       Evansville, Vanderburgh County, 85, 115, 199, 200, 202-206, 208, 211, 237
       Fillmore, Putnam County, 266
       Granger, St. Joseph County, 359
       Jeffersonville, Clark County, 356
       Lafayette, Tippecanoe County, 266
       Logansport, Cass County, 286
       Muncie, Delaware County, 62
       Newport, Vermillion County, 48
       Perry Township, Vanderburgh County, 205
       Plymouth, Marshall County, 192, 355, 359
       Princeton, Gibson County, 208
       St. Joseph County, 345
       South Bend, St. Joseph County, 151, 192
       Vanderburgh County, 202, 204
       Vermillion County, 48
       West Lafayette, Tippecanoe County, 266

Injuries, 35, 36, 37, 39, 40, 97-98
Intracoastal canal (waterway), 353
Iowa
       Cedar Rapids, Linn County, 82, 307
       Jackson Township, Benton County, 82
       Monroe Township, Benton County, 82
       Washington Township, Buchanan County, Iowa, 97
       Wilton, Muscatine County, 97

Ireland, Bandon, 328

J

Jackson, Laura (Stuple), 136
James
    Elizabeth, 14, 15
    Hannah (Thrall), 2, 4, 8, 11-13, 15, 17, 18, 22-25, 67, 93
    Simon, 14, 339
Jazz, 285
Jefferson National Expansion Memorial Association, 352
Jennings, Harriet (Bird), 327
Jesus, 24, 190
Jewett, Mary Julia, 8
John Brown Class (Methodist), 18
Johnson, Elsie M., 186
Jones
    Alfred C., 164
    B. Cornelia (Hauser), 164
    Carrie Frances (Thrall), 72, 73, 163, 169
    Emily E. (Hammer), 60
    Emily Martha (Thrall), 26, 60, 65, 72, 73, 182
    Kate (Gerking), 66, 181
    Robert H., 60, 65
    Sara Evelyn (Pfennighausen) Jones, 164
Joss, Elizabeth (Schriber), 185, 356

K

Kansas, 105, 183, 222
    Abilene, Dickinson County, 105, 150
    Cherokee County, 69
    Columbus, Cherokee County, 69
    Fredonia, Wilson County, 119, 122
    Hartford, Lyon County, 69, 72, 163
    Hartford Collegiate Institute, Lyon County, 69
    Independence, Montgomery County, 69
    Lyon County, 69, 72
    Montgomery County, 69
    Newton, Harvey County, 150
    Topeka, Shawnee County, 107
Kear, Mary Alice (Brown), 331, 332
Keaton, Marie, 314
Keeley Cure, 196
Keisling
    Charlotte Jane (Carter), 171-173
    Enola Loudicy (Thrall), 73, 171, 173, 177, 186-187
    Willard, 171-173

Kelley
    Evelyn May (Morgan), 207
    Hellein M. (Morgan), 208-209
Kelsoe, W. A., 68
Kentucky, 96, 206, 349
    Fort Taylor, 260
    Henderson, Henderson County, 203
    Owensboro, Daviess County, 208
    Paducah, McCracken County, 157, 321
    Pine Mountain Settlement School, Harlan County, 162, 346
    West Paducah, McCracken County, 318
King
    George Young, 148, 299
    Helen (-?-), 301
    Jefferson F., 299
    Margaret Louise/Lucille (Pifer), 133, 137, 147, 148, 299, 300
    Martha V. (Young), 299
Kirby, Mary Cynthia (Hooper), 106
Kiser, Mary (Hunter), 341
Kitchen, John S., 20
Klein, Lawrence, 342
Kloke
    Frances (Diefenbach), 202
    John Frederick, 202
    Nina G. (Morgan) (Rodgers), 202
    Philip, 202
Kohler
    Edward August Jr., 157, 321
    Edward August Sr., 321
    Grace (Rendleman), 321
    Mary Anna (Campbell), 157, 321
Krumsick, Leslie, 254
Kuno, 204
Kurz, Christina (Huck) 205

L

Labor strife, 261
Land and property sales, 16, 17, 29-31, 42, 79, 83, 118, 119, 140, 218, 241, 367
Landing Ship, Tank (LST), 356, 357 *see also* World War II
Landon, Alfred M., 262
Leach/Leech
    Rev. Daniel Bassett, 19-21, 238
    Lois M. (Sims), 237
    William S., 20, 21
Lee
    Grisom, 111

>Robert, 20
Leighton 43
>Daniel, 134
>Dora Sophia (Gould), 44, 133-135, 139, 141, 144
>Hope G., 135
>Louisa (Reynolds), 134
>Ollie, 135
>Robert Charles, 135, 140
>Virginia Susan (Brown), 139
>William H., 134, 139
>Willie Geneva (Pifer) (Stuple), 135, 136

Leighton-Pifer-Gould Connection, 43, 133-138
Lemon, George E., 80
Leoy, Bro., 64
Lescher, Dr. John J., 39
Letters (excerpts)
>Hannah James Thrall to daughters Mary and Laura, 22-24
>Edith Flint Thrall to Leonidas Thrall, 34
>Edith Flint Thrall to Leonidas Thrall, 61
>Edith Flint Thrall to Will F. Thrall, 63-64, 175
>William F. Thrall to newspaper (1902), 175-176

Libby's Foods (later Nestlé), 355, 359
Lighthouse for the Blind, 294
Lincoln, Abraham, 35
Linear Optimization, 342
Lions Club, 260

Lippert
>Ella (Gould), 144, 287, 289
>Leona (Walter), 287
>William F., 287

Lockwood, Guy, 16
Loomis
>Burton P., 319
>Charles H., 319

Los Angeles Rail Road, 244
Lough/Low, George, 20, 21
Louisiana, 47, 57, 152, 153, 309-311, 313
>Acadia Parish, 54
>Calcasieu Parish, 48, 151, 152, 155, 310, 313
>Crowley, Acadia Parish, 54, 149, 151
>Jefferson Davis Parish, 54
>Jennings, Jefferson Davis Parish, 151, 310
>Lake Charles, Calcasieu Parish, 26, 27, 48, 150, 152, 309-311, 314
>New Iberia, Iberia Parish, 152, 310, 311, 313, 315
>New Orleans, 310, 311, 314
>Opelousas, St. Landry Parish, 310
>Welsh, Jefferson Davis Parish, 54

Louisiana Conference of the Methodist Church, 311
Low, Dr. L. W., 39
Loyalty oath, 262
Lutes, Ada (Palmer), 361

M

MacLaren, Ian, 167
Maine, 349
Maller
    Alma (Sollod), 305
    Owen, 305
    Rosalie (Galeener) (Pifer) (Aukland), 305, 307
Management Science (journal), 342
Mannerchor (singing group), 348
Maps, 6, 10
Marr, Ruth Ann (Bisbee) (Teachout), 78, 80, 82
Marriott, Serena A. (Gould), 199
Marshall
    Beulah F., 4, 151, 152, 313
    Carrie Eleanor (Daughenbaugh), 152, 309
    Eleanor "Ellen" (Milton), 149, 150
    Etta J. (Campbell), 56, 310
    Harvey Centennial, 56, 149-152, 155, 310
    Robert N., 149, 10

Martin
    Areta Hope (Gould), 144, 295
    Emery H., 12, 144, 295
    Marion, 295
    Melissa (Moore), 295
Massachusetts, 3, 6, 21,
    Amherst, 226
Mathematics Genealogy Project, 343
Mattoon Hospital Auxiliary, 262
McDonald, Findley and Marjori, 84
McKendree College, *see* Colleges
McKnight
    Lucille Evangeline (Britton), 257
    Lucy Emily (Wilkin) 257
    Timothy Irle, 12, 124, 257
    William E., 257
McLennan, Nellie (Ross), 248
McNeill, Rev. J. W., 55
McNelly
    Hugh John, 11, 133, 137, 277, 278
    John O., 277

        Kathleen Virginia (Pifer), 131, 133, 137, 277
        Nanny Belle (Samson) McNelly, 277
Mead, Mary (Thrall), 14, 19, 95
Meeks
        B. F., 97
                Matilda Elizabeth, 97
        Mary (Beggs), 97
Meise, Catherine M. "Pat" (Morgan), 209
Menefee & Smith, 206
Methodist, 81
        Arbitration, 11
        Circuit riders, 10, 18
        Class leaders, 10, 18
        Deaconesses, 11
        Home for the Aged, Quincy, Adams County, Illinois, 60, 66
        Living wage, 11
        Methodist Hospital Nurses Home, Peoria, Illinois, 162
        Old Folks Home, Lawrenceville, Illinois, 139, 145, 146
        Old Peoples Home, Foster Avenue, Chicago, 161
        School for Negroes in Houston (Texas), 50
        Worker protection, 11
Meyer, Walter, 342
Michigan
        Albion, Calhoun County, 72, 166, 169, 323
        Ann Arbor, 341
        Battle Creek, Calhoun County, 167, 169, 327, 328
        Belding, Ionia County, 325, 328
        Bethel, Branch County, 78
        Big Rapids, Mecosta County, 167, 332
        Branch County, 78
        Calhoun County, 72
        Camp Custer, 305
        Charlotte, Eaton County, 325
        East Lansing, Ingham County, 328
        Hillsdale County, 72
        Holland, Ottawa County, 325, 328
        Iron Mountain, Dickinson County, 252
        Kalamazoo County, 332
        Lake Odessa, Ionia County, 167
        Midland, Midland County, 273-275
        Muskegon, Muskegon County, 325
        Parchment, Kalamazoo County, 167
        Midland, Midland County, 131
        Ovid, Branch County, 78
        Reading, Hillsdale County, 7, 325
        St. Joseph, Berrien County, 325
Migration, 5, 6 (map), 7, 16

Miller
  Carrie (Burdette), 292
  Eleanor (Gaunt), 251
  Philomene (Daugenbaugh), 309
  Sol, 140
Mills Prairie Class (Methodist), 18
Milton, Eleanor "Ellen" (Marshall), 150
Ministers
  Britton, Joseph Walter, 32, 117, 119
  Campbell, Charles W., 47, 55, 155
  Flint, John W., 221
  Gould, Virgil N., 44, 133, 135, 136, 140, 278
  Haney, Richard, 18
  Leach, Daniel Bassett, 238
  McNeill, J. W., 55
  McNelly, Hugh John, 131, 133, 137, 277
  Mooers, Charles, 72
  Thrall, Charles H., 66, 72
  Thrall, Harold L., 72, 356
  Thrall, Victor W., 72, 270, 325
  Unger, Paul, 187
Minnesota, 257
  Duluth, 248
  St. Louis County, 248
Minnesota Plan for Expert Testimony, 258
Mississippi River, 353
Missouri, 4, 120, 124, 288, 362
  Adair County, 53
  Atlanta, Macon County, 53
  Audrain County, 53
  Caldwell County, 54
  Columbia, Boone County, 221, 222
  Concord Village, St. Louis County, 319
  De Soto, Jefferson County, 144
  Glenwood, Schuyler County, 53, 121
  Greencastle, Sullivan County, 120, 124, 263
  Green City, Sullivan County, 54
  Greentop, Schuyler County, 121
  Hamilton circuit, Caldwell County, 54
  Jackson, Cape Girardeau County, 157, 317
  Kansas City, 105-6
  Kirksville circuit (Methodist), Adair County, 53
  Kirkwood, St. Louis County, 363
  Knox County, 53
  Laddonia, Audrain County, 53
  Lemay Township, St. Louis County, Missouri, 143
  Macon County, 53
  McRee Town, St. Louis, 367

Memphis, Scotland County, 120
Novelty, Knox County, 53, 120, 124, 259
Sappington, St. Louis County, 367
Schuyler County, 31, 53, 265
St. Louis, 38, 81, 101, 124, 154, 198, 221, 262-264, 271, 286, 288-290, 319, 352, 361, 365
St. Louis County, 319
Sikeston, Scott/New Madrid County, 130, 269
Sullivan County, 54
Vandalia, Audrain County, 53

Missouri Methodist Conference, 49
Missouri State Social Security Commission, 223
Mitchell, Bishop, 168
Modern Woodmen of America, 81
Monongahela River, 8
Montana, 241
Billings, Yellowstone County, 306
Great Falls, Cascade County, 138, 148, 304
Laurel, Yellowstone County, 306
Roundup, Musselshell County, 306

Mooers
Rev. Charles Ansel, 11, 72, 323, 324
Edith Flint (Thrall), 169, 323
George Ansel, 4, 169, 323, 325
Gertrude (Broome), 323, 324

Moore
Addie Claudia (Morgan), 209
Edith, 210
Henry, 210
Dr. Hugh, 306
John Butler, 210
Melissa (Martin), 295

Morgan
Ada Pearl (Vensel), 85, 217, 219
Addie Claudia (Moore), 209
Adele "Addie" (Gould), 85, 199, 202
Alice (??), 85
Allyn Theodore, 24, 28, 29, 31, 40, 87, 91, 92, 94, 95, 99-101, 147, 232
Amanda B. (Teachout), 31, 76, 78-80, 82, 83, 85, 214, 218, 219, 234
Amos B., 22, 25, 27, 28, 30, 31, 112
Ava B. [-?-], 115, 239, 240
Catherine Hazel (Crabtree), 208
Catherine M. "Pat" (Meise), 209
Clara Sophia (Huck), 205
Clementine (Clark), 31, 77, 85
Clemma (Hauschild), 203
Dixie (?), 241
Earl Amos, 4, 102, 225, 231

Edna Blanche (Wheeler), 114, 233-236
Edgar Alsinius/Ansel, 4, 79, 85, 91, 199-202, 205
Effie Gertrude (Bankston), 102, 225
Eliza Jane "Jennie" (Smith), 32, 109-111, 113, 114, 234
Elmina "Mina" Lois (Sims), 115, 237
Elsie P. (Drury), 102, 229
Eva (Brines), 102, 229
Evart/Everett William, 102, 229, 231
Evelyn Mae (Kelley), 207
Ezra Leonidas "Lon," 91, 93, 101, 221
Francis E., 4, 204
Glen Wilbur, 114, 237-241
Grace Clarine (Burgdorf), 203
Hale Eugene, 114, 233-235
Hallein M. (Kelley), 208-209
Ida, 105
Idella (Thrall), 107
Eliza Jane "Jennie" (Smith), 109, 113,114
Ellis G., 210-211
John M., 107
Lawson Allyn, 207
Lester "Reis" Morgan, 208
Louisa A. (Thrall) (Gash), 31, 87, 88, 94, 95, 101
Lucretia Ada "Crete" (Britton), 24, 32, 50, 91, 111, 117, 119, 128, 129, 160, 200, 260
Luther, 18
Lydia Haskell (?) (Rude), 27
Marion Wilson, 209
Martha Clementine (Clark), 31, 76, 79, 85
Mary Catherine (Schofield), 31, 87, 88, 94, 96-101
Mary Elizabeth (Thrall), 2, 16, 17, 23, 25, 27, 31, 42, 91, 121, 200
Mary Fletcher (Flint), 93, 221
Maxwell W., 30
Merle [-?-], 207
Mildred Eileen (Sims), 211
Milton Worthy, 24, 28, 31, 76, 79-82, 85, 86, 91, 112, 234
Minnie L., 101
Myrtle Bell (Collins), 80, 83, 85, 213, 214, 234
Nevelyn Edith (Perkins), 204
Nina G. (Kloke) (Rodgers), 202, 203
Raymond Lee, 83, 85, 217, 218, 234
Rebecca, 28
Roscoe Ralph, 101
Rosina Abigail (Smith), 31, 87, 90
Theodore, 27
Unknown, 85
Willard/Wilbur Amos, 9, 24, 28, 32, 83, 109, 111, 112, 114, 115, 118, 243, 245
William Turham, 105

Wilma Ann (Snider/Snyder), 115, 243, 244
Mormons, 176
Mosier, Alice (Vensel), 217
Moss
    Mrs. J. W., 98
    Lydia M. (Schofield), 99
Mothers pension, 89
Mull, Jennie (Brines), 230
Murdocks, 70
Music, 3, 133, 164

N

National Council of Teachers of Mathematics, 349
National Good Roads Association, 113
National Historic Mechanical Engineering Landmark, 338
Natural gas, 62
Neas-Sanderson Company, 201
Nebraska, 85, 112, 113, 174, 200, 213
    Antelope County, 78
    Battle Creek, Madison County, 82
    Bennett Village, Jefferson Precinct, Madison County, 79
    Cedar County, 97
    Dry Creek, Holt County, 80
    Lincoln, Lancaster County, 83, 214, 218
    Madison, Madison County, 79
    Madison County, 79
    Meadow Grove, Madison County, 85, 217
    Pilger, Stanton County, 81
    Platte County, 78
    Saunders County, 211
    Tilden, Madison County, 80
    University Place (now Lincoln), Lancaster County, 83
New England, 4
New Jersey, 337
    Bloomingdale, Passaic County, 281
    Highland Park, Middlesex County, 337
    Hurdtown, Morris County, 279, 282
    Lake Hopatcong, Morris County, 131, 277
    Milford, Hunterdon County, 278
    Montclair, Essex County, 208
    Paterson (Grace Church), Passaic County, 281
    Rockaway Valley, Morris County, 280
    Roselle (Wesley Church), Paterson, Passaic County, 281
    Tenafly, Bergen County, 281
New Mexico, Luna, Catron County, 175

New York
    Allegany County, 87
    Beacon, Poughkeepsie, Dutchess County, 280
    Ellenville, Ulster County, 280
    Fishkill, Dutchess County, 279, 280
    Ithaca, Tompkins County, 337
    Marlboro, Ulster County, 281
    Middle Hope (Newburgh), Orange County, 281
    Milton, Ulster County, 281
    Morsemere, Yonkers, Westchester County, 281
    New Hudson, Allegany County, 90
Nicaragua, 348
North Carolina, 73, 336
    Asheville, Buncombe County, 285, 300
    Chapel Hill, 73, 171, 177, 179

O

Occupations (*see also* **Farming**)
    Accountant, 243
    Account engineer, 322
    Adult educator, 353
    Agent, 201
    Agronomist and chemist, 324-325
    Air Force, 148
    Art and design professor, 353
    Artist, 325
    Assistant state attorney general, 254
    Assistant state's attorney, 255
    Attorney, 258, 260, 262
    Auto mechanic, 235
    Bank cashier, 200, 253
    Bank director, 332
    Barber, 231
    Beekeeper, 56
    Blacksmith, 19, 134, 266
    Cab driver, 203
    Cabinet maker, 19
    Cashier, 306
    Cattle man, 198, 366
    Cigar roller, 203
    Circuit Court judge, 262
    City attorney, 258
    Civil engineer, 266
    Clerk, 83, 156, 201, 218
    Clerk of court, 248

Coach, 301
Coffee roaster, 201
College professor, 176
Community field agent, extension service (farming), 223
Cook, 368
Corporate executive, 359
Country club manager, 208
Dairy laborer, 227
Department store cashier, 172
Die maker, 210
Dietitian, 289
Doctor, 15, 289, 346
Draftsman, 206, 318
Dressmaker, 83
Egg farming, 231
Electrical engineer, 198
Engineer aide, 322
Executive sales trainer, 362
Farm laborer, 96, 97, 215, 242, 368
"Figurehead" supervisor, 254
Freight and passenger agent, 310
Garage foreman, 235
Gas station attendant, 215, 219
Genealogist, 338-339
General store, 234
Grocer, 112, 173
Head Start local program initiator, 270
Helper beater (paper mill), 136
High-school principal, 180
Hog producer, 366
Horticulturist, 271, 329
Insurance agent/broker, 92, 253
Insurance company director, 258
Junior account engineer, 322
Laborer, 112, 151, 227
Latin teacher, 262
Laundry manager, 319
Law firm member, 255
Librarian, 177, 248, 270, 336
Logging, 35
Lot sales, 118, 119
Machine operator, box factory, 239
Machine operator, card company, 266
Machine operator, cigar factory, 202
Machinist (tractor factory), 239
Manager, Mechanics' Mutual Finance Corporation, 201
Materials engineer, 322
Mathematician and consultant, 342

Mathematics teacher, 186, 212
Mechanical engineer, 336
Merchant, 253
Milk peddler, 226
Minister *(see separate listing)*
Motorman (railroad), 244
Moving picture auto mechanic, 235
Musician, 153, 262, 263, 278, 283, 284, 301, 322, 353
Music teacher, 147, 182, 283, 285, 296, 300, 301, 353
Nurse, 36, 65, 66, 84, 314
Office manager 319
Orchardist, 271
Pension commissioner, 80
Photographer, 186
Planter (Louisiana), 152
Postmaster, 112
Police magistrate, 112-113
President, town board of trustees, 113
Psychologist, 305
Rancher, 215
Ranchworker, 215
Receptionist, 286
Refrigerator factory 202
Rubber worker, 217, 219
Sales, 83 (hardware), 84 (smoke house, gasoline), 175, 218, 332, 362
School administrator/supervisor/principal, 222, 270, 273, 293
School treasurer, 113
Sheriff, 253
Solicitor, 201
Special police (opera house), 201
State's attorney, 258
Stock man, 214
Supervisor, 322
Switchman for "steam railroad," 227
Teacher, 12, 118, 128, 146, 147, 161, 175, 176, 180, 182, 200, 222, 227, 244, 293, 296, 307, 328, 348, 362
Technician (hospital), 367
Tire builder, 219
Traffic engineer, 267
Vice-president and manager, 239
Wagon maker, 19
Warehouseman, 201
Wheelwright, 19

Odd Fellows Home, Mattoon, Coles County, Illinois, 156
Oertel, Anna (Snider/Snyder), 243
Office of Naval Research, 342
Ohio, 4, 6, 67, 127, 361, 362
    Cincinnati, 206

  Cleveland (1896 Methodist national conference), 63, 336
  Columbus, Franklin County, 323, 326
  East Cleveland, Cuyahoga County, 172
  Franklin County, 15
  Granville, Licking County, 4, 7, 13-15, 19, 25, 67
  Lebanon, 119
  Licking County, 6, 27
  Lorain, Lorain County, 138
  Mount Vernon, Knox County, 117
  Newark, Licking County, 67
  Sandusky, Erie County, 198, 361
  Winesburg, Holmes County, 356
  Youngstown, Mahoning County, 210
Ohio River, 5, 8
Oklahoma, 113
  Tulsa, Tulsa County, 231
Open Housing Covenant, 341
Oratory, 164

P

Pacific Northwest, 113
Paducah (Kentucky) Art Guild, 353
Palmer
  Ada (Lutes), 361
  Bernard Michael, 361
  Ruth Alice (Cover) (Hunker), 198, 361, 362
Parchet/Sarchet, Mary (Sande), 306
Parker
  Mary (Thrall), 19
  Thomas, 19
  Thomas [Jr.], 18, 19
Payne
  Annie (Cantwell), 153
Pearson
  Chester Edward "Jackie," 4, 157, 317
  Leona "Lena" Mae (Pearson), 157, 317
  Millie (Peterman), 317
  Roscoe, 317
Pennsylvania
  Bellevue, Allegheny County, 325
  Bethlehem, 65
  Connellsville (District Superintendent), 326
  Mount Washington, Pittsburgh, Allegheny County, 326
  Philadelphia, 6, 184, 341
  Pittsburgh, Allegheny County, 8
  Wynnewood Township, 306

Pension commissioner, 80, 90, 92
Peoria Astronomical Society, 349
Peoria, Decatur, and Evansville (railroad), 9, 10, 112
Perdue
    Rhodean Alice (Gould), 143, 283
    Samuel, 283
    Sophronia "Fronia" Jane (Thompson), 283
Perkins
    Alfred, 205
    Nevelyn Edith (Morgan), 204
    Stella (Thurnier), 205
Peterman, Millie (Pearson), 317
Peterson, Ross, Rall, Barber & Seidel, 258
Petting parties, 261
Pfennighausen, Mrs.O. C. (Sara Evelyn Jones), 164
Philips, John, 255
Phillips, Gordon, 352
Philosophian Literary Society, 182, 188
Pifer, 98
    Cecil Melvin, 4, 133, 137, 147, 148, 279, 303, 307
    Josephine H., 137
    Kathleen Virginia (McNelly), 131, 133, 137, 142, 277, 278
    Kathryn Inez (Williams) (Sande), 148, 304, 307
    Leo William, 135
    Lorine, 137
    Margaret Louise/Lucille (King), 133, 137, 147, 148, 299, 300, 304
    Rosalie F. (Galeener) (Pifer) (Maller) (Aukland), 303, 305, 307
    William Lee, 136, 148
    Willie Geneva (Leighton) (Stuple) 135, 136, 148
Pine Mountain Settlement School, Harlan County, Kentucky, 346
Piper, Mortimer, 305
Planned Parenthood, 341
Platonian Literary Society, 175
Poetry, 142
Politics, 139, 142, 261, 262, 297
Porter, Howell C., 119
Prairie Farmer (magazine), 129
Prohibition, 3, 69, 113, 142
Prohibition Party, 113
Property, *see* Land and Property
Public Savings Insurance Company, 201
Pulaski-Alexander County (Illinois) Cooperative Extension Service, 270
Pulaski County (Illinois) TB and Visiting Nurses Association, 270
Pulaski Farm Bureau (Illinois), 271

R

Race riots, 254
Radio set (=radio), 196, 227, 235, 239, 244, 266, 274, 296, 310, 368
RAND Corporation, 342
Randolph, John, 91
Raum, Green Berry, 80
Reck
    Grace (Watkins?), 252
    Hazel (Crocker) (Thorsness) (Britton), 123, 252, 253
    Peter, 252
Religious education, 181
Rendleman, Grace (Kohler), 321
Reserve Officers' Training Corps (ROTC), 306
Reynolds, Louisa (Leighton), 134
Rhode Island, 207
Robertson
    Minerva (Flint), 221
Rodgers
    Nina (Morgan) (Kloke), 202
    Onie/Orie, 203
Rohner
    Emil, 201
    Curtis, 201
Roosevelt, Franklin D., 262
Root, Charles, 20, 21
Rose Bowl, 3, 311
Ross
    Helen Gladys (Britton), 123, 248
    John G., 248
    Nellie (McLennan), 248
Round the World
    Airplane trip (1948), 262
    Boat trip (1960s), 338
Rude
    Alpheus, 20
    Edwin D., 29
    Lydia Haskell (?) Morgan, 27
    Pertamia, 18
Rumer, Mary (Hartman), 269

S

Saarinen, Eero, 352
St. Louis Philharmonic Orchestra, 285

St. Louis World's Fair, 175
Salem Methodist Episcopal Church, Edwards County, Illinois, 19
Samson, Nannie Belle (McNelly), 277
Samuelson, Paul, 342
Sande
    Charles B., 306
    Charles Bernard, 306
    Kathryn Inez (Williams) (Pifer), 138, 148, 304, 307
    Mary (Parchet/Sarchet), 306
San Francisco 1915 Exposition, 113
Satan, 142
Saunders/Sanders, Deanna (Honchin/Houchin) (Smith), 109, 110
Schaefer, Dr. Herman, 36, 39
Schafer, Lewis and Julia, 140
Schofield
    Abigail C. (Blackard), 99
    Agnes A. (Horton), 99
    Anna M., 99
    Charles, 99, 100
    Eunice B., 99
    George E., 99
    Hannah M. (Doty), 96
    Henry O., 99
    John Naylor, 99
    Lenora (Smith), 100
    Lucy Croker (Thrall), 99, 100
    Lydia M. (Moss), 99
    Mary Catherine (Morgan), 31, 88, 94, 96-101
    Ralph D., 99
    William Bobbitt, 96, 99, 100
Scholastic Bowl, 349
    Schooling, Years of, 82, 107, 113, 129, 140, 146, 156, 196, 202-204, 206-208, 210, 214, 226, 230, 234, 239, 244, 249, 253, 258, 266, 284, 289, 296, 301, 306, 318, 329, 332, 336, 359, 365, 368
Schriber
    Charles, Matthew Carl, 185
    Elizabeth (Thrall), 72, 73, 177, 184-187, 190-194, 346, 356
    Elizabeth (Joss), 185, 356
    Scotland, 167
        Glasgow, Lanarkshire, 336
    Seitz, Lewis, 201
    Seitz Smith and Company, 201
Shaffer
    Ada L. (Gould), 144, 291, 293
    Viola (Bumpus), 291
    William E., 291
Shannon, George W., 79
Shaw's Smoke House (Phoenix), 84

Shurtliff family, 29
Signatures
    Gould, Solon H., 41
    Morgan, Amanda M., 82
Simmons, Ava Marie (Goddard) (Cover), 199, 364, 368
Sims
    Dale Dwight, 4, 211
    Jesse D., 211
    John H., 237
    Lois M. (Leach), 237, 238
    Maud [-?-], 211
    Mildred Eileen (Morgan), 211
    Elmina "Mina" Lois (Morgan), 115, 237, 238
Small, Gov. Len, 251, 254
Smith
    Abner Turner, 109-111
    Benjamin F., 111
    Clarinda (McKrell), 91, 92
    Clark B., 87, 90, 91
    Deanna (Saunders) (Honchin/Houchin), 109, 110
    Ina, 100
    Eliza [-?-], 111
    Eliza Jane "Jennie" (Morgan), 32, 109-111, 113, 114
    Julia (Whittaker) (Henshaw), 90-92, 147
    Laura Henrietta (Hacke), 288
    Lenora (Schofield), 100
    Lewis E., 111
    Nathan E., 100
    Nora, 113
    Rosina Abigail (Morgan), 31, 87, 90, 91
    Sarah (Winchel), 87
Snider/Snyder
    Anna (Oertel), 243
    Charley, 111
    Elizabeth [-?-], 111
    Eliza J., 111
    Fanny J., 111
    James I., 111
    Mary, 111
    William, 111
    William (age 4), 111
    William H., 243, 244
    Wilma Ann (Morgan), 115, 243
Sollod, Alma (Maller), 305
Songs and Hymns
    "Come thou font of every blessing," 160
    "Scatter the seeds of kindness" 169
Southern Handicraft Guild, 329

Southern Illinois Electric Co-op, 271
Southern Illinois Methodist Conference, 49, 50, 55, 56, 69, 70, 140, 182, 183, 189
Southern Pacific Railroad, 309, 310
South Kansas Methodist Conference, 69
Spangler
    Henry W., 84
    Nancy Ann (Teachout), 84
Stanley
    Julius, 29
    William, 87
Stanley School House, 18
Stevens, Ernest, 258
Stone
    John Will, 96
    Leslie A., 96
    Minnie, 96
Stories, 46, 75, 180, 193-194, 346-348, 357 (*see also* World War II), 367
"Strawberry walk," 329
Studies in Philology, 177
Stuple
    Jacob, 136
    John Franklin "Frank," 135, 136
    Laura (Jackson), 136
    Mary Louise, 138
    Willie Geneva (Leighton) (Pifer), 135, 136
Subsistence homesteading, 329
Sunday School, 162
Sutton, Mary (Thrall), 88
Swiss, 186
Switzerland, Lausanne, 359

T

Taake
    Billie Jean (Cover) (Chamblin), 199, 364, 365, 367
    Clara (Will), 365
    Howard, 365
Tables
    Table 1, Etta birthplaces, 151
    Table 2, Leo birthplaces, 155
Tampa (Florida) Symphony, 285
Taxes, 15, 92-93
Teachout
    Amanda B. (Morgan), 31, 76, 78-80, 82, 83, 85, 214, 218, 219, 234
    Franklin, 83
    Nellie Ann (Spangler), 83, 84
    Raymond, 83, 84

Ruth Ann (Marr) (Bisbee), 78, 80, 82
William, 78, 82, 83
Tennessee, 327, 328
Crossville, Cumberland County, 328
Cumberland County, 329
Fountain City, Knoxville, Knox County, 167
Jackson, 37
Knoxville, Knox County, 73, 163, 166, 323, 324
Memphis, 38
South Knoxville, Knox County, 324
University of Tennessee Hospital, 169
Texas, 49, 57, 153, 343
Alvin, Brazoria County, 54
Houston, 341, 353
Houston Seminary, 49, 50
Wichita Falls, Wichita County, 56, 149, 152, 314
Thatcher, John, 18
Thompson
Maud (Haynes) (Brown?) (Clausen?), 138
Sophronia "Fronia" Jane (Perdue), 283
Thorsness
Hazel (Reck) (Crocker) (Britton), 123, 252, 253
Lionel G., 253
Thrall, 339
Aaron, 16
Albert Homer (A.H.), 106
Caroline (Cooper), 14-16
Carrie Frances (Jones), 72, 73, 163, 169
Charles Frankie, 191-192
Rev. Charles Haven, 11, 66-68, 72, 73, 181, 183, 184, 189
Cyrus, 25
Donna M. (Brown), 170
Edith Flint (Mooers), 169, 323
Edith Laura, 11, 64, 70, 72, 146, 159, 160, 174, 186
Edith Marie (Flint), 26, 34, 49, 59, 64, 65, 69, 72, 160, 174
Eliphas, 4, 14, 15, 19, 95
Elizabeth Rose (Henderson), 72, 189, 192, 345, 346
Elizabeth (Schriber), 72, 73, 185, 186-187, 190-192, 346, 356
Emily Martha (Jones), 26, 65, 72, 73, 182, 196
Enola Loudicy (Keisling), 73, 171, 173, 177, 186-187
Enola Rosalie (Carmichael), 335
Evelyn Grace (Bird), 72, 169, 327
Florence (Hooper), 105, 106
Frances Helen, 169-170
Gertrude (Gerking), 66, 67, 72, 73, 181, 182, 184
Hannah Caroline "Carrie" (Campbell), 12, 17, 19, 22, 26, 49, 50, 128, 151, 154
Hannah (James), 2, 4, 8, 11, 12, 13, 15, 17, 18, 22-25, 67, 93
Harold James "Jim," 2, 4, 72, 189, 192, 355, 356

Harold Leonidas, 11, 46, 64, 66, 73, 185, 188-191, 348, 356
Henry Clay, 106
Homer G., 88, 94, 95
Idella (Morgan), 107
Joan E. (Walker), 355
Joel, 7, 15
Laura Lucina (Gould), 8, 17, 23, 25, 33, 34, 42
Leonidas Worthy, 11, 17, 22-24, 26, 34, 37, 59, 63, 65, 70-73, 93, 159, 160, 174, 182, 189, 346
Louisa A. (Gash) (Morgan), 31, 87, 88, 94, 95, 101
Lucy Croker (Schofield), 99
Lyman, 16, 95, 99, 100
Mary Elizabeth (Morgan), 2, 16, 17, 23, 25, 27, 29, 31, 42, 91, 95, 121, 200
Mary (Mead), 14, 19, 95
Mary (Parker), 19
Mary (Sutton), 88, 94
Mary Virginia (Cover), 72, 73, 195, 196
Miriam Ruth (Foster), 72, 189, 192, 351
Nancy (??), 25
Natalie Elizabeth (Hunter), 184
Oliver, 7, 16, 22, 23, 67
Orilla (Brown), 14
Rachel Emeline, 22, 25
Rigdon/Royden/Bryden, 26
Robert McDowell, 12, 72, 184, 341
Rosalie (Carmichael), 172, 177, 179, 186, 338-339
Samuel, 3, 21
Unknown daughter, 170
Victor Worthy Jr., 4, 72, 170, 331,
Victor Worthy, 11, 34, 64, 65, 72, 163, 169, 174, 189, 190, 270, 325
Walter, 6
William, 2
William Flint, 12, 63, 70, 73, 160, 161, 171, 173-175, 177-179, 186
Worthy, 2, 3, 6, 7, 8, 11-19, 21-23, 28, 67, 93, 95, 99, 100, 238, 339

Thread
Elizabeth (Drury), 229
Robert Jr., 30

Thurnier, Stella (Perkins), 205
Tivnen, Bryan H., 260
To A Waterfowl., 188
Tornado, 16
Track meet, 180
Traffic clubs (New Orleans, Lake Charles, and Mobile), 311
Trees, *see "Allied Families"*
Troxel, Russell, 348

U

Unger, Rev. Paul, 187
University of Illinois Extension, 129
US populations, 5
USS *Olympia*, 338

V

Vector Spaces and Matrices, 342
Vensel
    Ada Pearl (Morgan), 85, 217, 219
    Alice (Mosier), 217
    W. J., 217
Vermont, 3, 5, 7
    Chittenden County, 6, 13
    Rutland, 6
    Underhill, 4, 13, 14
Veterans Administration, 305
Virginia, 7, 27, 28, 133, 135, 137, 138, 148
    Alleghany County, 134-136, 139
    Augusta Count, 136
    Botetourt County, 134
    Covington, Alleghany County, 131, 133, 134, 138, 139, 148, 277, 278, 300
    Shenandoah County, 136
    Upshur County, 6
Voight, E. L., 183
Voter registration, 215, 235, 239, 241, 245

W

Wabash River, 8, 9
Wales, 14, 339
Walker
    Lottie (Brown), 355
    Joan E. (Thrall), 192, 355
    Marie, 356
    Melvin, 355
Walter, Leona (Lippert), 287
Walton, Prof., 64
Ward, Alice E., 293
    Dorcas (Gould), 33
Washington
    Sunnyside Precinct, Yakima County, 234

Water conservation, 172
Watkins (?), Grace, 252
Watts
    Faith, 64
    Mary E. (Castile/Casteel), 247
Weber Sanitarium, Olney, Illinois, 98
Welsh, 4
Wentworth, H. G., 226
West Virginia, 6, 348, 367
    Fayetteville, Fayette County, 135
    Nitro, Kanawha County, 263
Wheeler
    Edna Blanche (Morgan), 114, 233
    John B., 234
    Minnie (Henderson), 234
Whitaker, Mrs., 65
White/Whyde, John, 16
Whittaker, Julia (Henshaw) (Smith), 90, 92
Whittenberg, Pernecie "Necy" (Cover), 195
Who's Who, 12
Wilkerson, Jeanne, 221
Wilkin, Lucy Emily (McKnight), 257
Will, Clara (Taake), 365
Williams
    Ann (Fraser), 304
    John G., 304
    Kathryn Inez (Sande) (Pifer), 138, 148, 304, 306, 307
Wilmore, C. A., 206
Wilson, Henry S., 38-40
Winchel, Sarah (Morgan), 87
Winnie Circuit, Texas, 54
Wisconsin
    Baraboo, Sauk County, 304
    DeForest, Dane County, 253
    Green Bay, Brown County, 252
    Marquette County, 90
    Spread Eagle, Florence County, 123, 251
Women, 8-9
    Women's Christian Temperance Union, 62, 114
    Women's Foreign Missionary Society, 62
    Women's suffrage, 61
Works Progress Administration (WPA), 318
    World War I, 4, 11, 12, 71, 168, 204, 226, 260, 263, 266, 289, 324
        4th Illinois National Guard, Company L, 284
    158th Depot Brigade, 266
World War II, 4, 168, 204, 212, 314, 318, 332, 346, 362, 366
    Operation Overlord, 357
    US Alaska Scouts, 212

        US Army Air Forces, 332
        US Naval Air Corps, 362
        US Navy, 321, 352, 356
        US Navy, USS *Farenholt*, 318
Wright, Mary Eliza (Collins), 213
Wyoming, Cheyenne, 210

Y

YMCA, 222
Yorkshire, England, 99
Young, Martha V. (King), 299
        Phoebe (Campbell), 48
Yungling, Rev. J. P., 94
YWCA, 289

www.ingramcontent.com/pod-product-compliance
Lightning Source LLC
Chambersburg PA
CBHW060542230426
43670CB00011B/1653